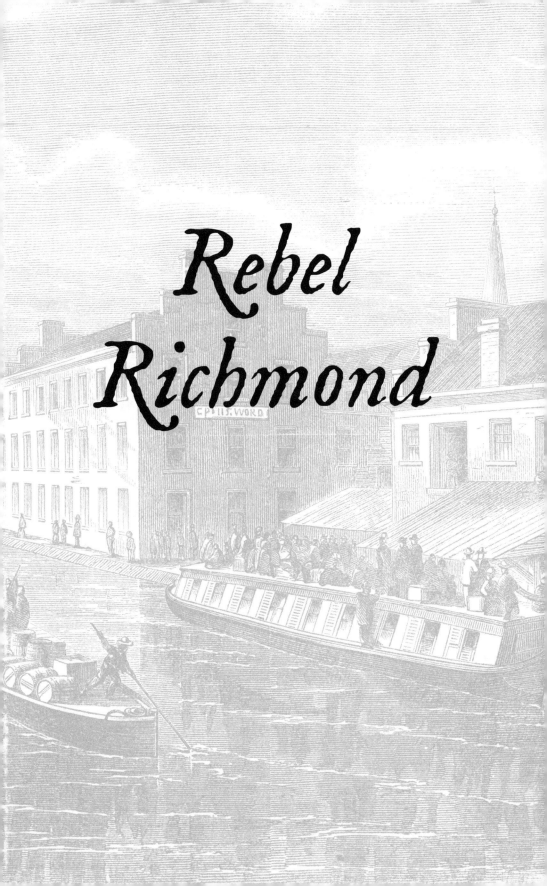

Rebel
Richmond

CIVIL WAR AMERICA

Peter S. Carmichael, Caroline E. Janney,
and Aaron Sheehan-Dean, editors

This landmark series interprets broadly the history and culture
of the Civil War era through the long nineteenth century and
beyond. Drawing on diverse approaches and methods, the
series publishes historical works that explore all aspects of
the war, biographies of leading commanders, and tactical and
campaign studies, along with select editions of primary sources.
Together, these books shed new light on an era that remains
central to our understanding of American and world history.

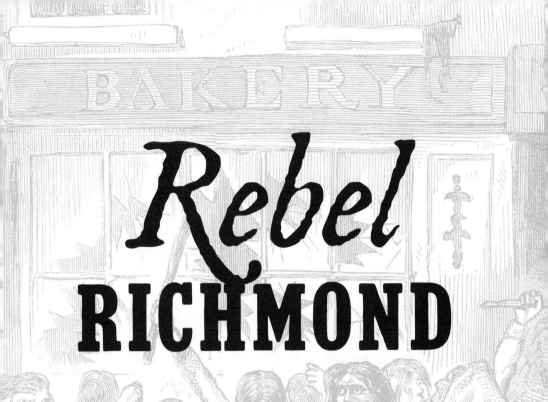

Rebel RICHMOND

LIFE and DEATH in the CONFEDERATE CAPITAL

Stephen V. Ash

THE UNIVERSITY OF NORTH CAROLINA PRESS

Chapel Hill

This book was published with the assistance of the William R. Kenan Jr. Fund of the University of North Carolina Press.

Designed by Jamison Cockerham
Set in Arno, Cutright, Fell DW Pica, Fell English, Scala Sans, and Brothers
by Tseng Information Systems, Inc.

Manufactured in the United States of America

The University of North Carolina Press has been a member
of the Green Press Initiative since 2003.

Jacket illustrations: passenger and cargo boats on the James River and
Kanawha Canal, Richmond, Va., sketched by J. R. Hamilton (1865), Library
of Congress Prints and Photographs Division; (sky background) *Sowing
and Reaping*, from *Frank Leslie's Illustrated Newspaper* (23 May 1863),
courtesy of the University of Virginia Library Online Exhibits.

LIBRARY OF CONGRESS CATALOGING-IN-PUBLICATION DATA
Names: Ash, Stephen V., author.
Title: Rebel Richmond : life and death in the Confederate capital / Stephen V. Ash.
Other titles: Civil War America (Series)
Description: Chapel Hill : The University of North Carolina Press, [2019] |
    Series: Civil War America | Includes bibliographical references and index.
Identifiers: LCCN 2019004289| ISBN 9781469650982 (cloth :
    alk. paper) | ISBN 9781469650999 (ebook)
Subjects: LCSH: Richmond (Va.) — History — Civil War, 1861–
    1865. | Richmond (Va.) — Social conditions — 19th century. |
    Richmond (Va.) — Economic conditions — 19th century.
Classification: LCC F234.R557 A84 2019 | DDC 975.5/45103 — dc23
LC record available at https://lccn.loc.gov/2019004289

for
Jeanie,
again

Contents

A gallery of illustrations begins on page 107.

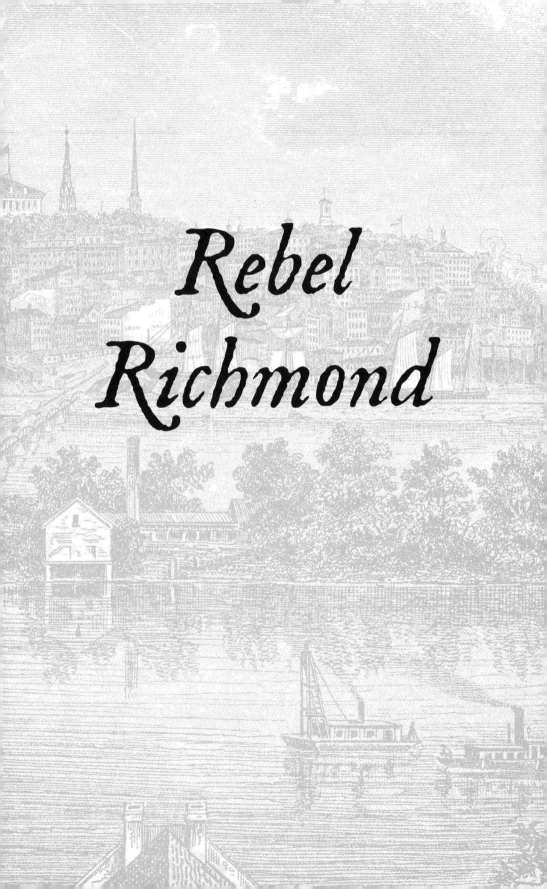

Rebel Richmond

Prologue

RICHMOND, VIRGINIA: THURSDAY, 11 APRIL 1861

The morning papers were crammed with urgent political news. It came from Washington, Montgomery, Charleston, and Richmond itself, where a convention of delegates from across the state was arguing over whether Virginia should join the seceded states. But most Richmonders had in mind more immediate concerns as they opened sleepy eyes and rose from bed.

The weather, especially. A four-day siege of thunder, lightning, and torrential rain had ended only the evening before. This act of God threatened Richmond far more than any political or military storm. The James River was flowing six to eight feet above normal. Some residents of the lower part of the city woke to find their cellars flooded. The water-powered flour mill of Haxall, Crenshaw, and Company, which sat at the river's edge, was inoperable. A part of George Sadler's tavern was six feet under water. The wharves at the downriver end of the city were submerged; the boats that steamed up regularly from Chesapeake Bay to deliver goods to Richmond and to carry away many of its manufactures would remain idle. The pumps that sent river water up to the municipal reservoir were disabled; although the reservoir was large and could slake the city's thirst for a week or so without replenishment, any longer hiatus could provoke a crisis.[1]

Beyond the city, the country roads had become channels of mud. Until they dried, the farmers and herdsmen of Henrico and neighboring counties whom Richmonders depended on for most of their fresh produce and meat would struggle to get their goods to the city's markets. The rain had also halted corn planting, threatening to curtail or at least delay this year's crop. And some of the wooden trestles of the Virginia Central and the Richmond, Fredericksburg, and Potomac Railroads had been washed out, interdicting all rail traffic between Richmond and points north.[2]

But the storm had been a blessing to the city in one respect: it had noticeably suppressed street crime and rowdiness. The police had made only two arrests the previous day, both for public drunkenness. The culprits were George Frost and Betsey Williams, both well known to the authorities for their habitual alcoholic sprees. They sobered up overnight in holding cells and then were marched to city hall to appear before Mayor Joseph Mayo at his regular morning court session. He was willing to let them go home if they could post a modest bond to ensure their future good behavior or find someone to post it for them. But both were poor and friendless, and so they went to jail.[3]

Also imprisoned in Richmond as dawn broke on 11 April were 175 men, women, and children who within a few hours would step onto an auction block and be sold to the highest bidder. No fewer than five of the city's numerous slave-dealing firms had scheduled sales for this day, in lots ranging from twenty to fifty human beings. Davis, Deupree, and Company advertised in this morning's *Enquirer* that it would offer "thirty likely slaves," who would of course be made available for inspection and interrogation by potential buyers before bidding began. The Odd Fellows' Hall on Franklin Street, where this auction would be held, was a popular venue: Pulliam and Company had reserved a room there to sell twenty-five people later in the day. How many of these transactions would forever separate husbands from wives and children from parents was anyone's guess; it was of no concern to the slave dealers or their customers.[4]

The flooding and the slippery streets notwithstanding, as the day progressed most Richmonders managed to go about their business. Housewives and house servants headed to the two municipal markets with shopping baskets in hand, although the vendors' stalls were rather sparsely stocked. Workmen white and black took up their tasks at the factories and artisan shops that had avoided the flooding. Clerks assumed their posts at the counters and desks of retail stores, business offices, banks, and hotels. By evening the river was subsiding rapidly and the damage was being repaired. Longtime residents of the city agreed that while this flood had been bad, it was much less destructive and disruptive than the big one of 1847 and even the lesser one of 1856.[5]

The storm had passed, and no other seemed to be in the offing. Richmonders retired for the night anticipating that the next day things would get pretty much back to normal.

The twelfth of April did not, of course, see normality restored. On that day a storm of a different sort broke. It would rage not four days but four years and would engulf not just Richmonders but all Americans.

This book is about the people of Richmond during those years of civil war, about how they lived and also about how they died. A remarkable drama unfolded in the city during that time, as its inhabitants were caught up in momentous events and profoundly unsettling changes. How Richmonders endured those tumultuous years is an intriguing and important story.

Rich in history but of modest size and modest political and economic significance on the eve of the war, Richmond abruptly became the capital of the new government of the Confederate States of America, its military headquarters, and its primary munitions producer, essential to the nation's survival. As the war got under way the population mushroomed, the economy was deranged by sea and land blockades, government and citizenry clashed desperately over the allocation of vital resources, and the city was targeted by a mighty enemy army.

This experience, it is fair to say, is unparalleled in American history. Richmond's wartime counterpart, Washington, D.C., certainly saw enormous governmental and population expansion and a vastly enlarged military presence, but it was not the primary manufacturing center of its nation's war effort, never endured blockades or scarcities that threatened the survival of government or citizens, and was never seriously endangered by an enemy army at its gates. Nor did any other Northern or Southern city in that era — or any era before or since — have to grapple with a comparable host of transformations and calamities. Civil War Richmond stands alone in the American experience in the nature and severity of the challenges it faced.

Earlier general histories of wartime Richmond emphasize the high politics of the Confederate government, the battlefield clashes of the armies defending and attacking the city, and the lifestyles and attitudes of the city's elites. Those histories leave much unsaid about how ordinary Richmonders fared in the maelstrom of war.

This book places national politics and military maneuvers in the background and turns the spotlight on Richmonders as a whole—the humble and the middling as well as the prominent and the powerful, the weak and the wicked as well as the strong and the decent. Drawing on rich sources untapped by previous tellers of the tale, it explores matters ranging from how the people responded to patriotic appeals and governmental dictates to how they fed and housed themselves amid grueling shortages and claustrophobic crowding, made a living in a turbulent economy and distorted labor market, wrestled with the problems of political dissent and war-weariness, confronted a deluge of crime and disorder, dealt with one another across the lines of race and class and gender, coped with the omnipresent specters of suffering and death, and sought the help of God in making sense of it all.

What happened in Richmond during the Civil War mattered. It mattered not just because eminent men decided lofty issues of war and state there, nor because enormous armies fought bloody battles over it, nor because polished ladies and gentlemen wrote memorable accounts of glittering balls and dinner parties there. Events and conditions in the city were reported in great detail by contemporary journalists and others and were followed closely all across America, by the Confederacy's foes as well as its friends, for the city was seen in many ways as the heart and soul of the Rebel nation and a key signifier of its destiny. Stories of Richmond's ordeal colored Americans' understanding of the war as a whole—not only while it was being waged but also after it ended.

Richmond's wartime experience was shaped by people of every class, color, sex, and age. The city's populace had always been diverse and became more so during the conflict. What Richmonders thought and said and did as the events of 1861–65 transpired spans the range of human nature, complicating any attempt to characterize them and categorize their behavior. Scholars seeking answers to the "big" questions about the Confederacy—for instance, whether it was sufficiently united to win the war or was doomed to defeat by internal divisions—may be frustrated by my reluctance (although not, I trust, complete failure) to address the debates or to situate the city in broader patterns. I hope the reader will understand that this reluctance reflects not indifference or ignorance on my part but rather my belief that Richmonders' Civil War experience was unique and multifaceted and that it ought to be understood and appreciated for its own sake and in all its variety. I am happy to let others draw what historiographical conclusions they will from what I offer here; they may well find evidence to support both sides of every issue.

America's Civil War was a people's struggle waged off the battlefields as well as on them. Nowhere was this truth more dramatically demonstrated than in the beleaguered capital of the Confederacy. If this book succeeds in bringing wartime Richmond to life as a city of flesh-and-blood men, women, and children of many sorts who responded in very human ways to extraordinarily trying circumstances, it will have fulfilled its purpose.

REBEL PATRIOTS

James Wright cheered the creation of the Confederate States of America. He perceived in it, for one thing, a personal opportunity. A forty-eight-year-old Richmonder, he lived in a rented home with his wife, five children, and two boarders. He was making a living as a house painter, but he dreamed of grander things. On 19 March 1861 he wrote to the Confederate secretary of war in Montgomery, Alabama, offering his services as a drum major—in which capacity, he proudly explained, he had served the U.S. Army for seven years and the Virginia militia for fifteen. But it was not just the prospect of once again donning a splendid uniform and shako and flourishing a baton in martial parades that excited Wright. An earnest Southern-rights man, he rejoiced in the birth of the Confederate republic: "My sympathies are with the *Southern States*, and as a native Virginian I, among many thousands, would be glad to see our old mother go *straight out*."[1]

James Wright's wish for his motherland would soon be granted, and a large majority of Richmonders would take their stand alongside him. Fervent Rebel patriotism would infuse the city and guide its course in the years that followed. But with the boon of Southern independence would come the curse of war, which would sternly test the commitment of Confederates such as Wright to the cause they championed.

The city where Wright made his home was, by American standards, middle-aged. Founded in the 1730s, incorporated in 1742, and designated the state capital in 1779, Richmond thrived economically thanks to its location at the falls of the James River. The interdiction of river traffic by the falls made

Richmond a natural entrepôt. Goods came down the river from Virginia's piedmont and highland regions and down the canal that eventually supplemented the river, while seaborne goods came up the river from ports around the world. Wholesalers, retailers, and warehousemen did a brisk business in the city. Industries developed in Richmond, too, their products flowing up the river and canal to the state's interior and down the river to the outside world.[2]

A wave of turnpike and railroad construction in the first half of the nineteenth century reinforced Richmond's commercial and industrial importance; it became one of the South's key road and rail hubs. Among the leading commercial enterprises in the city that benefited from the transportation boom was the slave trade. The primary industries were tobacco processing, flour milling, and iron manufacturing; they drew raw materials from Virginia's farms and plantations, from the coal deposits near the city, and from the pig iron furnaces beyond the Blue Ridge Mountains and were in many cases powered by the river rapids. Lesser industries emerged in great profusion as well. By 1860 Richmond ranked thirteenth among U.S. cities in industrial output—and first among those that would soon be part of the Confederacy.[3]

Newcomers were invariably struck by the topography. It was a city of hills. Each had a name: Union Hill, Church Hill, Oregon Hill, Navy Hill, and others. The highest, which offered a panoramic view of the city, was Council Chamber Hill, on the crest of which stood the impressive neoclassical state capitol designed by Thomas Jefferson. That building was at the center of Capitol Square, in or around which stood most of the other public buildings.[4]

The city stretched for two miles along the northern bank of the James (the left bank as one went downriver) and for a mile and a quarter inland at its greatest extent. It rose up dramatically from the river, which at that point, as described by one visitor, "is more than [a] fourth of a mile wide, but is much broken up with a multitude of rocky islets and bowlders, against which the waters are ever beating in angry fury and noise." A tributary of the James called Shockoe Creek bisected the city.[5]

Many thought Richmond beautiful, especially in the summer when the trees lining the streets were in full leaf. Winter bestowed a certain beauty, too, although it also brought vexation in the form of snow and ice that made the steep hills treacherous to pedestrians and vehicles. The city was laid out in a very regular pattern, with straight streets running (approximately) north–south that crossed east–west streets at strict right angles. The major thoroughfares were Broad Street and Main Street, which ran east–west flanking Capitol Square. The business houses and factories were mostly confined to the city's core, an area stretching from the riverfront up to Broad Street and from Shockoe Creek westward for a half mile or so. Surrounding the core were residential neighborhoods, each with its own nickname — Shed Town, Butchertown, Jackson Ward, and others — some of which took the name of the hill they occupied.[6]

Certain neighborhoods had a distinctive ethnic or racial tinge. Native-born whites made up only about half of Richmond's population on the eve of the war. Of the 37,910 inhabitants counted by the census takers in the summer of 1860, 11,699 (31 percent) were slaves, 2,576 (7 percent) were free blacks, and roughly 5,000 (13 percent) were foreign-born whites. Irish immigrants accounted for nearly half the foreign born, with Germans not far behind in numbers. Members of those two ethnic groups, along with the free blacks, tended to cluster with others of their kind in particular neighborhoods.[7]

But all the city's residents were swept up in momentous political developments from November 1860 to May 1861 that catapulted Richmond to greater prominence. The election to the presidency of Abraham Lincoln, a Republican, horrified many Southern whites, for he and his party were avowedly antislavery. Dismissing the Republicans' claim that they intended only to halt further westward expansion of the South's "peculiar institution," not abolish it, some white Southerners envisioned a nightmarish future in which the politically impotent South would have emancipation forced on it by the North. The result, they were certain, would be bloody havoc. Spurred by this fear, the seven states of the lower South seceded from the Union and sent representatives to Montgomery, where in February they formed a new nation, the Confederate States of America.

Many thousands of Virginians, James Wright among them, ardently desired to see their state join this exodus from the Union. But when Wright offered his services to the nascent Rebel army in March, he and his fellow secessionists were nowhere near a majority of whites in the Old Dominion. Yes, almost all white Virginians were disquieted by Lincoln's election; one Richmonder called it "the most deplorable [event] that has happened in the history of the country." But the fear of an imminent threat to slavery that seized the Lower South infected comparatively few inhabitants of the Upper South. White Virginians during that time, although as committed as any other Southern whites to protecting slavery, tended to see the incoming presidential administration as less of a threat to the peculiar institution than secession itself, which might trigger the chaos of a North-South war that would likely be fought out in the Upper South.[8]

But change came abruptly on 12 April. Early that morning Confederate artillery in Charleston, South Carolina, opened fire on Fort Sumter in the city's harbor, still held by the U.S. Army. The news soon arrived in Richmond by telegraph, convulsing that city as it did every other part of the South and North. Many conservative Richmonders, assuming that the attack made war inevitable, instantly reassessed their loyalties. "It is not doubtful which course the current of feeling is rapidly taking," wrote diarist John Jones, a Marylander who had arrived by train that day from Washington and had taken a room at the Exchange Hotel. "Even in this hitherto Union city, secession demonstrations are prevalent." Those trying to stand against the tide, said Jones, "are now stricken dumb amid the popular clamor for immediate action."[9]

Fort Sumter fell on 14 April. The next day President Lincoln proclaimed his intention to put down the Southern insurrection with troops to be summoned from the loyal states, thus dashing any remaining hope that war might be averted. White Richmonders, now forced to choose between waging war on the seceded states or joining with them to defend against invasion, overwhelmingly took their stand with the Confederacy. "The most hopeful unionists in Virginia have now given up," wrote a Richmond woman on 21 April. "Since coercion has become the policy of Lincoln's administration, combined resistance is our common duty." Three days later another Richmonder wrote to a relative in the North about the quick reversal of sentiment in the city: "You have no idea how hateful the word *Union* has become here."[10]

Richmond resounded for days with public demonstrations and street-corner orations. John Jones, who had intended just to pass through the city on his way south to the Confederacy, was caught up in the excitement and stayed on to chronicle it. "Business is generally suspended," he wrote on 15 April, "and men run together in great crowds to listen to the news." That day he saw "hundreds of secession flags . . . flying in all parts of the city"; that night he watched "a procession with banners and torch-lights." Politicians delivered rousing speeches, evoking "hearty responses from the people."[11]

Jones depicted a city celebrating jubilantly, but at least one other witness sensed a different tone. Observing the scene on the night of 19 April, Emma Mordecai perceived "no noisy exultation nor joyful spirit in the perfectly decorous throng that filled the streets. A deep earnest enthusiasm greatly tempered with sadness was the prevailing feature."[12]

For two months a convention of delegates from across the state had been in session in Richmond, debating and repeatedly rejecting an ordinance of secession. But on 17 April, two days after Lincoln's call to arms, the ordinance passed (subject to popular ratification), dissolving Virginia's ties to the Union. Eight days later the convention approved an alliance between Virginia and the Confederacy and ratified the Confederate Constitution. On 7 May, the Confederate Congress admitted Virginia to statehood. Virginia's electorate approved the secession ordinance by majority vote on 23 May. Three other states of the Upper South likewise hoisted the banner of the Confederacy.[13]

Meanwhile, the founding fathers in Montgomery, led by President Jefferson Davis, prepared for war. Selecting a permanent capital for their new nation was a matter of high priority, little Montgomery being deemed unsuitable by most. A number of cities vied for the honor, including Richmond. The Virginia convention formally invited the Confederate government to make Richmond its home, and the Virginia representatives to the Confederate Congress lobbied hard for acceptance. Two considerations were particularly influential in the eventual selection of Richmond. First, it would bring the government seat and army headquarters close to what would clearly be a primary theater of war, northern Virginia, rendering more efficient the military defense of the region. Second, Richmond would have to be strongly defended by Confederate forces in any event because of its strategic importance as a rail hub and industrial center. Congress approved the decision on 20 May. Government officials immediately began packing up and moving out of Montgomery by train. Jefferson Davis arrived in Richmond, amid great celebration, on 29 May.[14]

For some Richmonders, however, the conversion from Union to Confederate patriotism was no snap decision but a long, agonizing struggle. Jacob Bechtel was one. A thirty-six-year-old bookstore clerk, he had been born and raised in Pennsylvania but had lived in the South since he was twenty. His correspondence with his brother in the North during the spring of 1861 recorded the anguish of a man torn between two loyalties. On 1 April he condemned both the Lincoln administration and the "vaporing demagogues" working to get Virginia out of the Union, and he lauded the "brave and gallant spirits" in the Virginia convention who so far had stymied the secessionists. Twenty-three days later, with the state effectively out of the Union and the city ablaze with the spirit of resistance, Bechtel denounced "the War Proclamation of that stupid ass at Washington" but confessed that "I cannot bear to turn against the Old Flag." In early May he still deplored secession but deplored equally the North's determination to undo it by force: "The Union is gone, utterly, irrevocably gone. . . . Why then insist upon restoring the dead[?] Would a Union of bodies without a Union of hearts be desirable?" He prayed for a "peaceful separation" of North and South; it sickened him to think of the two sections "cutting each other[']s throats." Urged by his brother to return to the land of his birth and join the crusade to crush the traitorous Rebels, and warned that by remaining in the Confederacy he risked forever alienating his Northern kin, Bechtel replied, "I cannot forget that I have eaten and drank at the hospitable boards, and sat by the peaceful firesides of the South for sixteen years. . . . Here three of my children were born, and here the ashes of one repose. I cannot raise my hand against [Southerners]; even at the expense, as you say, of the sympathy of you all." By mid-May he had resolved to stay in Richmond and quietly accept things as they were. He vowed, however, that he would never voluntarily take up arms against the Union.[15]

Richmonders who rallied wholeheartedly to the Confederate banner had no doubt that their cause was just. They were taking up arms to resist tyranny, just as the Revolutionary patriots had done. "We are menaced with subjugation for daring to assert the right of self-government," wrote prominent Presbyterian minister Moses D. Hoge in June 1861. The Lincoln administration was a "military despotism" whose malevolent designs Hoge opposed "with my whole mind and heart." Another leading Richmonder, state attorney general John Randolph Tucker, affirmed that the Confederacy was waging "a war of *defence — not of aggression*. . . . We vindicate its rightfulness. We neither sought, nor provoked it. . . . We had no alternative, but to surrender our heritage [of liberty] to the wrong-doer, or to defend it to the death."[16]

Patriotic zeal, martial enthusiasm, and a spirit of sacrifice inspired many Richmonders to volunteer for military service. By November 1861 at least 2,500 were in uniform. Twenty-three-year-old Henry H. Fauntleroy spoke for many in a letter he wrote to Virginia's governor in June: "I am anxious to serve my country," he announced. A resident of the state's Eastern Shore when the war broke out, Fauntleroy had hastily moved to Richmond, "thinking that I could be of more service on this side of the bay in active duty." This had entailed a rather risky voyage "across the bay in an open boat, shunning the blockading ships." Fauntleroy had more to offer than the typical volunteer, for he was a graduate of the Virginia Military Institute, trained not only as a soldier but as a civil engineer. Suggesting modestly to the governor that he might make a good officer, he added that if no commission could be granted, "I intend to shoulder my musket & go as a private."[17]

Volunteers under eighteen years old, and there were many, were supposed to have parental permission to enlist. Some dodged that requirement by running away from home and lying about their age. In June 1861, sixteen-year-old James Oliver slipped away from his mother and made his way to Petersburg, where he joined an infantry company. This left his mother in dire straits. Recently widowed, desperately poor, and wholly illiterate, Ann Oliver had two other children to care for, both under ten years old; she would never have given James to the army willingly, for he was her sole support. But many other parents capitulated to the pleas of their underage sons, signed a consent form, and kissed them goodbye as they went off to war. Seventeen-year-old Levert Powell, son of a wealthy physician whose estate (Melrose) stood on the city's outskirts, quit school and joined the Richmond Howitzers just nine days after the news of Fort Sumter arrived. Less than two weeks later, eighty young Richmonders formed themselves into a military company and offered their services to Jefferson Davis; some were only sixteen or seventeen, none older than nineteen, but all had their parents' blessing. These youthful patriots were "ready to march at any moment," they informed the president, and were prepared "to bleed & die [for] the Southern cause."[18]

Some citizens volunteered with the understanding that they would serve only in and around the city. In the summer of 1861, 240 men joined together in a unit they dubbed the Home Artillery and offered themselves to the Confederacy with the proviso that they were "not to be called from Richmond or its immediate vicinity, unless on some special occasion of attack or defence, and then only to a convenient distance, and for a short time." This condition being accepted, they were equipped with cannons and horses. But a few weeks later, the Confederate high command, having reassessed its needs, proposed that the Home Artillery be assigned to the army posted at Manassas Junction, some ninety miles north. Its members refused consent, whereupon their cannons and horses were confiscated and the unit disbanded.[19]

A good many Richmond men of Confederate sympathies, military age, and sound health declined to volunteer. Although they were not required to serve before national conscription was enacted (except for limited periods in the state militia), social pressure to enlist was strong and some felt obliged to justify themselves. Their reasons varied. Powhatan Weisiger, a twenty-seven-year-old hatter, remained behind in 1861 when his five brothers and two brothers-in-law living in or near the city all went off to war; "I deemed my duty under the circumstances to stay at home," Weisiger explained, to care for the seven families of those who left as well as his own, which included his wife, two little daughters, and mother-in-law. A baker named John H. Pleasants likewise invoked family responsibilities along with financial necessity: a man "of moderate means" by his own estimate, he had a wife, three children, and a mother-in-law dependent on him. Only the vaguest of justifications was offered by George Dalney, who early in the war took a job with the Confederate Treasury Department because he did not feel "qualified to take the field." A city official named Charles Stuart, by contrast, deemed himself eminently qualified to take the field, writing Jefferson Davis several times during the war's first year to boast of his military education and experience, offer his services to the army, and trumpet his patriotism. ("I am heartily committed to the great struggle you are nobly conducting against fearfull [sic] odds," he proclaimed in one letter.) Stuart could have enlisted as a private at any time, but he chose to remain out of uniform as long as the commission he coveted was not forthcoming.[20]

In the months following the outbreak of war, Richmond became an armed camp. Although most of the troops who enlisted there or arrived from other parts of the Confederacy were soon forwarded to the front, many thousands of others remained, crowding into buildings taken over as barracks or into tents pitched wherever space could be found. Meanwhile the Confederate bureaucracy expanded, Richmond's existing industries grew busy with government contracts, new factories sprouted throughout the city, and the civilian population swelled. Army engineers took charge of constructing an elaborate network of fortifications to protect the capital from the Yankee invasion that was sure to come.

The first invasion was soundly repulsed at the Battle of Manassas on 21 July. This Confederate victory gave the capital a long respite from worries about its safety. But Rebel patriots who expected the U.S. government now to acknowledge defeat and accept Confederate independence were disappointed. The enemy nation instead began marshaling its vast resources in earnest and redoubled its efforts to crush the Southern rebellion. One of its primary strategic goals was capturing the Rebel capital. In the spring of 1862, a huge Union army was transported by sea to the tip of the Peninsula (between the James and York Rivers) and from there advanced northwestward toward Richmond.

Resigned now to a long, hard war and recognizing that volunteers alone would not keep the military ranks adequately filled, the Confederate government enacted, in April, a conscription law. This forced into the army many Richmond men who theretofore had declined to don a uniform. Not all the new enrollees went to the front, however. In the summer of 1862, the War Department, having had another change of heart on the matter of restricted military service, accepted for duty the Twenty-Fifth Virginia Infantry Battalion (generally known as the City Battalion), composed of Richmond men and boys and permanently assigned to the capital's garrison force. Here at last was a place for Richmonders who wanted (or were required) to serve in arms but wished to stay close to home.[21]

As the city assumed a war footing, many patriotic citizens ineligible to take up arms or excused from doing so did their part for the cause in other ways. Parlors, churches, and meeting halls hummed with the activities of civilian associations supporting the war effort. Women had a prominent role in this work. Sewing and knitting circles produced an endless stream of socks, scarves, pants, shirts, jackets, and even tents that went to the troops at the front. The Ladies' Aid Society of Richmond, headed by Mary Randolph, cooperated with the YMCA to receive and distribute contributions of goods sent from all over the South for the benefit of soldiers, especially those hospitalized in the city. Women also volunteered individually for hospital work, visiting the wards to comfort patients by reading to them, praying with them, or writing letters for them. Some took patients into their own homes when the hospitals were inundated. Two women, Sally Tompkins and Juliet Hopkins, founded private hospitals in Richmond early in the war, providing welcome aid to an army struggling to care for its sick and wounded.[22]

Men were active in voluntary work, too, and not only with the YMCA. The Richmond Ambulance Corps, established in 1861, rendered invaluable assistance to the Confederate army. Agents of the corps escorted sick and wounded soldiers from the front by train to Richmond and were on hand at the Richmond depots to ensure that each one was conveyed comfortably and speedily to a hospital. The Association for the Relief of Maimed Soldiers provided amputees with artificial arms and legs. Among that organization's directors was the Reverend Moses Hoge, who devoted himself to many other patriotic endeavors as well, including preaching regularly (often three times a week) at army camps in the Richmond area and, on one occasion, traveling to England on a blockade-running steamship to secure Bibles for Confederate troops.[23]

By late May 1862, the Union army advancing up the Peninsula was closing in on Richmond. The Confederate army that had triumphed at Manassas had since moved south to counter this new enemy threat and was manning the capital's fortifications. Now essentially under siege, Rebel Richmonders prayed for deliverance while military and civil officials pondered abandoning the city. The patriots' prayers were answered in late June and early July, when the Confederate army (under the command of Robert E. Lee) launched a counteroffensive that drove the enemy back down the Peninsula.

Lee's army subsequently moved north and for nearly two years kept the Union army well away from the capital. Richmonders' enjoyment of this lengthy reprieve was tempered, however, by the multiplying hardships of life in the city. An enormous influx of newcomers — many of them refugees from Southern regions invaded by Union forces — along with the Confederate War Department's insatiable hunger for provisions and manpower, the Union sea and land blockades, and the disruption of Virginia's transportation network, spawned critical shortages of food, housing, labor, and virtually every other essential commodity, not to mention a wave of crime and disorder that threatened to overwhelm the city authorities.

As the war continued, reports from the invaded sections of the country stiffened Confederates' determination to fight. The Yankees seemed bent on ravaging the South. "We hear of so many horrors committed by the enemy in the [Shenandoah] Valley," Richmonder Judith McGuire wrote in April 1862, "houses searched and robbed, horses taken, sheep, cattle etc., killed and carried off, servants deserting their homes, *churches desecrated*!" The threat to slavery was especially frightening. By the fall of 1862, it was clear that the U.S. government was making war on slavery, as many white Southerners had feared it would do ever since the 1860 election. Any lingering doubts on that score were put to rest by Lincoln's Emancipation Proclamation of 1 January 1863. In March of that year, Richmond minister William Norwood stood before his congregation and condemned the armies of the North for "set[ting] at defiance the received usages of civilized warfare; and . . . call[ing] to their aid all the horrors of servile insurrection."[24]

Knowing their struggle was just, Rebel patriots could rest assured that God was on their side. This was profoundly comforting to a people who sought to conform in every aspect of their lives to the Lord's will, for certainly no nation unblessed by divine providence could survive. The Reverend D. S. Doggett, minister of Richmond's Broad Street Methodist Church, reminded his flock repeatedly that Confederate victory was part of God's plan and that He would lend His mighty hand to achieve it. "It cannot be a matter of indifference to Him, whether the right or the wrong shall triumph," Doggett explained in September 1862. "In the bloody tragedies through which we have just passed . . . God has looked down from His throne upon us with paternal solicitude, and . . . has wrought our deliverance."[25]

A similar reminder of the justness of the South's war for independence brought peace of mind to one troubled Confederate soldier, a patient in a Richmond hospital with whom Judith McGuire spoke in March 1862. "I can't bear the Yankees," he told her, but "I believe some of them are Christians, and pray as hard as we do; . . . I don't know what to think of our prayers *clashing*." How, he wondered, can we be certain that God favors the South over the North? McGuire answered his question with another: "Don't you believe that God will hear us for the justice of our cause?" This struck the soldier powerfully. "Yes, it is just," he responded excitedly. "I never thought of looking at it that way before, and I was *mighty* uneasy about the Yankee prayers."[26]

In the spring of 1864, another massive Union offensive threatened Richmond, this one directed southward from northern Virginia. Lee's army fought desperately to repel it but was forced to give ground. By June the enemy army was as close to the capital's eastern limits as it had been two years earlier. But again the city was saved. Unable to breach its defenses, the Yankee host sidled southward, eventually besieging Petersburg, about twenty-five miles from the capital. There the two armies remained locked in a deadly embrace through the winter of 1865.

Richmond had once more avoided the enemy's clutches. But thereafter it enjoyed no real respite. From the summer of 1864 on, sizable Yankee forces remained within striking distance and repeatedly harried the capital with cavalry raids and infantry thrusts, keeping its garrison troops and emergency forces busy, its fortifications in constant use, and its inhabitants unceasingly anxious.

As the population burgeoned and the demands of war pressed ever harder, the sounds and sights of life in the city were transformed. Richmonders grew used to hearing the tramp of infantry companies, the clatter of cavalry squadrons, and the rumble of artillery batteries on the streets. From the army camps emanated the frequent roll of drums. From the sentinels who guarded government offices and prisons came the hourly cry of "all's well." Martial band music and the shouted commands of officers marked the regular drills and dress parades of the Local Defense Forces and the state militia, which were often held in Capitol Square and always drew a crowd. Alarm bells rang across the city to muster those troops whenever the enemy approached. The sound of cannon and musket fire from the fortifications periodically startled the populace.[27]

The city whose beauty had always been a source of civic pride grew shabby and dirty. The uncobblestoned streets became rutted, and the chain gang assigned to maintenance could not keep up. Garbage, especially fruit rinds, accumulated in the gutters, posing a slippery hazard to pedestrians and attracting packs of stray dogs. Worse filth piled up in the alleys, including dead dogs and cats. Annoyances that had long afflicted Richmond mushroomed: the dust stirred up by street traffic, the soot from coal fires, the flies that buzzed around in and out of doors.[28]

The city's deterioration proceeded inexorably as the war entered its second, then third, then fourth year. As supplies grew scarce and workmen were taken by the army, house paint cracked and peeled, gates hung awkwardly from broken hinges, and shattered windows were papered over rather than replaced. Carpeting disappeared as citizens donated it for use as hospital blankets and mattresses. Hotel guests noticed that the crockery and glassware provided them was cracked and chipped. The city gasworks, which fueled residential, business, and street lighting, failed intermittently due to equipment shortages, forcing many Richmonders to resort to expensive candles and, on moonless nights, plunging the streets into Stygian darkness.[29]

Want, suffering, and death took myriad visible forms. Patched pants, mended socks, and secondhand coats and dresses clothed many people who before the war would never have been seen in them. As the customary meat supplies diminished, the carcasses of deer, possum, and other wild game appeared in markets and eateries. Fodder ran short, too, and horses and other work animals took on skeletal looks. On the crowded sidewalks could be seen more and more one-legged or one-armed men in uniform. Women clothed in black likewise became a common sight. Military funeral processions wended their way along the city streets day and night.[30]

As the war stretched on and on and the enemy remained unvanquished, religion continued to offer comfort and certainty. Reverend Norwood, sensing his congregation's pain and perplexity as the contest entered its third year, confronted the problem squarely: "If our cause is so clearly just," he said, "why are we allowed to suffer such loss of property, such desolation of large tracts of country, such loss of precious lives?" The answer was plain: "For our sins! . . . While God may grant us final [victory], while he may . . . punish our enemies, he may, nevertheless, make use of them as instruments to punish us for our sins as a people."[31]

The notion that victory might be delayed and the Confederate people chastened until they became fully worthy in the Lord's eyes made sense to many Christians. "Our cause is just and God is with us," affirmed a young Richmond woman named Maria Peek. "But peace is stayed because as a nation our hearts are not prepared for it. There are too many evils of every description rife in the land." Seen in this light, hardships and military setbacks were not cause for despair but rather encouraging evidence that God wanted the Confederacy to win the war and establish itself as a righteous nation. Some of the South's afflictions, however, seemed inexplicable. When contemplating these, the faithful reminded themselves that while all of God's acts were benevolent, some were beyond human understanding and must simply be accepted obediently and patiently. The death in May 1863 of the brilliant general Thomas "Stonewall" Jackson, Lee's right arm, was one such mystery. "It comes so suddenly upon us," Richmonder Kate Mason Rowland lamented in her diary, "and seems such a grievous stroke to the Confederacy. But we must not question the wisdom of the Father who has called him."[32]

Even in the war's last months, as the Rebel armies in Virginia and elsewhere withered away and disaster after disaster battered the tottering Confederacy, many Richmond patriots kept the faith. In a January 1865 letter to his wife in Georgia, Congressman Warren Akin wrote, "Away with your fears. . . . We are in the hands of God, and if He is for us, what harm can befall us? . . . *I do not think we will fail*."[33]

Confederates as undaunted as Akin were fewer in Richmond by that time than in 1861. But even if Rebel victory no longer seemed certain to every patriot, hope for it endured. Perhaps God would see fit to work a miracle of salvation.

CITY OF STRANGERS

The war was only four months old when the editor of the Richmond *Daily Dispatch* expressed amazement at how it had changed the city. "We begin to feel as if we were really the metropolis of the South," he said. "We have with us the President and his Cabinet; Congress and its intellectual adjunct, and visitors by the thousand; soldiers are coming and going; strange faces and diversified uniforms meet us at every step, and we almost begin to forget the quaint, staid days . . . when every countenance was as familiar as the curbstones, and we felt like one family."[1]

That last part was hyperbole, of course. The days when everybody in Richmond knew everybody else were long past, beyond living memory; on the eve of the war the inhabitants numbered nearly 40,000. And at no time in the city's history had Richmonders "felt like one family." Yet there was a measure of truth in the editor's comments, for the war did usher in demographic change so sweeping and sudden that it left many of the old residents stunned. The city experienced a population explosion with few parallels in American urban history, as people of all sorts came there for reasons of all sorts. Of the many changes Richmond would endure in the war years, this was the most immediate and apparent.

Some of the newcomers came willingly, others reluctantly; some were soldiers, others civilians; some saw their move as permanent, others as temporary. But whatever their motives and sentiments, they came in great numbers. "The city is overrun," one of the newcomers remarked in early 1862. "Main Street is as crowded as Broadway, New York; it is said that every boarding-house is full." An Englishman who visited later that year described the city as "a very busy place. Its streets and hotels were literally crammed with soldiers, officers, and civilians, of all ranks." Of course, many who came to the city during the war soon moved on, but they were quickly replaced by others; there was constant turnover. Meanwhile, a good number of longtime residents departed, gone to the army or elsewhere. To those who remained, it seemed that Richmond had abruptly become a city of strangers.[2]

Richmond was not unfamiliar with rapid growth. Indeed, its population had increased 38 percent between 1850 and 1860. But that was a mere ripple compared to the flood of in-migration that began in the spring of 1861. Exactly how much the population subsequently grew is, however, unknown and unknowable, for no wartime census was taken. Various guesses were made during the war; these were based solely on anecdotes, hunches, unsystematic observations, and inconclusive documentation such as tax rolls but were probably not too far off the mark. A Confederate War Department clerk estimated in March 1863 that 100,000 people were then residing in the city. Five months later the *Dispatch*'s editor proffered the same figure, noting that it did not include the thousands of patients in the city's military hospitals. Other guesses ranged somewhat lower or higher. One visitor was told by Richmonders in late 1862 that the populace had doubled in the last two years to about 80,000; another War Department official reported in 1864 a total of 130,000. The continuous turnover of population complicated the head counting, but, all things considered, it is probably safe to say that on any given day between 1862 and the war's end, the number of people residing or staying temporarily in Richmond was at least double, and perhaps triple, what it had been when the war began.[3]

Confederate troops began arriving well before Richmond was named the capital and continued to come until the war ended. Many just passed through, but others remained for a time in training, in hospitals, or as part of the city's garrison. Jefferson Davis dispatched thirteen regiments to Richmond only five days after the Virginia convention voted to leave the Union—three days before the state formally allied itself with the Confederacy. As more volunteer units mustered throughout the South that spring and summer, many were likewise ordered to the nation's capital. They camped in tents wherever space could be found in and around the city or moved into temporary barracks in warehouses, lecture halls, and other buildings. "We are now in the midst of the din of war," one Richmonder remarked on 24 April. "Every train brings in hundreds of men.... We have now 5000 of them in Richmond with more & more pouring in continually." Another described the city that spring as "one vast encampment." Soldiers who could get away for a time from camps or barracks, with or without permission, could often be seen strolling along the city sidewalks, lounging in hotel lobbies, or crowding into saloons and gambling dens. Many of the officers brought along slaves to act as manservants or cooks; these black men and boys, some of them in uniform, also became a familiar sight around the city.[4]

By late May the trains that brought carload after carload of combat troops to Richmond also brought hundreds of Confederate civil and military officials, who immediately got to work establishing the national government in its new home. Most of the married men among them were joined sooner or later by their wives and children. The Confederate Congress, which had adjourned in Montgomery, reconvened in Richmond on 20 July; its members, and in some cases their families, trickled into the city in the preceding days and weeks.

The first congressmen and their successors would be a periodic presence in the capital through the war years. Once the provisional Confederate government gave way to the permanent government in February 1862, the legislature consisted of 132 senators and representatives. It held six sessions between then and March 1865, each lasting from one to five months and followed by an extended intersession. The Confederate civil and military bureaucracy, on the other hand, became a permanent — and vastly larger — presence. The executive branch, comprising the president's office and six departments (State, War, Navy, Treasury, Justice, and Post Office), required bureau chiefs and assistant chiefs, clerks of various sorts, aides, messengers, and other functionaries. Their numbers, substantial in 1861, multiplied thereafter as the national government expanded its powers and grappled with the demands of the world's first modern war. (The Confederacy had a judicial branch but never created a supreme court, and the number of judicial officers in the capital remained very small.)[5]

The Treasury and War Departments were the biggest government employers in Richmond. By 1864 there were well over 500 Treasury employees in the city, distributed among nine offices, or bureaus. The War Department comprised in 1861 eight bureaus with 50 employees; by 1864, nine bureaus with 176 employees. That department's presence in Richmond was, however, far greater than those numbers suggest, for its bureaus oversaw, besides the combat troops there, a huge array of quartermaster shops, commissary depots, hospitals, prisons, ordnance works, and other army facilities in the city, each with its own complement of supervisors, clerks, artisans, laborers, surgeons, nurses, guards, cooks, laundresses, and so forth, some of them civilians and others soldiers. Chimborazo Hospital, for example, employed several hundred people, as did the army shoe depot; the Confederate States Ordnance Laboratory employed 1,200.[6]

The combat troops who flooded into Richmond in the war's first months received a few weeks of instruction and were then forwarded to the army assembling in northern Virginia. After 1861 the city saw no more camps scattered about haphazardly and no more public or private buildings pressed into service as temporary barracks. But throughout the war, Richmond remained a depot for newly enrolled soldiers. In early 1862, the War Department established an official camp of instruction at the former fairgrounds one mile west of the city. Camp Lee, as it came to be called, was a reception and training facility for conscripts; sometimes it also housed sick or wounded Confederate soldiers no longer requiring hospital care but not yet healthy enough to return to their units, along with soldiers who had been captured and paroled by the Yankees but had not yet been formally exchanged and were thus forbidden to bear arms. Camp Lee was connected to the city by a rail line on which shuttles ran back and forth hourly during the day, and it was usually a busy, crowded place; there were rarely fewer than several hundred men quartered there at any given time and sometimes as many as 5,000.[7]

Also quartered in and around Richmond throughout the war was the city's garrison force. This revolving cast of Confederate infantry, cavalry, and artillery units manned defensive fortifications, patrolled the approaches to the city, and guarded bridges and government buildings. The garrison's strength varied over time; usually it counted between 4,000 and 5,000 men present for duty, not including the troops of the Virginia state military units that served in the city (who were mostly Richmond residents) or those of the Local Defense Forces (civilians who lived and worked in the city and mustered for duty only in emergencies).[8]

Far more numerous were the hospitalized Confederate soldiers. The War Department, noting the city's excellent rail connections and the plethora of large buildings, decided early on to make Richmond a military hospital center, primarily serving the main army in the eastern theater of war (commanded by Robert E. Lee after May 1862 and known as the Army of Northern Virginia). The Medical Bureau established dozens of hospitals in the city beginning in June 1861; several Confederate states and individuals established others. Until a sufficient number were in operation, patients were also cared for in private homes in the city. Early in the war, hospitals were set up in whatever buildings could be procured, in many cases former tobacco warehouses or factories. But these were eventually superseded by huge, specially built facilities called encampment hospitals. There were six of them, located on the city's outskirts. One was Chimborazo, which comprised 150 buildings on forty acres and could hold over 3,000 patients. Howard's Grove, Jackson, Louisiana, and Stuart were somewhat smaller. The biggest was Winder, which covered 125 acres and could accommodate over 4,000 patients.[9]

Sick Rebel soldiers came to Richmond from the front in a continual stream throughout the war. The wounded came mostly in waves following battles. The first wave hit the city in late July 1861, after the Battle of Manassas. Vastly larger ones struck the next spring and summer after Seven Pines and the Seven Days' Battles, which were fought very near the city. Second Manassas, Antietam, and Fredericksburg later in 1862, Chancellorsville and Gettysburg in 1863, and the Wilderness, Spotsylvania, and the clashes around Petersburg in 1864—each of these and many others generated a deluge of wounded Confederates who were sent to Richmond by ambulance or train. Over the course of the war, the city's military hospitals treated at least 200,000 sick or wounded Rebel soldiers, perhaps as many as 300,000. The typical patient's stay—whether he lived or died—was measured not in days but weeks; some remained for months. Quite a few who were ultimately discharged from the hospital but were unfit to return to the ranks (such as amputees), and were unable or unwilling to return home, stayed on in the city.[10]

Richmond's privately owned manufacturing establishments, like the Confederate government's facilities, were a rapidly expanding source of jobs that drew people in great numbers to the city, many of them with their families. The government needed war materiel and office supplies of every conceivable sort, and Richmond's factory owners were eager to provide them. Within weeks after the outbreak of war, manufacturers were signing contracts—especially with the various bureaus of the War, Navy, and Treasury Departments—and they continued to do so until the Confederacy's final days. The Tredegar Iron Works, owned by J. R. Anderson and Company, hired many new workers as the army called on it for cannon barrels and gun carriages. Other Richmond manufacturers that fattened on war contracts and were thus able to expand their workforce included Crenshaw Woolen Mills (makers of wool and cotton cloth for uniforms and tents), Haxall, Crenshaw, and Company (flour millers), Belvidere Manufacturing Company (producers of paper for government stationery, documents, and small-arms cartridges), Old Dominion Iron and Nail Works, and Eagle Machine Works, to name only a few. A sizable proportion of the newly hired workers, both skilled and unskilled, were slaves or free blacks. J. R. Anderson and

Company, among many other manufacturers, employed blacks in growing numbers during the war as white labor became scarce; by late 1864, hundreds were toiling at Tredegar.[11]

Entrepreneurs also flocked to the city, lured by the prospect of government contracts. Julius Baumgarten was one; an engraver and die cutter from Washington, D.C., he had moved to Montgomery when the Confederate government was founded and then followed it to Richmond, where in the summer of 1861 he began doing business with the Quartermaster Bureau, making stamps for letterheads and forms. Prostitutes by the hundreds made their way to Richmond, too, seeking business opportunities in a city teeming with soldiers and other men away from home. Rumor had it that the women came not only from other parts of the Confederacy but also from Baltimore, Philadelphia, and New York City.[12]

A lot of the newcomers who found work in Richmond were seeking not just a job but a refuge. The passions, enmities, and political and economic upheavals generated by the Civil War provoked a refugee crisis such as America had never known. Southern men, women, and children in vast numbers were driven from their homes, or chose to leave, and subsequently sought sanctuary in Confederate territory. Many of them headed to Richmond.[13]

Typically, these refugees were Rebel patriots who, through the fortunes of war, had found themselves suddenly in the hands of the enemy, or about to be. Like the wounded Confederate soldiers, they tended to come in waves. During the war's first weeks, many emigrated from Maryland, a Southern state that remained in the Union; many others in that time came from Northern states where they had previously taken up residence. As the war progressed, Yankee forces seized various parts of the Confederacy, and each of these military conquests triggered an exodus of refugees. In 1861, Virginia's Eastern Shore counties and some of its western counties along the Ohio River fell to the invaders. In 1862, the lower Shenandoah Valley, the Peninsula, Norfolk and vicinity, and the state's northeastern counties between the Potomac and Rappahannock Rivers also experienced invasion. Elsewhere in the Confederacy, many cities, towns, and rural districts fell to the enemy one by one between 1861 and 1865. These Union incursions, particularly those in Virginia, brought to Richmond many thousands of homeless men, women, and children trying to reestablish their lives.[14]

Most came by train, some in wagons, and a few on foot. The lucky ones brought along money and other personal property, or at least a marketable skill, which enabled them to settle in comfortably; the unlucky arrived with nothing but the clothes they wore and perhaps a little baggage. Robert

Hough was among the lucky. A prosperous, middle-aged tobacco merchant in Baltimore on the eve of the war, he left that city for Richmond in July 1861, accompanied by his wife and daughter (his two sons having already gone south to join the Confederate army). Although he had to leave behind much of his stock of tobacco, along with his account books and furniture, he managed to ship enough to Richmond before the Federal land and sea blockades tightened up to resume tobacco trading there, setting himself up in a building on Pearl Street. He did so well that before long he was able to branch out into the sugar trade.[15]

John A. Dugan did well, too, at least by his own standards. An ardent Rebel patriot in his late twenties and unmarried when the war began, he had quit his job as a clerk in the Shenandoah Valley town of Martinsburg and enlisted in an infantry company. A wound he suffered at the first Battle of Manassas left him permanently unfit for soldiering and he returned home. But when the Yankees invaded the valley in the spring of 1862, he refused to live under their rule. Determined to "follow the fortune of our beloved South," as he proudly asserted, he refugeed to Richmond. Although he had little or no tangible property, his useful talents enabled him to get a clerkship in the Quartermaster Bureau. Middle-aged sisters Susan and Ann Yerby, refugees from Maryland, likewise resumed their accustomed livelihood in Richmond. They had operated a boardinghouse in Baltimore, and when they left, they not only gave that up but also abandoned pretty much all their possessions. Yet, with the help of a third sister who had fled Missouri (another Southern state that did not secede), they managed to open a new boardinghouse in the Confederate capital, an upscale establishment on Fifth Street whose clientele included a number of congressmen.[16]

Other refugees struggled to survive in Richmond. Many found it impossible to resurrect the kind of life they once knew and had to settle for less. Francis R. Snapp, another Shenandoah Valley exile, had abandoned all his household goods and the tools and machinery of his foundry business when he fled to Richmond with his wife and three young children. This left him, as he lamented in 1863, "without a dollar in the world." He did find a job—Eagle Machine Works hired him to help manufacture artillery shells—but he got little satisfaction from it, for he was "compelled to labor as a common journeyman."[17]

Certain other refugees would have considered Snapp an ungrateful whiner, for he was at least able to make a living. Many could not. Among them was a Louisiana-born woman named Deady, whose husband, an Irish immigrant and a potter by trade, was languishing in a Northern prisoner of war camp. In December 1863, at age twenty-three, she left her home near New Orleans (which had fallen to the Yankees in 1862) because the military authorities had ordered that all citizens take the Federal oath of allegiance or depart to Rebel territory. How she made it to Richmond — with two little daughters in tow — is an unanswered question, for she was quite poor. Nor is it clear what she expected to do there. Perhaps she hoped to find a job of some sort, but either before or after arriving in the city she sustained an injury to her right hand that left her unemployable. By June 1864 she had exhausted what little money and saleable possessions she had brought with her and was desperate to get out of Richmond — even willing to return home (where she still had kin) and take the despised Yankee oath if she could get a Confederate passport and train fare. Petitioning the War Department got her the passport but not the fare. There were many such people, especially women with children, who refugeed to Richmond but then found themselves with no means of survival; some of them, unlike Deady, came from affluent circumstances and were well educated. A lot of them soon moved on.[18]

There were people other than refugees who also wanted out of Richmond but who, for one reason or another, were marooned there. Some had been visiting the city when their homes were captured by the Union army. Such was the fate of the West family of Norfolk, a husband and wife and four daughters who, in May 1862, suddenly found themselves homeless in the capital. After six weeks of fruitless attempts to make a living, Mr. West pleaded with the War Department to let the family pass through the Confederate lines and return home. He had no desire to live under Yankee rule, he said, but better that than to live "among strangers without [any] means [of support]," which he thought a "dreadful thing." Quite a few Confederate congressmen and Virginia state legislators found themselves stuck in Richmond during the long legislative intersessions because their homes had fallen into Yankee hands. A group of Richmond citizens, including the mayor and several city councilmen, thoughtfully hosted a holiday party for these unfortunates on Christmas Day in 1863, serving eggnog and edibles and, as the *Dispatch* reported, doing "much to make the strangers feel at home in Richmond."[19]

Certain others stranded in the city had been brought there against their will. L. C. McCalman was one of them. A fifty-two-year-old farmer from Carroll County, Georgia, with a large family dependent on him, he had conceived the idea of making some money as a civilian sutler catering to the troops in Virginia. In December 1862 he made the long journey from home, but by February he was in trouble. Caught selling liquor to soldiers at Hanover Junction, north of Richmond, he was arrested by the local provost marshal, who confiscated over $1,200 worth of his goods and sent him under guard to the provost marshal in Richmond. Penniless, unemployed, and with no means of getting home, McCalman wrote a plaintive letter to Jefferson Davis explaining his misfortune and pleading for the return of his property: "I am in a bad condition," he told the president. Anne Edwards, a resident of Culpeper County, Virginia, likewise ran afoul of local military authorities—how, exactly, is unrecorded—and was sent to Richmond, along with her children. After many months in prison she was released but was forbidden to leave the city. For the next two years, she lived by taking whatever work she could find and by continuing to draw rations from the prison. In the summer of 1864, the provost marshal finally relented, told her she was free to go home, and cut off her rations. By then, however (as she recounted in a written appeal dictated to a notary public, for she was illiterate), her house and other property in Culpeper had been destroyed by fire, leaving her "no home to go to." The provost marshal dismissed her plea to reinstate the rations, insisting that she had brought her troubles on herself by her "misconduct" in Culpeper.[20]

Edwards was one of the many thousands of people who at one time or another found themselves immured in the Eastern District Military Prison in Richmond. Castle Thunder, as it was generally known, was a former tobacco warehouse on Cary Street. Opened in August 1862, it replaced a short-lived facility known as Castle Godwin and was soon expanded to include some adjacent buildings. The War Department also maintained a smaller prison in the city called Castle Lightning. All three were under the direct authority of the Richmond provost marshal.[21]

Housed in these military prisons—in some cases for just a few days but not uncommonly for weeks or even months—were people of all sorts and from many different places (more than a few of them women) who had been arrested or detained by Confederate authorities. Most were Southern civilians charged with, or simply suspected of, disloyalty to the Confederacy in some form: uttering Unionist or abolitionist sentiments, aiding the Yankee army, dodging conscription, trying to pass illegally into enemy territory, and so forth. But the Castles also held other sorts of people whom the Rebel authorities wanted to keep locked up, including Confederate soldiers who had deserted or violated other articles of war, Union army deserters (who were confined separately from Union prisoners of war), Northern civilians caught in Confederate territory, and Southern civilians accused of counterfeiting, illegally manufacturing or selling alcohol, or other violations of Confederate law.[22]

Black men, women, and children were among the incarcerated. Like the white prisoners, they hailed from various places and had fallen into the Rebel authorities' clutches for a variety of reasons. Many were fugitive slaves apprehended by Confederate troops. A young boy named Robert, owned by a Culpeper County man, was one of these unlucky ones. After running off with a party of Yankee cavalry in June 1864, he enjoyed only one day of freedom before pursuing Confederates seized him and sent him to Castle Thunder, along with eight companions likewise frustrated in their bid for liberty.[23]

Recaptured slaves such as Robert rarely spent much time in the Richmond prisons; they were soon returned to their masters or otherwise put to work. But other blacks languished in the Castles for weeks or months on end. Lewis Going, a free black who made his home in Essex County, Virginia, and fished the Rappahannock River in a skiff for a living, was arrested in the fall of 1863 for ferrying white fugitives across the river to Yankee-held territory. Sent to Castle Thunder, he was still there more than six months later.[24]

Castle Thunder alone held, over the course of the war, some 40,000 prisoners, white and black. It got more crowded as time went on: there were about 300 inmates on any given day in late 1862, 600 in mid-1863, 700 by the spring of 1864, and perhaps 1,000 later on.[25]

Other involuntary Richmond residents in great numbers were to be found in the city's prisoner of war facilities. The War Department established sixteen of these beginning in the summer of 1861, of which up to half a dozen or so were in use at any one time. The most important were Libby Prison, opened in March 1862 in a former ship chandler's warehouse on Cary Street, and Belle Isle, a stockaded encampment erected four months later on an island in the James River near the city's western boundary. Several of the others were located in former tobacco-processing factories or tobacco warehouses.[26]

The Union soldiers who populated these prisons tended, like the refugees and the Confederate wounded, to arrive in waves. In the wake of every battle in the eastern theater of war (and even some in the western theater), great numbers of blue-uniformed captives came in by rail or on foot, guarded by Confederate soldiers. On 23 July 1861, for example, two days after the Battle of Manassas, 631 rolled in on the Virginia Central Railroad. Nearly 3,000 marched in on a single day in late June 1862, as the Seven Days' Battles were raging near the city. Some 2,000 tramped in on the Brooke Turnpike one evening in early May 1863, a fraction of those taken at the Battle of Chancellorsville. The 1864 battles brought thousands more to the city, including, for the first time, some black soldiers.[27]

The number of Union captives confined in Richmond varied widely over time, depending on not only the clashes of the armies but also the status of the prisoner exchange cartel between the C.S. and U.S. governments and the availability of prisoner of war facilities elsewhere in the Confederacy. But rarely were there fewer than 1,000 in the city and usually far more. In early November 1861, there were about 1,700; in mid-July of the following year, over 7,800; at the end of 1863, at least 13,000; at the beginning of 1865, almost 3,000. Libby, which housed mostly officers, held as many as 1,450 prisoners at one time, although its official capacity was 1,050. Belle Isle, used exclusively for enlisted men, held as many as 8,000 at a time.[28]

Nor does this complete the roll call of reluctant newcomers in Richmond. Soon after the outbreak of war, gangs of enslaved black men bossed by white overseers began arriving in the city and were put to work by state military engineers building defensive fortifications; their labor had been donated by patriotic Virginia slave owners. At the same time, local authorities in some Virginia counties and towns on their own initiative conscripted free black men and sent them to work on the capital's defenses. Such contributions failed to provide sufficient workers and in any event dried up after the initial flush of patriotic fervor passed, so the military engineers appealed to Virginia's slave owners to hire out their bondsmen to continue the work. But this too failed to secure enough labor, and eventually state and Confederate authorities resorted to impressing slaves and conscripting free blacks from all across Virginia to construct Richmond's fortifications.[29]

The elaborate network of trenches, redoubts, and obstructions that took shape around the city, and helped fend off the Yankee army for nearly four years, was the product of the sweat of many thousands of involuntary black laborers wielding picks and shovels and axes. They were quartered in or near the city and typically served for sixty days before being sent back to their owners and families, although some served considerably longer. The fortifications were continually improved and extended over the course of the war, and thus the demand for labor never ceased; the capital experienced periodic influxes of impressed black workers to the very end. Their numbers varied widely from month to month: at times there were few or none, at other times legions. In early November 1862, for example, some 5,000 were at work; ten weeks later, twice that many.[30]

Other enslaved people, not just men but women and children, too, were sent to Richmond in considerable numbers to keep them from running off to the Yankees or falling into their hands. Most came from peripheral regions of the Confederacy, particularly in Virginia, that were invaded or threatened by the Union army. Many were brought along by their refugee masters and stayed in the city serving them as long as the masters remained. Others were sent by masters who chose not to abandon their homes but feared for the safety of their human property with the Yankees near. In September, October, and November 1862, for example, carload after carload of slaves arrived in Richmond by rail from the endangered northern regions of the state, particularly the Shenandoah Valley and the Fredericksburg area.[31]

Those who came to Richmond unaccompanied by their owners were generally fated to be sold or hired out. The city was well equipped to deal with them, for it had long been a center of the Southern slave trade, second in importance only to New Orleans. Richmond brokers specializing in slave sales or slave hiring numbered in the dozens. Most of the black in-migrants who were hired out remained in the city, working as household servants, factory hands, fortification laborers, army wagon drivers, and hospital cooks and laundresses and in many other capacities; those put on the block were generally taken away to other parts of the Confederacy. So numerous were the latter in the fall of 1862 that the market became glutted and, to the disappointment of sellers and auctioneers, prices fell sharply.[32]

The men, women, and children sent to the city to be sold rarely spent more than a few days there. They were one small part of an ever-changing multitude that Richmonders called the "floating population," people who came for one purpose or another, remained only briefly—a day or two or three, perhaps a week—and then were gone. At any given moment during the war there were thousands in the city.[33]

Some were simply passing through on the railroads and found themselves forced to stay for a time awaiting a connection. There were, in particular, always a lot of soldiers going to and from home on furlough who needed overnight accommodation in the city; by the fall of 1862, the army was providing for, on average, 1,200 to 1,500 such men per night. But the typical short-term visitor came on business of some sort, drawn by Richmond's role as the new nation's government seat, military headquarters, and industrial center.[34]

Particularly plentiful were military men and aspiring military men seeking appointment, promotion, or reassignment. Such supplicants in fact began arriving in Richmond well before it became the national capital, for

Virginia set about raising a state army as soon as it seceded. (This army was turned over to the Confederate government in the summer of 1861 and became the nucleus of the Army of Northern Virginia.) G. W. Bassett Jr., for example, came to Richmond in late April from his home in Hanover County, north of the city, where he taught school. Introducing himself to the state army commander as a patriotic, unmarried, thirty-year-old native son of the Old Dominion who thought it "eminently my duty to be at the post of danger," Bassett requested a position—preferably a staff position, he added, for he knew nothing about drill or tactics.[35]

No sooner was the Confederate War Department established in Richmond than it was similarly besieged by applicants. William Skeen, a well-to-do lawyer from western Virginia, traveled to the city in mid-June, took a room at the Ballard House, and managed to get an interview with the secretary of war, from whom he asked authority to raise a guerrilla company to battle Yankee invaders and local Unionists back home. The stream of such applicants never let up as long as the Rebel capital endured. The *Examiner* remarked in the fall of 1863 that "there are now in Richmond upwards of two hundred officers without duty lying high and dry, and waiting for the flood tide of official orders to take them off and assign them to some field. . . . These officers . . . 'dance attendance' daily at the War Department, but their enquiry for orders is met with the caballestic [*sic*], 'Nothing yet.'"[36]

Other petitioners of every conceivable sort likewise haunted the offices of the Confederate government, particularly the War Department. On the very day that William Skeen was in town asking permission to wreak vengeance on Yankees and traitors, an elegant gentleman calling himself Camille La Valliere De Kalb was also there importuning the secretary of war. De Kalb, who claimed to be a grandson of the Revolutionary War hero of that name and a veteran of the Crimean War, had come from Canada to make a remarkable offer. He was willing, he said, to travel surreptitiously to Washington, plant sufficient gunpowder under the U.S. Capitol to blow it sky-high, and then detonate it while Congress was in session and President Lincoln was present. For this estimable service to the Confederacy he asked only modest compensation: a commission as colonel of topographical engineers and $1 million.[37]

De Kalb may have been the very first crackpot to buttonhole the Confederate secretary of war, but he was by no means the last. The great majority of favor seekers who descended on the capital were, however, on more serious business. In the late summer of 1861—a time when hope still abided for a short and relatively bloodless war—there came from Greene County,

Alabama, a Methodist minister named Elisha Phillips, who requested permission to examine War Department records and visit the army at Manassas Junction. He planned to publish a book as soon as the war was over containing a biographical sketch of every soldier who gave his life in Confederate service—a tribute, Phillips explained, to "the heroic Dead." In March 1862, a man named Metcalfe, representing a textile manufacturing firm in Middle Tennessee, presented himself at the War Department; he sought an order to protect the company's stores of cotton, for retreating Confederate troops in that region were burning every bale they could find to keep it out of the Yankees' hands. From Vicksburg, Mississippi, in late 1862 came a man named Marye requesting a permit that would allow him to pass beyond Confederate lines, slip into the North, and make his way to Boston, where he intended to buy shoes and blankets badly needed by the Rebel army; he was sure, he said, that he would be able to smuggle the stuff back into the Confederacy, leaving the Yankees none the wiser. F. N. Strudwick, owner of a large plantation and ninety slaves in Marengo County, Alabama, arrived in the capital in the summer of 1863 to plead for exemption from the draft; no one else was available, he claimed, to manage his place.[38]

Many who came had pathetic stories to tell. William B. Armstrong, a seventy-four-year-old blacksmith from Lincoln County, North Carolina, appeared at Christmastime in 1862 to beg for the discharge of his son Joseph, a conscript at Camp Lee who was sorely needed at home. The old man was too feeble, as he explained to the War Department, to work any longer; sometimes he could not even dress himself. His wife, Mary, too, was "old and helpless." If Joseph could not come home and keep the blacksmith shop going, not only his parents but his community would suffer. And besides, the father added, he had already sent eight sons to the army, one of whom would never return. A man named W. H. Ford traveled even farther—1,000 miles, from Texas—to ask the secretary of war to release his son from service. The seventeen-year-old had enlisted without his father's consent and marched away to war before he knew of it.[39]

The case of Mildred Hutton, a blacksmith's wife who lived some miles out in the Henrico County countryside surrounding Richmond, was another sad one. In October 1864 she came to the city to throw herself on the mercy of President Davis. Her husband, George, a conscript, had left Camp Lee without permission in order to go home and lay in a store of provisions for her and their three small children, who were facing starvation. The army charged him with desertion and now he sat in Castle Thunder, sentenced to imprisonment for the duration of the war. In a heartrending written plea,

Mildred told the president of her "poverty and distress" and begged him to release George, for she could not provide for the children on her own. "I pray god will tuch [sic] your kind and benevolent heart," she said, adding that if clemency was not forthcoming, "I can foresee nothing but nakedness and starvation." The harsh demands of war prevailed, however, and George remained in prison.[40]

Especially pitiful were the family members of sick, wounded, or missing soldiers who came to the capital to get information about them or help care for them. Every incoming train brought some of these unfortunates, all of them consumed with anxiety. "On the cars I met with many touching incidents," wrote Lucy Randolph, who traveled to Richmond from her Shenandoah Valley home in September 1862 to help nurse her ailing son. "One old woman had incurred much inconvenience & expense in leaving home & taking the journey with the hope of seeing her son who was sick at a hospital—another [was] looking for her husband who was wounded." Those who came with hope in their hearts were in many cases dealt a crushing blow. Cornelia McDonald, who lived in the Shenandoah Valley town of Lexington, suffered such a blow in 1864. Informed by letter that her husband, Angus, a Confederate officer, was in Richmond and very ill, she made the long journey there by canal boat and train. On arriving, she rushed from the depot to Angus's side only to find his corpse laid out with a wreath adorning it; he had died just the day before. Others came to Richmond without hope, having been notified of their loved one's death and desiring only to visit his grave, retrieve his personal effects, or make arrangements to ship his body home.[41]

The men and women who thronged Richmond on errands of business or mercy typically stepped off the train feeling overwhelmed, for the city was big and unfamiliar and intimidating. Thus the first thing many did was purchase one of the helpful guides for visitors published by Richmond entrepreneurs and available at the railroad depots and elsewhere. These booklets, such as *The City Intelligencer*, published in 1862, and *The Stranger's Guide and Official Directory*, published in 1863, provided the addresses of hotels, government offices (Confederate, state, and municipal), hospitals, prisons, cemeteries, banks, churches, and so forth. City maps were also for sale.[42]

Sympathetic Richmonders and the Confederate authorities stepped in to help, too, at least to help the many thousands who came to aid a loved one in uniform. In July 1861, in the wake of the Battle of Manassas, some citizens organized a committee to assist the wounded who were being brought to the city and distributed among hospitals and private homes. Inundated with inquiries from family members, by letter and in person, the committee set up an "intelligence office" that endeavored to maintain a record of where each patient could be found. In the spring of 1862, by which time the number of soldiers hospitalized in Richmond had multiplied vastly, an army chaplain named W. A. Crocker conceived a plan to formalize and improve this service. His appeals to the secretary of war and the surgeon general led to the creation of the Army Intelligence Office. Housed on the upper floor of the Bank of Virginia building on Main Street and staffed by a sizable contingent of clerks, this War Department agency kept registers, updated daily, of all patients in the Richmond hospitals and stood ready to assist anyone who came to the city in search of one. It also maintained a record of the current location of every Confederate military unit in the eastern theater to aid soldiers returning to duty after a long absence.[43]

Richmond's explosive population growth, unanticipated by the municipal and Confederate authorities, increasingly troubled them. The problem was threefold. First, getting enough food to the city to provide for the swollen populace, the hordes of visitors, and the numerous wards of the government (prisoners of war, inmates of the Castles, hospitalized soldiers, conscripts and others in Camp Lee, garrison troops, impressed black laborers) became more and more difficult as the war went on. Furthermore, every morsel thus consumed was one denied to the Subsistence Bureau, whose warehoused stockpiles of rations in the city were crucial to the Army of Northern Virginia's survival. Moreover, the presence of so many prisoners of war and political prisoners posed an internal threat to military security, especially when, as in the spring of 1862 and the spring of 1864, the Union army approached dangerously close to the city.[44]

These concerns were much discussed in official circles. In mid-1862 the city council considered calling on those citizens who could do so to move away voluntarily, to ease pressure on the food supply. In October 1863 Robert E. Lee urged Secretary of War James A. Seddon to remove all prisoners of war from the city. Lee repeated that advice the following April, and to the list of those who should be shipped out he added the Confederate parolees at Camp Lee, the Yankee deserters in the Castles, and all citizens not doing work essential to the war effort. Seddon endorsed these recommendations. Jefferson Davis and his cabinet took up the matter in April 1864, debating proposals to relocate a substantial portion of the government clerks to other cities and to encourage other civilians to leave voluntarily. Later that year the quartermaster general asked Seddon to consider removing Richmond's "surplus population." In early 1865, with the food crisis at its most intense, the city council discussed expelling the 5,000 or 6,000 women and children whose husbands and fathers had left them behind in the city when they fled to the Yankee lines.[45]

None of this came to much. The city council never got beyond talking about population removal, and the Confederate authorities did little more. In 1864 the Treasury Department transferred a few hundred employees to Columbia, South Carolina. The War Department removed the Confederate parolees that year along with thousands of prisoners of war. But the depopulation thus achieved in Richmond, with its many tens of thousands of inhabitants, was hardly enough to matter — and in the case of the prisoners of war was only temporary, anyway, for new prisoners soon took the place of those removed, or at least of some of them.[46]

Why so little was done to relieve a problem that everyone in authority agreed was critical is a question worth answering. For one thing, most officials probably recognized that urging the public to evacuate voluntarily was futile. As a Confederate functionary named Robert Kean explained after the president and cabinet shelved the idea in April 1864, "The *poor* would not have gone because they could not subsist elsewhere. The rich would not leave their property. Those in moderate circumstances have at great cost and trouble accumulated some store of provisions which they could not transport, nor could they buy elsewhere if they sold what they have. Hence they would have held to what they have here. The scheme would have been . . . a miserable failure."[47]

Any evacuation of the public would therefore have had to be forced. But this raised legal issues. The city council, uncertain of its powers in this regard, would not act without consulting the War Department. Secretary of War Seddon insisted on one occasion that he lacked authority to send away ordinary citizens against their will. However, he expressed no such reservation in his correspondence with Robert E. Lee and, given the extraordinary measures the Confederate government did take in Richmond and elsewhere under the doctrine of military necessity, it is doubtful that legal obstacles could have blocked population removal.[48]

The real obstacles were not legal but logistical. The government would have been obliged to resettle any citizens it forced out of Richmond or at least those who lacked the means to resettle themselves. This would entail transporting them, securing new housing for them, and thereafter either finding work for them or provisioning them as charity cases. Such an undertaking, if it involved numbers large enough to really make a difference in Richmond, was simply beyond the capacity of the hard-pressed Confederate government (not to mention the city government). So was the complete removal of prisoners of war: the War Department was never able to build and maintain enough prisons elsewhere in the Confederacy to allow those in Richmond to be closed down.[49]

The idea of moving the Confederate bureaucracy out of Richmond was scrapped in the cabinet deliberations of April 1864 (only to be hurriedly carried out one year later when the army abandoned the city). As Robert Kean explained, such an exodus "would produce a total dislocation of the public business." Another consideration was public morale. When a rumor swept the city in April 1864 that the whole Confederate government was about to pack up and move south (based no doubt on leaked, distorted reports of the cabinet discussion), a lot of Richmonders took it as a sign of impending military disaster and became alarmed; the actual removal of any substantial part of the government might well have sparked a panic (as indeed it did in April 1865). In any event, relocating the bureaucrats would not have eased the city's food crisis enough to justify the logistical effort and the administrative disruption.[50]

Thus Richmond saw no relief from the intense pressure of population. As long as it served the Confederacy, the city remained exceedingly crowded, a teeming hive where newcomers and old residents, soldiers and civilians, and the powerful and the humble all jostled one another on the sidewalks and vied for a share of dwindling resources.

Back when the war was very young, the editor of the *Dispatch*, reflecting the sentiments of many Richmonders, had welcomed the infusion of new blood and new life into the city. The conflict, he boasted, "has certainly given Richmond a start and a pace which she never had before. We hope it will be kept up until we are the Queen City of the South." Less than a year and a half later, in the last weeks of 1862, a visiting Englishman noted an altogether different attitude: "Strange to say, the people of Richmond are, I am told, not at all anxious that the seat of Government should be fixed in their city ultimately [i.e., permanently]. They have a notion that it will alter the character of the people, bring to the place a vast number of idle and vicious visitors, and, in short, change Richmond from a cozy, quiet country town to a busy, restless metropolis."[51]

He might have mentioned also the inhabitants' increasing distress over housing and food shortages, inflation, martial law, and other plagues being visited on their city. As time passed, more and more Richmonders began to wonder whether the stroke of great fortune they had celebrated in the spring of 1861, when their city became the new nation's capital, was in truth a curse.

City of Strangers

HOUSING THE MULTITUDES

"There are too many people here for the houses." Thus did War Department clerk and diligent diarist John Jones succinctly record in December 1862 a fact increasingly evident to everyone in Richmond. Housing in the city came under enormous pressure during the war as the population explosion multiplied demand while other factors restrained supply. The consequence was nothing less than a crisis that left few Richmonders untouched.[1]

Even before the war there never seemed to be enough housing. Carpenters and brickmasons stayed busy in the antebellum decades constructing new houses as the city's population grew, but more living space was always needed. The persistent shortage was only partly eased by the homeowners who rented rooms to lodgers in their houses or outbuildings. (Apartment buildings in the modern sense were unknown in Richmond in that era; almost every resident of the city lived in a house — though in some cases it was but a shanty — or in an outbuilding of a house. The only exceptions were the few who could afford to live in a hotel or who were accommodated in their workplace and those enrolled in boarding schools or confined in the city poorhouse or the state penitentiary.)[2]

Housing in Richmond on the eve of the war was a conglomeration of the old and the new. There still survived some of the elegant eighteenth-century homes built by the well-to-do; these were mostly wooden, with extensive lots and numerous outbuildings. A disastrous fire that swept the city in 1787 persuaded most home builders thereafter to use brick instead of wood, at least in the central districts. Growing demand for housing in the early nineteenth century led builders to divide up large lots and reduce the yard space and the number of outbuildings of new homes. By the late antebellum years, the typical dwelling in the city's core was a two- or three-story brick structure with a small front porch, a basement with windows at ground level (in many cases used as a dining room), and, in the backyard, a kitchen and perhaps another outbuilding (which if rented out to roomers or used to quarter servants was often called a "tenement"); the house sat close to the sidewalk and right up against its neighbor or with just a narrow space between the two. Beyond the city's center, the pressure on the land diminished, allowing for more space between houses; this in turn reduced the risk of a widespread conflagration and thus encouraged more wood construction, which was much cheaper than brick. Houses in the outer neighborhoods tended to be owned (or rented) by people of more modest means — many of them free blacks or immigrants — than those downtown; they were also generally smaller. Shoehorned in here and there in both the inner and outer districts were the leaky hovels of the poor.[3]

The new civilians who flooded into the city in the war's first months were hard-pressed to find accommodations. Normally an acute housing shortage of this sort would spark a housing construction boom, but wartime Richmond saw no such boom. Lack of land space was not the problem: there was plenty of vacant land on the city's periphery. The essential problem was the severe scarcity of materials and labor caused by the competing demands of the military — a problem that only grew as the war went on.

The army's voracious appetite for lumber — to build its own proliferating facilities in the city and the fortifications around it — strained the capacity of Richmond's sawmills, leaving little lumber for civilian use and driving its price sky-high. In May 1862, the president of the Richmond and Petersburg Railroad informed the secretary of war that lumber needed for work on the company's James River bridge was simply not to be had, for the city's sawmills were wholly occupied with army contracts. A state official complained in 1864 that the cost of lumber in Richmond was "going up almost daily." Sometimes army facilities themselves could not get what they needed. Phoebe Pember, a chief matron at Chimborazo, wanted to have storerooms built in which to lock up the hospital's medicinal whiskey but found that the excessive cost of lumber made it impossible. With such scarcity prevailing in Richmond — where military demands generally took priority over civilian demands anyway — a would-be home builder seeking lumber was doomed to frustration.[4]

Even if that builder somehow managed to round up lumber, he would almost certainly have been stymied by the shortage and high cost of nails. The city's primary manufacturer of that commodity, the Old Dominion Iron and Nail Works Company, located on Belle Isle, saw its wartime output, like that of the sawmills, pretty much swallowed up by the army (and to a lesser extent the navy, which built a shipyard, an ordnance laboratory, and other facilities in the city). Civilians seeking nails were as frustrated as those seeking lumber; growing scarcity predictably increased prices. Old Dominion, which in the summer of 1861 had charged $4.25 or $4.50 for a keg of nails, was charging $50 by May 1864; by the end of that year the price was $175. Inflation similarly hit other home-building supplies manufactured in Richmond, including hinges, locks, plumbing fixtures, gas pipes and fittings, and roofing and guttering materials.[5]

But even if hardware and lumber and all the rest had been plentiful and cheap, new home construction would have languished in wartime Richmond because skilled labor was so hard to come by. Many of the city's white carpenters, masons, plasterers, painters, plumbers, and others in the building trades volunteered for military service; many others, as old as fifty, were conscripted into the ranks. While a lot of these artisans were detailed to noncombat duty and remained in Richmond, they were required to do war-related work and were therefore unavailable for civilian needs. Moreover, the city's enslaved and free black building tradesmen, though exempt from military duty (aside from occasional impressment or conscription to work on the fortifications or do other tasks), were hired in great numbers by the War and Navy Departments and by private manufacturers of war materiel and were thus siphoned from the general labor pool. As long as Richmond was at war, men capable of constructing houses and available to do so were scarce.[6]

Neither government officials nor private entrepreneurs seem to have ever considered converting existing nonresidential buildings to housing. Early in the war there were quite a few unused warehouses, closed-down tobacco factories, vacant stables, and other structures in the city that, with a minimal investment of labor and materials, could conceivably have been turned into multiple-family dwellings, albeit of a very humble sort. Perhaps the notion of what would have been, in effect, apartment buildings was just too alien to mid-nineteenth-century Richmonders to suggest itself, even amid a housing crisis. But a likelier explanation is that in this respect, too, the ravenous military simply devoured the city's resources.

Some owners gladly sold or rented their real estate to the army or navy, while others had it taken from them by government fiat. Either way, a great deal of potential housing was sacrificed to the war effort. Warehouses and tobacco factories became Confederate hospitals, prisons, and quartermaster and commissary depots; private stables became army stables. The Richmond Female Institute, a private girls' school disrupted by the war, was reborn as General Hospital No. 4. Other hospital buildings were former wholesale or retail businesses, including the dry goods store of Kent, Paine, and Company. R. H. Bosher's carriage factory, too, was converted into a hospital, and when no longer needed by the Medical Bureau, it was turned over to the Quartermaster Bureau for use as offices. Even residential property passed into the War Department's hands, including two of the city's less fashionable hotels: the Saint Charles became General Hospital No. 8, and the United States became General Hospital No. 10 (a third, the Monumental, became a Treasury Department office building). On at least one occasion the Richmond provost marshal, citing military necessity, took possession of a house over the owner's protests.[7]

The consequence of all this was that throughout the four years of war, the multitudinous inhabitants of Richmond—save those who were wards of the Rebel government—had to cram into whatever housing existed at the war's outbreak. Houses therefore sheltered, on average, at least twice as many people as before the war. This was accomplished mainly by homeowners taking in lodgers. Some had long done so, of course, but now many more assumed the role of landlord. Few did it in a purely selfless spirit; most were driven to it by financial necessity. (Some wartime landlords were in fact renters themselves, having taken possession of an entire house and then subletting portions of it.) Certain homeowners declined to thus take in strangers, however, putting that much more pressure on those who were willing. "Lodgings were hired," Richmonder Sallie Brock recalled in her memoir of the war, "which seemed of india-rubber capacity, from the numbers frequently packed in them."[8]

A Mrs. Samuel, who had a house on Bank Street, was perhaps typical: she accepted four or five tenants. But one family in the Church Hill neighborhood opened its house to ten lodgers and was willing to take more. The rented portions of such places could be claustrophobically crowded. In some cases, single men, clubbing together to save money, slept six to a room. In many landlords' homes, rooms did double duty, serving as family parlors or dining rooms during the day and lodgers' bedrooms at night.[9]

Tenant families that could afford to do so, and that could find an agreeable landlord, would generally rent several rooms. If these included a parlor, dining room, and kitchen as well as sleeping quarters, a well-off family could essentially set up housekeeping apart from the landlord and, with the labor of its own servants or the landlord's, establish a semblance of the lifestyle it had known before the war. (Some landlords allowed lodgers to share the use of their home's parlor or kitchen without actually renting it out to them.) The Cary family, a mother and daughters who had refugeed from northern Virginia, rented such accommodations in a home on Third Street: downstairs they had a parlor in which to gather as a family and to entertain guests; just behind it was a large pantry where they ate meals (prepared in the backyard kitchen by the landlord's cook); and upstairs were their sleeping quarters and a bathroom. Mary Boykin Chesnut and her husband, James, mistress and master of a magnificent South Carolina plantation, rented an entire upper floor of a house at Twelfth and Clay while James was serving as a military aide to Jefferson Davis in 1863. It comprised a bedchamber, two good-sized rooms that they used as a parlor and a dining room, and two small rooms where their slaves Molly and Laurence slept. When the daughters of some friends came to live with them, the Chesnuts turned the dining room over to them for a bedroom and moved the dining table into the parlor, which also contained a piano. This seemed like cramped and humble quarters indeed to the aristocratic Chesnuts, but Mary accepted it philosophically: "We had no right to expect any better lodgings, for Richmond was crowded to suffocation—hardly standing room left."[10]

Few lodgers in wartime Richmond would have pitied the Chesnuts, for the vast majority had to make do with a single room. These accommodations ran the gamut from large, well furnished, and comfortable to tiny, unfurnished, and wretched. In December 1864, Confederate congressman Warren Akin secured a room in the home of merchant George Gretter at the corner of Fifth and Leigh, a quarter mile from the Capitol. It was spacious and Akin had it to himself, for his wife remained at home in Georgia and he wanted no roommate. It was also fully furnished, with a matching feather bed, washstand, and bureau along with a table, chairs (including a rocking chair), and a large mirror. The floor was carpeted, the walls papered, and the two windows had blinds and shades. It did tend to get chilly despite the coal fireplace, but landlord Gretter provided plenty of blankets; he also extended the house's gas line to Akin's room so the congressman could dispense with candles. Akin was quite happy with the place; in a letter to his wife he likened it to a good hotel room.[11]

Such luxury was rare in lodgers' quarters. More typical was the room rented by a woman who had given up a comfortable home in Alexandria, Virginia, when she refugeed to Richmond early in the war. A friend described the room as "uncarpeted . . . and so poorly furnished, that, besides her trunk, she has only her wash-stand drawer in which to deposit her goods and chattels." She did not complain, however; indeed, she was grateful to have found a place at all in Richmond and, as her friend wrote, "considers herself *nicely* fixed."[12]

Others could not abide so cheerfully their reduced standard of living. Clerk Henri Garidel, a refugee from New Orleans, took a room in September 1863 in the Sixth Street home of the Hester family. An eighteen-by-twenty-foot upstairs bedroom, it was fairly spacious by Richmond's standards and decently furnished. But to Garidel it seemed cramped, and he could not help comparing it to the home he had left behind. "My heart was very heavy when I entered that room," he wrote in his diary. "At age forty-seven I was renting a . . . room for the first time." He soon moved. In the winter of 1865 he found himself forced by circumstances to take an attic room in a dirty, dilapidated house on the far western end of Main Street—"a dark, isolated neighborhood," as he described it, a long twelve blocks from his office downtown. This place gave him reason to wish he had never left the Hesters' home. The room was sparsely furnished, had a sloping ceiling so low that he could barely stand upright, lacked gas lighting, and had but one window. It was not only depressingly dim but cold—"a genuine icebox," Garidel complained—because four of the window's twelve panes of glass were missing and no amount of stuffing with fabric or covering with paper could keep the frigid wind from whistling through. One night a bowl of water he left sitting out froze solid. He referred to this room as his "prison cell" and spent as little time there as possible.[13]

Accommodations for working-class lodgers, white and free black, were generally no better than Garidel's attic and often worse. Shoemaker and Irish immigrant Joseph McCarthy, his seamstress wife, and his fourteen-year-old stepdaughter all squeezed into a single room on the upper floor of a small, cheaply built house on Cary Street in which two other families roomed. This structure (it may in fact have been a "tenement" outbuilding) did not even have an entrance hallway or indoor stairs; to get to their room, the McCarthys had to go around to the back, where an outdoor stairway gave access to the second floor. Many enslaved people also lived in such accommodations, for masters who hired out their slaves in the city often allowed them to secure their own lodging. The slaves of masters who were themselves lodgers generally lived with them, although few had the luxury of a private sleeping chamber like the Chesnuts' Molly and Laurence; a cramped nook beneath a staircase or the hard floor of a kitchen or pantry was more likely to be their nightly resting place.[14]

The proliferation of unfurnished and semifurnished lodgings stoked the demand for furniture of all sorts. A great deal of furniture was manufactured in wartime Richmond but little was available to the civilian population, for the Confederate military demanded so much of it. The civilian demand was at least partially met, however, by the emergence of a lively market in used furniture, both for sale and for rent. War Department clerk Jones rented furniture for the multiroom lodgings he and his family occupied from 1861 to 1863, until he could afford to purchase what he needed. When he started buying, he did so piecemeal from various householders willing to part with a chair here, a table there, and so on. He mused in his diary that "a history of the household goods we possess . . . if it could be written" might be interesting to read. "I think we have articles belonging in their time to twenty families." The editor of the *Daily Richmond Enquirer* noted in late 1862 that "superan[n]uated furniture is at a premium. . . . The auction houses are stocked with [it] daily, and . . . every article commands a sensational price." He claimed to have witnessed a recent sale in which a washtub had gone for five dollars, a table missing a couple of legs for ten, and a tablecloth for twelve.[15]

No matter how many lodgers landlords took in, there were always more people needing a place. Every day they could be seen trudging around the city, ringing doorbells, and inquiring anxiously about accommodations. Frustration and exhaustion were often their lot. "Every house in this city is full, from cellar to roof," lamented newly arrived Burton Harrison in March 1862, "and it is almost impossible to get any room at all." Judith McGuire, a refugee from northern Virginia, came to Richmond earlier that year with her husband, staying temporarily in the home of a cousin. While her husband toiled in his office (a prominent Episcopal clergyman and delegate to the state secession convention, he now had to settle for a clerkship in the Post Office Department), she set about finding a permanent abode. "Spent this day in walking from one boarding-house to another," she wrote in her diary on Thursday, 6 February, "and have returned fatigued and hopeless. I do not believe there is a vacant spot in the city." Friday was the same: "Walking all day, with no better success. 'No vacant room' is the universal answer. I returned at dinner-time, wearied in mind and body." Pursuing a couple of tips from acquaintances, she tried again on Saturday, but to no avail: one place had already been let, the other had never been available—she had gotten a false lead. At that second place she had to endure not only frustration but humiliation. The lady of the house "had 'never dreamed of taking boarders,' was 'surprised that such a thing had been suggested,' looked cold and lofty, and meant me to *feel* that she was far too rich for that."[16]

McGuire made two more calls that day. The first was fruitless but the second generated a glimmer of hope. Come back Monday evening, the landlady told her, and a room might be available. McGuire did so, was shown the room (on the third floor, in the rear), judged it satisfactory, and was set to close the deal—until the landlady told her the rent: "I stood aghast!," for it was "twenty dollars more than the usual price, and three dollars less than our whole salary per month." She protested that she could not afford it and tried to negotiate, but the landlady was unmovable: "I can fill my rooms at any time" was her insouciant response. McGuire left, "feeling forlorn and houseless." Several days later she finally was directed to a place on Grace Street where she found a "small, but comfortable," room, available and affordable. She and her husband moved in on 19 February.[17]

McGuire was lucky in some respects. It was a seller's market and, as she learned on that Monday evening, landlords set the terms and often felt no compulsion to bargain. Many refused to accept lodgers with children. Many also turned away single women for fear they might be "loose." And even those hat-in-hand applicants who survived the landlord's scrutiny and secured accommodations often faced further exasperation. Some landlords, knowing they could easily get other roomers, treated those they had highhandedly. In 1862, before they got the place at Twelfth and Clay, the Chesnuts had lodged for a time in a home owned by what Mary acidly described as "some 'decayed ladies' forced by trouble, loss of property, &c to receive boarders." Very soon after they moved in, they began to wish they had not. "The house was comfortable and the table good," Mary acknowledged. "But [we] paid the most extravagant price, and [we] were forced to assume the patient humility of a poor relation. So fine was the hauteur and utter scorn with which [we] were treated."[18]

Many other landlords offered considerably less than a comfortable house and good table and blithely ignored their lodgers' complaints. (Some in fact offered no table at all, leaving lodgers to find board elsewhere.) Henri Garidel was chronically at odds with his various landlords. In the spring and summer of 1864, he and his fellow roomers endured a plague of bedbugs that the landlord did nothing to remedy. "They are devouring us," Garidel wrote. That landlord, moreover, provided but one bathtub for a home accommodating at least ten people. The house was messy, too—"a real pigsty"—and, once the warm months passed, it was always cold. At the end of

1864 he moved to another place, the home of a thirty-year-old unmarried woman whom he came to detest, referring to her in his diary as "that horrid old maid." She, too, tolerated dirt, clutter, and frigid temperatures, and Garidel stayed with her only a month before moving out in disgust. But his next place (that of the attic room with missing windowpanes) gave no more satisfaction: "I have never seen anything to equal the filth and the massive disorder," he wrote in March 1865. The condition of the bathroom was particularly revolting; eventually he refused to use it and instead would wait until he was at work "to satisfy certain pressing needs."[19]

Thus landlord-tenant conflicts multiplied in the crowded city. But tenants were not the only aggrieved parties. Many landlords found themselves saddled with unsavory roomers, including deadbeats. Ann Jones, proprietor of a house on Broad Street, placed a notice in the *Dispatch* in 1862 warning others not to take in a certain M. B. Tyler, who until recently had lodged with her and whom she had kindly indulged as he kept making excuses for not paying her. When his debt reached $32.50, he disappeared. Jones provided a description of the culprit, adding that "he is nothing but a Yankee, and ought to be arrested, and sent [to] the other side of Mason & Dixon's line." Some landlords tried to avoid such problems by requiring prospective tenants to furnish references.[20]

Many tenants who fell behind in rent were, however, more to be pitied than condemned. Isabella Straub was one. The wife of a soldier serving at the front, she rented two rooms of a house owned by Charles Loat. In 1863, when she found herself unable to pay—a predicament common among wives dependent on a soldier's paltry stipend—Loat determined to get rid of her. Legal eviction being impossible in this instance (a state law passed in 1862 protected soldiers' wives and children from it), Loat seized Straub's key and tried to hound her out; she resisted and took her case to the mayor's court. There she received justice: the mayor rebuked Loat, threatened him with jail, and, as the *Dispatch* reported, "held him to bail for his future good behavior in the sum of $150."[21]

Friction between landlords and tenants in wartime Richmond is unsurprising given the housing crisis. What is more remarkable is that in many cases they got along quite well. "Mr. Gretter and his family are very pleasant people," Congressman Akin wrote not long after moving in with them, "very attentive and polite, and free and easy in their manners, and I feel quite at home." John Jones likewise complimented his landladies, three widows who rented out rooms in their home on Clay Street; not only were they personable but "they lend us many articles indispensable for our comfort."

Hospital matron Phoebe Pember had some complaints about the accommodations she secured in October 1863—a third-floor room without carpeting or gas and, in her opinion, overpriced—but she quickly put them aside and embraced her landlords, Samuel and Martha Skinner, as warmly as they embraced her. "Instead of a boarder I am made one of the family," Pember wrote, "and a very pleasant family too." Samuel, a fifty-four-year-old steamboat captain (perhaps now idled by the Yankee blockade of the James River), "is a very pleasant well informed man, highly cultivated." He and Martha had three daughters living with them, ages eleven, sixteen, and eighteen. The whole family, in the eyes of Pember (a South Carolinian), "are Virginia[ns] all over, . . . kind hearted, generous, thoughtless [i.e., absent-minded], lazy, untidy people, who never have anything in its place or a place for anything." Their foibles, which would have given Henri Garidel fits, only endeared them the more to Pember. "If they get hold of your dress by accident . . . [they will] as likely [as not] put it on, always expecting you to do the same. If my room is more convenient for dressing or sleeping or talking, why in my room they all congregate and I am fortunate if no one carelessly mistakes my tooth brush for theirs—indeed I carry it in my pocket for fear of accidents."[22]

The housing shortage inevitably drove rent skyward, although many people blamed greedy landlords rather than the ineluctable laws of supply and demand. One frustrated newcomer trying to secure lodging damned Richmond as a "shameless city of extortion." In early 1862, a furnished room for one person, with board, could be had for $20 a month. By mid-1862, the cost averaged $30 to $40; by the beginning of 1863, $60 or more; by early 1864, $200 to $300. (Scarcity of housing alone did not generate this inflation, of course; it operated in tandem with the scarcity of food, firewood, coal, and gas and the profusion of Confederate currency.) Lodgers who made other arrangements for meals still paid a steep price. By 1864 an unfurnished room without board commanded at least $30 a month; by 1865, $50. Furnished rooms cost much more: an average of $75 in 1863 and $90 or $100 in 1864. Wages and salaries failed to keep pace. In 1864 a typical Confederate government shoemaker made $3 a day, a government clerk from $125 to $250 a month. For single men and women, even those sharing a room, it was hard enough to survive with rent eating up so much of their pay; breadwinners with unemployed dependents found themselves desperately squeezed.[23]

Rent hikes, disagreeable accommodations, and insufferable landlords left many tenants disgruntled and unsettled. At any given time, a large proportion of them were restlessly scouting the city for better lodgings. Moves were frequent: wagons piled with trunks and furniture could be seen lumbering along the city's streets every day. Henri Garidel moved four times between September 1863 and January 1865. For some, facing an abrupt rent increase they could not afford and a landlord with no patience, the search for a new place could be anxious, even frantic. Judith McGuire told of the plight of her friend Mrs. Upshur, an elderly widow and refugee, who in April 1864 "called to ask me to assist her in finding a room to accommodate herself, her sister, and her little grandson. Her present room, in the third story of a very nice house, suited her very well, but the price was raised every month, until it had become beyond her means." McGuire "cheerfully promised her to do what I could" but in her diary expressed misgivings: "To obtain a room is a most difficult task." James Mondy, a twenty-seven-year-old machinist with a large family, was informed by his landlord just before Christmas in 1864 that on 1 January his monthly rent would rise from $64 to $100. Mondy was on emergency duty with the Local Defense Forces at that time and had to beg his commanding officer for a ten-day leave to find new lodgings, for the increased rent was far beyond his ability to pay. The leave was granted, although what sort of accommodations for himself and his six dependents Mondy might by then have been able to secure, for the little he could afford to pay, is grim to contemplate.[24]

How many wartime Richmonders lived unburdened by rent hikes and landlord-tenant disputes because they owned a house and declined to take in lodgers is impossible to say—but there were some, as illustrated by Judith McGuire's encounter with the haughty lady whose doorbell she rang in February 1862. However many there were, their number undoubtedly dwindled over time as the scramble to survive amid shortages and inflation forced more and more of them either to accept tenants or to leave Richmond. Some newcomers to the city, blessed with sufficient money, managed to achieve a kind of quasi-independent householding by renting an entire house and keeping it for their exclusive use. Thereby, they avoided both having to rub elbows daily with a landlord and having to deal with subletters, although they did not avoid the inevitable squabbles over rent. Their number could not have been great, for the expense was far beyond the means of most people. John Jones complained in 1863 that an unfurnished, "small, dirty, dingy, dilapidated house" commanded $800 a year; a decent unfurnished place, suitable for a respectable middle-class family like his own, went for $1,200 to $1,800 a year. By 1865 some were paying $6,000. Maintaining an appropriate standard of living in such a home required, of course, the services of one or more servants. Any middle-class or elite householder who did not own slaves had to hire help. In 1864, hiring one enslaved domestic cost about $250 a year; in 1865, $400.[25]

Some wealthy newcomers, including the Chesnuts when they first came to Richmond in July 1861 and many Confederate legislators whenever Congress was in session, chose to live in a hotel. There were six first-class hotels in the city when the war began: the Exchange, Ballard House, Spotswood, Columbian, Powhatan, and American. All were well appointed and well managed, but the first three were particularly noted for their elegance, even drawing comparisons with New York City's fabled Astor House. One visitor in 1861 praised the Exchange, with its ornate façade, marble floors, mirrored corridors, French chandeliers, and plush furniture, as "the finest building I was ever in." It stood directly across Franklin Street from the Ballard House, to which it was connected at the second story by an enclosed pedestrian bridge (the two hotels were owned by the same proprietor). The five-story Spotswood, Jefferson Davis's first Richmond residence as well as the Chesnuts', was built around a great atrium; from the indoor balconies on each upper floor, guests could gaze down on the lobby, the dining room, the billiard room, the bar, and other public rooms.[26]

Hotel living was of course very costly, although the expense was partially offset by the dining, maid, valet, and laundry services that allowed guests to dispense with personal servants. The daily rate in 1862 for one adult at a first-class hotel, which included room, board, and services (except laundry and shoeshines, which were extra), averaged $3 (for a child, $2). By 1863 it had climbed to $6; by 1864, to $25 or $30. Over time, hotel rooms became not only costlier but scarcer, for the increasingly desperate food crisis crimped the ability of the hotels to provide meals and killed them off one by one. By late March 1865, only two, the Spotswood and the American, remained in business.[27]

People of lesser means could secure good accommodations by renting houses or rooms in the countryside surrounding Richmond, where lodging was much cheaper. The drawback, of course, was a lengthy walk or ride to work, but for many it was worth the trouble. The Henrico County court magistrates reported in March 1865 that in "that portion of the County which surrounds the City of Richmond, with its Cordon of villages, the houses . . . are crammed from bottom to top with occupants," many of them "refugees and sojourners." An extreme example of a suburban commuter was Thomas Loockerman, who refugeed to Richmond in 1861 from Maryland's Eastern Shore and took work as a Treasury Department clerk. With a wife and several daughters to support, he could not afford to live decently in the city so instead rented a comfortable cottage in the village of Ashland — a good fifteen miles to the north, in Hanover County. Whether he depended on a horse or on the Richmond, Fredericksburg, and Potomac Railroad for transportation, Loockerman must have spent hours a day going to and from work. Some breadwinners compromised by lodging their families in the countryside while themselves staying in the city. E. C. Howard, a Treasury Department employee struggling to get along on a salary of $83 a month in 1862, resorted to this expedient, although it most likely meant that he saw his wife and children only from Saturday evenings to Monday mornings.[28]

Another alternative to paying the exorbitant cost of lodging in the city, although available to only a lucky few, was securing quarters in one's workplace. A number of War Department clerks slept in their offices. Many army hospitals set aside space to house employees. Fannie Beers, a matron at the Second Alabama Hospital, a former tobacco factory on the eastern end of Franklin Street, was provided with two rooms that had been the factory owners' offices. One became a bedroom for herself and her young son (her husband was in the army), while the other doubled as her sitting room and office. The massive Winder encampment hospital included a large staff dormitory with a partition dividing it in two; on one side were rooms for surgeons, on the other rooms for matrons and nurses, two people sharing each room. These were Spartan quarters, to be sure: the building was of unpainted pine, the interior walls were unfinished, and each room had but a single window and scant furnishings (two cots, two chairs, a table, a washstand, and a tub). But some, such as volunteer aide Constance Cary, who roomed with her mother, a matron, were able to make their place homey enough. With the addition of a rug, curtains, a mirror, a little more furniture, and a flower box in the window, Cary deemed the room livable by the standards of wartime Richmond.[29]

The city's poorest inhabitants, or many of them, made do in tiny, freestanding shanties, paying minimal rent or simply squatting rent-free. These were plentiful in antebellum Richmond, and a few more may have been built during the war, for they could be thrown together at almost no expense using unskilled labor, scrap lumber, and a handful of nails. The death of a twenty-two-year-old prostitute named Parmelia Robertson in October 1863, in the wharf district known as Rocketts on the city's east side, brought the coroner to the scene and afforded the public a glimpse inside one such abode. It was "a miserable hovel," the *Dispatch* reported, "about twelve by fourteen feet in size, the front part used as a doggery and the rear occupied as a lodging room" by Robertson and two other women. The body lay in the back room "on a pile of dirty rags" surrounded by "filth." It was, perhaps, a fittingly dismal place for Robertson to end her short, unhappy life: the coroner determined that she had killed herself with a deliberate overdose of laudanum.[30]

More wretched even than the shanty dwellers were Richmond's homeless. Their numbers were never large, for the municipal authorities maintained a poorhouse even during the worst travails of war, but they were always a part of the city's population. Ann Thacker, described by the *Dispatch* as "a street wanderer" and "an idiotic white woman," was arrested and charged with vagrancy in October 1861. The mayor sent her to jail, presumably for her own good and preparatory to committing her to the poorhouse. Three months later, the *Dispatch* reported the death of Leah Jones, who had "been leading a vagrant kind of life" since her husband's death several years earlier. Her body was pulled from the canal the morning after she fell into it in a drunken stupor. Most pathetic of all were the children adrift in the city. Mary Jenkins, "a meek looking girl of twelve or fourteen years," as the *Examiner* described her, was taken into custody in the summer of 1864 when it was discovered that she had "no home, no place to stay, no mother, no father, no kindred." She refused to tell the authorities where she had come from or why she was in Richmond. Noting "her sun-bonnet and browned face," the newspaper surmised that "she might be a country waif, blown by some domestic hurricane outside of the home circle and cast down in the slough of this wicked city" — in plain words, a runaway. Eight-year-old George Griffin was brought to the police station in 1863 by a citizen who had found him wandering the streets alone. When questioned, the boy said he was from Memphis, that both his parents had died, and that with "no home and no friends" he had attached himself to a unit of soldiers and tagged along with them to Richmond. The mayor put him into the hands of the overseers of the poor.[31]

Housing the "floating population," the hordes of men and women who came to the capital on some errand or were forced to spend a night or two when passing through, further strained the city's resources. For people of means, the hotels stood ready to provide not only accommodations but transportation: each had its own omnibus to shuttle guests to and from the railroad depots. Cheaper but still expensive were those boardinghouses (a minority) that accepted short-term lodgers. In early 1862, one in the Church Hill neighborhood offered room and board for "gentlemen" by the day ($1.50) or week ($7), "washing and candles extra." Two years later a short-term boarder could expect to pay $8 to $12 a day.[32]

Those who could not afford such costs but felt compelled to come to the city anyway depended, in many cases, on the kindness of strangers. One poor family from western Virginia showed up at Chimborazo Hospital, having come to see a wounded kinsman, and pleaded so persistently for a place to stay that Phoebe Pember finally bent the rules and put them up for six nights in a laundry room. Two sisters from Alabama arrived in Richmond in 1863 to bring home their brother, who had lost a leg at Chancellorsville, but having exhausted their funds just getting to the city, they found themselves helpless and stranded until a well-to-do woman learned of their plight and took them under her wing. A North Carolinian named Eliza Watkins likewise found a guardian angel in Richmond, in this case no less a personage than the first lady of the Confederacy, Varina Davis. In July 1862, on learning that her husband had suffered a head wound in the Seven Days' Battles, Watkins rushed to the city with no means of subsisting herself there and no idea of where to find her husband (the Army Intelligence Office was not yet in existence). Her inquiries at various hospitals proved fruitless. Mrs. Davis happened to see her on the street looking so forlorn that she stopped to ask what was wrong. Hearing the sad tale, she invited Watkins to stay in her home (by then the Davises had moved from the Spotswood to a house) while she continued her search. The same issue of the *Dispatch* that reported this touching incident also carried Watkins's appeal for news of her husband—one of many such advertisements in the Richmond papers that month—under the heading INFORMATION WANTED. (This story had no happy ending: Sgt. John M. Watkins of Company C, Third North Carolina Infantry Regiment, succumbed to his wound in a Richmond hospital, possibly even before Eliza arrived in the city.)[33]

The many Confederate soldiers who had to stay overnight in Richmond when traveling between the army and home on furlough posed a problem, too, for few had the money for a hotel or boardinghouse. Early in the war, some individual citizens and benevolent organizations, including the YMCA, stepped in to help by providing free lodging, but there was never enough for all those in need. Thus, as the *Dispatch* reported in February 1862, many were "compelled to walk the streets during the entire night, or lay [sic] down in the first locality that presents itself, whether eligible or otherwise." This and other editorial scoldings eventually shamed the War Department into establishing the "Soldier's Home" on Cary Street, which provided meals and sleeping quarters for up to 2,700 sojourners in uniform. Some may have preferred to spend the night under the stars, however, at least in the warm months, for those accommodated in the "Home" were required to assemble for meals at the summons of a drum, submit to roll call, and muster each evening for dress parade.[34]

Accommodations for the many tens of thousands of Rebel government wards whose stay in Richmond was longer varied widely. Camp Lee, which housed army conscripts in training, unexchanged parolees, and convalescents, presumably provided barracks built of planks or logs (although some of these may have been unwalled shelters of the barest sort) and probably employed tents, too, when the camp's population outstripped the barracks' capacity. Whether it was more uncomfortable in the winter or the summer was debatable; one soldier who was there in June 1863 thought it "the most disagreeable Camp in the C.S. It is in the open Fair Grounds, without shade, and while we were there we were exposed to the hot sun and a severe wind, which blew the sand everywhere." Richmond's garrison troops occupied a variety of housing at many different places in and around the city. The men of the Surry Light Artillery battery, for example, spent part of the war in good frame barracks with bunks, fireplaces, and brick chimneys. But most others slept in tents in the warm months and crude log huts in the winter, just as the men of the field armies did; some of the officers, however, avoided roughing it by lodging in private homes near their troops' campsite. The impressed or conscripted black men brought to Richmond to work on the fortifications were sheltered throughout the year in tents, which could be easily packed up and transported as the men were moved around to different sections of the lines. With pine boughs beneath them, a blanket over them, and a fire at each tent's entrance in the winter, they were deemed by the army sufficiently comfortable, although reports of suffering on cold nights were common.[35]

Hospitalized Confederate soldiers got the best accommodations their government and its citizens could provide. In the earlier part of the war, almost all the Richmond hospitals were situated in former warehouses or factories or other large buildings taken over by the army, most of them multistory brick structures. Whether operated by the Medical Bureau or private associations, they were generally kept very clean and orderly — especially after women began to be accepted in large numbers as nurses and matrons — and as well supplied as possible. A visitor who had a look inside one in 1862 saw "rows of neatly-furnished iron bedsteads all down the long floors" and complimented the hospital authorities on their capable management. He felt compelled to add, however, that each bedstead was "occupied by a pale, anxious face," and he confessed that despite its efficiency and cleanliness, the place was "among the most depressing sights" he saw in Richmond. Moreover, even the most attentive hospital staff could not relieve every discomfort. Window screening being unknown in the city in that era, flies plagued the hospitals (as they did homes and every other place). Going up and down stairs was a hardship for many patients and a burden for the staff. And while the buildings were adequately warmed in the winter with heating stoves or furnaces, little could be done to cool them in the summer. Windows were generally few and poorly placed to catch breezes. In hot weather, patients and staff alike sweltered.[36]

The army encampment hospitals that eventually replaced these early hospitals were a vast improvement. Designed on the "pavilion" model, they comprised individual, single-story wards. These were frame structures built of pine, well separated from one another, bountifully ventilated, and oriented to catch the prevailing winds. Chimborazo, for example, had ninety-eight wards (along with at least fifty other buildings housing kitchens, laundries, storerooms, offices, and such). Every ward was twenty-eight by eighty feet in size, whitewashed inside and out, with ten windows on each long side, two on each end, and six doors. The windows had sliding shutters, readily opened and closed as the weather dictated. Within, individual wooden bunks arranged in four rows of eight held thirty-two patients, who lay on straw-stuffed mattresses or, if likely to soil the bedding, on straw alone. Stoves provided heat. Sheets were washed, bedding was aired, floors were scrubbed, and patients were bathed frequently. Walls inside and out got a fresh coat of whitewash every few months. Strict rules of behavior for patients and staff and a highly structured daily routine of meals and medical attendance were enforced, as was segregation in various forms: the wounded, the sick, and the convalescent were generally assigned to separate wards; officers and enlisted men were kept apart; and all patients from a given state were assigned to a particular hospital or division of a hospital.[37]

The Yankee prisoners of war held in Richmond endured living conditions ranging from barely decent to agonizingly harsh. There was no deliberate, systematic mistreatment of these prisoners by the Confederate army (or more specifically, by the Richmond provost marshal's office, which had charge of them), although there were individual instances of abuse; the suffering was fundamentally a product of the extreme scarcity of resources available to provide for the unexpectedly large number of prisoners.[38]

Housing for the Belle Isle prisoners, all enlisted men, devolved over time from tolerable to appalling. When the prison camp was built in mid-1862, lumber was in such short supply in Richmond (much of it siphoned away by the huge encampment hospitals under construction) that the War Department could provide only tents, not barracks, to house the prisoners. The area they were confined in comprised about four acres, surrounded by a wooden palisade. (The island was considerably larger than that, but much of it was occupied by civilian dwellings and the Old Dominion Iron and Nail Works.) It was a breezy spot amid the James River's roaring rapids, the camp sat atop a knoll, and the island was well drained. Under the right circumstances this could have afforded the prisoners an acceptable measure of comfort—those circumstances being a prison population no greater than about 3,000 and the use of the prison only in the spring, summer, and fall. And such was the case in the first year of the prison's existence. But after the exchange cartel with the U.S. government broke down in the latter part of 1863, the Confederate authorities had to crowd prisoners into Belle Isle beyond its proper capacity and hold them there year-round. By early 1864, 8,000 or so were crammed in, and the pleasant winds of summer had become the frigid gales of winter. The tents leaked and there were not enough blankets to go around. The tents were also too few, forcing many men to sleep outside. Firewood was provided, but no amount of it could keep the cold at bay on the worst winter nights. Inept administration aggravated the prisoners' suffering. Fearful of escape attempts, the authorities prohibited the use of the latrines (which were outside the palisade) at night; thus, human waste accumulated around the tents in amounts that even the mandatory daily cleanup of the camp could not fully dispose of. And, too, the authorities did nothing to suppress the organized band of thugs in the camp, many of them veterans of New York City's notorious antebellum gangs, who preyed on their fellow prisoners, assaulting and robbing them.[39]

Libby Prison, where captured Union officers were confined, kept all inmates indoors, provided baths and water closets, and was free of organized prisoner violence and thievery; but in other respects it rivaled Belle Isle as a miserable abode. It was a three-story brick building, a former warehouse on Cary Street east of Shockoe Creek. The prisoners were held on the second and third floors, each of which comprised three rooms. Each room was a little over 100 feet long, 44 feet wide, and 8 feet high. The windows were barred to keep the prisoners in but were unshuttered and thus unable to keep the winter winds out. There were bunks in one room, which was used as the prison hospital, but the others had none; all prisoners except the sick slept on the floor. Some had a blanket or overcoat for warmth, but many had neither. No benches or other furniture were provided and the prisoners were never allowed outside for exercise. Thus they spent their days, including mealtimes, sitting, standing, or lying around on the floor. Like Belle Isle, Libby grew crowded in the latter part of the war. By November 1863 the prisoners numbered 1,044, giving each an average floor space of about six by four and a half feet. The rooms were cleared of rubbish daily and the prisoners could stay clean thanks to the baths, but no amount of policing of quarters or bathing of bodies seemed to have any effect on the lice, which infested every room and every prisoner.[40]

Lice, overcrowding, cold, a scarcity of blankets, and hard floors for beds were likewise the lot of the Castle Thunder prisoners. These were mostly Confederate civilians accused of disloyalty or draft dodging, along with Rebel and Union army deserters and recaptured fugitive slaves. The prison comprised three adjoining buildings (two former warehouses and a tobacco factory, all multistory brick structures), and like Libby Prison it consisted mainly of large, bare rooms where the prisoners lived, ate, and slept. But unlike Libby it had some small rooms and also an enclosed yard in the rear where prisoners were allowed to get fresh air and exercise for a half hour each day. Segregation of the prisoners was the rule, though not always strictly enforced: white male civilians and Confederate soldiers were confined in one building, Yankee deserters in another, and white women and blacks in the third. Prisoners caught stealing, trying to escape, or violating any other rule were subject to rigorous punishment, including ball and chain, tying up by the thumbs, whipping, and solitary confinement in an eight-by-eight-foot windowless room dubbed the "sweat house." Reports of abuse of the inmates by prison officials prompted a congressional investigation in 1863 that found a good deal of supporting evidence but resulted in no sanctions.[41]

Whatever their living accommodations, all Richmond residents depended on heating fuel—mainly firewood and, to a lesser extent, coal—for survival during the cold months. Firewood was plentiful and cheap before the war, for the country districts surrounding the city were rich with timber and the roads, railroads, and canal provided ready access to it. But the expanding wartime populace needed firewood in unprecedented quantities, while the Confederate government, with its vast array of offices, factories, hospitals, prisons, and other facilities, not only absorbed a great deal of the available firewood but also claimed much of the space in railroad cars and canal boats in order to bring in all the other supplies it needed. And, too, the army impressed many draft animals used for hauling civilian wagons, along with some of the slaves who drove them and some of those who felled and chopped timber for the wood suppliers. Wood remained bountiful in the rural areas, but what was transported to the city was never enough. The market price rose inexorably. A cord—roughly the quantity needed to comfortably heat a typical one- or two-room residence for one winter month—could be had in January 1862 for $8. A year later the price was $18, and a year after that nearly $40. By the last winter of the war, dealers were demanding $100 to $150.[42]

Coal users likewise struggled to maintain a supply sufficient to avert suffering, even though there was plenty of coal within easy reach of the city. Wartime transportation and labor problems bedeviled the coal suppliers as they did the wood suppliers. Inevitably, consumers paid an increasingly burdensome price. In early 1862, the going rate in Richmond was fourteen to eighteen cents a bushel; by early 1863 it was fifty cents, and by the end of that year, a dollar.[43]

Gas, which was used exclusively for streetlamps and indoor lighting, also became scarce and costly as the war went on. The Richmond City Gas Works, a municipal facility located in the Rocketts district, was the sole supplier of this commodity. It manufactured gas from coal, which it needed in huge quantities and struggled like every other coal consumer to obtain. The gasworks struggled, too, to obtain the specialized equipment and materials it needed: iron retorts, firebricks, lime, and a particular kind of clay tile available only from a Georgia manufacturer. The price of gas, which was set by the city council, remained at its prewar level of $3 per 1,000 cubic feet until November 1862, when it was raised to $3.50. After that, it soared precipitously, like the price of everything else: $6 by February 1863, $15 by July 1864, $30 by September 1864, and $50 by February 1865. Beginning in 1862, there were occasional interruptions of service due to equipment failure. By 1865 gas production had declined drastically and street lighting had been wholly sacrificed in order to maintain indoor service. Many a night found the city wrapped in impenetrable gloom. "I have never seen anything darker than the streets of Richmond when there is neither gaslight nor moonlight," Henri Garidel complained. "You can't see where to put your feet."[44]

By that last winter of the war, the oppressive costs of housing and fuel were forcing a great many Richmonders to make painful choices. Pay the rent on time, or spend the money instead on wood to fire up the cold stove and enjoy some blessed warmth? Move to cheaper lodgings—meaning tinier, dingier, barer, more dilapidated, and farther from work—or stay put and pray that the landlord would be patient when the rent was overdue? And looming alongside these uncertainties was another no less agonizing: how to keep body and soul together amid a food crisis that threatened to starve the Rebel capital.

FEEDING THE MULTITUDES

Commissary General Lucius Northrop, head of the War Department's Subsistence Bureau, was cantankerous, stubborn, and widely resented in the military and government as one of Jefferson Davis's pets. But he knew his job, and he perceived clearly the bitter fact confronting those responsible for wartime Richmond's food supply. He expressed it forcefully in November 1863 in a discussion with fellow War Department bureau chief Robert Kean. At issue was the secretary of war's decision to allow the city council to draw on commissary stores in Richmond to help feed the city's suffering poor. Northrop opposed it and asked Kean to urge the secretary to reconsider. Kean refused: "I told [Northrop that] I did not agree with him," he wrote in his diary, "that I thought it of very great importance that the city should be fed." But Northrop was adamant. "He said very earnestly that the alternative was between the *people* and the army, that there is perhaps *bread* enough for both but not *meat* enough, and that we have to elect between the *army* and the *people* doing without."[1]

Few matters generated more impassioned debate and desperate exertion in wartime Richmond than food. The same forces that created the unforeseen housing shortage—the population explosion and the competition between government and populace over limited resources—also put enormous, unanticipated pressure on the food supply, pressure intensified by external forces.

Like any other city, Richmond depended on outside sources of food. Before the war, provisions were plentiful and cheap. The fresh produce and dairy products that Richmonders consumed came mostly from the farms of Henrico and the counties abutting it, as did much of the grain, meat, and fodder; the Shenandoah Valley also provided a great deal of those last three commodities. In both of those regions and others that supplied Richmond with food, the farms were a mix of small to middling-size family operations—which aimed at self-sufficiency and sold only whatever surplus they might raise—and large, commercially oriented plantations reliant on slave labor. Many farmers, especially the big planters, rotated among grain, tobacco, and grass, reinvigorating their fields periodically with South American guano; some increased their yield of grain by using mechanical seed drills, reapers, and threshers.[2]

Antebellum Richmond had an abundance of transportation channels by which food could be brought in. The road network, essential for drawing provisions from the surrounding countryside, was by mid-nineteenth-century Southern standards a good one. Besides the many country roads feeding into the city (dirt thoroughfares maintained by county governments, which marshaled the labor of local citizens and slaves), there were a number of turnpikes (privately owned toll routes, generally graded, ditched, and macadamized or planked). Daily along these roads and turnpikes, horse- or mule-drawn carts and wagons trundled from the farms to the city loaded with garden vegetables, fruit, milk, butter, eggs, corn, wheat, hay, and poultry, jostling for space with droves of cattle, hogs, and sheep.[3]

The rail network, on which provisions were brought from afar, was the envy of the South. Five railroads served the city, linking it to points north, east, south, and west. These were the Virginia Central; the Richmond, Fredericksburg, and Potomac; the Richmond and York River; the Richmond and Petersburg; and the Richmond and Danville. Each had its own depot in the city. (None of the five connected to any other, a hindrance to through traffic but of no consequence for the provisioning of Richmonders.) Commodious and speedy only by comparison with wagons and canal boats— a locomotive could typically pull no more than ten or fifteen loaded freight cars and rarely averaged better than fifteen miles per hour between stops (somewhat faster if pulling passenger cars)—trains nevertheless played a key role in feeding antebellum Richmond. They demanded a lot of maintenance, however, and vast quantities of supplies. Rails, which were made not of steel but of wrought iron, wore out frequently, as did iron spikes and wooden crossties and trestles. Locomotives required enormous amounts of chopped wood to fuel their boilers (none were coal powered). The rails and locomotives were almost all imported from the North or Great Britain. All five railroads depended almost entirely on slaves (mostly hired rather than company owned) and free black men for the heavy, unskilled labor needed to repair tracks and trestles, cut timber, and load and unload freight, and they depended on them in part for essential skilled labor, including as brakemen, firemen, and mechanics.[4]

As trains rumbled and screeched and hissed into Richmond bearing grain, fodder, and cured meat, cargo of the same sorts quietly glided in aboard canal boats. The James River and Kanawha Canal connected Richmond, through a series of ninety locks, to a point almost 200 miles west, passing through Lynchburg, an important rail junction. Fifty feet wide and five deep, the canal was a privately owned toll route. The boats that plied it (some designed for passengers, most for freight) were owned by various packet companies that paid the toll and passed the cost along to their customers in addition to their passenger-per-mile and ton-per-mile transportation charges. The boats were pulled by teams of horses or mules that trod towpaths along the canal banks. From Lynchburg, 136 miles away, a boat could reach Richmond in about seventy-two hours. The canal demanded substantial labor. Maintaining the mortared granite blocks that lined it, the wooden lock gates that dammed it, and the wooden bridges that spanned it kept a good number of quarrymen, stonecutters, masons, carpenters, blacksmiths, and common laborers busy. On the eve of the war, the canal company employed 455 men, the great majority of them black. The packet lines employed many more blacks and whites as boatmen and team drivers.[5]

Unprocessed wheat and corn transported to Richmond were delivered to the city's numerous mills for grinding. (Far more came in than was needed to feed the inhabitants, for antebellum Richmond was a major exporter of flour.) From there, the flour intended for city consumption went to local grocery stores and bakeries. The beef, pork, and mutton that came in on the hoof were sold to butchers, who in turn sold most of their product in the two municipal market houses. Almost all the vegetables, fruits, dairy products, and poultry brought in to provision the city were likewise retailed at the municipal markets. When Richmonders went food shopping they spent most of their time at the markets.[6]

Each market was a two-story brick building nearly a block long, owned and administered by the city. The First Market House was at Main and Seventeenth, just east of Shockoe Creek; the Second Market House was about three-quarters of a mile north of there, at Marshall and Sixth. Two municipal clerks, overseen by the city council's First Market and Second Market committees, were on hand whenever the markets were open to enforce the ordinances regarding hours of operation, sanitation, weigh scales, and so forth. Six days a week (they were closed on Sundays), the markets were crowded with basket-laden shoppers and noisy with the palaver of haggling and the coming and going of wagons and carts. Inside and clustered around the market buildings were dozens of stalls, each leased for a year at a time to the highest bidder. Most of the hucksters were city butchers or farmers from the surrounding countryside. Typical of them was Mary Jackson, age thirty-five in 1861, a Second Market huckster who peddled products from the small farm west of the city that she and her husband, Elisha, operated. She no doubt also peddled the products of neighboring farms whose owners had no stall.[7]

Antebellum Richmonders did not, of course, live by bread, meat, and produce alone; no less essential was their water supply. The city was blessed in this respect too. Besides the many privately owned wells in the backyards of houses and elsewhere, there was a municipal water supply. The water-works was located a little beyond the western city limit, adjacent to the canal and river. There, water-powered pumps drew water up to a 4 million–gallon reservoir, where it was filtered. Gravity and pressure then forced the water through underground main and branch pipes to various parts of the city. Thus did water flow to public fountains and hydrants and to any homes, businesses, and institutions whose owners or managers were willing to pay for the convenience.[8]

Wartime scarcity soon rendered prewar plenty a distant memory. Either the civilian population explosion or the War Department's insatiable demand for provisions would have caused a serious food shortage; together they provoked a crisis. The crisis deepened as food production in the regions supplying the city diminished and transportation was disrupted. War Department clerk and diarist John Jones was one of those who, like Commissary General Northrop, recognized the impossibility of simultaneously appeasing the hunger of Richmond's swollen civilian population, the hunger of its vast numbers of garrison troops, conscripts, hospital patients, military prisoners, and impressed slave laborers, and the hunger of the Army of Northern Virginia, which depended heavily on the provisions stockpiled in Richmond's commissary depots. Jones put it starkly in 1863: "The army must be fed or disbanded, or else the city must be abandoned."[9]

Every shipment of food to Richmond after the spring of 1861 stirred the envy of those not entitled to it. The War Department claimed a large share of space on incoming freight trains for its provisions and other supplies and required the railroads to give military cargo priority over civilian goods. (In an act of patriotic generosity, all the Richmond railroads agreed in 1861 to grant the Confederate government a 50 percent reduction in freight and passenger rates for the duration of the war—a decision they came to regret.) The War Department likewise gobbled up space on the packet companies' canal boats, even after the Quartermaster Bureau assembled its own fleet of sixteen or more boats that hauled army supplies exclusively. War Department bureaus competed not only with Richmond's civilians for food but with each other: late in the war it was discovered that the Quartermaster Bureau was appropriating rail shipments of corn clearly designated for the Subsistence Bureau.[10]

The army also nearly monopolized the output of Richmond's grain mills and bakeries. The largest milling operation in the city, the Gallego Mills owned by Haxall, Crenshaw, and Company, had what clerk Jones described in 1862 as a "gigantic contract with the government to furnish flour, and . . . have a preference of transportation by the contract." For a time, the War Department even forbade shipping to Richmond any unground wheat not intended for the army; on one occasion in March 1863, it abruptly impressed every barrel of flour in the city's mills, warehouses, and groceries that was not already claimed by the army, paying only a government-set price well below market value. The bakeries, too, were heavily committed to army contracts. The American Bakery, the largest in the city, was by late 1863 supplying Libby Prison and Castle Thunder with up to 7,000 loaves daily; whatever it produced in excess of the two prisons' needs it offered to the public, but, as the *Examiner* noted, "the supply is always exhausted before the demand ceases." In the spring of 1864 the same paper reported that "nearly all the bakers have ceased to bake for the public, and have turned their attention to supplying the hospitals. The public, we suppose, will have to take care of itself."[11]

The War Department also drew provisions directly from the municipal markets. Chimborazo Hospital had an agent whose job was to go to one of the market houses at sunrise six days a week and stay there as long as it was open, shopping for edibles to augment the patients' diets. Libby Prison guards were dispatched to the markets for groceries to help feed the Yankee officers in their charge. Subsistence Bureau agents tasked with provisioning the Army of Northern Virginia shopped there too. An influx of several thousand enemy prisoners of war in January 1863 triggered a surge in prices at the market hucksters' stalls—beef, for instance, jumped from forty to sixty cents a pound literally overnight—because, as John Jones affirmed, the prisoners "are subsisted from the market." In some cases, army agents refused to pay the hucksters' prices, declared the goods subject to impressment, and took what they wanted, paying only the government rates.[12]

Some Richmonders protested what they perceived as the War Department's high-handed snatching of food from civilians' plates. In December 1862 the president of the Richmond, Fredericksburg, and Potomac Railroad complained to Secretary of War Seddon that he could not get enough rations for his hired slave laborers; the problem, he said, was that so much of the food supply was "monopolized by [the] government." That same month, a representative of the flour-milling firm of Dunlop, Moncure, and Company addressed Seddon concerning the recent order barring incoming grain shipments that were not under War Department contract, a measure intended to secure more railroad cargo space for the army; the order, he said, would inflict a "heavy loss" on the company, which still produced flour for the civilian market. Three months later, a petition was laid on Seddon's desk, signed by Governor John Letcher, Mayor Joseph Mayo, and other prominent Richmonders, objecting to the impressment of meat in the markets. In January 1864 the city council appointed a committee to call on Seddon and convey the council's concerns about that same matter. The owners of some of the flour seized in March 1863 obtained a state court injunction against further impressment—and thereby dared the War Department to defy the sacred principle of states' rights.[13]

These protests availed little. It was not that the War Department was unsympathetic; from the secretary on down, its officials acknowledged and regretted the difficulties that the army's demand for food imposed on Richmonders. When Robert E. Lee urged removing all the prisoners of war because their presence "increases largely the amount of supplies to be transported to the city, and thus employs transportation which might be used for the benefit of the citizens," Seddon earnestly concurred. But neither he nor the other secretaries of war before and after him could find any way out of the dilemma, any way to fully satisfy the needs of Richmond consistent with their duty to sustain the army. In replying to the plea of Dunlop, Moncure, and Company, Seddon could say only that cargo space for army supplies was a military necessity that would continue as long as the war and that the consequent hardships should not be "complained of by loyal citizens."[14]

A host of factors conspired to curtail the productivity of the farms that fed Richmond, divert much of what they did produce to other purposes, and disrupt the transportation channels between farm and city. The sea and land blockades imposed by the Union navy and army immediately after the war began cut Virginia's farmers off from sources of guano and from the Northern manufacturers that had long supplied plows, drills, reapers, threshers, and the spare parts that kept them working. The consequent scarcities, especially of plowpoints, which required frequent replacement, impaired agricultural production. Even more injurious was the scarcity of labor that plagued the farms by 1862. Yeoman farms were deprived of hands as white men volunteered for, or were drafted into, the army; plantations were likewise deprived of overseers. Plantations suffered further from the loss of black labor. Across the state, slaves were impressed periodically to work on the fortifications at Richmond and other points. In regions invaded by the Union army, thousands were permanently removed by refugeeing masters while thousands of others escaped and found their way to freedom. Henrico, on which Richmond especially depended for food, was among the counties hit hard by the loss of black field hands. In early 1865, after the army issued yet another call for slave laborers, the Henrico authorities pleaded for exemption, pointing out that the number of able-bodied male slaves in the county had declined by half since 1861 due to removal or flight and that many planters consequently were struggling to produce a crop.[15]

Enemy incursions not only depleted the black labor supply but, in many instances, severed Richmond from the farms that provisioned it. Some of Virginia's most productive agricultural regions, including the lower Shenandoah Valley, were occupied periodically or permanently by the Union army. Even in areas not actually occupied, the nearby presence of the Yankees or just the threat of invasion prompted many farmers to abandon their homes. In some cases, farms were ruined by the construction of Confederate defensive works. Here again, Henrico was particularly hard hit. In the same 1865 petition in which they begged for exemption from slave impressment, the county fathers stated that "the enemy now hold possession in force of a large portion of the territory of our County, believed to be one third of it; in addition to this a large portion of the County between the hostile lines [or] occupied by our Army is nearly uninhabited."[16]

Even farms well within the bounds of Confederate control could fall victim to sudden, destructive enemy raids. Isabella and Cornelius Atkins, a free black couple who operated a fifty-acre farm fourteen miles from Richmond, endured an ordeal of that sort in the summer of 1864, when Union cavalry swept through their neighborhood. The hungry troopers dug up the Atkinses' one-acre truck garden, taking potatoes, onions, and cabbages no doubt intended for the Richmond market. They also seized nine hogs, a cow, a horse, poultry, crops of corn and oats still in the field, stored grain and meat, fodder, fence rails, two plows, and a farm cart. "They took all we had,"

Isabella testified after the war. "They stripped us completely." Many other Virginia farmers could have told a similar story.[17]

Farms near large concentrations of Confederate troops—especially those around Richmond—also suffered frequent pillaging by poorly disciplined soldiers (and sometimes by good soldiers too long on poor rations). Indeed, many farmers found such visitations to be more destructive than anything the Yankees ever inflicted on them. One who lived not far from Camp Lee complained to the War Department in August 1862 that troops were stealing fruit from his orchard and green corn from his fields "in open day, in full view of the officers, without any apparent effort on their part to prevent them." They were also carrying off fence rails for firewood, which left the growing crops exposed to grazing livestock: "Fences that have been repaired one day are torn down the next." Similar complaints piled up on the secretary of war's desk. The *Dispatch* warned in the summer of 1863 that such depredations were seriously reducing Richmond's civilian food supply and driving up market prices and demanded that the army do something about it. The army tried: stern orders against plundering were issued by the commander in chief, the secretary of war, and subordinate officers at every level. But the problem persisted as long as the war went on.[18]

Farm produce in even greater quantities was taken by the army quite legally. In 1863 the Confederate Congress enacted an in-kind tax that demanded of farmers one-tenth of their annual yield of grain, vegetables, cured meat, and fodder; the goods were to be delivered to local depots established by the Quartermaster Bureau and from there went to feed the armies. On top of that, farmers were subject to the impressment of crops, livestock (both food and work animals), and wagons—in fact, anything militarily useful—by quartermaster and subsistence agents and field and post commanders whenever military necessity demanded. Impressment fell hardest where the Confederate army's presence was largest. In the fall of 1864, the Henrico County official charged with provisioning the poor—nearly all of whom were wives and children of men in the ranks—wrote an anguished plea to Secretary Seddon: there was hardly a grain of surplus wheat left in the county, he said, thanks in great part to the relentless impressment agents, and he feared for "the suffering families of the soldiers."[19]

Transporting agricultural produce from Henrico and surrounding counties to the Richmond markets became more difficult even as the supply dwindled, for country roads and turnpikes deteriorated badly as armies overburdened them and county authorities and turnpike companies failed to maintain them. The constant movement of Rebel and Yankee infantry, cavalry, artillery, supply wagons, and ambulances in the Richmond area for four years put an enormous burden on the road network. A toll keeper on the Richmond, Williamsburg, and Central Turnpike, dutifully logging Confederate army traffic in order to bill the War Department properly, recorded that between April 1863 and August 1864 the pike was traveled by 10,882 four-horse supply wagons and 7,221 two-horse ambulances. (Because there was no charge for pedestrians, he did not bother to note the tens of thousands of infantrymen who also trod the pike.) Even under normal circumstances, roads needed a lot of maintenance: dirt thoroughfares were rutted by heavy wagons, silted up by erosion, and washed out by freshets; turnpikes required regular clearing of drainage ditches and patching of macadam and planking. But the same wartime shortage of white and black labor that plagued agricultural production also left the county authorities and turnpike companies hard-pressed to keep their roads in repair. Nor could local officials and private proprietors readily repair or replace the many bridges and ferryboats wrecked by troops of both sides.[20]

Citizens and soldiers alike bemoaned the condition of the roads around the city. An army officer described them in June 1862 as "deplorably bad. Artillery can scarcely be moved at all; and the supply wagons are gotten along with great difficulty & loss." A civilian who rode four miles out on the Mechanicsville Turnpike later that year observed that "so completely . . . had it been cut up by the incessant passage of artillery, stores, and troops, for a year and a half, that it was getting into very bad condition." The Manchester and Petersburg Turnpike was deemed by its own director in 1863 to be "unfit for travel" and very nearly "impassable." Bad enough in dry weather, after a rainfall or snowmelt the untended roads turned into morasses. Farmers and hucksters who supplied the city markets were, like the army, frequently stuck in the mud. John Jones recorded after a snowfall melted in March 1863 that "the roads are very bad. No food is [now being] brought to the market." More than once the Dispatch castigated the Henrico authorities for failing to do their duty in this regard; the egregious condition of the county's roads, said the editor, was seriously impairing the movement of provisions from farm to market.[21]

Rail transportation, on which Richmonders relied for a great deal of their grain, cured meat, and fodder, was also impaired. Here, too, the severe scarcity of labor wreaked havoc. After 1861 the railroads had to compete fiercely with the War Department for white and black manpower. The pool of unskilled labor available to cut timber, repair tracks and trestles, and load and unload cars shriveled, as did the pool of skilled labor available to maintain cars and locomotives and drive the trains. The superintendent of the Virginia Central warned in August 1862 that lack of fuel would very soon shut down the line unless more woodchoppers could be secured. Later that year the president of the Richmond, Fredericksburg, and Potomac echoed that warning; the impressment of black axmen, he said, had left the line desperately short of fuel, crossties, and trestle beams. The skilled workforce of the Richmond and Danville's machine shop dwindled by April 1863 to a mere four men, nowhere near enough to keep the rolling stock in repair; the company's president begged the War Department to release conscripted railroad mechanics from field duty and assign them to the shop. The railroads were also crippled by shortages of critical materials. Cut off from their Northern and European suppliers, they had nowhere to turn for new rails, cars, locomotives, and spare parts; the few Southern facilities capable of making them (such as Tredegar) were busy producing munitions. As track and rolling stock wore out, the railroads were hard put to replace or repair them, often resorting to cannibalizing spurs or sidings for rails and less efficient locomotives and cars for parts. The railroads suffered, too, from the theft of fuel and cargo from wood depots and freight cars insufficiently guarded due to the labor shortage and from the destruction of track, trestles, and rolling stock by the Union army.[22]

Starved for labor, fuel, and equipment and deteriorating day by day, the Richmond railroads struggled to meet the demands imposed on them. By early 1864, three of the nine locomotives owned by the Richmond and Petersburg had given out and been withdrawn from service; of that company's forty-one freight cars, eleven were by then on their last legs, as were six of twenty-one flatcars. To stretch out the life of their iron rails, some of the Richmond railroads were forced to restrict cargo weight, reduce engine speed, or cut the number of daily runs. Worn rails that could not be replaced were kept in use beyond safe limits, resulting in frequent accidents and delays. The Virginia Central suffered four derailments in the space of five days in early 1863.[23]

The James River and Kanawha Canal, too, experienced shortages of labor and materials. Nevertheless, it managed to operate fairly efficiently until near the war's end. Volunteering and conscription deprived the canal company and the packet lines of almost all their white workers, but increased recruiting of black labor made up most of that loss. Recognizing the critical economic and military importance of the canal, both the state government and the War Department stepped in to help it. In March 1862 the Virginia General Assembly approved a grant of $200,000 to the canal company, much of which was used to hire additional free and enslaved black workers. The War Department, for its part, liberally granted exemptions from slave impressment to the canal company and packet lines. It also permitted the canal company to buy (at below-market prices) picks, shovels, wheelbarrows, carts, and other tools and equipment from the army; it even delegated authority to the company's chief engineer to impress slaves, horses, and mules as needed along the route of the canal.[24]

Thus bolstered, the canal continued to deliver food to Richmond until early 1865, when nature and the Yankee army dealt it heavy blows. In January the James River flooded, submerging parts of the canal and rendering it unusable for days. Hardly had it resumed operation when, in February, a cold snap froze it up for more than a week, again bringing boat traffic to a halt. In early March, Union cavalry raiders struck, wrecking thirty-four locks and disabling an eighty-nine-mile stretch of the canal. Thereafter nothing came into the Confederate capital by canal from farther than thirty miles away.[25]

Beset by burgeoning demand, declining production, and faltering transportation, Richmond's food supply was spread thinner and thinner. The inevitable consequences were soaring prices. In 1860 a market shopper could buy a pound of butter for twenty-five cents. By January 1862, that price had doubled; a year later it was $2; by March 1865, $20. Other staples followed roughly parallel paths. Bacon, twelve and a half cents a pound in 1860, cost twice that in January 1862, $1.25 in early 1863, and $20 in March 1865. A barrel of flour, $6.50 in 1860, cost $13.50 in mid-1862, $30 in early 1863, and $1,000 or more by the end of the war. Sometimes there was no food to be had at any price. Meat, in particular, periodically disappeared from the markets. John Jones, a regular grocery shopper, noted in March 1864 that "the market-houses are deserted, the meat stalls all closed, only here and there a cart, offering turnips, cabbages, parsnips, carrots, etc., at outrageous prices." Eleven weeks later no relief was in sight: "There has been no meat in [the] market for a long time, most of the butchers' stalls being closed during the last three months." Shortages eased somewhat thereafter, only to return in force during the last winter of the war. "The markets are now almost abandoned," Jones wrote in late February 1865, "both by sellers and purchasers." A month later, another Richmonder echoed Jones: "The stalls of the great market-house, [once] so famous for their abundant supplies of fish, flesh and fowl, are a sight now, so empty are they. For many days nothing but 'greens' is to be seen there, and even our 'bacon and greens' lacks the *bacon*."[26]

Boardinghouse residents, although not directly dependent on the markets for food, were in no way sheltered from the inflation and scarcity, for their landlords simply passed along the rising prices and served less generous and less varied meals. And as time went on, more and more boardinghouse operators, weary of the expense and difficulty of feeding hungry lodgers three times a day, quit doing so, telling them they could stay on as roomers but henceforth must get their meals elsewhere. In September 1863 a Post Office Department clerk named W. F. Smith complained that boarding-house keepers "have nearly universally given up their establishments as un-profitable and impracticable at the present rates of living, and have resorted to room renting." He and his family, like many others in the same predica-ment, reluctantly signed on as "day boarders" (also called "table boarders") at a lodging house that still served meals and thereafter had to sleep and eat in two different places.[27]

Meanwhile, the price of board moved upward and the quality downward. By early 1864, a single person could expect to pay, as one outraged Rich-monder reported, from $150 to $200 a month "for meals alone & wretched ones at that." Only a few months earlier the going rate had been $75 to $100. War Department clerk Henri Garidel, who moved to the Confederate capi-tal in July 1863, complained after nine months of boarding there that "since I have been in Richmond I have never eaten my fill. The meals are very small and very badly prepared." One evening months later, when he came home to his boardinghouse "dying of hunger," Garidel was "rewarded by a very bad dinner. A soup that Drink [a household pet] would not have eaten and a piece of meat as tough as a horse." When he and his fellow boarders sat down to dinner five days later, they found "some [watered-down] soup, a plate of turnips, and a plate of beans. That was our entire meal."[28]

There were alternatives, most of them in one way or another unsatis-factory. Some lodgers were allowed to cook food in the fireplace in their room or use the landlord's kitchen, but that of course required buying provi-sions in the market. Many people turned to the city's eating establishments, of which there were four kinds. The least expensive were the "cookshops"; with no waiters and little or no seating, they sold prepared food mainly to go. The most expensive were restaurants, which only the prosperous few could patronize regularly. In between were bars that served food as well as liquor (known as "eating saloons," their clientele almost exclusively male) and hotels, most of which had a dining room where, after purchasing a meal ticket from the desk clerk, a customer could sit down beside others at a long table and eat in boardinghouse style. As the number of boardinghouses and hotels in the city dwindled, the number of other eateries, especially cook-shops, multiplied. But they, too, of course, contended with the hard realities of the food supply, and their customers decried the poor fare and high prices.[29]

Richmond's water supply was strained by enormous wartime demand but held up much better than the food supply. Citizens without access to wells drew heavily on municipal water, whether they lived in houses connected to a main or relied on public fountains and hydrants. Most War Department facilities within the city, including Libby Prison and Castle Thunder, were connected to mains and used municipal water. (Those on the city's outskirts—Camp Lee, Belle Isle Prison, and the encampment hospitals—had wells.) The waterworks experienced some labor and equipment shortages but remained in full operation save for a few occasions when high water in the James flooded the pumps; even then, the reservoir's six-to-seven-day supply usually allowed water to continue flowing through the mains until the river subsided. The city council, worried that the increasing demand would eventually overwhelm the waterworks, eased the burden on it by authorizing construction of a number of municipal wells and by funding maintenance and repairs on any privately owned well whose owner agreed to let the public use it.[30]

The spiraling cost of food in Richmond demanded the attention of Confederate, state, and city authorities, but they never solved the problem. It may have been insoluble. Or perhaps there was a failure of imagination: for one thing, no one ever considered rationing, which could have brought prices down by forcibly constricting demand. One thing the authorities did try was limiting food prices by fiat, a scheme probably doomed to fail even if carried out systematically and energetically, which it was not. On 7 April 1862, the military department commander, Gen. John H. Winder, armed with extraordinary power by virtue of President Davis's recent proclamation of martial law in the city, imposed a price cap on four staples (butter, eggs, potatoes, and fish) whose prices had escalated egregiously. But the city's market hucksters and grocers—who would lose money selling at the mandated prices—responded by refusing to offer those goods for sale. The public complained loudly, and on 30 April, Winder revoked his order. He tried and failed again in July 1862, decreeing a ceiling on the price of corn, which provoked similar resistance. The War Department then decided that even under martial law it had no authority to fix retail food prices. In the fall of 1863, the state and municipal governments, prodded by a petition from Richmond workingmen, took up the idea. A bill was introduced in the legislature that would cap not only the food prices in the capital but also the prices of manufactured goods. This was too much for citizens schooled from infancy in the virtues of small government and free markets: the city council held a public referendum on the bill, the Richmond electorate condemned it by a vote of 867–296, and the legislature scuttled it.[31]

In the summer of 1862, the city council approved a plan, proposed by a Richmond clergyman named Jeremiah Jeter, to increase the supply of food in the markets and reduce its price. With the cooperation of the Richmond and Danville Railroad, a special train would run daily from the capital to Burkeville (forty-five miles away), stopping at every station along the way. On board would be an agent of the city who would take in charge any food-stuffs that local farmers were willing to consign for sale in the city markets. On returning to Richmond, the agent would see that the goods were carted to market and sold; he would also collect the proceeds, and on the next trip down the line would pay each farmer what he or she was due. (Alternatively, any farmer who so desired could climb aboard the train and accompany his or her goods to market.) The city would cover the costs of rail transportation and cartage and would take no cut of the proceeds. A similar deal would be arranged with one of the canal packet lines, and the plan would be well pub-licized to alert farmers along the rail and canal routes. This scheme would no doubt have had a beneficial (albeit modest) impact on market supplies and prices in Richmond, but it fell through when the city failed to secure the nec-essary transportation from the hard-pressed rail and packet lines.[32]

With food prices rising without restraint, most Richmonders could en-joy good, satisfying meals only in proportion to how much money they had. Those who had plenty ate well, even in the war's most desperate months. This provoked the envy and resentment of those less fortunate. Clerk Jones wrote in early 1863 that "none but the opulent . . . can obtain a sufficiency of food"; a year later, "meal is the only food now attainable, except by the rich." Judith McGuire reported in January 1865 that some of the wealthy were host-ing parties "where the most elegant suppers are served—cakes, jellies, ices in profusion, and meats of the finest kinds in abundance." Stories like that were not just rumors. Mary Chesnut, mistress of a grand South Carolina plantation, recounted in detail some of the sumptuous meals she partook of while she and her husband lived in Richmond. The Chesnuts not only had lots of money but could draw on their plantation for provisions; shipments of rice, potatoes, butter, eggs, pickles, ham, and wild game came to them by rail every few weeks. On Christmas Day 1863 their dinner began with oyster soup, which was followed by "boiled mutton, ham, boned turkey, wild ducks, partridges, [and] plum pudding," accompanied by four kinds of wine. A few weeks later Mary and some other ladies lunched at the home of the first family of the Confederacy, where Varina Davis served "gumbo, ducks and olives, supreme de volaille, chickens in jelly, oysters, lettuce salad, chocolate jelly cake, claret soup, champagne, &c." On another occasion around that time, Mary easily came up with seventy-five dollars to purchase "a little tea and sugar." The Chesnuts' slaves Molly and Laurence, who came with them to the city, also ate well (if not so elegantly), as did the slaves of other wealthy Richmonders.[33]

Other people in the city, however, had to reckon with the soaring cost of food. Better off than most were skilled workers not subject to conscription, especially the self-employed, for they could set their own compensation and to some extent keep their income in step with inflation. A free black cobbler told John Jones in April 1863 that he was averaging ten dollars a day mending shoes. Saddlers were making ten to twelve dollars a day in late 1863—at least 30 percent more than a War Department bureau chief, as bureau chief Robert Kean noted in his diary. Shoemakers at that time were getting sixteen dollars to sole a pair of shoes; they could average close to two pairs a day, and the manufacturers who employed them provided the leather and thread. The city's barbers, who were nearly all free black men, were likewise among the favored. Henri Garidel paid three dollars for a haircut in June 1864, when he himself was making only about eleven dollars a day as a War Department clerk; some barbers by that time were charging four dollars. Women with sewing expertise could also do well. In late 1863, dressmakers were demanding, as Richmonder Catherine Cochran complained, twenty-five dollars "for the plainest dress." Cochran, raised among the South's elite, noted with a touch of bitterness the relative prosperity of some of the city's skilled working-class residents, many of whose social superiors were scrambling to get enough to eat: "Go to market," she wrote, "& you see the poorest looking men & women carrying off their plates of butter and full supplies of meat & vegetables."[34]

Much less prosperous, in many cases, were Richmond's middle-class civilian breadwinners. A large proportion of them were employees of the Confederate, state, or municipal government, and their salaries, fixed by law and only infrequently raised, invariably lagged far behind inflation. As time passed they struggled ever harder to keep food on the table. Most of the clerks in the War, Treasury, and Post Office Departments, for example, made between $1,000 and $1,500 annually in the second and third years of the war. Among the Richmond municipal employees in that period, the captain of the night watch earned $1,000 a year, the city assessor and city attorney $1,500, and the gasworks superintendent $1,800. Single men might live decently at those rates, especially if they roomed with others, but men with dependents found it very hard to do so. W. F. Smith, the post office clerk who had to secure separate boarding for himself and family after his landlord stopped providing meals, was one of twenty-one clerks in his department who petitioned the government for relief in September 1863. Rent alone now absorbed $75–$100 of their monthly pay of $125, they said, leaving nothing close to the amount needed for clothing, fuel, and food. "It is no exaggeration to say, that the majority of the clerks . . . are . . . at the present time, only half fed and half clothed; [and] that they have been compelled to borrow money till their credit is gone." Unless something was done to remedy this situation they would soon "be reduced to a state, if not of actual starvation, at least of severe and pitiable suffering." War Department clerk Jones grimly chronicled in his diary the relentless rise of food prices and the failure of government salaries, including his own, to keep pace. "We are in a half starving condition," he wrote in July 1863. "I have lost twenty pounds, and my wife and children are emaciated to some extent." Eight months later, by which time his adult son was also bringing in a salary, Jones was still distressed: "My income, including Custis's, is not less, now, than $600 per month, or $7200 per annum; but we are still poor, with flour at $300 per barrel; meal, $50 per bushel; and even fresh fish at $5 per pound." In November 1864 he noticed that "our fireside conversations at night" were becoming fixated on a single theme: "They relate mostly to the savory dishes we once enjoyed, and hope to enjoy again."[35]

Even worse off were the unskilled and semiskilled, who made up the majority of the city's civilian workforce. In early 1863 most of the hundreds of women and girls employed at the Confederate States Ordnance Laboratory (a War Department facility that manufactured firearm cartridges and caps) made $1.65 a day; none made more than $2.50. At the former rate, an employee who never missed a day of work could earn no more than $45 a month, or just over $500 a year; at the latter rate, less than $68 a month, or about $800 a year. The laboratory's minimum wage rose later in 1863 to $2.40 a day, but by then food prices had risen proportionately far more. The several thousand semiskilled needlewomen hired by the War Department's Clothing Depot to make uniforms averaged, in late 1863, about $50 a month (doing piecework at $2 for a jacket and $1.50 for a pair of pants). Of the two night watchmen employed at the War Department in the latter part of 1862, one was paid about $70 a month, the other $50; the department's four messengers were paid between $26 and $42. In early 1864, a female attendant at one of the encampment hospitals earned $30 a month.[36]

In the winter of 1864–65, the head of the War Department's Richmond Arsenal appointed a three-man board to assess the living expenses and pay rates of the arsenal's employees. The board's report tabulated the average monthly expenses of one breadwinner with a single dependent at prevailing prices. Assuming $50 for rent (for one unfurnished room), $100 for firewood, $45 for candles, and $40 for soap, nonfood expenses added up to $235 a month. Food for a month cost much more: a bare minimum — sixty pounds of meal, twenty of bacon, half a bushel of potatoes, and a little rice and salt — came to $355. At that time, some unskilled laborers in the city were earning as little as four dollars a day, or slightly over $100 a month. Even Confederate government clerks, some of whom got a raise in February 1865 that brought their annual salary to $5,500 (about $458 a month), could not meet such expenses if they had any dependents.[37]

The many Confederate government wards in Richmond, among them the Union prisoners of war, the civilian and military inmates of the Castles, the garrison troops, and the impressed slaves and conscripted free blacks who labored on the fortifications, were generally entitled to the same provisions as Rebel soldiers in the field. The task of feeding them fell mostly to the Subsistence Bureau and (where the fortification workers were concerned) the Engineer Bureau. These bureaus and the secretaries of war made a good-faith effort to provide the prescribed daily ration — which was less than bountiful but sufficient to sustain health — and for the most part succeeded. But even with the War Department's extensive power to procure and transport food, its supplies in Richmond sometimes ran short, especially in the latter part of the war, and its wards consequently suffered. In 1864 several dozen Confederate soldiers being held on various charges in Castle Thunder petitioned President Davis about their food, which at that time amounted to a half pint of rice soup, ten ounces of bread, and six ounces of "very bad meat" per day. "We could not be treated worse if we were convicts," they declared, adding that the prison authorities were undoubtedly "trying to starve us to death." Similar protests were voiced by the Yankee prisoners at Libby and Belle Isle. The government's supply of meat, in particular, frequently ran out. The Belle Isle prisoners went meatless for long periods in the winter of 1863–64 — a matter that the secretary of war brought to the attention of Commissary General Northrop, who replied that they were no worse off in that regard than Confederate soldiers. This was true: an artilleryman whose battery was part of the Richmond garrison reported in April 1864 that he and his comrades had gone without meat for up to fourteen days at a time during the last few months; he proffered this fact to justify their nocturnal raids on citizens' chicken coops. The repeated shortfalls in provisions were particularly hard on the impressed slaves and conscripted free blacks because, as the Engineer Bureau admitted, even their full ration was inadequate, for on average they worked considerably harder and longer each day than soldiers.[38]

Confederate soldiers posted to Richmond for other than garrison duty suffered, in some cases, as badly as the hungriest civilians, for the War Department did not provision them directly but instead expected them to provision themselves. The enlisted men among them were mostly either hospital convalescents (a lot of them assigned to hospital duty) or artisans such as shoemakers and machinists, whose skills were so critical for the war effort that they were not sent to the field but rather detailed to one of the private or government factories producing for the army. Instead of rations, these men received a "commutation of rations" monetary allowance and a per diem allotment (essentially a wage, paid by the employer but set by the government). Both were raised periodically in response to inflation but were never much better than paltry by the standards of wartime Richmond: the commutation of rations allowance during the last year of the war was $2.50 a day; the per diem through most of 1863 and 1864 was three dollars (raised to eight dollars thereafter but only for the most skilled artisans). Even when combined with the soldier's basic pay (eleven dollars a month for a private until mid-1864, eighteen thereafter) and other commutation allowances (for quarters, fuel, and clothing, items usually provided directly only to soldiers in the field), these stipends could not cover the expenses of even a single man in the capital, much less one with dependents. When in 1864, twenty-six detailed enlisted men at Howard's Grove Hospital begged the Confederate surgeon general to do something about their plight, the hospital's head surgeon earnestly endorsed their petition, affirming that the disparity between their incomes and the price of food in the city had left them "in a starving condition." Many officers posted to Richmond, especially junior officers, were hardly better off, for even though they were paid considerably more than enlisted men and received the commutation allowances for quarters and fuel, they were not entitled to those for rations or clothing nor to any per diem.[39]

The hundreds of thousands of Rebel soldiers who at one time or another were hospitalized in the city were generally well fed, for the Confederate government and people agreed that caring for the nation's sick and wounded defenders must be a priority. While the hospitals received some provisions from the Subsistence Bureau, for the most part each took responsibility for feeding its own patients. This was accomplished, first, by establishing a "hospital fund" that pooled the commutation of rations allowances of all the patients and any cash donations that came in. With this money, agents of the hospitals not only went to the city markets daily to purchase provisions but also traveled beyond Richmond (sometimes far beyond) to buy in bulk at prices well below those prevailing in the city. What they procured was transported to the hospitals by wagon, rail, and especially canal (Chimborazo and Winder Hospitals in fact owned and operated their own canal boats). Almost as important as the hospital funds were the contributions of food that the hospitals solicited and received in great quantity and variety. Fresh produce, dairy products, and other items came from generous citizens in the Richmond area; nonperishables came from all over the Confederacy. Hospitalized soldiers commonly enjoyed luxuries that few other people in Richmond could afford, including tea, oranges, and jelly. The flour and cornmeal procured was often turned into bread on site and served warm from the oven, for many hospitals set up their own bakeries. Richmond's hospitals did, however, experience periodic food shortages as Rebeldom's transportation network deteriorated.[40]

As food became scarcer and costlier, Richmonders high and low, in and out of uniform, struggled to get along. Desperation spurred many to extraordinary exertions to keep themselves and those in their charge decently fed. As the war went on, the city witnessed a multiplicity of responses to the crisis.

Many women were driven by want to abandon certain customs of gender, class, and even morality that had always defined their lives. Formerly well-to-do women sold off the jewelry, gowns, and silverware whose display had once affirmed their social rank. Some reluctantly took work outside the household as government clerks, loath to announce thus their loss of status and dreading the prospect of accommodating themselves to a radically different daily routine, yet grateful that office jobs were becoming available to women and that they had the requisite literacy, numeracy, and penmanship to fill them. One was Judith McGuire, who in December 1863 secured a clerkship in the Subsistence Bureau. Noting in her diary that as a condition of employment she had to attest that she truly needed the work, she added wryly that the bureau could surely dispense with that requirement, "as no lady would bind herself to keep accounts for six hours per day without a dire necessity." McGuire also told in her diary of Richmond women of her class forced to stoop even lower. She knew several "brought up in the greatest luxury" who were now engaged in making and selling straw hats. Another, a refugee from Maryland who had left behind extensive landholdings,

McGuire found one day "sitting at her sewing-machine, making an elaborate shirt-bosom"; she had resorted to taking in sewing because she and her husband could not live on his income as an army captain.[41]

Many working-class women and girls in Richmond had had to take jobs outside the household even before the war, although probably not a majority, especially among the wives and daughters of skilled tradesmen. But during the war, with many husbands and fathers gone to the army and even those still at work in the city struggling to cope with the rising cost of living, a far greater proportion of working-class females entered the workforce. Poorly educated for the most part, wholly illiterate in some cases (especially Irish immigrants), and generally lacking any but basic homemaking skills, they were excluded from the clerkships and hospital matron positions that middle-class and elite women filled. They labored instead as Clothing Depot needlewomen, C.S. Laboratory cartridge makers, hospital attendants and laundresses (many of these free blacks), and the like. So poorly paid were they that some were driven to supplement their income by selling their bodies. A letter sent to the secretary of war in September 1863 alerted him to this "deplorable evil" and asked him to raise the wages of the female manual laborers working for his department. "Many of these poor girls & women are lapsing into prostitution," explained the anonymous letter writer (an upperclass woman, on the evidence of prose style and handwriting), "from their total inability to feed & clothe themselves with the pay rec'd by them, their necessities inciting bad men to allure them into a state which has been aptly styled the 'pathway of Hell.'"[42]

Other Richmonders eased the pangs of hunger by producing their own food. As time went on, more and more backyards in the city turned green with growing vegetables. In the spring of 1863, John Jones laid out a twenty-five-by-fifty-foot garden behind his rented house, tilled it well, and proceeded to plant potatoes, beets, tomatoes, lettuce, lima beans, squash, cabbages, red peppers, parsnips, okra, and turnips. Tending it diligently every day after work and on Sundays, he was ultimately rewarded. By late summer he and his family were dining daily on the produce. "My little garden has been a great comfort to me," he affirmed in September, and had well repaid his efforts; he estimated that it would save him $150 in food expenses that year. Only the potatoes had failed. The next year Jones planted again, adding corn, collards, and eggplants.[43]

Vegetable production was taken up in some cases on an institutional scale. Even as John Jones was tilling and sowing his little plot in the spring of 1863, Castle Thunder's commandant ordered that a garden be established

Feeding the Multitudes

in a vacant city lot next door to the prison. Inmates would be permitted to help cultivate it for exercise, he decided, but the produce would be enjoyed only by the Castle's employees. The army encampment hospitals undertook to make themselves self-sufficient in vegetables and thus save a good portion of their hospital funds. Winder and Jackson planted gardens big enough to justify the purchase of plows and harrows; Jackson's took up most of a forty-acre field adjacent to the hospital. Patients convalescing at the hospitals did much of the cultivating. Winder Hospital went even further: frustrated by periodic shortages of milk in the city markets, the head surgeon ordered in 1864 that a hospital dairy be established, with sixty cows that would produce 150 gallons of milk every day. (In this case Winder was relieving itself of one shortage only to perhaps create another: the cows would require hundreds of thousands of pounds of hay annually for feed, which would have to be brought in on the hospital's canal boat.)[44]

As scarcities persisted, some of the city's large private employers, perhaps taking their cue from the hospitals, began putting to use their resources of money and personnel to buy food in bulk beyond Richmond for the benefit of their civilian employees, offering it to them at cost or giving it to them in lieu of wages. Some had long engaged in food procurement to feed their hired slave hands, as they were contractually obligated to do, but now they extended it to include free workers. J. R. Anderson and Company, which operated the Tredegar Iron Works, began doing so in the fall of 1862; its agents traveled as far as Tennessee, Georgia, and the Carolinas to purchase great quantities of corn, wheat, pork, and beef at prices well below those of the Richmond markets. In time, the Virginia Iron Manufacturing Company, the Virginia Central Railroad, the Richmond, Fredericksburg, and Potomac Railroad, and other firms adopted the practice. Samson, Pae, and Company, an iron manufacturer, was by late 1864 issuing to each of its free civilian workers a biweekly ration of seventy pounds of flour, ten pounds of beef, and a half gallon of molasses, for which it deducted sixty-seven dollars from the worker's pay — ninety-nine dollars less than the current Richmond market cost. The company estimated that these quantities were sufficient to allow an average-size family to avoid buying any of those foodstuffs in the marketplace. When it could procure other items, such as potatoes or beans, the company offered them to employees at half the market price. Savings such as these spared many workers and their families from dire hunger.[45]

Smaller companies and even individual citizens also reached beyond Richmond for provisions. Although lacking the large firms' resources, some did manage to procure modest amounts of goods at prices well below those demanded in the city. In 1864 the superintendent of Hollywood Cemetery, deploring "the extortionate and increasing price of flour in this market," undertook to buy from a supplier elsewhere in Virginia five barrels for each of the twelve gravediggers he employed, all of them family men barely able to survive on their wages. Richmonder William Liggon arranged, through his son-in-law in southwest Virginia, for the purchase and transport from there of 500 pounds of bacon to help feed his family of eight whites and three slaves. Citizens of very limited means sometimes pooled their money for such endeavors. Among them were Ellen O'Brien and four other women, "all poor" by their own account and some with husbands in the army. O'Brien herself acted as their agent, traveling in the fall of 1864 to Staunton in the Shenandoah Valley, where she bought ten barrels of flour for the group and arranged for shipment to Richmond on the Virginia Central.[46]

Some civilian employees of the Confederate government in Richmond, including a number of Post Office and War Department clerks, likewise organized informal purchasing cooperatives and dispatched agents into the hinterlands in search of cheap provisions. Others, joined by many detailed soldiers, pleaded for permission to draw on the Subsistence Bureau's large stores of food in the city. The government, committed above all to the welfare of Lee's army, resisted these pleas for a long time but eventually relented. Beginning in late 1863, detailed men working at the C.S. Arsenal and the C.S. Armory were permitted to buy limited amounts of rations from the commissary depots, paying the same well-below-market rates that the army's impressment agents paid to farmers. This privilege was thereafter extended to other detailed men and, very late in the war, to the government's civilian employees. War Department clerk Henri Garidel made his first purchase of commissary supplies in February 1865: twelve pounds of flour, four of bacon, five of rice, and a quarter gallon of molasses, for which he paid $21.50 — the market value at that time being $120.50. Moreover, a few of the government facilities in the city, including the C.S. Laboratory and the Naval Ordnance Works, adopted the practice of procuring their own foodstuffs in bulk for sale or in-kind payment to their employees.[47]

In the latter part of the war a good deal of food was smuggled into Richmond from Union states and Yankee-occupied Confederate regions by people known as "blockade runners." Most operated by land rather than water. Loading a wagon with tobacco or cotton (commodities abundant in the Confederacy and in great demand elsewhere), they would set out from Richmond, surreptitiously enter enemy territory, swap their goods for foodstuffs, and make their way back to the city. The Confederate government permitted such trade, with certain restrictions, and the Richmond provost marshal gave blockade runners passes to get through the Rebel army's picket lines. The Richmond, Fredericksburg, and Potomac Railroad helped feed its employees this way; in late 1863 it got permission to send an agent into the Union-held counties of northern and eastern Virginia, where in return for 3,000 pounds of processed tobacco the company could obtain 6,000 pounds of bacon. These ventures were of course hazardous — the Union army, determined to interdict the trade, apprehended many blockade runners and confiscated their goods — but the potential profit was enticing.[48]

Whatever expedients succeeded in getting more food to Richmond, the fact remained that a good many people there had not a penny to pay for it. Like any other city, Richmond had always had to deal with the problem of the destitute. Their number swelled during the war. In July 1862 the War Department received a poignant plea for help from a woman named Ann Hargrove, who lived in an upstairs room on Third Street and whose husband was in the army. She was desperate: too sick to work, without friends or family to help her, out of money, out of food, dreading the landlord's next knock on the door, and now "in necessity and affliction" obliged "to call on strangers for assistance." There were many like her, including Bettie Myrtle, an unmarried woman who came to the city as a refugee with her widowed mother and two young siblings. She had gotten a job and managed for a time to support the family, but then she and her mother both fell ill. In September 1864 she wrote President Davis — having no one else to turn to, she said, for not only her father but her brothers had died "since this cruel war [began]. . . . All i ask is bread. . . . if you can not send me flour please send me the means to get it. . . . i am to[o] weak to walk out [my door]. . . . we have nothing to eat."[49]

Poor relief in Richmond had always been primarily the work of private charitable organizations, and so it remained during the war. The municipal government did maintain an almshouse for those wholly unable to care for themselves, but otherwise it preferred just to fund the private charities (which of course also relied on donations from the public, not only of money but of food, clothing, and fuel). The Union Benevolent Society, an organization of Richmond churchwomen, was the chief beneficiary of city government funding before and during the war. Also active in poor relief through the war years were the YMCA and the Church and Union Hill Humane Association. New organizations arose in response to wartime need: the Richmond Soldier's Aid Fund Committee, which assisted the wives and children of men in uniform; the Richmond Soup Association, which doled out vegetable soup to the poor (the broth derived from beef shinbones provided by an army slaughterhouse); and the Citizen Relief Committee, formed late in 1864 to coordinate the efforts of all the city's charities. As far as possible, the relief societies avoided the Richmond markets when purchasing provisions for the poor, endeavoring instead to buy in bulk beyond the city.[50]

A brief but alarming outbreak of violence on the streets of Richmond in April 1863, perpetrated mainly by working-class women protesting high food prices, spurred the city council to take a more direct role in poor relief. At a meeting eleven days after the riot, the council passed an ordinance establishing a city-operated market stall where indigent citizens could receive a weekly ration of free food. The municipal overseers of the poor (who supervised the almshouse) were instructed to procure the necessary provisions, determine who was eligible for the handout, and issue them tickets to be presented when they applied at the stall. The city council also made coal and firewood available to indigents. Twenty thousand dollars were appropriated to pay for all this, supplemented by another $50,000 two months later and more as the war continued.[51]

With the very neediest citizens thus provided for (as well as possible, for the city authorities faced the same obstacles as everyone else in procuring food, and sometimes their supply ran short), attention turned to the many not poor enough to receive the free distribution but not sufficiently well-off to eat adequately at prevailing prices. In the fall of 1863 the city council created a board of supplies, composed of five councilmen and three private citizens and funded by the city, whose task was to purchase provisions in quantity (mostly from beyond Richmond but partly, with the War Department's permission, from local commissary depots) and sell them at or below cost to "those who, while able to pay moderate prices and unwilling to be the recipients of charity, are not able to pay the excessive rates now demanded." The board set up a depot, known as the city supply store, for distribution. In 1864 the city council essentially turned over the administration of the free and reduced-cost food programs to the Citizen Relief Committee and other private charities while continuing to fund them.[52]

Wartime Richmond experienced hunger, to be sure, but the unremitting efforts of civil and military authorities and ordinary citizens, especially in the latter half of the war, saved the city from starvation. There was no further bread rioting after the outbreak of April 1863, and, as John Jones noted repeatedly in his diary, there were no beggars to be seen on the streets. Two scanty meals a day of the plainest sort of food became the rule in many a household, and some citizens, as Jones observed, appeared "gaunt and pale with hunger." But Richmond survived.[53]

WORKING

What enabled wartime Richmond to avoid starvation and beggary, besides the extraordinary efforts to bring food to the city, was the abundance of civilian jobs. The editor of the *Examiner* made this point in December 1863. Although food had certainly been much cheaper before the war, he said, labor had been "too plentiful," driving down wages and leaving many willing workers unemployed. Now, however, there was no lack of work for the physically able of whatever age or sex. "The war has opened up an [*sic*] hundred branches of industry in the place of the few callings that have been rendered profitless by the war, and which, in times of tranquility and plenty, furnished employment and food for the poor. Now, though the head and elder sons of a poor family be in the service, the mother, daughters, and younger children . . . are almost sure to find ready employment."[1]

From 1861 to 1865, the great majority of Richmond's civilian residents — a considerably larger proportion than before the war, at least among women and children and the elderly — engaged in remunerative work, compelled to do so in many instances by the escalating cost of living and the absence of customary breadwinners. And jobs were generally available in plenty; indeed, most employers found themselves by the second year of the war desperate for workers as the Confederate bureaucracy grew, government and private factories and other facilities multiplied and expanded, and the army siphoned away more and more men. The shortage of labor thus joined the food and housing shortages as a key factor shaping the experience of the

Rebel capital. Like those other crises, it provoked bitter contention and spurred an urgent search for remedies.

As the *Examiner*'s editor noted, however, the derangement of the city's economy by the onset of war did throw some people out of work. The land and sea blockades took a heavy toll on businesses dependent on trade with the North or foreign countries. As early as June 1861, a number of mercantile houses closed their doors, thus idling clerks, porters, and other employees. Particularly hard hit—in fact, nearly wiped out—was the tobacco industry, which fell victim not only to the blockades but to a state law limiting tobacco cultivation in order to encourage more grain production. When the war began, the city boasted fifty-two tobacco factories employing well over 3,000 people (the great majority of them hired slaves); by 1863 only a half dozen or so were still in operation.[2]

The wave of Confederate volunteering among white men in the city immediately following the outbreak of war, along with the exodus of Northern-born and foreign-born Richmonders who refused to live in the Confederate States of America, left some employers short of hands. But until the spring of 1862, the jobs of these departing workers were readily refilled. For every clerk who donned a Rebel uniform or fled to Yankeeland, for example, there were others who chose not to do so and were ready to take his place. The closing of some Richmond mercantile houses and most tobacco factories, as noted, left clerks looking for work. The influx of refugees, which included a good number of U.S. government employees who had resigned their positions in Washington, expanded the pool of available clerks in the Rebel capital, as did the idling of many teachers in the Richmond area whose male students had abandoned their studies and gone to war.[3]

Replacements for the skilled working-class men who joined the army or renounced the Confederacy were somewhat harder to find. Their loss was felt acutely by many employers. Less than two weeks after the surrender of Fort Sumter, Tredegar Iron Works superintendent Joseph Anderson complained to Governor Letcher that two of his most valued hands, blacksmith Lewis Ogden and cannon rifler John McDonald, had left to join the Virginia volunteers. Nine days later he wrote Letcher again, listing more craftsmen who had departed and warning that armament production would suffer if the hemorrhaging of skilled labor was not stanched. The firm of Mitchell and Tyler, watchmakers who branched out into sword and bayonet production soon after the war began, severely felt the absence of employee Isaac Goddard, an early enlistee who was not only an expert watchmaker but also a chemist.[4]

The loss of such men was partly offset by the inflow of refugees, among whom were craftsmen of all sorts anxious to find a job. But at least as important was the War Department's willingness to discharge or detail soldiers with skills needed by Richmond employers engaged in war-related work. The respite from enemy military pressure enjoyed by the Virginia theater of war from late July 1861 to the spring of 1862 encouraged a liberal policy of releasing soldiers at the request of manufacturers and other employers if the public good would thereby be served. (Governor Letcher was similarly liberal in granting exemptions from state militia service in the war's first year.) Joseph Anderson's appeals secured the discharge of cannon rifler McDonald, who returned to his old job at Tredegar. Likewise successful was the petition of printing firm Ritchie and Dunnavant for the discharge of one of its former "principal hands," now needed back at the shop to help fill contracts with the War, Post Office, and State Departments. James Acree, serving with the Fifteenth Virginia Infantry, received a discharge and returned to work in Richmond at the request of the butcher who had previously employed him as an assistant and who now needed him back to help supply the army hospitals with meat. So generous was the War Department's policy regarding such appeals that when the president of the Richmond Stove Works (provider of heating stoves to army hospitals and barracks) asked that two iron molders previously employed at the works now be detailed there—which would mean that the two would remain enrolled in the military—the secretary of war just went ahead and discharged them.[5]

As the business of war in Richmond burgeoned in the summer, fall, and winter of 1861–62, many employers found that simply retrieving prewar employees from the army was insufficient. They asked for other skilled men, as did the managers of the many new war-production facilities that sprang up. Army authorities generally obliged. In the same appeal that won the release of his two previously employed molders, the president of the Richmond Stove Works asked for the detail of three others currently in uniform of whom he had learned; these men, too, were quickly discharged and dispatched to Richmond. Joseph Anderson likewise stayed alert for tips about useful skilled workers in the army; he succeeded in getting a number of machinists and blacksmiths discharged and gave them jobs at Tredegar. Pvt. E. M. Hall of the Nineteenth Virginia Infantry, a shoemaker in civilian life, returned to that work in September with discharge papers in his pocket at the request of a Richmond entrepreneur who had a contract with the Quartermaster Bureau for 400 pairs of brogans. Two soldiers of the First Virginia Infantry, Michael Kehoe and Timothy Burns, likewise got discharged that month and headed to the capital, in their case to work for the Richmond and Petersburg Railroad. When workers were requested for a specific project rather than long-term employment, the War Department was accommodating but granted details rather than discharges. Thus, for example, when Richmond iron founder Philip Rahm agreed to construct a machine the government bakery needed to produce hardtack, the War Department detailed eight machinists to him with the stipulation that they would return to their regiments as soon as the job was done.[6]

When it came to filling the unskilled and semiskilled jobs in Richmond that were vacated by departing white men or created by the expansion of war production, the War Department offered no help (except to help itself to the labor of black men impressed or conscripted to build fortifications). White male refugees who came to the city met some of the need, but over time both private and government employers came to rely increasingly on slaves, free blacks, and white women and children.

Black men and women had long worked in Richmond's industries, of course, but after the outbreak of war their numbers swelled. The pool of available black laborers, especially slave laborers, was large in the war's first year. The collapse of tobacco manufacturing freed up thousands for war work, and thousands more were brought or sent to the city from the hinterlands by masters fearful of Union invasion. Richmond's numerous slave-sale and slave-hiring agencies helped put them to work where they were needed. At Tredegar, which had employed no more than eighty blacks on the eve of the war, there were by January 1862 some 135, a handful of them free but the rest all hired slaves. (A few were not unskilled but skilled, including seven blacksmiths and a carpenter.) The Virginia Central and other Richmond railroads likewise expanded their black workforce as white hands departed and business boomed. And, too, many free and enslaved blacks, women as well as men, were hired to work in the wards, kitchens, and laundries of the army hospitals; by early 1862, Chimborazo alone employed over 50 black cooks and bakers and more than 200 nurses. But domestic work continued to absorb much black labor. Before the war, the majority of black workers in the city had been household servants. During the war the proportion was probably somewhat less, but the number of black domestics surged in response to the influx of upper-class white families and the proliferation of boardinghouses.[7]

White women and children had also labored in Richmond's antebellum industries but not in great numbers. As the war got under way, they were an increasingly common sight in the city's privately owned shops and factories and government facilities. By July 1861 some 370 women and girls were assembling rifle and pistol cartridges at a factory on Bird Island in the James River. The Crenshaw Woolen Mills put women on the payroll, too, along with some children as young as ten. The army hospitals hired unskilled white women as nurses and laundresses. Tredegar took in fifty boys as apprentices during the war's first year, nearly triple the number accepted during the two years before the war. Hundreds of women signed on as government needle-workers to sew uniforms, knapsacks, and such: this was a particularly attractive opportunity for women with small children, for they could do the work at home, picking up the materials at an army depot and then returning the finished product there, for which they were paid by the piece.[8]

With the coming of spring in 1862, Richmond's labor market was transformed. From that time until the end of the war, the city's employers, government and private alike, confronted an increasingly critical shortage of workers, especially skilled workers. The primary cause was the imposition of national military conscription, which took more and more white men from the city even as the expanding industry and bureaucracy demanded more and more labor.

The Conscription Act of April 1862 made all able-bodied, white, male residents of the Confederate states ages eighteen to thirty-five subject to military service. The War Department put in place a system of conscription agents (known as enrolling officers), examining boards, and camps of instruction to gather draftees, confirm their eligibility and fitness, and give them basic training. Also enacted by Congress and implemented by the War Department was a complex and repeatedly revised set of regulations exempting certain classes of men from conscription. This was intended to keep enough artisans and professional men at home to carry on industrial and agricultural production, to allow local, state, and national governments to function, and to ensure the welfare of the civilian populace. Exempted men included, at one time or another and with various stipulations, blacksmiths and other metalworkers, railroad engineers and brakemen, millers, tanners, shoemakers, plantation overseers, Confederate government clerks, municipal and state officials, teachers, ministers, physicians, druggists, newspaper editors and printers, and others. The law also allowed a conscript to avoid service by purchasing a substitute, i.e., paying another healthy, military-age man (one not subject to the draft, such as a foreigner) to take his place.[9]

As the Rebel nation's military situation deteriorated, the army's demand for manpower grew more voracious. The War Department's willingness to discharge able-bodied soldiers to work on the home front consequently evaporated. Congress raised the maximum draft age to forty-five and then fifty, lowered the minimum to seventeen, slashed the number of draft-exempt classes, and abolished substitution. Skilled white employees of military age in manufacturing and transportation, in particular, were eventually almost all conscripted; those whose work was deemed "absolutely indispensable to the public service" (as determined by the War Department, case by case) were permitted to stay on at their jobs as detailed men, but their entitlement to this privilege was carefully scrutinized and had to be frequently recertified.[10]

The heavy hand of conscription fell on Richmond's white, male workforce with increasing severity. Charles Werner and Cornelius Starkey, employees of Mathias Altmeyer, who supplied the Quartermaster and Subsistence Bureaus with candles and soap, were conscripted in late 1862 and denied detail to Altmeyer's shop despite his insistence that they were essential to its operation. The War Department held rigidly to its rule that no details would be granted to any contractor who could not attest that the employees in question would devote 100 percent of their labor to producing for the government. Because Altmeyer sold a portion of his products on the market, Werner and Starkey went to the army.[11]

Examining boards grew stricter over time, particularly about medical exemptions. Many a man initially declared physically unfit for service was subsequently given another look. Phillip Tabb Jr., a forty-three-year-old Confederate government clerk who suffered from a bad back, testicular disease, and neuralgia, had been excused from service in 1862 but in the summer of 1863 found himself conscripted, judged fit for duty by the Richmond examining board, and ordered to report to Camp Lee. An appeal by his supervisor failed to win Tabb a discharge, although it did get him a sixty-day detail to his clerkship with the possibility of renewal. Less fortunate was Thomas M. Heltzhimer, a Richmonder who served in the army until September 1862, when he was discharged and sent home by reason of a hernia that rendered him unable to march. This reprieve lasted only until May 1864, when—still plagued by the hernia—he was drafted, approved for duty, and ordered to Camp Lee. Another among the lame and halt sent to the front as the army grew more desperate was Harvey Luttrell. A middle-aged private in the Tenth Alabama Infantry, Army of Northern Virginia, he was so debilitated by asthma and rheumatism by the spring of 1863 that he was detailed to Richmond for light duty as a hospital clerk and nurse. There he lived and worked until the fall of 1864, by which time the army was in dire straits. "There is now a great call for soldiers," Luttrell wrote his wife from Howard's Grove Hospital on 4 October, "and the examining board are sending a great many to the field who have heretofore been considered unfit for duty and I am one of that class." Nine days later he was in the trenches at Petersburg.[12]

Conscription in Richmond was enforced by the district enrolling officer and the city provost marshal; each had a body of troops at his command. They were called on frequently by other War Department officials. In September 1863, for example, the superintendent of the Ordnance Depot learned that Christopher Brown, an Army of Northern Virginia artilleryman with leatherworking skills who was detailed to a saddlery on Broad Street, had failed to return to his unit when the saddlery's contract with the Ordnance Bureau expired. The superintendent immediately wrote the provost marshal asking that Brown be arrested and turned over to the army; he helpfully appended directions to the saddlery and to Brown's residence on First Street.[13]

With labor increasingly scarce, employers of every sort deluged the War Department with petitions for details. Few were satisfied with the response. Government and private manufacturers of munitions and other supplies for the army were given priority, but even they could not get all the workers they needed. The superintendent of the Ordnance Depot fought a running battle with the secretary of war (and with Gen. Robert E. Lee, to whom the secretary often referred such matters) to get more soldiers detailed to him and to hold on to the ones he had. In November 1864 he complained that "the shops have been depleted [of manpower] so much already, that we must now stop the drain, else the army will suffer for necessary supplies." Two months later he requested the detail of fifty saddle and harness makers, without whom it would be "impossible to meet the demands of the army & provide even a scanty supply for the opening of the [spring] campaigns." Joseph Anderson of the Tredegar Iron Works likewise struggled to keep his operations adequately manned. Again and again he was told that "the condition of the army forbids the department to entertain any proposition to reduce its effective strength by details." By late 1864 the free labor force at Tredegar, which had numbered nearly 1,000 in 1861, had dwindled to less than half that.[14]

Employers not directly engaged in producing army materiel got even shorter shrift — even those whose services were vital to the war effort. Charles Ellis, president of the Richmond and Petersburg Railroad, beseeched the secretary of war in August 1862 for the detail of one of the company's former mechanics now in the Army of Northern Virginia. The military demands on the railroad were onerous, Ellis explained, and he had too few skilled workmen to keep all the engines and cars running. But the secretary refused him even that single man, citing General Lee's request that no more of his troops be detailed for now except to government facilities. Two months later Ellis tried again, asking for the same man, but the secretary would not budge: there would be no details while Lee's army was "in front of the enemy." On occasion, when the army was not so hard-pressed, the secretary relented and granted details requested by the Richmond and Petersburg and other railroads; but these were always temporary and subject to revocation at any time. Ellis protested vehemently in the fall of 1864 when five artisans detailed to his Richmond repair shop were abruptly ordered to lay down their tools and report to Camp Lee.[15]

The James River and Kanawha Canal Company also butted heads with the War Department over labor. When its president requested the detail of four soldiers to construct canal boats in Richmond, the secretary of war said no, even though the petition was endorsed by Virginia's governor. The army needed those men more than the canal did, the secretary insisted; the company would have to find boatbuilders not subject to conscription. The War Department's own telegraph office in Richmond was chronically short of trained telegraphers and its appeals for details were repeatedly denied. In July 1862 the beleaguered superintendent of the office asked that four such men be detached from their units in the Army of Northern Virginia and sent to him "without a moment's delay." The secretary of war forwarded the request to General Lee, who replied that he could not spare a single soldier at this time and suggested that the telegraph office try to get along with fewer telegraphers. Even the Richmond hospitals suffered from the loss of conscripted workers and the reluctance of the War Department to grant details. In 1863 John Belvin, who was employed by two hospitals to bury deceased patients, asked for the detail of his assistant, a forty-three-year-old coffin maker named William Chandler, who had been conscripted thanks to Congress's act raising the age limit to forty-five. This case never reached the secretary of war's office: the Conscription Bureau's local enrolling officer looked into it and ruled — despite the earnest endorsement of Belvin's request by a captain in the Quartermaster Bureau — that Chandler's work was not important enough to keep him out of the ranks.[16]

Employers whose business did not directly aid the army were the most frustrated of all those who petitioned for details. They tried to make the case that they bolstered the war effort by providing essential goods or services to the civilian populace or by keeping up home-front morale, but the War Department was rarely persuaded to part with any frontline soldiers for their sake. The firm of Mitchell and Tyler, maker and repairer of watches and clocks, was threatened in early 1864 with the loss of its only remaining watchmaker, Isaac Goddard. He had served for a time in the army but was eventually certified as physically unfit and went back to his trade. The local examining board having recently reevaluated him, he was now deemed capable of active duty. The proprietors of the firm begged the secretary of war to detail Goddard to them "for the public good," pointing out that he was in charge of repairing and adjusting all the public clocks in the city — including those at the railroad stations, without which the railroads could not function. They enlisted the support of a number of railroad company executives, who sent in their own petition asking that Goddard be allowed to remain at his job. The secretary of war referred the matter to the local enrolling officer, who replied that there were a number of draft-exempt men in the city who could do that work; Goddard, he said, should go into the ranks.[17]

L. B. Thomas, a Richmond apothecary with a shop on Broad Street and a large clientele, was by late 1862 debilitated by illness and falling behind in his work. Unable to find a qualified person in the city available to act as his assistant, he wrote the secretary of war asking for the detail of the man who had served him in that capacity for years before the war, now a soldier in the Forty-Sixth Virginia Infantry. Thomas, too, obtained endorsements, in this case from no fewer than seven Richmond physicians who testified to the importance of his business for the citizenry. The petition was rejected.[18]

George and Hugh Watt, whose iron foundry was devoted principally to manufacturing plows, tried in the fall of 1862 to persuade both Jefferson Davis and the secretary of war to allow their conscripted molders, blacksmiths, and woodworkers to remain at work, citing the critical scarcity of plows in Virginia now that Northern manufactures were unobtainable. The secretary dismissed the appeal, remarking that too many men were being excused from duty at the front. Moreover, he said, a plow could last a long time but the pool of available soldiers was fast being depleted. The Watts' skilled workforce consequently dwindled as employees were taken by the army; by early 1863 the firm was turning away potential customers for lack of sufficient hands to keep up production.[19]

Banks were also hit hard by labor shortages. The conscription laws provided no exemptions for the Confederacy's bank workers, and bankers were thus forced to plead with the War Department for details as their draft-eligible tellers, cashiers, clerks, bookkeepers, and watchmen were called to duty. In June 1862 the president of the Traders' Bank of Richmond sent the department a list of six such employees whom he deemed "indispensably necessary to carry on the operations of the Bank." If he were to lose them, he warned, "the Bank must close." Later that year, the president of the Bank of the Commonwealth submitted a similar request, stating that he had been desperately shorthanded for months and that the loss of any more employees would force him to suspend operations. If that happened, he added slyly, the bank would have to call in the substantial loans it had made to the Confederate government in order to refund the depositors' money. Such pleas left the secretary of war unmoved; the banks would have to get along with whatever properly trained men could be found who were exempted from conscription by reason of age, nationality, or disability.[20]

Publishers likewise struggled to keep their operations staffed. Acknowledging the importance of newspapers, the Confederate government exempted their editors and pressmen from the draft; it did not extend that favor to periodicals, of which Richmond was home to quite a few. Some of them, like so many other employers, appealed to the War Department. A coproprietor of *Southern Punch* told the chief of the Conscription Bureau of his fruitless attempts to hire the additional employees he badly needed (a printer, engraver, and draftsman). "Our business," he said, "is often seriously injured by delay in publication." He went on to assert the importance of his magazine for the commonweal: "Its circulation tends to keep both civilians and soldiers in good spirits diverting their minds from the necessary hardships of war." The proprietors of the *Southern Literary Messenger*, in a plea to the secretary of war for three details, similarly extolled the moral benefits of their magazine — to no avail, for their request was denied.[21]

Beset by labor shortages and denied details, employers turned more and more to draft-exempt white males. Boys, older men, the physically disabled, and foreigners (including refugees from Maryland) were in great demand. In his plea to the Conscription Bureau, the coproprietor of *Southern Punch* swore that he had done his best to staff his office with exempt men. Four were currently in his employ: a leg amputee, a discharged soldier with a bullet-shattered arm, a deaf-mute, and a Canadian. The C.S. Laboratory had hundreds of boys on its payroll by late 1863; many others were hired by private manufacturers such as the Old Dominion Iron and Nail Works. Employers with sufficient resources even reached beyond the Confederacy seeking laborers. In the fall of 1862, Tredegar Iron Works, which was chronically short of skilled workers, dispatched recruiting agents through the Federal land and sea blockades to Maryland and Europe. They returned empty-handed, but other Richmond employers had better luck. Entrepreneurs William Crenshaw and Charles Hobson managed to entice a Dubliner, Michael Long, to move to Richmond in 1863 to manage their snuff factory. Long got not only free transportation across the Atlantic and a good salary but also a War Department certificate confirming his exempt status as a foreign national, which kept the enrolling officer and provost marshal off his back. The Confederate government, confronted with a critical scarcity of engravers needed by the Treasury Department, likewise sent agents across the Atlantic — even before conscription was enacted. Among their recruits were Englishmen George Dunn and William Gellatly, who came to Richmond in March 1862 with the assurance that their families, too, would eventually be brought over at government expense. Even in the highest reaches of the Rebel bureaucracy the pressure to replace militarily eligible men with exempt men was strong. By mid-1864, of the 176 male clerks, supervisors, and other functionaries employed in the central offices of the War Department's nine bureaus, 96 were certified as over- or underage, disabled, or otherwise unfit for military duty. (The other eighty, all liable to conscription, received special exemptions only because their "services are considered absolutely necessary.")[22]

Castle Thunder proved, interestingly enough, to be a rich source of labor. Many of the Union army deserters held there, and some of the Northern civilians, were quite willing to work for the Rebel war effort in exchange for freedom. The War Department approved this arrangement in early 1863, and thereafter hundreds of such men (almost all foreign born) were released to work in Richmond's manufacturing shops and other facilities. (Less successful were efforts to recruit workers from among the Southern political prisoners in the Castle and the Yankee prisoners of war in Libby, Belle Isle, and elsewhere.) In October 1863 a Confederate official named Isaac Carrington, who had examined all the prisoners currently in the Castle, compiled a list of seventy-six Union army deserters who, he said, were "very anxious to go to work." All were immigrants — mostly Irish, English, German, or Canadian — and the majority claimed to be unwilling draftees who had "deserted at the first opportunity." Among them were carpenters, blacksmiths, shoemakers, machinists, and iron molders, along with unskilled laborers. Carrington recommended, and the War Department subsequently ordered, that these men be released as soon as suitable employers could be found. Nothing was required of them except an oath — not of fealty to the Confederacy but merely "to obey state & Confederate laws & military regulations."[23]

Typical of such men were John Kane and Frederick Beresford, whom Carrington interviewed in September 1863. Both were Irish born. Kane, age twenty-eight, had come to the United States five years earlier. Drafted on 30 July 1863, he was ordered to the Union Army of the Potomac, then operating in northern Virginia; there he was assigned to a New York regiment. On his second day in the ranks he deserted. He subsequently fell into the hands of the Rebels and was committed to Castle Thunder. Beresford, a thirty-three-year-old common laborer, had been in America for sixteen years. Drafted about the same time as Kane while residing in Connecticut, Beresford, too, was ordered to the Army of the Potomac. He never reached it: he jumped off the train south of Alexandria and was eventually picked up by Confederate scouts. The Old Dominion Iron and Nail Works offered to hire both him and Kane, and they readily assented.[24]

Another Richmond employer glad to have such men was Tredegar, which by the summer of 1864 employed no fewer than forty. Others were hired by the army's Clothing Depot and by a furniture-manufacturing shop under government contract. The army hospitals, too, welcomed Castle inmates willing to take the oath and hire on. Around the time he secured the release of Kane and Beresford, Carrington did the same for several foreign-born civilians who had worked for the Union army until they were captured by Confederate forces; these men were bakers, their skills much in demand in the hospital kitchens.[25]

As time passed, Richmond employers dipped more and more into the pool of black labor. The railroads were especially thirsty for black hands. Between 1862 and 1864, the Richmond and Danville expanded its black workforce from 328 men to 700, almost all of them hired slaves; in 1863 alone, the Virginia Central added 98 men to its force of hired slaves, bringing the total to 322. The canal company and the packet lines also relied increasingly on blacks as their white labor force dwindled. So did manufacturers, including Tredegar Iron Works, the Virginia Iron Manufacturing Company, the Old Dominion Iron and Nail Works, and Watt and Company. By late 1864 the number of blacks at Tredegar was more than double that employed three years earlier. Some employers acquired blacks by purchase rather than hire. The municipal gasworks, plagued by labor shortages, was one; in October 1862 the city council appropriated $30,000 to buy slaves for the works.[26]

The War and Navy Departments also relied more and more on black labor. The army's Ordnance, Medical, and Quartermaster Bureaus were especially active recruiters of black hands (along with the Engineer Bureau, which put thousands of impressed slaves to work on the Richmond fortifications). In October 1862, the C.S. Arsenal in Richmond had at least 150 slaves at work producing ordnance materiel. By 1863 some 445 black men and women, free and enslaved, were at work at Chimborazo Hospital and another 280 at Winder. Of the many Quartermaster Bureau facilities in Richmond, a shop overseen by Maj. R. P. Archer was perhaps typical. There, some

55 white men and almost 200 black men manufactured and repaired army wagons, ambulances, saddles, and harnesses. Half of the blacks were artisans hired from their owners. Among them were Henry, a harness maker, and George, John, Jim, and Dick, blacksmiths; for each of these men the bureau paid $1200 a year.[27]

Most of the slaves hired in Richmond during the war were rented out gladly by their masters, and most of the free black workers offered their services willingly. But such voluntarism failed to meet the demand for labor, and the government therefore turned increasingly to coercion. A series of local, state, and Confederate laws passed between 1861 and 1864 made Virginia's slave men liable (as property) to impressment and its free black men liable to labor conscription. Deferring to the slave owners' needs, the Virginia legislature and the Confederate Congress restricted the number of slaves that could be impressed and limited the length of service to sixty days. But no such consideration was extended to free blacks. Under the Confederate conscription act of early 1864, all able-bodied free black men ages eighteen to fifty not already employed in war-related work were to be rounded up by the Conscription Bureau, parceled out to employers who needed them, and held to labor for the duration of the war.[28]

A large proportion of the black men impressed or conscripted in Virginia went to Richmond. The slaves were almost all put to work on the fortifications, as were the free blacks conscripted in 1861. Later in the war, the free blacks were generally assigned to jobs according to their skills. In the spring of 1864, thirteen conscripted freemen were detailed to Samson, Pae, and Company, a foundry that manufactured ordnance for the navy. Another freeman, John Randolph, was detailed to the firm of Haxall, Crenshaw, and Company, flour millers under contract with the Subsistence Bureau. William Mundin, a barber, was detailed to cut hair at General Hospital No. 4.[29]

The pool of black labor was not inexhaustible. In the latter half of the war, Richmond's employers were plagued by a dearth of black workers nearly as critical as that of white workers. Private employers competed with the government for black hands; government bureaus competed among themselves. When the Treasury Department relocated its offices in 1863 and needed some heavy iron safes moved, no laborers could be found for hire, forcing the secretary of the treasury to ask the secretary of war to lend him eight slaves for a few days from among those at work on the fortifications. In 1864 a wood dealer in the city who employed a number of slaves as wagon drivers pleaded with the War Department for the return of one who had just been impressed and sent to the fortifications; firewood was very scarce in the city now, the dealer said, and many citizens relied on him for their supply. Tredegar Iron Works was repeatedly vexed by the impressment of its hired slaves, including some of its key skilled hands, as were Chimborazo and other hospitals.[30]

Labor-hungry employers also expanded recruitment of white women and girls. By early 1863 such workers, some as young as nine, comprised about half of the 600 employees of the C.S. Laboratory. Among them was eighteen-year-old Mary Ryan, who assembled percussion caps and friction primers. Another was Elizabeth Ashmore, an impoverished forty-six-year-old seamstress with no husband who had lived in the city since before the war; her job at the laboratory was sewing powder bags for cannon shells. In a nearby building, Ashmore's fifteen-year-old daughter, Emma, made revolver cartridges. The C.S. Clothing Depot's force of needlewomen doing piece-work grew to nearly 3,700 by late 1863; thousands more would have been hired if the depot had been able to secure enough cloth. The army hospitals increased their hiring of unskilled white women and girls as nurses and laundresses. Typical of them was Mary Jenkins, not yet fifteen years old, a country girl who came to Richmond and found work in 1864 as a nurse at Howard's Grove.[31]

The shortage of men eventually forced the Confederate government to hire educated women for certain skilled positions, namely hospital matrons and bureau clerks. (A number of women had in fact been supervising private hospitals since the beginning of the war.) As many as 350 were eventually employed in the army hospitals as ward matrons, assistant matrons, and chief matrons. Even more, perhaps 400 or 500, took clerkships with the Treasury, War, or Post Office Departments. The replacement of men with women in the bureaucracy proceeded inexorably in the latter part of the war, under orders from the very highest levels. When a post office functionary begged the secretary of war in 1864 to return the department's clerks now in the ranks, whose absence was crippling the movement of mail, the secretary responded bluntly, "This matter has been decided directly by the President. Ladies will have to be employed in the P[ost] Office."[32]

For women aspiring to such jobs but unqualified, training became available. In June 1864 a man residing on Third Street and calling himself "Professor" C. M. Ligget posted an ad in the *Dispatch* announcing his intention to offer instruction in double-entry bookkeeping, recordkeeping, and penmanship "to a few pupils (male and female)." Five months later the War Department's telegraph office set up a school to train young women as telegraphers.[33]

Wartime Richmond's workplaces, whether offices, large factories, small artisan shops, hospitals, or other sites, were agitated by tension and conflict. The sources of discontent were many, but chief among them were wages and salaries. Few employees saw their pay keep pace with the galloping inflation. Struggling workers deluged employers with pleas and protests. In the fall of 1862 a group of War Department clerks, bewailing the "exorbitant prices" for food and clothing and citing the raise recently granted to certain other government office workers, petitioned for equal salaries. In 1863 journeyman shoemakers employed by government contractors demanded a raise from sixteen to eighteen dollars a pair for soling shoes. That same year a number of post office clerks, noting Congress's failure to grant them raises before its last adjournment, asked permission to draw rations from commissary depots. They appealed for help not just for themselves but on behalf of "the *starving* or *freezing* of all clerkdom."[34]

Appeals of this sort sometimes persuaded employers but often met resistance. At least one of the firms employing the journeyman shoemakers who sought a raise flatly rejected it and warned that the company would "withhold work from all those who demand the advance"—a stance applauded by the *Examiner*, which insisted that the shoemakers were already well paid and urged that "if they are not content with reasonable profit on their labour" they be sent to the army. Some petitioners won the support of their immediate supervisors only to be rebuffed at higher levels. Such were the fates of blacksmith V. V. Vaughan and five other artisans employed in a Quartermaster Bureau shop, all of them detailed conscripts who found their paltry monthly pay and daily stipend insufficient to sustain themselves and their families; their November 1863 plea for a raise was endorsed by two quartermaster officers but subsequently ran into a stone wall of bureaucratic regulations. At least one petitioner lost not only his appeal but his job. S. D. Boyd, a married man struggling to get by on the fifty dollars a month he earned as a War Department courier, invoked the "enormous high price of living" in Richmond when he asked for a raise in September 1862. Unfortunately for him, this request spurred the department to reconsider the need for his position. The secretary of war himself made the decision: "Pay off and dismiss the courier."[35]

On occasion women added their voices to the employees' appeals. A petition for a raise submitted by Medical Bureau clerks in 1864 was signed by twenty men and—in a separate column—five women. These and other female government clerks had every reason to feel aggrieved, for by law they were paid 25–50 percent less than their male counterparts for the same work.

And the systematic discrimination against them went beyond the matter of salaries. Skeptical about the character of any woman seeking entry into the traditional male sphere, bureau chiefs expected female job applicants to provide letters of recommendation (from men) attesting not only to their intelligence and their need for the job but also to their moral rectitude — a requirement not applied to male applicants. Once hired, the women faced further prejudice and suspicious oversight. Ordnance Bureau clerk Henri Garidel, who sympathized with his female coworkers and thought "they do very good work," was disgusted when a supervisor promulgated a code of conduct to be applied to female clerks only: "Office hours from 9:00 to 3:00. Recess at 12:00 to be limited to thirty minutes. Punctual attendance is required. Conversation during office hours to be limited to the business of this office. A non-compliance with this order will ensure the dismissal of the party or parties reported by the clerk in charge as disregarding the same." Garidel, a product of Louisiana's Creole culture who relished the lax oversight of male clerks in his office, considered this decree "ridiculous. These Americans don't have the respect for their women that we do. They are brutes."[36]

Even where such blatant discrimination was absent, some women found offices and hospitals to be hostile work environments. Phoebe Pember, who became a chief matron at Chimborazo in late 1862, recounted a surgeon's reaction on the day she was hired: in a loud whisper meant for her to hear, and "in a tone of ill-concealed disgust," he informed a colleague that "*one of them had come.*" The idea of a woman in a position of authority provoked a good deal of muttering among the hospital's male staff members about "petticoat government," and some tried to undermine Pember's position. But she stood her ground, most notably in a hard-fought, drawn-out battle over control of the hospital's medicinal whiskey supply (by law within her purview), confounding her adversaries and eventually winning the respect and cooperation of many of the men.[37]

Once the Confederate government opened up clerkships and hospital supervisory positions to women, there came a flood of applications vastly out of proportion to the available jobs (an exception to the general rule of labor shortage in wartime Richmond), for there were thousands of educated women in the city facing privation and desperate to earn some money. The secretary of the Treasury remarked in 1863 that "one [clerkship] vacancy will bring a hundred applications." When Jefferson Davis intervened to try to find a place for a woman who appealed to him personally in 1864, one after another of his bureau and department chiefs informed him that nothing was available; the quartermaster general, for one, replied that he already employed "as many Ladies as can be of use in this Bureau" and had applications on file from 100 others.[38]

The scramble for these positions generated frustration, anxiety, and rivalry. Octavia Taylor, a refugee from the Peninsula, wrote Davis in 1863 after her application for a Treasury clerkship (accompanied by recommendations from several prominent Richmonders) was rejected. She suspected that she had been turned down not only because there was a long waiting list for the job but because she "was not a *personal* friend" of the secretary of the Treasury. "All I ask is *work*," she implored, adding that she was an unmarried orphan, her only brother was in the army, and Federal invaders had seized her property. "Is there not some way in which I can serve you?" Catherine Baxley, a thirty-seven-year-old refugee from Baltimore who described herself as short of food and fuel and "almost out of *hope*," complained of favoritism of a different sort at the Treasury Department when she wrote to the president in January 1864. She and a number of other very needy older women employed there had recently been let go while certain other females — "*young and pretty girls*" — were retained. These girls did not really need the work, Baxley insisted; they sought merely "a little 'Pin Money'" or funds to maintain a horse "with which to 'promener *a cheval aux environs*'" with one of the many gallant *little officers now sojourning in the City.*"[39]

Fierce competition for a limited number of jobs also characterized the piecework needle trade on which the C.S. Clothing Depot relied. The Quartermaster Bureau mandated that this work was to be reserved for women (white women, that is) with the greatest need. Some who were denied work protested that they were more deserving than some of those employed, spurring the depot superintendent to investigate everyone on the payroll and to dismiss those who could survive without the job; by late 1863 he had fired some 500. The next year, still besieged by far more applications for work than he could grant, he set forth a strict order of priority in hiring: first, the wives, mothers, and daughters of soldiers in the field; next, widows and orphans; and last, dependents of soldiers detailed to work in Richmond. Eventually he enlisted the help of the Visiting Committee of the YMCA (which also assisted the city government in identifying citizens entitled to poor relief); the committee interviewed applicants in their homes and to each one deemed eligible granted a certificate, which she had to present at the depot when picking up the materials to be sewn.[40]

Discontented workers whose skills were in great demand and short supply frequently took advantage of that enviable circumstance to quit their job and move on to a better one. The superintendent of the Ordnance Depot warned in November 1862 (before women began to be hired in great numbers in government offices) that unless his clerks, who were currently making $1,200 a year — "a mere pittance in these times to a man who has a Family" — were granted a raise, he would be unable to keep his office staffed; one of his best employees had recently left for a position in a bank at $1,600. A few months later he reported the same problem with his artisan workforce: "The men in our shops are using every means in their power to get away from here, because they cannot live at the present rate of wages." Many workers quit to secure not better pay but a draft exemption. John and George Gibson, manufacturers under contract with the Medical Bureau to make hospital beds and other furniture, advised the bureau in October 1862 that their operations were endangered by the loss of skilled hands. Liable to conscription while in the Gibsons' employ, men were leaving at the rate of several a week to take jobs at the C.S. Arsenal and other government facilities, where they were immediately provided with exemption papers. W. A. Bass, who clerked for the Richmond and Danville Railroad, left abruptly in September 1863 to return to his previous place of employment, the *Daily Richmond Enquirer*, where he was exempted by law. Bass's supervisor at the railroad, who was less than satisfied with his work, nevertheless lamented his departure because Bass at least knew the office routine and "at this time clerks of any kind are difficult to procure." The restless moving around of employees declined over time as women with no other options took over government clerkships and as draft exemptions were curtailed, leading to many skilled workers being conscripted and then detailed to their jobs; but it persisted to the end of the war among men safe from the draft by reason of age, disability, or citizenship.[41]

Even detailed men sometimes walked away from their jobs and took others or in other ways defied their bosses. This was risky, for they were not free workers but soldiers under orders and subject to military authority and punishment. Those who took the risk probably calculated that their labor was so valuable and scarce that employers would put up with their disobedience and protect them from the army's wrath. Some labor-starved employers did in fact bend over backward to accommodate fractious detailees, but they bent only so far. The issue first came to the government's attention in late August 1862, when the superintendent of the Ordnance Depot informed his chief that some of his detailed men, apparently regarding themselves as basically exempted, had gone off and taken jobs elsewhere. The War Department reacted swiftly: General Orders No. 64, dated 8 September, decreed that detailed conscripts "who leave their employment without authority will be arrested as deserters." Employers, whether government officials or private contractors, were thereafter required to report the names of detailees absent without leave. But the threat of arrest and punishment was no sure deterrent. In June 1863 the assistant superintendent of the Naval Ordnance Works informed the Conscript Bureau that no fewer than four of his detailed men had left their jobs in the last two weeks, most recently William Jones, "a first class machinist and a valuable man." Similar reports kept the enrolling officer and provost marshal busy to the end of the war. On 17 February 1865, George Minnick, a soldier in the Twenty-Eighth Virginia Infantry detailed to the Ordnance Depot's harness shop, was granted a seven-day leave to visit his family in Botetourt County; eighteen days later he was still absent from work and his supervisor suspected that "he does not intend to return." The usual outcome of such cases, when the culprit could be apprehended, was not a court-martial but a speedy return to the ranks.[42]

At least eight times during the war, disgruntled Richmond workers banded together and went on strike — a flurry of labor activism the likes of which the city had not seen since the late 1840s and early 1850s. The intention in every case but one was to win a raise. Some of these strikes succeeded; others failed. Irish foundry workers at Tredegar struck in September 1861; pointing out that they could easily get work at the nearby C.S. Armory at a higher wage, they forced Tredegar to match what the armory was paying. Seven months later, journeyman lithographers at a print shop with a Treasury Department contract struck in protest over management's decision to bring in apprentices to assist in the work. This was ill timed, for Richmond was under martial law just then and the Confederate government was in no mood to countenance the disruption of its business. The strikers were arrested by military authorities and held in jail until they agreed to return to work. Three months later, in July 1862, skilled workers at the Virginia Central Railroad's Richmond shop walked off the job and marched to the company's headquarters at Seventeenth and Broad, where they demanded a raise — which the management, hard-pressed by military and civilian transportation needs at the time, immediately granted. The next month the *Daily Richmond Examiner*'s printers struck over a wage issue but met determined resistance from management. August 1863 saw the only recorded instance of a strike by office personnel, when post office clerks refused to perform their duties any longer without a raise — a bold but quixotic effort that fizzled out almost as soon as it began, for their salaries were set by law and Congress was not even in session at the time and would not reconvene for months.[43]

Late in 1863, hundreds of female operatives at the C.S. Laboratory facility on Brown's Island staged a sit-down strike, calling for an increase in their minimum wage from $2.40 a day to $3. The fifteen or twenty who refused to join the strike were threatened by the others with a dunking in the river. The laboratory's managers quickly convened a meeting to consider the demand and apparently gave in without resistance. Ten months later, with their wages still lagging behind inflation, the laboratory women and girls struck again. This time management fought back, rejecting the demands and posting newspaper ads announcing the immediate hiring of hundreds of women to replace the strikers. But after five days, during which work at the laboratory was entirely halted, management surrendered, reckoning that bringing in so many untrained hands would cripple production and possibly compromise the quality of the caps, primers, and cartridges manufactured there.[44]

One strike turned violent. In July 1864, Hollywood Cemetery's grave-diggers, Irishmen all, laid down their picks and shovels and refused to work unless their seven-dollar-a-day wage was increased. James O'Keefe, the cemetery superintendent, promptly hired some black men as scabs. But when they showed up at the cemetery, the Irishmen attacked with clubs and ran them off. O'Keefe then procured some black convicts from the state penitentiary, who set to work accompanied by armed guards. But in the meantime he negotiated with the strikers, who returned to work when he offered them a raise of $1.10.[45]

Few black workers in Richmond were in a position to challenge their employers openly, no matter how disagreeable their circumstances. Those who were enslaved, whether working for their owners, hired out, or impressed by the government, were expected to do as they were told without a murmur and faced a whipping if they disobeyed. No better off were the many free blacks conscripted for government labor. And yet black workers slave and free did find ways to resist. Some did so by running away. Free black men conscripted by state and city authorities in the summer of 1861 to work on the Richmond fortifications deserted in droves. Isaac Pleasants, taken from his small farm nine miles below the city, labored for twenty-six days on the fortifications before slipping away and returning home. Joseph Atkins was marched away from his Henrico County farm to the fortifications by armed guards, but he managed to desert after two weeks and make his way back home. Seaton Anderson, a Richmonder, got away after only two hours of work. By August 1861 the list of free black men absent without leave from the fortifications contained 150 names. Such desertions continued in the latter part of the war, by which time free blacks were being conscripted under Confederate authority for various sorts of labor. Two white Richmonders under contract with the Subsistence Bureau to fish the James River reported in March 1864 that of the thirty-eight free black conscripts assigned to them, nine had disappeared. Enslaved workers ran away too — especially from fortification work, which was exhausting and often unhealthy, requiring laborers to slog through mud or wade through waist-deep water. Some headed to the Yankee lines, and others tried to get home or just hid out in the woods. Each of these choices was risky, for Rebel civil and military authorities were always on the lookout for runaways, and many were apprehended, flogged, and sent back to work.[46]

Hired slaves could sometimes improve their circumstances by appealing to their owners. In 1862, a number of slaves leased to the Subsistence Bureau's hardtack bakery in Richmond complained to their owners about the job and asked to be sent elsewhere. To the disgust of the bakery's superintendent, who had spent much time and effort training these hands in the intricacies of the baking process, the masters granted their slaves' wish and declined to renew the leases when they expired at the end of the year.[47]

In the latter half of the war, Richmond's workplaces were increasingly agitated by the demands on workers enrolled in the Local Defense Forces (LDF). Established by Congress in the late spring of 1863, the LDF consisted of white male Richmonders not on active military duty but capable of bearing a musket — clerks and artisans, supervisors and menials, exempted men and detailed men. Comprising six infantry battalions (later reorganized into three battalions and two regiments), each embracing a number of companies, the LDF was an emergency Confederate military force mustered only when the enemy directly threatened the capital. It was intended to serve for very limited periods and only in the vicinity of the city.[48]

Enrollment in the LDF, at first voluntary for everyone but War Department employees, was eventually required of all physically able white men of military age in the city. (Some younger and older males joined willingly.) Most LDF companies were made up of employees of a particular workplace, bureau, or department. The men of Company D of the Third Battalion, for example, were Treasury Department clerks; those of Company G, post office clerks. Most of the companies of the First Battalion consisted of Ordnance Bureau employees; those of the Fourth Battalion, Navy Department employees; those of the Sixth Battalion, Tredegar employees.[49]

The LDF's strength varied over time. At its peak, in the spring of 1864, it could muster about 3,000 men for duty. When called up, its battalions and regiments became full-fledged units of the Confederate army; the men wore uniforms, held military rank, carried muskets and accouterments, and were subject to army authority and discipline. Between call-ups, they attended to their jobs as usual but were expected to participate (armed and in uniform) in weekly drills and occasional public parades for formal review and inspection.[50]

In its first year of existence, the LDF was mustered infrequently and for only a few days at a time, in response to small-scale Federal raids. Nevertheless, complaints were heard from workers and bosses alike about problems generated by LDF service. The weekly drills were a burden that some members thought unnecessary. "They are all willing to fight, when the enemy comes," War Department clerk John Jones remarked in his diary in September 1863, "but they dislike being *forced* out to drill." A quartermaster officer with the Clothing Depot asked in October that his employees be exempt from drills, reviews, and inspections because their absence on those occasions interfered with the depot's operations; the quartermaster general endorsed this request, noting that such disruptions were "becoming a serious evil." A lot of the men stopped showing up for drills and parades, offering one excuse or another or none at all.[51]

During the final year of the war, beginning with the great Union offensive in Virginia in the spring of 1864, Richmond was subjected to enemy pressure so formidable and relentless that it strained the Army of Northern Virginia and the capital's garrison troops beyond their ability to defend the city. Repeated emergencies triggered call-ups of the LDF far more frequent and lengthy than anyone had anticipated when it was created. Workplaces of every sort were thrown into turmoil. On 25 June 1864, by which time most of the Confederate government's clerks had been in the field with the LDF for four weeks or more, the secretary of war warned General Lee that "we are suffering here very serious inconveniences. . . . Their absence greatly impairs the vigor of administration in almost every department of the Government." War Department clerk Jones (too old to shoulder a musket) expressed it more pithily in his diary that same day: "The clerks are still kept out . . . the government, meantime, being almost in a state of paralysis." A few days later the *Examiner* reported that "the derangement of the [city post office] is getting worse and worse every day, and unless the regular clerks be speedily returned, mail transportation and delivery must soon come to a stand still." Newspapers and journals suffered too. Jones noted on 30 September that "none of the papers except the *Whig* were published this morning, the printers, etc., being called out to defend the city." In early December the proprietors of the *Southern Literary Messenger* begged the secretary of war to return their last remaining hand, W. H. Crews, a private in

Company A, Third Regiment, LDF; his absence from work since 29 September had brought their operations almost to a halt. Even critically important manufactories were impaired. The superintendent of the C.S. Arsenal asked his bureau chief in December to try to secure the return of his skilled hands in the LDF, gone more than two months now: "The work of the Arsenal," he said, "is getting hopelessly behindhand." Three months later Joseph Anderson reported that Tredegar's operations had basically ceased because "all our [white male] hands are now in the field." He could not even bill his customers, for every clerk was absent.[52]

The men in the ranks all grew weary, many angry, some mutinous. "We have been 26 days out this time," wrote Lycurgus Caldwell in a letter to his daughter on 27 June 1864, "and many of us are tired of marching[,] building breastworks and felling forest trees." Caldwell, a post office clerk and sergeant in Company F of the Third Battalion, insisted that "I do military service cheerfully from a sense of duty," but he acknowledged that some of his comrades were "skulkers" who "pout and grumble like children." The grueling toil that active duty entailed was not the LDF troops' only grievance. Many resented what they saw as the fundamental unfairness of extended call-ups. One wrote anonymously to the secretary of war in November 1864, as his unit marked its forty-fourth consecutive day in the field. "Is there no way to satisfy the government[?]," he demanded. "Are not our services at our legitimate businesses sufficient[?]" No, he continued in answer to his own questions, the government had apparently decided that "life[,] limb, or health alone can suffice. . . . We have for two years worked for you at starving wages, our families have suffered, and this is the reward of our services and suffering." John Jones reported around that same time that "the poor clerks in the trenches are in a demoralized condition." The government, when it forced them into the ranks, had "assured [them] that they would only be called out in times of great urgency, and then be returned to their offices in a few days. They have now been in the front trenches several months." There was perceived injustice, too, in the duty assignments of the LDF. Certain powerful men in the government "are quietly having their kinsmen and favorites detailed back to their civil positions," Jones wrote, while "the poor and friendless" remained in the trenches.[53]

As morale eroded, discipline in the LDF broke down. Many men, perhaps tacitly encouraged by their employers, began dodging not only drills and parades but call-ups. A summons to duty on 16 August 1864 brought out only about one-fourth of the men on the LDF rolls. When another came in late December, not a single man of Company A, Third Regiment, responded.

Even more troubling were the outright desertions at the front. John Jones noted in November 1864 that "hundreds of the local forces, under a sense of wrong, have deserted to the enemy."[54]

Those who did their duty in the field not only endured physical hardship but, like all other frontline soldiers, faced the ever-present risk of death. A number of men lost their lives while serving with the LDF, but Richmonders were particularly touched by the death on 4 October 1864 of Jacob Bechtel—the bookstore clerk who in the spring of 1861 had agonized over the question of loyalty, torn between the North of his birth and the South of his long residence. In June 1863 he enrolled, apparently without compulsion, as a private in Company A, Third Battalion, LDF, thereby forsaking his earlier personal vow never to voluntarily take up arms against the United States. In the spring of 1864 he went to work for the government as a clerk in the adjutant general's office of the War Department. That fall he was with his unit in the fortifications near Chaffin's farm, seven miles south of the city. On the last afternoon of his life he and a comrade, seeking a closer look at some skirmishing going on beyond the fortifications, moved forward to an exposed position despite being warned of the danger. Suddenly Bechtel collapsed: a bullet fired by an enemy sharpshooter had struck him in the chest, killing him instantly. His body was taken to Richmond, to the home he shared with his wife, Sarah, and their seven children. He was buried the next day. The *Examiner* eulogized him as "a worthy and respected citizen," and friends raised a fund of several thousand dollars to help his grieving family.[55]

Even more lethal to the working people of Richmond than Yankee rifle and cannon fire were workplace accidents. Manufacturing and storage facilities, especially those handling any of the myriad sorts of ammunition and other explosives produced in the city, could be hazardous places to earn a living. The war was less than three months old when a chemist named Joseph Laidley, engaged in making gunpowder for the army, committed some act of carelessness—possibly involving a lighted cigar—that leveled the building he was working in and literally blew him to pieces (his right hand was found 200 yards away). In February 1862, two young white men died after days of suffering from injuries sustained in an explosion at an Ordnance Bureau workshop; Charles Schop was nineteen, John Fitzpatrick only seventeen. In November 1864, the inadvertent detonation of artillery shells being loaded into wagons at a munitions storage site near the river killed three black laborers instantly, one of them a slave named Randall, while mortally wounding another, along with their white boss.[56]

The C.S. Laboratory facility on Brown's Island was the scene of one of the deadliest workplace accidents in American history. Employed there were hundreds of white women and girls, along with a few men and boys. Some assembled bullets, paper, and gunpowder into rifle and pistol cartridges; others disassembled faulty or damaged cartridges so the bullets and powder could be reused; still others prepared the percussion caps and friction primers used to fire small arms and cannons. There was always a lot of loose gunpowder and fulminate lying around inside the various buildings on the island, and the air was thick with combustible dust.[57]

Employee Mary Ryan had been seen on occasion roughly handling the wooden blocks that held friction primers under preparation. This was dangerous: the primers were very sensitive, easily ignited. Some of Ryan's coworkers warned her to be more careful, but she paid no heed. It was she who touched off the explosion heard all across the city a little before noon on Friday, 13 March 1863.[58]

The fiery eruption blew out the sides of the building Ryan was working in, bringing the roof crashing down. The falling roof may have killed some, but most of those who died were burned to death. As many as ten people perished almost instantly, while others ran from the building to throw themselves into the river, screaming in terror and pain, their skin blackened and their hair and clothing on fire. Mary Ryan was found alive in the rubble but lived only until Monday. Dozens of other injured workers succumbed after lingering for a longer or shorter time in unimaginable agony, their skin burned away. The death toll was reckoned at forty-five—until a month after the explosion, when another victim's body was found floating in a nearby millrace. All but three of the dead were women or girls.[59]

The laboratory disaster shocked Richmond and provoked a great outpouring of sympathy and charity. But it barely interrupted the busy pace of life in the city. There was too much else to do, too many crises to grapple with, too many desperate demands to be met, too many other deaths to be dealt with, to allow the luxury of dwelling on this single tragedy. The victims and their families aside, Richmonders quickly put the matter behind them and got on with the task of living.[60]

View of Richmond, mid-nineteenth century. Spanning a cluster of hills overlooking the picturesque falls of the James River, Richmond was founded in the 1730s and designated Virginia's capital in 1779. By the time this print was published, the city was well connected by road, canal, rail, and river to all parts of the state and to the outside world and had become a major Southern industrial and trade center. (Library of Virginia)

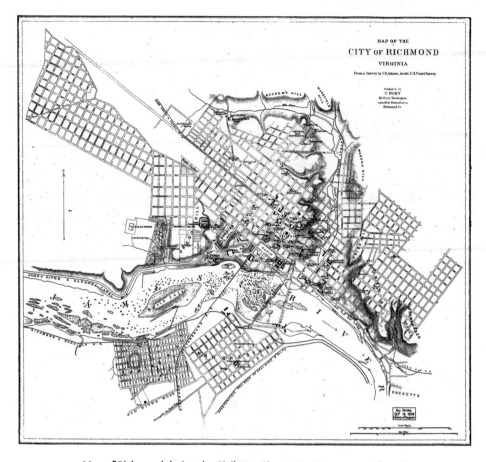

Map of Richmond during the Civil War. The city's streets were wide and straight. Laid out in a grid pattern on the steep hills, they posed a challenge to pedestrians, vehicles, and draft animals when covered with snow or ice. The city's civic heart was Capitol Square, in and around which most of the state and municipal government buildings were located. Surrounding the square and extending down to the river was the commercial district. Beyond that, to the west, north, and east, were residential neighborhoods. (Library of Congress)

Main Street, spring 1865, looking west from the intersection with Eighth Street.
This was a part of Richmond's commercial district. Visible are business signs
illustrating the diversity of the city's entrepreneurial enterprises, including those
of a barbershop, an art supply store, a restaurant, and a cigar store. In public
spaces such as this, black behavior was strictly policed: slaves and free blacks were
forbidden to smoke in public and were required to give way to white people on
crowded sidewalks and flagstone crossings—the latter being much used in rainy
weather, when Richmond's unpaved streets turned to mud. (Library of Congress)

Unidentified soldier of the Richmond Howitzers, one of thousands of Richmond men who fought in the Confederate army. Many who donned a Rebel uniform were under eighteen; those unable to get their parents' permission resorted to lying about their age. The soldiers of the Richmond Howitzers served in the field with the Army of Northern Virginia throughout the war, but many other Richmond men and boys served in and around the city as members of the garrison, the Local Defense Forces, or the militia. (Library of Congress)

View of Richmond, spring 1865, looking northwestward from Church Hill. The large building on the horizon is the state capitol, the meeting place of the Confederate Congress during the war. The brick residences in the foreground were typical of wartime housing. Mostly single-family dwellings before the war, homes of this sort were often crowded with tenants during the war as the city's population burgeoned and homeowners took in lodgers to help make ends meet. (National Archives)

First Market House, Main and Seventeenth Streets, in 1865. This and the Second Market House at Marshall and Sixth were the primary venues for the sale of fresh meat and produce in Richmond before and during the war. The city government owned both market houses and enforced strict rules regarding sanitation, weights and measures, and hours of operation. After 1861, as the swelling civilian populace and the voracious Confederate army competed for the city's diminishing food supply, the market hucksters' stalls often had little to offer. (*Harper's Weekly*)

Richmond terminus of the James River and Kanawha Canal in 1865. On the right is a passenger boat, on the left a freight boat. Stretching nearly 200 miles westward from Richmond, the canal was a privately owned toll route. As the railroads deteriorated during the war, the canal assumed greater importance for bringing food to Richmond from distant points. It also brought in coal, pig iron, and other supplies for the city's industries. (*Harper's Weekly*)

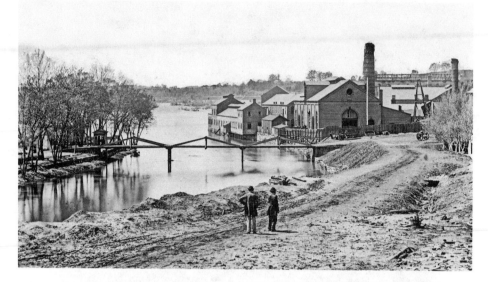

Tredegar Iron Works on the James River in Richmond, spring 1865. One of the Confederacy's major ordnance producers, Tredegar employed many hundreds of workmen, skilled and unskilled, white and black. Like the city's other factories, it struggled to retain sufficient labor as the Confederate army demanded more and more men to fill the ranks. After the spring of 1862, the white workers of military age at Tredegar were almost all Confederate soldiers detailed to their ironworking jobs. This kept them out of the field forces, but they were required to enroll in the Local Defense Forces and man the city's fortifications during military emergencies. (Library of Congress)

John H. Winder, Confederate brigadier general and military chief of Richmond until early 1864. Under his authority were the Richmond provost guard and a detective squad; together they acted as the capital's military police and investigated civilians suspected of treason or other violations of Confederate law. Winder was the designated executor of President Jefferson Davis's martial law decree of 1 March 1862, in obedience to which he tried but failed to close down all the city's saloons. He also made two unsuccessful attempts to regulate commodity prices amid the city's soaring inflation. (Library of Congress)

One of the three buildings of Castle Thunder, 1865. Officially known as the Eastern District Military Prison, Castle Thunder held Southern civilians suspected of disloyalty, Confederate and Union army deserters, Northern civilians apprehended in Confederate territory, runaway slaves who had been recaptured, and various other people who had run afoul of the Rebel authorities. Forty thousand men and women were confined here over the course of the war, as many as 1,000 on any given day. As labor grew scarce in wartime Richmond, Union army deserters and Northern civilians imprisoned in the Castle were recruited to work in factories. (Library of Congress)

Black Richmonders, April 1865. Slaves and free blacks made up almost four-tenths of the city's population on the eve of the war. Subordinated by law and custom and (in the case of the slaves) liable at any time to be separated from their families by sale, they nevertheless established strong family and community ties. During the war they seized on new circumstances to expand their limited sphere of autonomy. Always an important part of the city's workforce, skilled and unskilled black men and women assumed even greater importance as white workmen went to the army and employers grew desperate for labor. Hundreds of Richmond slaves managed to flee the city and take refuge with the Union army, but the increasingly repressive mechanisms of racial control ensured the survival of slavery in the capital until the day Federal forces captured it. (Library of Congress)

Joseph Mayo, wartime mayor of Richmond. Scion of an old and prominent Richmond family, Mayo was a voice of the white upper classes in all his official dealings. His daily court sessions gave him the opportunity to scold and punish the city's malefactors, especially rowdy drunks, flagrant prostitutes, insubordinate blacks, and other Richmonders of the "lower sort" that he so disdained. Like all other elite Richmonders, Mayo was stunned by the April 1863 bread riot, perpetrated mainly by working-class white women. He and the city council subsequently took steps to forestall a recurrence, but until the war's end they remained fearful of unrest among the white masses. (Cook Collection, The Valentine)

Moore Hospital, Main and Twenty-Sixth Streets, April 1865. Also known as General Hospital No. 24, this was a former tobacco factory taken over by the Confederate army's Medical Bureau in 1861. It and other military hospitals set up in Richmond's preexisting buildings were generally poorly ventilated, fiercely hot in summer, and hard for the patients and staff to get around in because of the stairs. They were ultimately replaced to a great extent by "encampment hospitals" such as Chimborazo, designed for maximum patient comfort and ease of access. All the hospitals employed white and black women as nurses, laundresses, and cooks; educated white women were hired as matrons. Patients were very well cared for, on the whole, except in the immediate aftermath of major battles, when the hospitals were deluged with wounded men. (Library of Congress)

Those who have lost friends in the ARMY, will please preserve this circular for reference.

EMBALMING THE DEAD.

PRESERVING

AND

PETRIFYING THE DEAD.

The undersigned will attend in all the details to the preservation of the bodies of the DEAD entrusted to their charge, and every embalment will be conducted under the supervision of a skilful surgeon.

PERSONS AT A DISTANCE

Desiring to have the bodies of their deceased friends, on the field of battle or elsewhere, disinterred, embalmed, disinfected, or prepared and sent home, can have it promptly attended to by application to the undersigned, at the office of

J. A. BELVIN, Undertaker,

GOVERNOR and 12th Streets,

RICHMOND, VA.

N. B.—The process being the original Rousseau Process, perfect satisfaction is guarantied.

Embalments or disinfectants made at private residences, or upon the field.

Doctors MACLURE & GERRADY,

Care of JOHN A. BELVIN,

Governor and 12th Streets, Richmond, Va.

Wartime circular advertising the services of Richmond embalmers. The capital was one of the very few places in the Confederate South where embalming was available. Only a small proportion of the bereaved families of soldiers who died in and around the city could afford to have their loved one's body embalmed and shipped home. "Doctor" Maclure supplemented his income by smuggling Confederate deserters and draft dodgers out of the city, hidden in coffins—until he was caught by one of General Winder's detectives and locked up in Castle Thunder. (National Archives)

Confederate soldiers' section of Oakwood Cemetery, 1865. A plain coffin, unceremonious burial, and crude wooden headboard were all that the hard-pressed Confederate authorities could provide for the tens of thousands of Rebel soldiers who died in Richmond's hospitals and whose families were unable to see to their interment. By the war's end, Oakwood, a municipal cemetery, held the bodies of at least 16,000 soldiers; the privately owned Hollywood Cemetery held thousands more. Both donated a section of their land to the government for that purpose. The dead were buried wearing nothing but their underwear, for the army reissued their shoes and outer garments to soldiers in the field. (Library of Congress)

Women in mourning garb viewing the burned section of Richmond, April 1865. Black-clad women were a common sight on the city's streets during and after the war, most honoring a father, brother, husband, or son who had sacrificed his life in service to the Confederate cause. The fire whose results these two are surveying was touched off during the Rebel army's evacuation of the city. It destroyed nine-tenths of the commercial district, crippling the city's economy in the immediate postwar years. (Library of Congress)

DISSENT AND DESPAIR

Confederate loyalty was by no means the unanimous political sentiment of wartime Richmond. Dissenters included men and women who adhered to the Union cause on principle, those who had no love for either the United States or the Southern nation, and those whose early Rebel patriotism waned as the government's demands grew onerous and its ability to survive questionable. These "traitors" provoked fear and wrath among the stalwart Confederates, and the authorities battled incessantly to suppress them or force them to aid the cause. As the city struggled to fend off the Yankee army and cope with hardships, it was roiled by disaffection and by anxiety about enemies within.

Most Richmonders with unyielding Union convictions left the city soon after the outbreak of war. The majority of these fugitives were of Northern or foreign birth. Robert Granniss, a twenty-one-year-old sales clerk who had moved to Richmond in 1858 from his native Brooklyn, packed his bags and headed north by train just five days after Lincoln's war proclamation. Granniss had felt quite at home during his three years' residence: he had made many friends, courted a Richmond belle, and even joined a volunteer militia company. He was not wholly unsympathetic to the arguments of the secessionists, but in the end, as he wrote in his diary, "I cannot be expected to bear arms against home and kindred."[1]

Facing Rebel retribution if they declined to convert, nearly all the Unionists who stayed in the city concealed their sentiments. Some, including a well-to-do, Richmond-born woman named Elizabeth Van Lew, a New

Jersey-born tool manufacturer named D. W. Hughes, and a Scottish-born baker named Thomas McNiven, eventually became part of a loose underground network of dissidents in and around the city who smuggled messages to the Union army about Confederate troop movements and helped prisoners of war and disaffected Richmonders escape to the Yankee lines. They did so, of course, fully aware that if caught in the act they could end up swinging at the end of a rope.[2]

Publicly silent, too, were black Richmonders. Very few of them, whether enslaved or free, had any affection for the Confederacy, for they all knew that preserving slavery and white supremacy was the Rebel nation's raison d'être. But when the war began, probably none were actual Unionists, for the United States government — which had enshrined slavery in the Constitution and statute law and denied even free blacks the privilege of citizenship — had certainly never done anything to earn the gratitude, much less the loyalty, of black Americans. But in time, as it became clear that the North's war against secession was also a war against slavery, the Union cause won the hearts of Richmond's black men and women. Thomas Johnson, one of the few slaves who could read, often met surreptitiously with fellow slaves in the city to discuss the war and to tell of what he had learned from newspapers. In hushed voices he and his friends celebrated Union battlefield victories and prayed for the day when the Northern hosts would march triumphantly into Richmond. Even when the war news was discouraging, those assembled took comfort in Johnson's readings of biblical prophecy, especially Daniel 11:15: "So the king of the north shall come . . . and the arms of the south shall not withstand."[3]

Hardly had the cannons at Charleston Harbor cooled in the spring of 1861, when Richmond's secessionists began worrying about the enemies among them. "There are persons in this city disloyal to Virginia, and desirous to give 'aid and comfort' to the Federal Government," the *Dispatch* warned on 19 April. "The police and private citizens should keep a sharp look-out for these spies and Tories." In another call to action the very next day, the *Dispatch* urged that subversives, men and women alike, be identified and exposed, for they were "more dangerous than any [foe] that can be found on the battle-field."[4]

The city council moved quickly. On 22 April it passed an ordinance requiring Richmonders who suspected someone of harboring "sentiments that render such person suspicious or unsafe to remain in the City" to notify the mayor. The accused would be brought before the mayor's court and, if judged guilty of "entertain[ing] such opinions," would be "dealt with as a vagrant or person of evil fame" — meaning jail or expulsion. The council took steps, too, to protect essential facilities in the city against sabotage, authorizing guard patrols at the reservoir and gasworks and extending the hours of street lighting around railroad stations, flour mills, wharves, and militia depots and stables. But fearing that the public ferment might encourage mobbing, the council also ordered that the mayor "suppress . . . all committees of vigilance or safety or other collection of men, who without authority arrest or threaten any person who may be suspected."[5]

Meanwhile, Richmond secessionists were forming a volunteer home guard. This was no vigilante gang: it had the city council's blessing and consisted of respectable, law-abiding citizens, among them lawyers, doctors, merchants, and even ministers. Established just days after the outbreak of war and fully organized by mid-May, the home guard enrolled some 400 men, all over age forty-five and armed at their own expense. It held frequent drills and stood ready to help the authorities secure the safety of the city as the younger men went off to war. Now and then the guard marched publicly to assure right-minded citizens that they were safe from internal threats and to cow the otherwise-minded into submission.[6]

Richmonders under suspicion soon began to feel the heat. "I received your letter yesterday," Jacob Bechtel wrote to his brother on 24 April, "and read it with *great caution*. The sentiments therein expressed were so foreign to those at present in vogue here that I deemed it prudent to commit it to the flames immediately . . . lest by dropping out of my pocket, it might put my neck in danger of a hempen collar." Still cleaving at that point to the old flag, Bechtel had kept his mouth shut about politics since Lincoln's war proclamation nine days earlier; any Unionist who dared to speak out now, he said, was "a *marked* man." But he could not be certain that his silence would ensure his safety: "My position here has become very precarious." In a subsequent letter he told his brother, "Don't write me any thing about politics[;] all letters [to or from those under suspicion] are scrutinized, and any strong expressions might involve me in trouble, as a traitor & holding trait[o]rous correspondence."[7]

Bechtel was not alone in believing that the Richmond mail was being monitored, although that may have been a baseless rumor. Tobacco merchant Daniel Von Groning wrote to two of his customers in Germany on 3 June giving them business news but declining to say anything more: "I cannot indulge in any remarks about politics, all our letters being liable to be opened." But whether mail tampering was fact or fancy, some Richmonders were heeding the calls of the press and city council to watch for dangerous

Dissent and Despair

characters. Harriet Baker wrote the governor on 18 May to warn of a Northern woman she had met in April. The woman had been in the city only briefly before returning home, but she had let slip enough information to convince Baker that she was a "Black Republican." Suspecting that she might return to Richmond, Baker gave the governor a detailed description of her, adding that "this beautiful country is surrounded & (I fear) *permeated* in some degree by traitorism."[8]

A disturbing incident that very night of 18–19 May struck many Richmonders as proof that subversives were at work in their city. Sometime before midnight, soldiers who were bivouacked on a hill overlooking the Tredegar Iron Works spotted flames rising from a building that housed the works' pattern shop. They quickly gave the alarm and the fire was extinguished before it spread. Just a few hours later, however, Tredegar watchmen came upon two other fires, these in the very heart of the works; they, too, were put out before they spread—even though the closest hydrant had been sabotaged.[9]

Vigilance redoubled in the aftermath of the Tredegar fires. Fear of subversion consumed the whole Confederacy during this time, but it was especially intense in Richmond, the nation's primary industrial center and newly designated capital. Through May and June, nearly every day saw one or more suspects hauled before the mayor and interrogated about their loyalties. Some were freed, but many were locked up in the city jail—rarely on the basis of any meaningful evidence of treasonable activities but because they could not prove their innocence to the mayor's satisfaction or had simply spoken their minds about sensitive political matters. This egregious violation of civil liberties was accepted without protest by the Richmond public as a whole. The *Enquirer*'s editor voiced the thinking of many: "These are not the times for maudlin sentimentalities [about legal rights], but for the utmost activity in ferreting out all whom we have good reasons to believe inimical to our interest." In late June, with the national government established in Richmond, Confederate officials took over this mission. An army provost marshal was appointed to deal with the city's internal enemies, among other matters, and the municipal jail was superseded by Castle Godwin (and eventually Castles Lightning and Thunder) as the place of confinement for suspected spies and traitors. This transition to Confederate authority did not restore the traditional rules of law: in the succeeding months, men and women continued to be arrested in Richmond without evidence of traitorous acts, although most were soon freed.[10]

Strangers in the city, especially Northerners like the object of Harriet Baker's suspicions, endured particularly close scrutiny. But even if they were long-established in Richmond, those guilty of Northern birth attracted the attention of authorities. New Jersey–born manufacturer D. W. Hughes — a devout Unionist, to be sure, and later an outright subversive, but at this point involved in no treasonous activities — was arrested and held in Castle Godwin for five months. Richmond's German immigrants, long suspected of insufficient enthusiasm for slavery, also became targets of special attention and frequent arrest in the war's early period.[11]

An *Examiner* editorial in mid-July articulated the worries of many Richmonders and suggested a remedy. "There are upwards of fifteen hundred Yankees and Hessians in this city," the editor declared, "some of whom are known to be Abolitionists[;] the balance, we believe, with one exception, were *Union* men as long as it was safe to express that political faith. There is not a doubt that these men would hail with exceeding joy the successful invasion of our capital by the myrmidons of Lincoln." With the city now rendered vulnerable by the departure of so many militiamen and volunteers, it was not unlikely that "these [Northern and German] fellows will take matters into their own hands, maltreat our families, destroy our public works, and perhaps, lay our homes in ashes. . . . Shall we be content to leave them in the same city or county with our unprotected wives and children, surrounded by a dense negro population?" The editor stopped short of an overt call for expulsion, but no reader could have missed the point.[12]

Such concerns were voiced across the Confederacy. The government soon responded. The Alien Enemies Act, passed by Congress on 8 August and supplemented by a presidential proclamation six days later, decreed that all males in the Confederacy age fourteen or older who had been born in a Northern state must swear an oath of Confederate loyalty or leave the country by 23 September; those failing to do so were subject to arrest and imprisonment or forcible expulsion. (Persons born in the nonseceding slave states of the United States, such as Maryland, were exempted.) Immigrants from other nations were not addressed in the law; subsequently, however, those unwilling to become Confederate citizens were required to register with the government and swear an oath to submit to Confederate authority.[13]

Northern-born Richmonders who refused to swear fealty to the Confederacy and had not already abandoned the city now went north (with a few exceptions, most of whom wound up in one of the Castles). The other Yankee natives in the city presumably took the Rebel oath as required — some, such as Jacob Bechtel (by now fully converted to the cause), in good faith; others, such as D. W. Hughes (who stayed on through the war), in bad faith. No amount of oath taking, however, could put Richmonders' fears to rest. The provost marshal, who had at his command not only a force of troops (known as the provost guard) but also a special detective squad, stayed busy investigating suspicious persons, especially strangers, Yankees, and immigrants. As 1861 gave way to 1862, rumors abounded about a planned Unionist uprising in the capital, which gained strength in the late winter as Richmonders got news of serious military reversals in the western theater and contemplated the prospect of a major Union offensive in Virginia in the spring. Congressman T. S. Ashe, among many others, took the rumors seriously; he warned Jefferson Davis on 28 February that "there are designing men in this City plotting treason" and recommended "strong and decided" action to "destroy the scheme in embryo."[14]

Ashe wrote knowing that the president now possessed extraordinary power to deal with traitors, for just a day earlier Congress had authorized him to declare martial law and suspend habeas corpus in any place threatened by enemy armies. Davis acted swiftly: on 1 March he declared these drastic security measures to be in effect in Richmond.[15]

The provost marshal and his minions immediately began rounding up suspected subversives who had so far avoided arrest or been freed by habeas corpus proceedings. By mid-March, thirty of them were locked up in Castle Godwin (formerly McDaniel's Negro Jail, a holding pen with barred cells used by slave dealers). Fifty-nine-year-old John Minor Botts, whose only offense was publically avowing his Unionism, was seized at his home in a predawn raid on 2 March and held in solitary confinement for eight weeks with no visitors allowed; after enduring repeated interrogations and the confiscation of his personal papers, which turned up not a scrap of evidence of treasonous activities, he was released from prison but held under house arrest. Also taken into custody was the Reverend Alden Bosserman of the Mayo Street Universalist Church; he had been under suspicion since the previous July, when he refused to open the church on the Sunday of national thanksgiving designated by President Davis after the victory at Manassas. Bosserman, like some of the others swept up in the March dragnet, was Northern born; also well represented among those arrested were German Americans, including a prominent restaurateur named Valentin Hechler.[16]

The suspension of habeas corpus was rescinded by mid-September 1862 and never reimposed in Richmond. But the army authorities there, including the successive secretaries of war, commanders of the military department embracing the city, and provost marshals (who reported to the department commander), acted until the war's end on the assumption that Richmond remained under martial law—a notion much debated but never specifically overruled by the president, Congress, or any judge. It was always a restrained sort of martial law, however, far from a military dictatorship. The city council, courts, and police force continued to operate as usual. Newspapers were not censored. Moreover, the War Department imposed its own partial check on tyranny by appointing officials known as habeas corpus commissioners, civilian lawyers whose job was to examine all prisoners held in the Castles on suspicion of disloyalty and recommend whether they should remain in custody. A good many people accused on weak evidence were freed by the War Department on the commissioners' advice. But a good many others stayed in prison or were repeatedly rearrested, even if proof of treason was lacking or if their offense was merely criticizing the government or harboring Union sentiments.[17]

In other ways, too, Richmonders felt the hand of martial law. By decree of Brig. Gen. John H. Winder, the department commander for most of the war and the designated executor of the president's 1 March proclamation, all civilians entering or leaving the city had to have a military passport, to get which they had to convince a passport office clerk that they were on legitimate business. Winder also required the railroads to give the provost marshal the names of arriving passengers and the hotels to give the names of arriving guests. He furthermore forced Richmonders to surrender all privately owned weapons. Moreover, he ordered that the city's innumerable saloons be shut down, and he banned the sale, distillation, and importation of liquor (measures aimed at suppressing not subversion but rowdiness). The provost marshal was responsible for enforcing all these commandments; his mufti-clad detectives, who by 1864 numbered twenty-six, and his uniformed provost guard became familiar sights as they patrolled the streets and lurked around the railroad depots and hotel lobbies checking passports and questioning anyone who looked suspicious. Many Richmonders complained about Winder's orders, especially the onerous passport requirement, but they generally put up with them — except for the saloon and liquor decrees, which were so widely disobeyed as to be virtual dead letters almost from the start.[18]

However rigorous the measures to secure the city from internal threat, Richmond never rested easy. Rumors of Unionist treachery continued to circulate and citizens still eyed strangers warily. Three Frenchmen who visited the capital in the late spring of 1862 aroused considerable suspicion, prompting the provost marshal to lock them up for investigation. As they sat in prison, one Richmonder urged the authorities to throw away the key, for he was certain that the three were "hirelings of the Lincoln Government.... The villainy they will perpetrate when the opportunity offers will be our down fall. For God['s] sake do not allow them to go forth. . . . Be warned—take no strangers in your midst—plots of the darkest dye is being enacted." Another Richmonder wrote anonymously and breathlessly to the secretary of war in June 1863 to warn of a storekeeper in the city named Hallock, who supposedly had declared that "he would not give a fig for Jeff. Davis and his whole cabinet [and] that the Government was just got up for robbery, and that he has one negro and he would be willing to lose her for the Yankees to get possession of the City . . . [and] believes they certainly will get here and he has a union flag he means to run up on their arrival." A man who checked into the Spotswood Hotel that year was summoned to General Winder's office for questioning simply because someone had reported seeing a map of the James River and Kanawha Canal in his room; fortunately for him, he was able to prove that he was a stockholder in the company.[19]

No one in the city, of whatever rank or patriotic credentials, was entirely safe from suspicion. "I have again and again," wrote an anonymous informant to the War Department, "heard both citizens and soldiers say there was a traitor somewhere in Richmond holding an important office . . . else how is there so much important intelligence communicated to the enemy[?]" When some of the cannons and shells produced by the Ordnance Bureau were found to be defective, War Department clerk Jones hinted darkly in his diary that the explanation was not shoddy workmanship but disloyalty, for the bureau chief was a native Pennsylvanian. Even General Winder was regarded doubtfully by some, for he hailed from Maryland, a Southern state but Unionist dominated.[20]

All these fears were exaggerated, although certainly not baseless. There were indeed seditious Southern Unionists and Northern spies in the city. But the harm they did to the Confederacy was negligible compared to that done by certain other people in the capital, few if any of whom regarded themselves as friends of the U.S. government. These were the men who illegally evaded conscription or deserted from the army.

There were thousands over the course of the war. "A great many *skulkers* from the army are seen daily in the streets," John Jones noted in July 1862, "and it is said there are 3000 men here subject to conscript duty, who have not been enrolled." Some were Richmond residents; others gravitated to the teeming city hoping to disappear there. Among the deserters were detailed men who left their jobs and did not report back to their units. Other deserters, those who slipped away from their units in the field, were especially numerous when the Army of Northern Virginia was operating near the capital.[21]

The task of apprehending all these fugitives from the ranks fell mainly to the provost marshal, although the district enrolling officer also went after draft dodgers. From the advent of conscription in April 1862 to the end of the war, the provost guardsmen and detectives devoted far more effort to this work than to rooting out Unionist traitors and Yankee infiltrators. With the power of martial law behind them, they made life hard for those trying to avoid military duty, for they were authorized to stop and question any man in civilian clothes they came across who might conceivably be of military age and any man in uniform whose reason for being in the city was not obvious; they were also authorized to haul in for further questioning or just take straight to Camp Lee anyone who failed to answer satisfactorily. Their diligence — indeed, ruthlessness — was notorious. Innocent men, even those with army discharge papers, medical examiners' certificates of disability, exemption papers, furlough orders, military or hospital passes, or certificates of foreign nationality, were frequently harassed and sometimes incarcerated. On one occasion in 1864, provost guards accosted two gentlemen in mufti, interrogated them, and, finding that both were in their forties and neither had papers to establish innocence, prepared to take them into custody as draft evaders; the two escaped that ordeal only because they eventually managed to prove that they were the Confederacy's postmaster general and attorney general.[22]

The risk of being nabbed on the street drove a lot of draft dodgers and deserters underground. Some were able to avoid discovery; others were apprehended, thanks in some cases to sharp detective work or tips from the public and to the fact that neither the provost marshal nor the enrolling officer seems to have been obligated to obtain search warrants. A number of fugitives were taken by surprise when their hideouts were raided. One was a deserter named Bowlar who, in April 1864, holed up in a house in a disreputable neighborhood known as Screamersville. Acting on a tip, a squad of provost guardsmen descended on the place (very likely a brothel) and searched every room but failed to find their quarry. Still suspicious, they returned to a room where two women lay in a bed purporting to be sick. A closer look revealed that the bed frame held not one but two mattresses, one atop the other. Between these, the guardsmen found Bowlar — who by then was probably glad to be caught, for he was nearly suffocated.[23]

Some of those in the city who were obliged to serve but loath to do so invested their hope not in eluding the authorities but in deceiving them. Lying about one's age was a common ploy. When Philip Weber, a willowware manufacturer and longtime Richmond resident, was taken as a conscript in June 1864, he insisted that he had been born in 1807 and was therefore past the maximum draft age of fifty. The date was recorded, he said, in his family Bible (which, alas, he could not offer as evidence for it was not in his possession). He even swore to that date of birth in a notarized document and got two old friends to confirm it before the same notary. These avowals apparently convinced the Conscription Bureau, but they were almost certainly false: four years earlier, in June 1860, Weber had declared to the federal census taker that he was forty-six.[24]

A thirty-five-year-old man named Timmerman, German born but a naturalized American citizen who had run a saloon before the war, took advantage of the conscription law's exemption of teachers. In early March 1864 he started a school in a back room of the Lutheran church on Fifth Street. But according to a well-informed Richmonder who wrote to the district enrolling officer later that month, it was a sham, perpetrated with the connivance of the church's pastor, whose loyalty was suspect. The law stipulated that anyone claiming this exemption must have been teaching for at least two years. Timmerman had no such credentials; his teaching career had begun the day he started the school. Furthermore, he dismissed the students each day after just an hour or two of instruction. He was, said the informant, nothing but a "skulker from our flag and from the service."[25]

Some of the men in Richmond trying to avoid military service were truly desperate, none more so than one who, on a Sunday afternoon in April 1864, made his way to the Richmond and York River Railroad track near the gasworks. Whether he was a recent conscript or a convalescent soldier who had walked away from a hospital (accounts differed), his purpose became clear when he lay down next to the track and placed his left forearm over the nearer rail as a train approached from the east. The engineer and passengers saw him but too late; the locomotive's front wheel severed his hand. He then stood up and ran off, gripping the bleeding stump with his other hand. What became of him after that was not recorded, but he had certainly gotten himself out of the army.[26]

Desperate, too, were the men who made up their minds to desert from the Local Defense Forces (LDF) and flee to the Union lines. Not only would they face imprisonment or worse if caught in the act, but, even if successful, they would be abandoning their jobs and homes and families in Richmond. Nevertheless, some made the attempt.

They were driven, many of them, by anger over the repeated and extended calls to duty that they had to endure from the spring of 1864 on. Army authorities were well aware of this anger and its consequences, for they were warned about it often. An Ordnance Bureau inspector told his chief in October 1864 that many LDF members employed in munitions manufacture had gone over to the enemy and many more planned "to avail themselves of the first good opportunity," for they were "much dissatisfied with their position here, being as it is half mechanical & half military." In early 1865 an anonymous "Friend to the South" wrote President Davis a letter (forwarded to the secretary of war) deploring the "suicidal policy of forcing mechanics while in Government employment to the front." The LDF troops, he said, were sick and tired of being told "that each week [on active duty] would be the last." Who could blame them for deserting? "These men will not serve faithfully in the double capacity of soldier and mechanic."[27]

Hard-pressed in those months, the army would not let the LDF stand down. Instead, it tightened security in those parts of the fortifications manned by the LDF. Cavalry scouts patrolled those sectors regularly. Orders went out decreeing that any person spotted going even three paces beyond the picket lines was to be shot without warning. Nevertheless, LDF men continued to run off to the enemy, most of them at night and while themselves on picket duty. The commander of the LDF reported in late October that, on average, two or three were deserting daily. War Department clerk Jones confirmed that figure in early November, noting that, in the last two months, the LDF had lost through desertion no fewer than 100 men and perhaps as many as 200.[28]

Not all the LDF soldiers who fled to the enemy did so while on duty in the fortifications; nor did all the Confederate deserters and draft dodgers in Richmond remain there hoping to avoid detection. Some got out of the city and into Yankee-held territory with the help of certain men willing to guide them — willing, that is, for a price commensurate with the considerable risk involved. By 1864 several human-smuggling operations were active in the city, underground railroads offering a way out of the Confederacy for those who could pay.[29]

Most of the smugglers traveled by night, leading the fugitives on foot or hauling them as quietly as possible by wagon, evading the Confederate pickets and scouts beyond the city who would demand to see papers and inspect cargo. But other smugglers operated openly by day, bluffing their way past the Rebel lines. One of the more successful — until the provost marshal's office got suspicious and laid a trap for him — was a Richmond embalmer named William Maclure. Part of his very active wartime business involved the bodies of Union troops who had died in or near Richmond and whose families had arranged (through the U.S. Army, under flag of truce) for their retrieval. Maclure would disinter the corpses, place them in coffins, and haul them by wagon to the enemy lines — with the permission of Confederate authorities, who gave him a passport. Exactly how many of the coffins he transported contained not corpses but rather the live bodies of men who had paid to be sneaked out of the city was never determined, but on his last attempt the detective who surprised him on the road discovered two. Maclure and his two customers ended up in Castle Thunder, after the detective reportedly declined the embalmer's offer of $1,000 to let them pass.[30]

During the last two years of the war a lot of people in Richmond besides soldiers and conscripts also tried to get out of the city and into the Union lines. Their motives varied. Many were destitute, unable to work or so poorly paid that the escalating cost of food and shelter and everything else was out of reach. Others were draft-exempt men fearful that the government would revoke their exemptions. Still others were married women seeking to join husbands who had already gone to Federal territory.[31]

For some, abandoning the Confederacy was relatively easy and quite legal. Unnaturalized foreign-born men and women were not, as a rule, held in Rebeldom against their will. Their applications for passports to the enemy lines were granted routinely, in some cases over the protests of employers who wanted to keep them. A boss at the C.S. Armory fumed in December 1863 about his immigrant workers' ready access to Yankeeland, "there being no obstacle of importance in the way"; he had lost several recently, including two grinders, a machinist, and a highly valued draftsman named Schumann who had gone to live with relatives in the North. British subject John Halloran, a carbine factory hand unable to support himself and his wife, child, and mother-in-law on six dollars a day, got a passport for the whole family in 1864; when his supervisor appealed to higher-ups, insisting that the man was irreplaceable, he was told flatly that Halloran was free to go where he wanted.[32]

Also readily granted passports to go north were Richmond's prostitutes, many of whom had moved to the city from New York, Philadelphia, or Baltimore after the war began. In July 1864 a sizable number of them, by then soured on life in the Confederate capital, applied for permission to leave. A passport office clerk recorded the name and age of each and also her occupation: "fancy woman," "woman of the town," or, in the case of twenty-five-year-old Mollie Thompson, "a broken down public woman." The *Examiner* hailed this "exodus of the *cyprians*" and claimed that "some of the former notorious brothels are [now] nearly depopulated."[33]

Passports always specified the bearer's destination. Many people leaving Richmond with permission to go north were passed to the Potomac River. They could usually travel as far as Fredericksburg by rail and there hire a wagon and driver to take them the rest of the way; when the railroad was cut, wagons and drivers could be procured in Richmond (the prostitutes reportedly paid $600 apiece to be carted from there to the Potomac). Many others exiting Richmond and the Confederacy were passed to a designated landing on the lower James River, where a United States boat bearing a flag of truce put in regularly to take passengers and mail to Fort Monroe (on the tip of the Peninsula) and nearby Norfolk and Suffolk, all held by the Federal army; from there, seagoing vessels sailed to Northern ports. People permitted to leave Richmond to go to Europe (there were quite a few, especially among the foreign born) could avoid dealing with the Yankees by getting a passport to travel by rail to Wilmington, North Carolina, and there taking passage on a blockade-running steamship.[34]

The Richmond military authorities' policy on granting passports out of the Confederacy was ad hoc and inconsistent. People who might have significant knowledge of the city's defenses or other military matters and who could not be trusted to hold their tongues once they were in Union territory were in some cases denied passports, even if legally entitled to leave by reason of nationality; so, too, were healthy men of military age and men with special skills, for fear the North would put them to use. Married women with absent husbands came under particular scrutiny. Mrs. E. F. Killian, struggling to support herself and her two-year-old on paltry earnings from sewing, applied for a passport, explaining that she wanted to join her husband in the North; he was a Rebel soldier who had been captured at the Battle of the Wilderness and interned in a Yankee prison camp—until he took the U.S. oath of allegiance and was released. Better for her had she been less forthcoming: she was promptly informed that no passport would be given, for granting her one would encourage other Confederate prisoners of war with wives at home to do as her husband had done. Even women whose husbands were still serving loyally in the ranks were denied permission to go north, lest the men be inspired to go over to the enemy. One was Bridget Macauley, another Richmonder struggling to survive, who in August 1864 sought a passport for herself and her five children to Washington, D.C., where she had relatives. Macauley, Killian, and other women in like circumstances were essentially held hostage in Richmond.[35]

Some Richmonders with no legal way out of the Confederacy turned to other means. The human-smuggling operations that spirited away army deserters and conscripts also transported civilians who could pay the fare. Others got away using forged or altered passports (available on the black market for prices ranging from hundreds to thousands of dollars) or legitimate passports that they got by lying convincingly about their nationality. Still others deceived the authorities by obtaining a passport for travel within the Confederacy and then making their way to the Union lines at some point less heavily guarded than Richmond. John Delano, a fifty-seven-year-old carpenter who, in November 1863, was denied permission to go north, got a passport to Petersburg in January with the secret intention of proceeding from there on foot, presumably to Suffolk or Norfolk. He was caught twenty-five miles beyond Petersburg, however, far short of his goal; his journey ended not in the United States but in Castle Thunder. W. L. Pettit, a boilermaker at the Richmond Navy Yard, had better luck. Dispatched on official business to North Carolina in February 1865, he made his way instead to Suffolk and there entered the Union lines. Pettit was not only a master artisan but a captain in the Fourth Battalion of the LDF.[36]

Many men who got out of Richmond illegally and headed for the enemy lines left behind wives and children. Most did so not intending to abandon them permanently but hoping that the authorities would eventually allow the women and children to join them. That hope was rarely gratified. In the latter part of March 1865, a Richmond councilman reported, as related by the *Examiner*, "that there were now in the City between five and six thousand women and children whose husbands, fathers, and natural protectors had gone off to the Yankees and left them here a burden upon the City." The newspaper's editor was certain that these unfortunates "would hail with joy an opportunity to follow [their husbands and fathers] North," and he applauded the council's decision to petition the secretary of war to let them go. Nothing was done about the matter, however, in the few days that Richmond remained the Confederate capital.[37]

The decision to flee Rebeldom was for many not just personal but political, a confession of patriotic exhaustion and loss of faith in the Confederacy's ability to nurture its citizens or even to survive as a nation. In early 1864 an anonymous Richmonder wrote a congressman to tell him about "what is now going on secretly in this city." There was, he said, a dangerous "party of employees in the various [government] departments." They were laboring men unable to support themselves and their families on their current wages. Their pleas for a raise or access to government foodstuffs having been rebuffed, they were now conspiring to run off to the enemy, evading Confederate pickets and scouts if they could but taking them prisoner or even killing them if they had to. "They say furthermore that when their labor won't [provide] them a living they do not want to live under such a government."[38]

The hardships of life in Richmond were better endured when news from the military fronts was good, but by the fall of 1864 Confederate patriots had little to celebrate. Lee's army still held out under siege at Petersburg, and Richmond's garrison troops, the LDF, and militia still managed to keep the enemy at bay, but elsewhere the military situation was deteriorating alarmingly. Moreover, Abraham Lincoln's reelection ended all hope of a negotiated peace that would leave the Confederacy standing with slavery intact. As the leaves of the capital's trees withered that autumn, so, too, did Rebel morale. "There is more despondency in Richmond now than I have before observed," said post office clerk and LDF soldier Lycurgus Caldwell. War Department clerk Jones also sensed it: "There is deep vexation in the city — a general apprehension that our affairs are rapidly approaching a crisis such as has not been experienced before."[39]

Yet hope abided among many. When Sunday, 1 January, proved to be a dazzlingly bright and cloudless day that put an end to a long period of rain and snow, War Department bureau chief Robert Kean prayed "that it may be an omen and that the affairs of this unhappy nation may from this day begin to improve." Under no illusions about military affairs, however, Kean acknowledged in his diary that "there is . . . little reason to found the hope upon, except the goodness and mercy of the All Wise." Government and civic leaders tried to stiffen Richmonders' resolve; in speeches, sermons, and editorials through the frigid winter of 1865 they sought to rally sagging spirits and put fears to rest, even as reports from the battlefronts told of one disaster after another. God was much invoked, but the repeated assurances that He was on the Confederacy's side were less and less convincing. So were the repeated assurances that Lee's army was invincible. A sense of approaching doom gripped more and more citizens, periodically inflamed to near panic by rumors that the Confederate government and army were preparing to abandon the city.[40]

"I am so anxious," clerk Henri Garidel admitted in his diary in mid-February. "The news gets worse every minute. I have little faith in our winning." Ordnance Bureau chief Josiah Gorgas, although not himself giving in to despondency or alarm, described on 2 March the Richmond public's state of mind: "People are almost in a state of desperation, and but too ready to give up the cause. . . . There is [a] sentiment of hopelessness abroad, a feeling that all our sacrifices tend to nothing." Four days later he wrote that "the crisis of our fate is rapidly approaching, and men's minds are harrassed [sic] with doubts, fears & perplexity. The weak are for submission and those who have more fortitude are affected by the fears of the timid. . . . Wherever three or four are gathered together there are ominious [sic] whispers & dubious shakings of the head. Even those whose faith remains unshaken find it difficult to give a reason for their faith."[41]

The abrupt abandonment of Richmond to the enemy on 2 April and the surrender of Lee's army a week later extinguished the last hopes of the city's Confederate patriots. Well before then, however, many had begun to ask not *whether* the cause was lost but *why*. There was much pointing of fingers: various political and military leaders were denounced for bungling the tasks of creating, sustaining, and defending the nation. But other Richmonders were certain the explanation lay elsewhere. The dream had failed, they insisted, because Confederates were unfaithful to their God. Defeat was the wages of sin.

DISORDER, CRIME, AND SIN

Antebellum Richmond was no stranger to rowdiness and lawlessness, but these problems mushroomed in the hothouse environment of war. The population explosion and the acute scarcity of necessities, along with other factors, enormously complicated the civil authorities' task of making the city safe to live in. And to the afflictions of burgeoning disorder and crime was added, at least in many Richmonders' judgment, the disintegration of civic and private virtue.

The consequences of all this were grave, and not just for the victims of the criminals and hooligans. The overtaxed city police force came to rely increasingly on the military to secure public safety; this in turn burdened the military, which had many other problems on its hands and thus was stretched thinner and thinner. And, too, like the crises of housing, food, and labor, the crises of disorder, crime, and sin fueled the feeling among many Richmonders that the city was under siege by more than just the Yankee army, and they raised agonizing questions about the competency and endurance of Richmonders' government and the righteousness of their cause.

Off-duty soldiers with bellyfuls of whiskey perpetrated most of the rowdiness. Military orders prohibiting enlisted men from drinking, and liquor purveyors from serving them, were routinely flouted. Soldiers could readily purchase whiskey by the drink in groggeries or by the canteen from hucksters. In June 1861 some Florida volunteers, newly arrived in the city and craving refreshment, met up with a Richmond slave named Walker willing to serve as a guide; only after two of the Floridians were accosted by the police for excessive noisemaking did the authorities discover, as the *Dispatch* reported, that Walker "had been going around with parcels of drunken men in uniform, piloting them to different localities where they could indulge in spreeing." Alcohol-fueled brawls were common. Recounting one in September 1861 that resulted in the arrest of ten men, the *Dispatch* declared itself "sick of the work of recording the rows of the soldiers." Mayor Mayo seconded that sentiment two months later, announcing that he was fed up with the daily parade of soldiers brought before him for drunkenness and fighting.[1]

Off-duty soldiers often carried weapons, orders notwithstanding. A visitor in early 1862 was appalled at "the scene presented in Richmond daily. The city is crowded with re-enlisted soldiers on furlough. A hundred whiskey shops are in operation on Main-street and the side alleys. Drunken men reel in and reel out, tumble into the gutters, sprawl over the sidewalks, [and] brandish knives and pistols." A few months later the *Dispatch*'s editor saw "five drunken [cavalrymen] riding about the streets, cutting and slashing with their sabres, and raising a row at nearly every corner." Philip Brown, a desk clerk at the American Hotel, had to deal with so many armed and uniformed drunks carousing in the hotel bar, staggering through the lobby, and spoiling for a fight that he kept not only a billy club close at hand but also a loaded derringer and revolver.[2]

Drunken soldiers plagued Richmond from the earliest weeks of war. It took longer for the surge of civilian lawbreaking to inundate the city, but by 1863 Richmond was awash in petty and felonious crime. No single class of people was responsible; the perpetrators included women and children as well as men, blacks as well as whites, and gentlefolk as well as roughnecks.

For pickpockets the crowded, bustling city was a godsend, a veritable orchard of wallets ripe for plucking. These skilled criminals infested wartime Richmond, especially the railroad depots, hotel lobbies, and auction houses. Shoplifters, too, found good pickings. The *Examiner* remarked in late 1864 that "the mania for shoplifting may be said to amount to an epidemick [*sic*] in this city." Dry goods stores, millineries, shoe stores, and groceries were the favorite targets of the shoplifters — most of whom were women, a lot of them amateurs driven to desperation by the spiraling prices of necessities. "We might enumerate cases," the *Examiner*'s editor continued, "where females, heretofore considered ladies and highly respectable, have been detected in shoplifting." Some of the bigger retail houses, recognizing that their busy, distracted clerks and managers could not contain the problem, hired undercover detectives "to roam round the salerooms . . . and keep watch and ward over suspicious customers and the store stock."[3]

Other frequent targets of theft were backyard vegetable gardens, smokehouses, chicken coops, and storage sheds. These were plundered almost always while the city slept. War Department clerk John Jones arose one freezing January morning in 1865 to find his woodshed broken open; he was lucky, in a way, for the thief had taken only two sticks of firewood—worth ten dollars at current prices—leaving him seven. Somewhat less common, but still rampant by antebellum standards, was the burglary of houses and stores. This, too, was generally a nighttime undertaking, but some bold perpetrators worked in broad daylight. In the fall of 1863 there was a rash of thefts committed by poor white women who were going door to door on residential streets pleading for a handout or some other favor; if a servant answered the bell, the caller would ask to see the lady of the house, and when the servant went off to fetch her, the caller would slip inside, grab everything of value she could carry, and quickly depart. By that stage of the war, burglaries were so common that some Richmonders were loath to leave their home unattended, even for a short time. On Christmas Day 1863, John Jones's wife and children went off to church without him, he having decided to remain behind because "it would not be safe to leave the house unoccupied."[4]

Much thievery, although by no means most, was the work of slaves. Two hired by Winder Hospital, William and Lewis by name, were eventually caught after making off, a little at a time, with bed linens and clothing from the hospital's stores; when their cache was discovered it amounted to, as the *Examiner* reported, "at least a four-horse wagon load." An enslaved man named Christopher broke into a house in early 1864 and temporarily got away with $2,500 worth of jewelry and clothing. Ill-gotten goods such as these were generally fenced (unless, like William, Lewis, and Christopher, the thieves were caught before they could sell them); certain shopkeepers in the city, including a white couple named John and Sarah Gormley, who had a store on north Second Street, quietly made themselves available to receive stolen property.[5]

The thieves and rowdies of wartime Richmond were not all adults. Juvenile delinquency had disturbed the city's peace in the antebellum years—particularly rock-throwing battles between informal, neighborhood-based gangs such as the "Butcher Cats" of Butchertown and the "Hill Cats" of Shockoe Hill—but once the war began the problem swelled. The absence of many fathers gone to the army was undoubtedly a factor, as was the dearth of schools available to the multiplying number of children in the city.[6]

The youth delinquency of the war years was more often just annoying than seriously harmful. The rock battles continued: "Union Hill fights Church Hill, and Church Hill fights Rocketts," the *Dispatch* reported in February 1862, having noted four months earlier that the combatants included "not only the rag-tag-and-bob-tail boys, but lads who wear good clothes and stand-up collars." Juvenile vandalism and pranks also provoked grumbling: "The statue of Henry Clay has been mutilated," the *Examiner* huffed in 1863, "by the vicious boys who have the free range of the Capitol Square." The next year that paper condemned "the outrageous conduct of the boys who infest the neighbourhood of Franklin street, between Fourth and Fifth. . . . They steal the door mats from the residence fronts, [and] wrench off the door knobs and bell-pulls." Not all the young offenders were white. Oscar, Paul, and Charles, "three negro imps," as the *Examiner* labeled them, were brought to the mayor's court in June 1864, "charged with heaving stones in the public streets to the annoyance of citizens, and to the danger of human optics and window glass"; their antics cost their owners five dollars apiece.[7]

But more serious juvenile offenses cropped up increasingly. The regular Sunday evening rock fight between the "uptown boys" and the "Rocketts boys" took a dangerous turn in November 1861, when several of the participants pulled out pistols and fired; fortunately, no one was hurt. Some of the pickpocketing and a lot of the shoplifting that plagued the city were the work of children, as was some of the burglary. In May 1864 two white boys, John Minter and George Green, were arrested for breaking into a home and making off with $2,000 in cash.[8]

The scariest aspect of the wartime crime wave was the muggings or, as they were known, "garrotings." These violent robberies were carried out almost always at night on unlit streets, of which there were more and more as the gasworks deteriorated. Working often in teams of three, the garroters would approach their victim—usually a lone, prosperous-looking male—stealthily from behind; one would seize and hold him while the others went through his pockets. If the victim cried out or resisted he would be choked or beaten, sometimes fatally. While some of the "night owls," as they were nicknamed, simply prowled the streets seeking random prey, others thoroughly planned their assaults, spying on potential victims to learn their routines and keeping tabs on the habitual movements of the police.[9]

By late 1862, garrotings were frequent enough to unnerve many Richmonders and discourage nocturnal strolls. Soldiers and civilians alike confessed their anxiety. James Graham, an infantry officer serving with the capital's garrison force, declared in June 1863 that "this city of Richmond is one of the worst places I ever saw. Hardly a night passes but some one is knocked down and robbed of all he has. I would rather be in the army [at the front] and marching almost every day than to be camped any where near this place." Congressman Warren Akin wrote his wife on 27 December 1864, a month after he arrived in the city, noting that he had "not been out at night, but once (except to church) since I have been here, and then I had two members of Congress to come home with me. I am afraid to walk the streets at night. . . . A man, not long [ago], was knocked down in the street, killed and robbed." Two days later, the House of Representatives resolved to hold no more night sessions for the time being. Akin explained why: "The weather is bad, the streets not lighted, some members not well, and [there is] danger of assassination in the streets."[10]

As unruliness, crime, and violence burgeoned, Richmonders sought explanations and solutions. To some, the root causes seemed obvious: the enormous influx of riffraff, in and out of uniform, and the omnipresence of liquor. The *Dispatch* warned in January 1862 that the once-orderly city was getting "a reputation for rowdyism" and blamed the proliferation of groggeries, which was attracting "an entirely new population" of unsavory characters. Later that year an English visitor heard similar complaints: "The Richmond people asserted that all this disorder was owing to the fact that Baltimore had discharged her tainted population, male and female, upon them; and that the 'plug-uglies,' 'dead-rabbits,' 'shoulder-hitters,' gamblers and sharpers, and a hundred other classes of villains . . . had emigrated to Richmond." Others blamed New Orleans, which allegedly spawned a host of louche sorts who had gravitated to the Confederate capital. Among them was a unit of colorfully uniformed infantrymen known as Zouaves. "It was composed of the most lawless and desperate material which that city could send forth," Richmonder Sallie Brock Putnam avowed in her memoir. "It is said that its Colonel, with the approval of the Mayor of New Orleans, established recruiting booths in the different jails there, and each criminal was given his option either to serve out his time or join the battalion. . . . From the time of their appearance in Richmond robberies became frequent. Wherever a Zouave was seen something was sure to be miss[ing]. . . . Always finding means to effect their escape from their barracks at night, they roamed about the city like a pack of untamed wildcats."[11]

The Zouaves were ordered to the front in early 1862, to the great relief of Richmonders. But the city's travails continued, as did the finger-pointing.

In February 1864 a hustings court grand jury was concerned enough to take upon itself the task of identifying, in a formal report, the causes of "the great increase of crime" in the capital. "The most fruitful source," the jurymen concluded, "is the large number of licensed and unlicensed drinking houses and low groggeries with which our city is infested." A few days later Governor William Smith forwarded to the general assembly a copy of that report with an endorsement in which he blamed the vast majority of crime in Richmond on the "wretched habit of intoxication" fostered by the innumerable "tippling houses."[12]

Military and civil authorities both grappled with the problem of public drunkenness but with little success. The army's initial response was to try to keep soldiers away from liquor by confining them to camps or barracks and strictly limiting the number allowed out on passes at any one time. But it was not hard to slip past the sentries at night ("run the blockade," in soldier lingo) or to forge passes; many men did so and made their way directly to a bar. So the army also put the provost guard to work on the city streets checking uniformed men for passes. In the latter part of the war, two lieutenants and nine enlisted men of the provost guard were assigned exclusively to this duty. But in a city as big and crowded as wartime Richmond, it was hardly difficult to dodge a patrol of that size. Off-duty soldiers, with or without passes, continued to sneak into groggeries or buy whiskey from obliging hucksters.[13]

Finding it impossible to keep soldiers from frequenting saloons, the army eventually took aim at the saloons themselves. The municipal authorities, exasperated with drunken civilians as well as drunken soldiers, did so too. The city council passed ordinances in 1861 requiring tippling houses to be closed all day on Sunday and after 10:00 P.M. all other days—the Sabbath and late nights being the times liquor-fueled revelry most often got out of hand. But these ordinances were hard to enforce and often flouted, and before long the council began considering a more drastic step. On 1 March 1862, it directed a committee to prepare for council review "an ordinance for the purpose of [permanently] closing the drinking houses in the City."[14]

The committee was saved the trouble of drawing up that ordinance by the Confederate government, which that very day put Richmond under martial law. This decree not only suspended habeas corpus in order to crack down on Unionist subversion but also banned the sale, distribution, and distillation of alcohol in order to suppress drunken rowdiness. In the following weeks the provost marshal, supported by the municipal authorities, waged war on the capital's liquor sellers. Some of those not complying voluntarily were raided. One foray took place on the night of 19 March, when 120 provost guardsmen, reinforced by the city police, swooped down on a one-half-square-block area along Cary Street where a number of dives were dispensing liquor and the drinkers were particularly noisy. Cordoning off the whole area, the minions of the law then marched into each establishment, confiscating whiskey and arresting vendors and customers alike — eighty-nine of them altogether.[15]

Liquor selling was not wholly extinguished by these efforts, but it was curtailed and driven underground, and the city grew noticeably quieter. This reign of peace and sobriety proved, however, to be but a brief interlude. The heavy, sustained pressure required to keep the problem in check in a large city of thirsty soldiers and civilians was simply beyond the manpower resources of the provost guard and police, who had much else to do. The *Enquirer* remarked as early as 24 May that enforcement was getting laxer and groggeries were multiplying and reappearing above ground.[16]

The city authorities, although never explicitly acknowledging so, apparently concluded that eradicating liquor was impossible and the attempt thus pointless. It made more sense to return to the old system of licensing its sale (a source of considerable municipal revenue) and tolerating a certain level of drunken disorder while endeavoring to rein in the worst offenders. With the restoration of habeas corpus in the latter part of 1862, which the city authorities interpreted as the lifting of martial law (the War Department disagreed), they felt free to institute their own policy. By early 1863 the city was granting tippling licenses on a limited basis and by mid-1863 quite freely: "Bar-rooms are springing up in almost every neighborhood in the city," the *Dispatch* reported in July. The military authorities eventually ended their war on groggeries, too, although they continued to try to keep soldiers out of them.[17]

In late February 1864 Governor Smith told the general assembly that Richmond now had 161 licensed tippling houses (and, by some estimates, more than 300 unlicensed ones). Appalled by the resulting surge of public drunkenness, he for one was ready to give prohibition another try. The city authorities being unwilling, he urged the state legislators to act. They did so within a few weeks, prohibiting any further municipal licensing of groggeries. All current licenses in Richmond expired on 30 April, and so on that day saloons again became illegal. But the law's only effect was to drive the liquor vendors once more underground and deprive the city of revenue. At year's end, Congressman Akin gave his wife a report on sobriety in the national capital: "You can form no idea of the drunkenness here. One would think now that whiskey is five dollars a drink, that not much would be drunk, but the drinkers will have it; and when they pay so much for a drink, I am told they take a large one."[18]

Running in all the disorderly drunks would, by itself, have kept the municipal police busy during the war; having to deal also with the pickpockets, shoplifters, burglars, garroters, and other criminals at large in the city taxed the force far beyond its abilities. Comprising two units, the day police and the night watch, the force was headquartered in two station houses, one at each city market. From the beginning of the war to the end, it was woefully undermanned. In April 1861, the day police numbered eight and the night watch forty-four. As Richmond's population swelled, the force failed to keep pace. Not until December 1861 did the city council authorize additional hiring, bringing the day police up to eleven men but leaving the night watch unchanged. In December 1863 two more day policemen were authorized and hired, but the night watch's strength remained at forty-four. There was no further enlargement of the force during the war; in fact, its effective strength, sapped by the army's demand for conscripts, dwindled by early 1864 to eleven day policemen and thirty-six night watchmen.[19]

These few dozen men did their best to stem the tide of crime that engulfed the city. In 1860 the day police and night watch together had averaged 171 arrests per month; from April 1861 through January 1864 the monthly average was 338. But the tide was overwhelming, forcing the city authorities to rely more and more on the military to preserve public order. By 1862 the provost guard was devoting a considerable portion of its efforts to basic policing. It even teamed up formally with the night watch, assigning a musket-bearing guardsman to accompany each watchman on his rounds. It also assisted the day police, routinely turning over to them the civilian drunks and malefactors it apprehended.[20]

The Richmond courts were overburdened, too, for every civil arrest required judiciary attention. Mayor Mayo played a key role in this matter, and he gave long hours to it in addition to his other official duties. All persons arrested were taken to one station house or the other and held there in a cell (dubbed a "cage"). Early each morning, six days a week, Mayo visited the station houses and decided which prisoners would be brought before him later at the mayor's court. The others were discharged or, in the case of slaves he deemed guilty of very minor offenses, were dispatched immediately to the public whipping post at the First Market House to receive a designated number of lashes and then be sent home. The mayor then went on to city hall, on Broad Street near Capitol Square, where his court convened each day, Sunday excepted, at 9:00 A.M. The arrestees not released earlier awaited him there, having been removed from the cages and marched to the courtroom with a police escort, a daily ritual that never failed to attract spectators along the way.[21]

The mayor (or, in his absence, the city recorder or a councilman) then heard the cases one by one. If the offense was serious and he found evidence of guilt sufficient to prosecute, he ordered the accused to appear before the hustings court at its next term; in the meantime, unless bail was met, the accused was confined in the city jail, on Marshall Street three blocks east of city hall. For lesser offenses, most commonly public drunkenness, disorderly conduct, or petty theft, the mayor dispensed justice on the spot, often accompanying it with a stern lecture aimed at the perpetrator or a wry commentary on the state of affairs in the city. The usual sentence was a fine or peace bond (levied on the parent or master in the case of children and slaves). Those unable to pay—including soldiers, whom the mayor did not hesitate to punish just like civilians although he usually turned them over to the provost marshal instead—were given a jail term of up to twelve months.[22]

Not surprisingly, the jail was crammed. Designed to hold 100 prisoners, by the latter part of 1862 it held 200 (among them juveniles and women, for whom there was no separate facility). Putting able-bodied male inmates to work on the municipal chain gang, to repair streets and remove rubbish, relieved the crowding to some extent but only during the daytime. The city council addressed the matter in the fall of 1862, ordering a committee to investigate conditions in the jail; the committee subsequently advised, "in view of the present large and unprecedented number of prisoners," that six additional cells be constructed. The council ordered this done, but the jail remained overcrowded. A riot erupted there one night in February 1863, during which prisoners destroyed much property and threatened the jailor's life. Reporting the incident, the *Dispatch* remarked that "the jail is now, and has been a long time, filled to overflowing with an assortment of the grandest scamps in the Confederacy."[23]

The hustings court, which dealt with the serious criminal cases, faced an ever more crowded docket while, like the police force, being drained of personnel by the army. In 1863 the court's judge, William H. Lyons, implored the secretary of war to exempt one of his deputies liable to conscription, explaining that the court's business had swelled to fifty or sixty felony cases per term; this required summoning between 500 and 1,000 jurors, not to mention numerous witnesses. Add to that, Lyons continued, the task of escorting the accused criminals from the jail to the courtroom and back, and then to the penitentiary if convicted, and it must be obvious that he could not spare a single deputy. The secretary was unmoved.[24]

As they confronted the surge of rowdiness, property crimes, and violence, Richmonders also endured a plague of corruption and immorality. That, at least, is how many perceived it, although they may have exaggerated the problem in this time of profound anxiety. Whatever the case, as the war continued many people worried that civic and private virtue were in decay and sin in the ascendancy. Dismayed by the failure of their calls for moral reformation, the Confederate patriots among them trembled at the thought that God might lose patience with the Rebel nation, for they believed that it could not survive without His sanction and that He was watching it closely for signs of infidelity to His commandments. Never abandoning their faith in His righteousness, some lost faith in the Confederate cause.

The national government's pervasive presence in the city created countless opportunities for official malfeasance, and many functionaries were tempted. Enough were caught in the act to prove that the myriad rumors of corruption that circulated around the city all through the war had some basis. The government received many tips, often in anonymous letters, alleging official misconduct. Especially common were reports of army officers neglecting their duties in favor of indulging in the amenities of life in the capital. Identifying himself only as "a citizen," one Richmonder vented his spleen in a letter to the secretary of war concerning certain staff officers of the Quartermaster Bureau, "worthless, scheming representations of humanity, who have slunk from service in the field . . . [and] whose sole occupation is [horseback] riding with ladies of very doubtful character and easy morals." He was fed up with seeing "these pseudo military geniuses with all the trappings of gold lace—riding at break neck pace thro' the streets of this city." Indolent officers often congregated in the hotel bars, especially the elegantly appointed and very welcoming bars of the Spotswood and the Exchange. The army high command was aware of this and, in the spring of 1862, seriously considered closing down those two hotels for "offer[ing] inducements to [officers] to be absent from their posts."[25]

The government property amassed in the capital tempted some of those in charge of it. Theft and rumors of theft were rife. Signing himself "A Friend to Honesty," one informant warned the War Department about William Sledd, a man of "degraded character," recently appointed to the provost marshal's detective squad but formerly employed as superintendent of the government slaughterhouse in Richmond. In the latter capacity he had been investigated for stealing cattle and subsequently fired. But he may have gotten away with a fortune: the letter writer swore that Sledd had been penniless before taking that job, which paid only $100 a month, but now was worth $75,000. Another informant accused a clerk at a hospital for prisoners of war of stealing delicacies donated by Northerners and sent to Richmond under flag of truce for the patients: "He gave a party some months [ago] at his Residence[;] the nice things they had can not Be Bought in our city such as amons [i.e., almonds] lemons . . . different kind[s] of jelly preserves maple sugar loaf sugar all kinds of cakes and many other things such as the north affords."[26]

The power wielded by certain Confederate officials was a seductive invitation to bribery. Many were accused of graft; some were guilty. War Department clerk Jones asserted in November 1861 that palms were being greased in return for looking the other way when certain Richmond merchants or their agents sneaked into Union territory to buy goods subsequently resold in the city for enormous profits. Later, after the issuing of passports was regularized, they were sometimes quietly offered for sale. In 1863 the lieutenant in charge of the passport office was arrested after evidence surfaced that he was getting $100 apiece for them. Quartermaster officials also came under suspicion. The anonymous citizen who denounced the joyriding staff officers also claimed that "the greatest corruption exists" in the administration of the army stables in the city: certain private citizens — "jobbers and sports in and around Richmond" — were being permitted, presumably in exchange for some under-the-table gratuity, to stable their horses at government expense; one in particular "has nothing to do but apply and his horse is immediately installed, and at once an imaginary colonel, doctor, major, captain, or somebody of that description is created [in the official record] and the horse is of course well fed, groomed, [and] shod." Most disturbing of all were rumors, of which there were plenty, that well-heeled men desperate to stay out or get out of the army were buying exemptions and discharges from venal officials. One was alleged to have bribed the members of the Richmond examining board to the tune of $11,000 for a medical exemption (a charge the War Department immediately investigated and declared false).[27]

The most notorious official scandal involved the provost marshal detectives. Recruited in the summer of 1861 by General Winder himself, they were mostly former policemen from Baltimore and points north — which made them instantly suspect in the eyes of many Richmonders. Clerk Jones, who fulminated against them repeatedly in his diary, described them as "illiterate men, of low instincts and desperate characters," habitués of "bar-rooms, ten-pin alleys, and such places"; their chief, Samuel Maccubbin, was supposedly "reared in the mobs of Baltimore." They enjoyed a windfall after the prohibition decree of March 1862, according to rumor, for they drank all the liquor they confiscated. The allegations grew more serious over time; Congress and the newspapers took notice. Among other transgressions, Winder's "Plug Ugly alien policemen" (Jones's epithet) reportedly used their access to the general to get his signature on blank passports, which they sold. By the fall of 1862 the detectives' "monstrous crimes" (Jones again) had become "the theme of universal execration." General Winder—probably guiltless himself but loath to admit the delinquency of his pets—was forced to act. On 29 October he fired the whole squad. (He subsequently organized a new one, rehiring a couple of the original members he judged honest.)[28]

The denunciations of corrupt government officials, fierce though they were, could seem gentle next to the wrathful excoriation of the civilian men of commerce who gouged the suffering people of Richmond. These "speculators" and "extortionists" hoarded great quantities of food, fuel, and other necessities, according to popular belief, biding their time, exulting as prices went skyward, and ultimately making a killing in the market. Almost never were they specifically identified: dark, spectral shapes, they worked their evil out of the public eye—and did so with impunity, for there were no laws against such activities (save General Winder's ill-fated and short-lived regulations capping certain commodity prices). They were declared guilty not of criminality but of unpatriotic greed and sinful mammon worship.[29]

The idea that the impersonal laws of supply and demand might be responsible for the inflation and shortages that tormented the city was never acknowledged: Richmonders blamed human depravity. "It is not the scarcity of food which causes the high prices," John Jones insisted. "It is an insatiable thirst for gain." In 1863 workingmen of the city came together in a mass meeting that condemned "the spirit of extortion and speculation now so rife in the community" and called on the general assembly to pass legislation "suppressing speculation in the prime necessaries of life." Newspaper editors and sermonizing ministers also took up the cry, as did some businessmen. Tredegar director Joseph Anderson, for one, was certain that speculators were behind the escalating costs of nails and other items essential for the works' production. Clerk Jones was appalled not only by the seeming invulnerability of the malefactors—"The government appears to be no match for them"—but by their mercilessness, for they took pity on no one: "The extortioners prey upon every victim that falls within their power."[30]

The speculator demonized in the public mind was not only avaricious, unpatriotic, and heartless but also cunning, always alert for new opportunities to enrich himself at the expense of ordinary citizens. In early 1865, when the Confederacy's last major blockade-running port (Wilmington, North Carolina) was threatened by a Yankee fleet, rumors flew around Richmond that speculators were buying up every pound of coffee and sugar in the city with the aim of jacking up the price, gleefully anticipating the cessation of foreign imports. Some Richmonders swore that the speculators were bound in a sinister conspiracy, acting together to monopolize critical supplies and maximize their profits. The city is "infested with gangs of speculators," the *Dispatch* declared in 1862, who are "working in concert."[31]

A lot of Richmonders were also convinced that many or most of the speculators were Jewish. Antebellum Richmond had been relatively uninfected by anti-Semitism, and the city's small Jewish population (which supported three synagogues) was well represented among the Confederate patriots who joined the ranks or in other ways aided the cause. But the wartime economic strains, the public's insistence on blaming human villains, and the persistence of ancient stereotypes spawned ugly accusations. "The Jews are at work," John Jones wrote in September 1861. "Having no nationality, all wars are harvests for them. It has been so from the day of their dispersion. Now they are scouring the country in all directions, buying all the goods they can find. . . . These they will *keep* until the process of consumption shall raise . . . demand." A year later he claimed that "the Jew extortioners" were amassing immense fortunes and doing the Confederacy more harm "than the armies of Lincoln. . . . If we gain our independence, instead of being the vassals of the Yankees, we shall find all our wealth in the hands of the Jews." In 1863, commenting on the plight of the "poor refugees" in the capital, Jones condemned "the flint-hearted Shylocks of Richmond, who have extorted all their money from them."[32]

The moral rot that so many Richmonders sensed was not confined to the iniquities of rich speculators and corrupt officials. As the war went on, more and more ordinary citizens and soldiers seemed to stray from the path of virtue. The liquor problem was especially disturbing. Drinking not only begat rowdiness and crime but also, according to popular wisdom, lured decent people from their duty, turning them into wastrels who were neglectful of family and comrades, burdensome to society, and useless in the struggle for Southern independence. The hustings court grand jury report of February 1864 denounced tippling houses not only because they bred criminality but because they "demoralize and ruin soldiers and others." Governor Smith, forwarding this report to the legislature, added his own thoughts:

"The young and unsuspicious soldiers who come to spend a pleasant hour [in drinking establishments] are the most common victims," he said; shutting down these places would "save many a citizen & gallant soldier from ruin & disgrace." A young Richmond woman named Maria Peek deplored "the beastly and disgraceful conduct" of certain army officers: "I mean the worship at the shrine of that enticing god—Liquor!" That women as well as men were indulging was particularly abhorrent to some. The *Dispatch* commented on the arrest of one woman for public drunkenness in 1863: "It is certainly bad enough to see a man under the influence of liquor, but for a white woman to be found in a drunken condition nothing can be more revolting."[33]

The Richmond chapters of the Sons of Temperance, active in the antebellum era, continued their battle against drunkenness into the war years, even though (as the *Dispatch* remarked in November 1861) they now must "fight against heavy odds." The Sons hailed General Winder's prohibition decree of March 1862 as an endorsement of their crusade and a long stride in the right direction. The subsequent abandonment of military and civil attempts to abolish saloons disappointed them, but they persevered, certain that the city needed their help now more than ever. In the fall of 1862 they appointed one of their number, a dry goods merchant named William H. Christian, to appeal directly to President Davis. "You no doubt know that this society is composed of men of sobriety," wrote Christian, altruists "who have the welfare of mankind as the basis of their action." Hoping that General Winder might renew the war on saloons, Christian made an earnest request of the president (one that few other Richmonders would have seconded by that point): use your influence "to bring about the protraction of Martial Law in this city."[34]

As they lamented the ravages of alcohol, some Richmonders worried about another path to dissipation: gambling. It was outlawed in the city, but men of all classes embraced it enthusiastically and the ban was only sporadically enforced. Gaming establishments, ranging from sordid dives to elegant parlors, were numerous in the antebellum years and more so during the war. Faro was the game of choice, and whether the patrons were rough workingmen or cultured gentlemen, they generally drank while they played and sometimes got violent.[35]

In the fall of 1863 the city authorities decided to stamp out gambling. Police raids closed many of the gaming places. But not for long: the *Dispatch* reported in mid-December that the business was already reviving, spurred

Disorder, Crime, and Sin

by the reconvening of Congress and the state legislature, many of whose members were avid gamblers. The editor castigated the mayor and police for their laxness: "To any who doubt our charge against the authorities that the 'law to punish gaming' is transgressed nightly in this city, let them closely observe Main street at midnight.... [Behold the] mysterious appearance of men, singly and in pairs, from heavy closing doors that lead to interiours [sic] that give forth no light or sign of habitation.... Notice the unaccountable popularity of side alleys that ostensibly lead nowhere in particular. If the observer use his ears as well as his eyes, he will catch the lingo of the faro-table, as some lucky or unlucky one wends his way from its presence, cursing his ill-luck or blessing his good fortune. Faro is still exhibited in Richmond, and no rod is soaking for the backs of the exhibitors." That game of chance (along with others, including poker and three-card monte) remained popular and accessible in the capital through the end of the war.[36]

Richmonders who virtuously shunned the gambling den and the tippling house might still go astray, moralists warned, by stepping into the third portal of hell, the theater. The city had several theaters; popular before the war, they drew bigger and bigger crowds with the immense influx of soldiers and civilians beginning in the spring of 1861. Offering a variety of entertainments including minstrelsy, orchestral music, dance, comedy, melodrama, and Shakespeare, they attracted customers of every class, sex, and race. Some of the customers misbehaved, particularly those occupying the cheap seats in the "pit"; the night watch was frequently summoned to subdue drunken, cursing, belligerent, egg-throwing rowdies in the audience, many of them in uniform. Quieter sorts of misbehavior went on in the notorious "third tier," where prostitutes and the men who sought them congregated. The acts on stage were sometimes objectionable, too (at least in the eyes of "respectable" Richmonders), laced with vulgar double entendres meant to appeal to the coarser sorts. The performers, male and female alike, were also objects of scorn, branded in the respectable public's mind as a disreputable lot.[37]

The theaters came under increasing moral scrutiny during the war. On Sunday, 8 February 1863, Pastor J. L. Burrows of Richmond's First Baptist Church devoted his entire sermon to the matter. He was moved to do so by the much-ballyhooed opening of the New Richmond Theatre, which would take place the next night. It had risen from the ashes of the original Richmond Theatre, destroyed by fire thirteen months earlier (an act of God, some said; others suspected arson). Burrows began by denouncing the large troupe of male performers boasted of in the theater's newspaper ads, healthy men of military age who were somehow managing to avoid service: "No cripples from the battlefields are these—they can sing and dance; they can mimic fighting on the stage. For the serious work of repelling a real enemy they have neither taste nor heart." He then described what the city could expect once the New Richmond was in business, starting with "the multiplication of drinking saloons all around the theatre." This was, he said, "just as sure to happen . . . as buzzards are sure to gather around carrion," for "those who visit the theatre are the thirstiest mortals for strong drink to be found." And liquor would of course be brought into the New Richmond itself, probably even sold there on the sly, because "all theatres, with rare and intermittent exceptions, are grog-shops." The alcohol would encourage the depravity of the miscreants who were invariably drawn to theaters. "Look round upon the audience," Burrows urged the theatergoers in his congregation. "For whatever there is of debasement, vice and crime in the community is there represented. There are found certainly the lowest and most vicious human beings, white and black, that the purlieus of a city can vomit forth." The theater not only embodied the worst of human behavior but nurtured and propagated it: "The apprentice to vice can gain in the theatre new insight into the principles of his chosen trade. They are developed in the curses and blasphemy of 'the pit'—in the shameless impudence of the 'third tier'—in the drunkenness and riot of the gallery, and often in the fashionable ribaldry of the boxes." And to those who insisted that theaters offered edifying entertainment he had this to say: "Among the lessons of the stage are very often such as these: simple honesty and truth are folly and vulgarity—religion is bigotry or hypocrisy, and the humbly pious are fools and fanatics—fraud and falsehood are justifiable as means to an end—murderers and duelists are model men—suicides are worthy of high eulogium—libertines and seducers are noble and generous—chastity is prudishness or affectation. . . . Away, then with the . . . preposterous plea, that the theatre . . . is a school of morals. It is, what it always has been, a school of immorality and vice. . . . You cannot visit the theatre and love it and remain innocent and pure."[38]

Burrows would have damned the theaters in any circumstances, but other Richmonders found them troubling only in the context of war. Benjamin Jones, an artilleryman in the city's garrison force, attended a number of shows at the New Richmond but eventually questioned "the propriety of permitting the play-house to be open at times like these. When we reflect upon the great struggle that we are engaged in, and the frequent reverses that our arms have sustained, and also come to think of the hard lot of our soldiers, and the many deaths that are constantly taking place in the hospital and on the battle-field, it does seem to me that such diversion as the theatre offers us should be prohibited. It looks very much like Nero fiddling while Rome is burning."[39]

Some felt pangs of conscience about other amusements that in peace-time had seemed innocent. Mary Chesnut chronicled the growing discomfort her husband, James, had with the social gatherings that she loved. She frequently invited friends to her lodgings, where "we danced to the music of an old ramshackle piano — and had a good time generally." She also went out with friends to enjoy other sorts of entertainment, accompanied at first by her husband. But "I knew it could not last — [James] going everywhere with us, to parties, to concerts, to private theatricals, even to breakfasts." Finally reaching his limit, he "denounced us for being so dissipated." Mary persisted in enjoying herself, however, until James laid down the law after she hosted a party in November 1863: "We are to have no more festivities. This is not the time or the place for such gaieties." She dutifully bowed to this decree, for her husband was "decidedly master of his own house." But a few weeks later, encouraged by a friend who promised to keep James occupied one evening, she surrendered to pleasure and had some friends over "for eggnog and casino." The plan miscarried: James "came straight home and found the party in full blast." To Mary's relief, he did not make a scene. But the next day he lectured her sternly: "No more parties. . . . The country is in danger. There is too much levity here."[40]

Another moral issue stirred up by the war was proper relations between the sexes. Certain traditions were severely tested. One was unchaperoned outings of young, unmarried men and women — a practice accepted in ante-bellum Richmond (at least among middle-class and elite whites), unlike in many other parts of the country. In his memoir of life in Richmond during the war, Thomas De Leon explained this as a "village custom" that survived because the city's population remained relatively small before the war and families within a given social class knew (or knew about) each other well enough to rest easy when their daughters went out for walks, rides, or picnics or to indoor entertainments with male acquaintances. But the massive influx of strangers and exodus of old residents that began in the spring of 1861 obliterated whatever remained of village communalism in Richmond. Suddenly young men of unknown background and character were calling on young women, a state of affairs in which, as De Leon put it, "a wolf might . . . readily have imitated the guise of the lamb." Many elders worried about this, he recalled; some wondered if the custom should be discontinued and chaperonage required. This did not happen: unchaperoned dating persisted in wartime Richmond—as did, presumably, the anxiety about it.[41]

Richmonders worried, too, about women (of all ages but especially younger ones) coming into physical contact with male strangers. The formal and informal rules that segregated the sexes in certain circumstances outside the bounds of kinship and friendship were frequently challenged by wartime necessity. It was customary, for example, for passenger trains to have a separate "ladies' car" for women and children; no men were allowed on it except those escorting female passengers. But the enormous wartime demands on Richmond's railroads often nullified that rule. In many cases passengers were too numerous and cars too few to allow setting aside a ladies' car, and women thus found themselves cheek by jowl with strange men; even on those trains with a ladies' car, men desperate to get aboard when the other cars filled up sometimes managed to get seated with the women. The hiring of female clerks in the government bureaus was worrisome too. Although their desks were set apart from those of the male clerks, generally in separate rooms, they could not wholly avoid close contact with the men, especially on the narrow stairways of the office buildings. A Richmond woman familiar with the Quartermaster Bureau headquarters warned President Davis that it was "no fitting place for *young* ladies. Married ladies, or ladies of a certain age only should be employed there," for the women "are compelled to occupy the same building as the gentlemen there employed, using the same stairs and at the same hours." Some Richmonders fretted about the women lodged in the city jail, where overcrowding left them very close to the male inmates; the *Dispatch* argued in 1863 that propriety demanded a separate facility for them. Employing women as hospital nurses and matrons evoked especially deep anxieties, for they had to deal with strange men in the most intimate ways— changing bandages, giving baths, emptying chamber pots. Some moralists continued to oppose it even after the critical need for female hospital labor became evident and the women had proved their worth.[42]

Of all the transgressions manifest in wartime Richmond, most disturbing in the eyes of some was Sabbath breaking. While much of it was an undeniably necessary accommodation to the demands of war—soldiers of the garrison and the Local Defense Forces could hardly devote Sundays to rest and devout reflection while in the trenches fending off enemy attacks, and many government and private facilities engaged in war work (including hospitals and prisons) had to operate seven days a week—much of it seemed gratuitous, further evidence of moral decay. Sabbath profanation troubled artilleryman Benjamin Jones even more than theatergoing; he thought the excuse of military necessity, while sometimes legitimate, was often abused. In a letter to a friend in 1863 he quoted a bit of verse that had been much on his mind lately:

A Sabbath well spent,
Brings a week of content,
And health for the toils of to-morrow;
But a Sabbath profaned,
Whatsoe'er may be gained,
Is a sure forerunner of sorrow.

He urged his friend to "pray for the spread of religion in the army. Pray for those in authority, that all of them may become pious and God-fearing men; and pray for the Sabbath to be respected and honored by all, both high and l[o]w."[43]

What tormented Jones was the vision not just of lost souls but of a lost cause. The sinning he lamented was not confined to the nation's capital; it plagued the whole Confederacy and tarnished it in the sight of God. "With me this Sabbath profanation is a serious matter. I have my fears of what the final issue of this war will be, wholly on this account. I fear God will not continue to bless our cause . . . unless this sin is turned from by all in authority. If our cause fails, at last, I believe it will be due, in great part, if not entirely, to our own national mistakes and sins in regard to the law of the Sabbath day, and not because our fight is not just and upright."[44]

Other Richmonders agreed that the unchecked transgressions of the Confederate people threatened to turn God against them, but not all deemed Sabbath breaking the cardinal sin. Maria Peek agonized over intemperance. Drunkards failed to understand "the blackness of this crime," she thought; they must "repent and devote their lives to a nobler purpose." If they persisted in their debauchery, "God's wrath will fall yet more heavily upon this afflicted people and the innocent suffer with the guilty." For War Department clerk John Jones, the great menace was speculation. "May God put it into the hearts of the extortioners to relent," he pleaded. "I fear a nation of extortioners are unworthy of independence, and that we must be chastened and purified before success will be vouchsafed us." Rector William Norwood of St. John's Episcopal Church was of the same mind. In a sermon entitled "God and Our Country," he condemned a number of national sins but singled out speculation for special censure. This abomination was begotten of avarice, he explained, and "avarice is declared by God's word to be idolatry, because it estranges the heart from him. The avaric[i]ous man worships mammon, and our Saviour declares, 'ye cannot serve God and mam[m]on.'" Moneygrubbing of other sorts likewise imperiled the Confederacy, Norwood warned: many people were abandoning the virtues of piety, charity, and moderation in pursuit of riches. "And will not God judge for this, and may we not expect still heavier chastisements, unless this demoralizing, this degrading, and idolatrous spirit of gain is repressed, and we humble ourselves before God for this sin?"[45]

These anxious patriots who beseeched the Confederacy's sinners to cease and repent, lest they provoke divine fury and national ruin, were doomed to disappointment. As the war went on, there was no perceptible lessening of Sabbath breaking, drunkenness, or greed nor of the other iniquities that the war seemed to nurture: gambling, theatergoing, frivolity, hedonism, and sexual impropriety. As their jeremiads went unheeded, and as the Rebel nation's military disasters multiplied and its prospects for survival dimmed, the prophets could only conclude that the Confederacy had fallen from grace. And as they contemplated that calamity, they had to reckon with challenges to another sacred obligation: preserving the racial order.

WHITE SUPREMACY AND
BLACK RESISTANCE

When he was in his midforties, Thomas Johnson recalled how he had come to understand, at a very early age, that he was a slave. Born in rural Virginia in 1836, he spent most of his youth in Alexandria and Washington. Describing in his autobiography his childhood up to about age eight, he told of "how happy I used to be [at first], playing in the yard with other children like myself, not knowing we were slaves." But as he grew and his awareness of the world sharpened, he "began to see that there was a great difference between the white and the coloured children. White people were free — 'free born' — but black people were slaves, and could be sold for money. What seemed worse than all was the discovery that our mothers, whom we looked upon as our only protectors, could not help us." In 1853 Thomas was sold to a new master in Richmond, and there he remained through the war.[1]

Like other enslaved children, Thomas also learned that white people could not wholly subjugate black people, either in body or in spirit; there were ways to resist. His mother gave him his earliest lessons in this regard. "She first taught me the Lord's Prayer. As soon as I was old enough, she . . . told me if I would learn how to read and write, some day I might be able to get my freedom; but all this must be kept a secret. . . . She [also] told me what she knew about heaven, where there would be no slaves — all would be free. Oh! I used to think how nice it must be in heaven — 'no slaves, all free,' and GOD would think as much of the black people as He did of the white. Then she would talk of Africa — how that we were all free there, but white people stole us from our country and made slaves of us." The injustice of slavery, the possibility of securing a better life on earth (by subterfuge when necessary), and the certainty of an afterlife of freedom and equality: these lessons comforted those held in servitude and emboldened them to resist oppression.[2]

Johnson turned twenty-five the year the Civil War began. It would ultimately liberate him and the 4 million other Southern slaves; their freedom would not have to await their arrival in heaven. But emancipation was no simple, straightforward, or uniform process. Each part of the South had a distinctive experience depending on its particular circumstances. In some places slaves gained freedom early in the war, in others late, and in still others only weeks or months after the Confederacy's demise. The wartime experience of slaves (and free blacks) in Richmond was shaped to a great extent by the factors peculiar to the city, especially the enormous expansion of population and industry, the critical labor shortage, the pervasive Confederate military presence, and the proximity of Union forces. Opportunities arose that the black populace eagerly seized, easing the burdens of subjugation to some degree and, for a fortunate few, even opening paths to freedom well before the Rebels abandoned the city to the Yankees. But almost every overt assertion of black autonomy, even the mildest, sparked the wrath of white Richmonders and provoked a backlash.[3]

Southern whites before and during the Civil War were convinced that slavery and white supremacy were not only necessary for the safety and prosperity of society but also morally beneficent, and they created a vast network of racial laws, institutions, and customs to enforce their will. In Richmond, no less than in other parts of the South, a rigid caste system undergirded by force and violence subordinated blacks, both bound and free, and ensured the dominance of whites.[4]

Few white Richmonders had any qualms about slavery. In May 1863 state attorney general John Randolph Tucker delivered an address to the Richmond YMCA that summed up white racial assumptions. His purpose was to justify secession, and the heart of his argument was that the Yankee abolitionists' crusade against slavery was absurdly misguided and profoundly threatening to the South. He first set forth the indisputable "facts" about the descendants of Ham: they were "incapable of amalgamation with the white race, by natural law, fixed and unalterable; incapable of political or civil equality with the white race, by original inferiority, and the debasement of centuries; incapable of freedom, except to be licentious and brutal and savage, and only fit to be enslaved, if order and security were to be conserved."

White Supremacy and Black Resistance

Slavery was therefore "our social necessity. Its disturbance would be a social disaster—might be our social ruin." Furthermore, slavery benefited the white South beyond restraining the bestial impulses of African Americans. By unifying all whites in a superior caste, it "saved us from the grinding conflict between capital and labor" that plagued societies with no permanently bound class to do the dirty work.[5]

These truths alone were enough to vindicate slavery, Tucker believed, but there were more. Slavery was a blessing not just to Southern whites but to the enslaved themselves. In its nurturing embrace, "the African has been civilized and [C]hristianized to a greater extent, than under any other educational process to which he has ever been, or can be, subjected." Slaves owed their enslavers a debt of gratitude, for in the South "kindness to the slave is the rule, and cruelty the exception," and "the master has been elevated, by discipline, for the high duty of guardianship to an inferior race." Abolitionists who quoted the Bible in their favor were deceived or disingenuous: God "ordained [slavery] for us, and . . . never condemned it, but prescribed regulations for it, as [H]e did for all other lawful relations in life!"[6]

Slavery being manifestly necessary and salutary, those black people beyond its grip troubled the minds of whites. With their naturally depraved impulses unconstrained by a strict but loving master, free blacks could hardly be expected to live upright and productive lives. That the vast majority actually did so made little impression on whites, who firmly believed that free blacks as a class were worthless. The editor of the *Whig* admitted in 1862 that some of those in the city were respectable and industrious but insisted that the majority were "thriftless and lazy vagabonds." The *Dispatch*'s editor concurred, acknowledging that there were some decent free blacks in Richmond but that most seemed "idle, trifling and good for nothing." Moreover, black men and women free to manage their own lives were a bad example to those enslaved, liable to corrupt them and make them dissatisfied with their lot.[7]

Municipal and state laws and law enforcement embodied white racial assumptions. The justice system as it applied to Richmond's people of color had always been stringent and biased, but it became more so as the sectional crisis deepened, Northern abolitionists grew more active, and Southern blacks were perceived as increasingly restless. By 1861 the legal restraints on black Richmonders were many and onerous.[8]

These restraints had two purposes. The first was to prevent a black uprising. The city had experienced one in 1800 (known as Gabriel's Rebellion); that event remained vivid in the consciousness of Richmond's whites, as did the bloody Nat Turner Rebellion of 1831 (which took place about seventy miles from the city) and the abolitionist raid on Harpers Ferry (in the Shenandoah Valley) in 1859 led by John Brown, a failed attempt to touch off a slave revolt. The law thus forbade Richmond blacks (enslaved or free) to possess a gun, ammunition, sword, or bowie knife, on penalty of up to thirty-nine lashes at the public whipping post. They were forbidden even to carry a cane at night, unless necessitated by "age or infirmity." Lashes were likewise to be inflicted on any blacks who organized a "secret society" or attended a meeting of one. In fact, no private gathering of any sort involving five or more blacks was permitted without white supervision. No slave was to be away from home at night without a written pass from his or her owner or employer. Free black men and women residing in the city were required to register annually with the hustings court and carry their registration papers at all times. To enforce these laws, the authorities had at their disposal not only the day police and night watch but also the Public Guard (created by the legislature in the wake of Gabriel's Rebellion and overseen and funded by the state), a standing armed force of ninety men charged with keeping a close eye on black Richmonders and defending the capital's public buildings in the event of an insurrection.[9]

The other purpose of the racial laws was to keep black people from asserting any sort of social equality with whites. Whether enslaved or free, they were expected to live and behave as befitted members of a servile caste, and this meant that they were denied all sorts of routine freedoms enjoyed by whites. Richmond's municipal code specifically forbade free and enslaved blacks to smoke in public or to walk through Capitol Square or a white cemetery or any other place where whites enjoyed recreational strolls (unless on an errand for owner or employer). It furthermore forbade slaves to possess liquor or to ride in a "licensed hack or carriage" without the written permission of their owner or employer. Slaves and free blacks must give way to white people on sidewalks and on the flagstones at intersections, stepping into the street if necessary; they must not "use provoking language, or use or make insolent or menacing gestures to a white person, or speak aloud any blasphemous or indecent word, or make any loud or offensive noise by conversation or otherwise" in public. Slaves were not permitted to hire themselves out or to secure their own lodging or board apart from their owner or employer; these matters, when necessitated by circumstances, must be directly arranged, paid for, and closely supervised by the white persons responsible for the slaves.[10]

The Richmond authorities were determined to enforce all these rules sternly—especially Joseph Mayo, who was elected mayor in 1853 and repeatedly reelected for more than a dozen years. On first taking office, he proclaimed his intention "to make all negroes and mulattoes know their places and obey the laws." During his administration, the public whipping post saw ever-increasing use; slaves and free blacks he deemed guilty of even the most minor offenses often received the maximum allowable mayor's court punishment of thirty-nine lashes. When black Richmonders talked among themselves, they referred to him contemptuously as Old Joe Mayo; they "looked upon him as their Nero," one recalled, "a man without a heart."[11]

The paternalism that Attorney General Tucker boasted of was not, however, entirely a figment of the white imagination. In Richmond, as throughout the South, the harshness of the racial caste system was often tempered by the conscience and kindness of individual whites. One was a prosperous merchant named William Brent. It was he who purchased Thomas Johnson in 1853. Johnson, who had suffered many a beating from his previous master and an overseer, recalled in his autobiography that "from this time [on] I received better treatment. I was never flogged after coming into the hands of Mr. William Brent." Brent was "always . . . kind to his slaves, and every member of the family followed his example," including Brent's son Thomas, to whom Johnson was assigned as a personal servant, and his wife, Caroline, who inherited Johnson after Brent's death in 1862.[12]

To slave owners such as the Brents, their bondsmen were not just part of the household but members of the family. When Richmonder William Liggon sought permission to ship 500 pounds of bacon to the city from the Shenandoah Valley in 1864, he affirmed that the goods were not intended for resale but for family use: "I . . . have eight whites and three blacks in [my] family." In some cases, masters and slaves were literally kinfolk. Richmond slave dealer Silas Omohundro, who died in 1864, left a will granting freedom and a substantial financial gift to "my woman Corinna Omohundro," who "has always been a kind, faithful and dutiful woman to me"; the will furthermore freed "her five children, . . . who are also my children." Although Silas's relationship with Corinna (who had served as his housekeeper) and the children may not have been a secret among his white intimates, the public revelation of it no doubt came as a surprise to many other Richmonders, for the light-skinned Corinna had for years been passing as white and living under the name Corinna Hinton in a dwelling next door to Silas's.[13]

The racial paternalism manifested by many whites, however benevolent, was rarely altogether selfless. Even the kindest always kept in mind the need for obedience and labor from black people. In April 1864, Richmonder Mary Doggett, wife of a soldier, came to the defense of her slave William, who had been convicted in the hustings court of abetting the attempted escape of another slave. The court sentenced William not only to "receive nine and thirty lashes on his bare back, to be well laid on by the sergeant at the public whipping post," but also to be sold and transported out of the state, so he could never again endanger slavery in Virginia. Anxious to save William from this awful fate, Doggett petitioned the governor for a pardon, insisting that William was innocent. Moreover, she said, he was a lifelong "family servant," raised by Doggett's mother, and had always had an "irreproachable character." It was not just the well-being of her helpless dependent that concerned Doggett, however. As she further informed the governor, William was her "only source of support," as she had hired him out as a barber for $400 a year. If he were sold, the sum she would receive (after taxes and fees were deducted) "would amount to scarcely nothing [sic]," and the interest it would earn would be too little to live on. If a pardon was out of the question, Doggett added, perhaps the governor might reduce the sentence to corporal punishment alone — "severe if you please" — and let William return to his barbering.[14]

A similar blending of humanitarian with practical concerns marked the religious efforts of the white clergymen who ministered to black Richmonders. (A state law passed after the Nat Turner Rebellion forbade blacks to preach.) The Reverend Robert Ryland, pastor of the First African Baptist Church before and during the war, embodied this dual impulse. Deeply committed to bringing the blessings of salvation to his black flock, he was equally committed to upholding the racial caste system. Like Attorney General Tucker, he deemed slavery not only a necessity for whites but a boon for blacks, seeing in it "the mysterious hand of God leading the African to Jesus." Sundays afforded him the opportunity to preach not only the gospel of Christ but also the gospel of white supremacy. Earnestly he explained to his congregation that "God has given this country to the white people. . . . They are the lawmakers — the masters — the superiors. The people of color are the subjects — the servants — and even when not in bondage, the inferiors. . . . God enjoins you to your submission." Thomas Johnson heard a lot of sermons like this in Richmond. The Bible-quoting white ministers, he recalled, "never failed to keep us informed about Abraham's servants, and 'servants obey your masters,' and what the Angel said to Hagar" (this last being the command to a runaway servant to "return to thy mistress, and submit thyself under her hands").[15]

Paternalism was not much in evidence in Richmond's thriving slave auction houses. One of slavery's worst horrors — the abrupt and perma-

White Supremacy and Black Resistance

nent separation of husbands from wives and children from parents — was an everyday occurrence there. Silas Omohundro presided over many such tragedies even as he nurtured his own black family. The enslaved people of Richmond, like those everywhere else in the South, lived in constant fear of family separation, for even the kindest masters might find themselves in financial straits that necessitated selling off their valuable black property or else might die, leaving their bondsmen to be parceled out among heirs or converted to cash to meet creditors' demands. An Englishwoman sojourning in the city in late 1860 and early 1861 recorded a conversation she had with a slave named Pete, who, with his wife, Charlotte, and three young children, was owned by the Englishwoman's landlady. Blacks were normally very reticent when questioned by whites on racially sensitive matters, but Pete opened up on this occasion when the subject of slave sales arose. "Oh! Mistress Jones," he said, "we can none of us tell when our turn will come. I was sold away from my father when I was so young that I shouldn't know him now if I was to meet him. That's a mighty hard thing to think of. And my brother, he went to another part, an' I hain't never seen him since. . . . [It] may be [that] I'll lose my children as my father lost me."[16]

Many black Richmonders endured physical as well as emotional torments. Few whites, even the sincere paternalists, saw anything wrong with corporally punishing blacks who misbehaved. But almost all drew a line between the "moderate correction" permissible in the interest of subordination and obedience (the definition of which was broad, encompassing even thirty-nine flesh-rending lashes at the post) and the unconscionable violence that a few slave owners and other whites inflicted. Most of the worst incidents never came to public notice, but those that did, if egregious enough, sometimes provoked the authorities to act. In the summer of 1864 a slave owner named Jacob Hoeflick, a confectioner by trade who kept a grocery store at Tenth and Cary, was brought before the mayor to answer a charge (as reported by the *Examiner*) of "unlawfully, cruelly, inhumanly and brutally beating a small negro girl named Joe, or Josephine, a slave infant belonging to him, and aged about four years." Several of Hoeflick's neighbors "testified that the child had been beaten habitually and frequently" with a foot-long leather strap "laid on with such severity that the sound of the flagellations could be heard for a considerable distance from the house." A policeman who had gone to Hoeflick's home the previous day to investigate testified that he found the child "cold and [nearly] pulseless," her "eyes . . . glazed and fixed," and concluded that death was imminent. He was right: even as he spoke in court little Josephine lay dead.[17]

Southern whites, the humane and inhumane alike, regarded blacks as primitive human beings, by nature desiring little more than the satisfaction of basic animal needs. As the *Examiner's* editor put it in 1864, "A negro fears nothing so much as that which robs him of the several senses of existence — sleep, food and the gratification of the passions." These necessities being amply provided under the benign system of Southern slavery (along with the perquisites of civilization and Christianity), whites saw no proper reason for enslaved people to be discontent, unless they were among the unfortunate few cursed with a cruel master.[18]

Whites professed to see everywhere evidence of slavery's benevolence and the slaves' contentment (such professions growing louder and more frequent as slavery came under increasingly heavy attack from outside the South before and during the war). "The negroes are the best-clad people in the South," War Department clerk John Jones insisted in 1862. "They are well fed, too, at any cost, and present a happy appearance. And they are happy. It is a great mistake of the Abolitionists, in supposing the slaves hail their coming with delight; on the contrary, nearly all the negroes regard their approach with horror." The editor of the *Dispatch*, of like mind and well aware that his newspaper was read in the Union as well as the Confederacy, issued a warning in June 1861 to "A. Lincoln and his horde of Abolitionists": "The vast majority of the colored people in all the Southern States," he claimed, "will be true to their masters and true to their country."[19]

Yet there was no denying, either before the war or (especially) after it began, that certain slaves manifested unhappiness with their lot, some even going so far as to run away. Most white Southerners took this as evidence not that their assumptions about slavery were wrong but that insidious provocateurs were tampering with the institution, stirring up the normally docile and loyal but highly suggestible slaves with false notions and turning them into restless malcontents — the usual suspects being free blacks and outside agitators.

Southern whites were constantly alert for signs of tampering. In 1864 Richmonder Maria Clopton wrote President Davis about a free black named William Smith, an employee of one of the army hospitals, who she claimed "exerts a most pernicious influence over my slaves." She had known him for years, was certain he was working to undermine slavery, and regarded him as "injurious to the safety of the City." Recently she had taken her case to the mayor's court, hoping to get Smith jailed or removed from the city, but had succeeded only in having him put under a peace bond. Now she turned to the Confederate government, pleading "the urgency of the matter." The gov-

White Supremacy and Black Resistance

ernment took this complaint seriously: the president referred it to the War Department, which decreed that Smith be conscripted and "sent to some distant point." Six weeks later, however, it was discovered that Smith had managed to elude arrest and "continues his vexatious proceedings" in the city. The secretary of war himself then stepped in, telling the Conscription Bureau to find the miscreant, turn him over to the Nitre and Mining Bureau, and see that he was taken far away; this matter demanded "special attention," the secretary insisted, "as the man is believed to be dangerous and mischievous to the community." Within days, Smith was in custody and gone from Richmond.[20]

Certain outsiders likewise attracted scrutiny and blame. The Englishwoman who managed to get Pete to speak frankly in private had to be cautious about satisfying her curiosity regarding slavery, for "all English people were looked upon as 'abolitionists,' added to which the fact of my having so many relatives in the Northern States, drew upon me not a little suspicion, if not the positive ill-will of some members of the [landlady's] family; and I found myself closely watched whenever I addressed a slave." When two of Jefferson and Varina Davis's hired house servants, Jim and Betsy, absconded to the Union army in 1864 — to the astonishment of the paternalistic Davises — their friend Mary Chesnut pointed out that the two slaves were known to have had a good deal of money stashed away and concluded that they had been bribed by Yankee secret agents in the city in the hope that they would divulge inside information about the Confederate government; Chesnut could imagine no other explanation for their flight to the enemy.[21]

Tampering likewise explained, to white people's satisfaction, organized slave uprisings. Although only a handful had occurred in the more than two centuries of Southern slavery's existence, the threat of a bloody rebellion haunted the white psyche. Alarming rumors of plots arose now and then, but with rare exceptions they proved groundless. Richmond experienced a panic at Christmastime in 1860 that provoked a militia muster but quickly subsided when no evidence of insurrectionary intrigue could be found.[22]

That was the last slave uprising scare that Richmond ever endured. While whites in other parts of the Confederacy, especially where slaves were densely concentrated, continued to worry about revolts throughout the war — their anxiety much aggravated by the absence of so many white males gone to the army — those in the Rebel capital rested easy, for the expansion of the slave population there was more than matched by the huge influx of troops. Whatever revolutionary plots the free black and Northern instigators supposedly at work in the city might be trying to persuade the slaves to join mattered not, for white power was unchallengeable there. "You need not entertain . . . any fears about the tobacco here," Richmond merchant Daniel Von Groning assured a European customer in July 1861. "It is perfectly secure. The enemy cannot come here and as regards a negro insurrection you will agree with me that that is out of the question when I tell you that we have a permanent camp here in Richmond of 25,000 troops. 500 men would be ample to keep our negroes in check even if they had a disposition to revolt which they have not." In May 1864, even as the great Union army offensive against Richmond got under way, John Jones observed that "there is but little fear of an insurrection" in the city—although by then he suspected that "the enemy would be welcomed by many of the negroes, both free and slave," should the capital fall.[23]

Contrary to white belief, slaves required no subversive meddling to turn them against slavery and spark a desire for freedom. As Thomas Johnson's recollections reveal, such sentiments became a part of enslaved people's consciousness as soon as they were old enough to begin to understand the world around them. Every day of their lives they saw the contrast between their condition and that of whites and wondered why it must be so. "Hardly a day passed without some one of my own long-oppressed people being led to the whipping post," Johnson remembered, "and there lashed most unmercifully. Every auction day many were sold away to Georgia, or some other of the far-off Southern States, and often they could be seen in companies, handcuffed, on their way to the Southern markets, doomed, doomed to perpetual slavery." These scenes deeply troubled and perplexed Johnson, moving him to seek answers in religion and to dream of liberty. A visit to Richmond in 1860 by the prince of Wales, who was touring the United States, led the wistful twenty-four-year-old slave to fantasize: "If I could only see the Prince, and tell him my desire for freedom," Johnson imagined, the prince would surely purchase him and take him to England, where he would be free. The slave Pete likewise yearned for freedom and escape from the South, confiding to the English boarder in 1861 that "if I'd had *my* will I'd a gone to Liberia."[24]

Expressing such sentiments openly was of course dangerous. With rare exceptions, slaves in the presence of whites wore masks of contentment and deference. Pete's English confidante, observing his interactions with his owner and her family, was struck by his "gracefulness and polish of demeanour, blended with obsequiousness and humility, that was almost painful to contemplate." Another English visitor, who spent a good deal of time in the city in 1862 and attended a black church service and even a slave auction, never got a hint that slaves were anything but satisfied with their lot: "Go through the streets, and into the negroes' church of Richmond," he wrote, "and you will say, happy is the 'coloured race.'"[25]

Until the war took a course that offered real hope of emancipation, the enslaved people of Richmond were forced to accept bondage as a given in their lives. They accommodated themselves to it when they had to, pushed back against it when they could. The Christian faith professed by many tempered the harshness and grief of servitude. A fifteen-year-old girl named Frances, who was Pete's sister-in-law and owned by the same mistress, told the Englishwoman of the joy she was experiencing since her recent conversion: "The Lord's mercy saved me," she declared rapturously. "Now I ken hope for Heaven; I have a home there, and if I git sick and die, I go to heaven for a home.... Now I'm happier than ever I was before." Whatever else might be denied her as a slave, this amazing grace was hers to cherish: "Jesus cares for *all*," she affirmed, "He died for *all*." Not long after this, the Englishwoman attended a black church service at which a member of the congregation, permitted by the minister to offer a prayer, ended it thus: "An' dough we'r tied an' boun wid de chain ob our trubbles in dis worle below, make us to 'member dat our Saviour was sore 'flicted and heabby griebed, an' dat we shall reap de joy in season in Heaven for ebbermo'!" The prospect of an eternal life of bliss by God's side, after the travails of earthly life ended, comforted many slaves even in the worst circumstances. A twenty-year-old woman named Margaret, condemned by the Richmond Hustings Court to hang for murdering a white infant, stood calmly on the scaffold in January 1863 before a crowd of hundreds, insisting to the end that she was innocent and that God would judge her fairly. An eyewitness paraphrased her last words: "She was prepared to go; and though the mode was horrible, she trusted [that] when the pain of the body was over her spirit would rest in Heaven."[26]

Looking beyond worldly woes to future rewards did not mean utter resignation to one's temporal circumstances; nor did it mean accepting the white interpretation of biblical allusions to servitude. Black Christians, while welcoming their white ministers' assurances about the good news of salvation, quietly scoffed at their admonitions about their servile obligations. One was overheard to mutter disgustedly, on being told yet again by Reverend Ryland that God had ordained white supremacy and black submission, "*He be d——d! God am not sich a fool!*" Thomas Johnson was born again in 1857, an experience that brought him profound joy and a measure of inner peace, but he never forgot that "while I had a free soul, my body was in slavery." Twice thereafter, when hired out by his master to wait tables at a seaside summer resort, he tried without success to escape to freedom.[27]

The black churches of Richmond were not just places of Sunday sermonizing. They were the pulsing heart of the city's black community, a community that embraced both enslaved and free people of color and enriched their often grim lives. There were five such churches by 1860, four Baptist and one Methodist, the oldest founded in 1841. All were offshoots of formerly integrated churches, whose white leaders had granted the black congregants' request for a separate institution of worship. On the eve of the war, the membership of the four Baptist churches alone totaled roughly 4,600 — well over a third of the city's black adults — and many nonmembers also attended services. Church membership swelled during the war, as black newcomers to the city joined. A wave of revivalism in the summer of 1863 also added many names to the rolls. Ebenezer Baptist, for example, had 429 members in September 1861; three years later it boasted 635.[28]

The five churches had white ministers, as the law required, and were supervised by their parent churches, but black members played important roles as deacons. Sometimes they took on other roles as well. Reverend Ryland, who for all his homilies about black obedience wanted his First African Baptist congregants to take charge of the church's affairs as much as possible, encouraged them to select the Sunday hymns and to offer prayers before and after his sermon — opportunities they eagerly grasped. And he had no objection when they lingered in the pews for more fellowship, exhortation, and song after he exited. (Never blinded by his missionary zeal, Ryland knew full well that his flock relished these moments far more than his sermons.)[29]

The black churches fostered community through various activities besides the Sunday gatherings, activities modeled on those of their parent churches. They sponsored Sunday schools, raised funds to aid the needy — not just needy free blacks but also slaves of neglectful masters — and oversaw black baptisms, weddings, and funerals, some of which were quite elaborate and attracted large assemblies. Moreover, the churches disciplined their errant members and adjudicated disputes among them.[30]

Each church's deacons met regularly to consider members' charges and complaints, hear testimony, and dispense justice. They took very seriously not only matters that put the congregants' souls at risk but also those that threatened the harmony of the church or the family. The penalty for the worst offenders was exclusion from the church. In December 1861, for ex-

White Supremacy and Black Resistance

ample, as recorded in the minute book of Ebenezer Baptist, "Richard Tunstall was excluded for having two wives." In September of that year, Philip Green was dropped from membership for fighting, and early in 1862 Charles Jones suffered the same fate for theft. In February 1865 the Ebenezer deacons expelled Ann Harris "for using profane language towards sister Sampson and associating with lewd persons" and Ann Eliza Price "for associating with women of evil fame, and disobeying [her husband] & leaving her husband's house." The deacons were not always of one mind: in June 1862, for example, following "a long and warm debate," they decided by a mere 5–4 majority to expel Brother Morton "for disagreement with his mother [and] sister, and suspicion of adultery." Some charges were dismissed. Pinky Judah, investigated by a church committee after a rumor arose of her "leaving her father's house and mingling with persons of doubtful reputation," was found innocent by the deacons in January 1864. Furthermore, the decree of exclusion could be voided if the sinner demonstrated repentance and a desire to return to the fold. Isaac Priddy and his wife, excluded in early November 1862 "for unlawful intimacy before they were married," were "restored to fellowship" before the year ended. It took Mahala Brooks, "excluded for fornication" in December 1861, a longer period of contrition and a marriage to make things right with the church, but in December 1862, now Mahala Johnson, she was welcomed back.[31]

Institutions besides the churches also nurtured black communalism. Fraternal organizations, of which there may have been ten or more in the city when the war began, brought blacks together for camaraderie and mutual assistance. One was the Union Burial Ground Society, founded by free blacks in 1848 to advance (as its constitution declared) "the welfare of our race and . . . [its] morality, and . . . for the interment of the dead." Annual balls sponsored by some of these associations were a highlight of black social life before and during the war. Less formal fellowship thrived in the neighborhoods where free black homeowners clustered. Many of them took in boarders, free and enslaved, and presided over a lively domestic life. Neighborhood residents also gathered in local groceries and cookshops to gossip and in alleyways to gamble.[32]

Strengthened in many ways by faith, family, and community, black Richmonders resisted however they could the constraints and dehumanization of slavery and white supremacy. Many slaves routinely evaded the laws forbidding them to drink or to go about at night without a pass; free blacks in large numbers ignored the requirement to register with the authorities; slaves and free blacks alike paid little heed to the ban on gatherings of five or more without a white person in attendance. The efforts of the mayor, police, and Public Guard to enforce these ordinances had only modest success. Nor were the ordinances banning self-hire and independent lodging and boarding by slaves well enforced, for many masters were happy to let their bondsmen and women defy those rules to save themselves the trouble of arranging matters.[33]

Achieving literacy was another way to counter oppression. A small proportion of black Richmonders managed to do it, despite the odds. Most whites thought it best for blacks to remain unlettered, fearing that a command of reading and writing would encourage dissatisfaction with their ordained status and allow them to read abolitionist literature and to forge passes and freedom papers. State law forbade whites to teach slaves or free blacks to read or write. But this law was sometimes ignored by sympathetic whites. (Reverend Ryland, for one, quietly encouraged reading by his congregants, deeming it a shame that they should be denied firsthand knowledge of the Bible and religious tracts.) A very small number of blacks taught themselves to read. Thomas Johnson, urged by his mother when he was a child and later inspired by his search for God to want to read the Bible, secretly and laboriously explored the mysteries of the written word, eventually acquiring a copybook and a spelling book and often getting help from his unwitting young master by "innocently" inquiring about the boy's school studies. By the time Johnson reached his midtwenties he could make sense not only of the Bible but of newspapers, and he shared what he learned in clandestine meetings with fellow slaves.[34]

Subtle assertions of dignity also mitigated the degradations of the caste system. Slave surnames were one example. Generally (there were exceptions), whites did not acknowledge them; in official and unofficial dealings alike, a slave's given name and the full name of his or her owner were all the identity whites cared to grant. But among themselves, slaves claimed last names. For instance, every slave mentioned in any connection—longtime member, new member, excluded member, redeemed member—in the wartime minutes of Ebenezer Church had a surname, and rarely was it that of the slave's owner. The other side of this coin was deflating the dignity of whites. Recounting a good joke at the expense of one's master or boss or some other white person enlivened many a black gathering. A Richmond woman's memoir recorded what could only have been an elaborate practical joke played on Varina Davis on no less an occasion than her husband's inauguration in February 1862 as president of the permanent Confederate government. It involved the "arrangement for her progress to Capitol Square made by her negro coachman. When they set out, at a snail's pace, she observed, walking solemnly and with faces of unbroken gloom, on either side of her carriage, four negroes in black clothes, wearing gloves of white cotton. Demanding impatiently of the coachman what in the world this performance meant, she was informed: 'This, madam, is the way we always does in Richmond at funerals and sich-like.'"[35]

Black Richmonders' affirmations of dignity, pride, and equality were mostly covert. But when they could get away with overt manifestations they did so, although these sometimes tested the tolerance of whites. Visitors to the city, before and during the war, were often struck by the fine, fashionable clothing worn by some free and enslaved black men and women at church services and other dressy occasions. Free blacks were often seen being driven through the city in hacks, and they were a regular presence at the city's theaters, although they were required to sit or stand in designated sections away from "respectable" whites. Congregants of the black churches, whose own cash contributions and outside fundraising supported the churches financially, made sure their facilities were furnished and maintained in a manner that not only honored God but reflected well on them.[36]

The money that such things required was not lacking, either before or (especially) during the war. The city's black community as a whole, while certainly not affluent, was never penniless. Many free black men earned good wages as artisans; they were particularly prominent in the building trades and they monopolized barbering. Free black men and women in considerable numbers operated profitable groceries, cookshops, and groggeries, licensed and unlicensed. A lot of slaves, too, had some cash at their disposal. Tipping of house servants, carriage drivers, porters, and hotel and restaurant waiters was quite common, even expected in some cases. Many skilled and unskilled slaves hired out by their masters were permitted to keep a portion of their wages, especially that earned by "overwork," that is, voluntary labor in excess of what the employer required and for which a premium was paid. Some masters gave their slaves money to drop into the collection box at church on Sundays. And, too, some slaves pilfered money or saleable items from their owners or employers.[37]

Some free people of color acquired substantial property. Fields Cook was one. Born a slave around 1814 in rural Virginia, he came to Richmond as a young man and earned money for his owner and himself as a barber and "leech doctor." By 1850 he was free, having probably been allowed by his master to purchase himself. Eventually he purchased his wife and son too. His master may also have taught him to read and write; in any event, by the

1840s Cook was literate and had undertaken to write an account of his life. In that decade, too, he started buying real estate. In 1860, by which time he had given up barbering and leeching and was employed as a waiter, his three pieces of real property (one of them no doubt his home, the others likely residences rented out to tenants) were worth $1,500 dollars. More than 200 other free black real estate owners resided in Richmond at that point, of whom seventy had, like Cook, at least $1,000 worth; altogether, the free black holdings in the city on the eve of war were worth nearly $185,000.[38]

The war offered even more opportunities for the free and enslaved black people of Richmond to make money. The labor shortage created by the siphoning away of white male workers to the army was a great boon for many blacks, as was the concurrent expansion of industry and population. Of course, black men were siphoned away too, slaves being impressed for fortification work and free men conscripted for various jobs; however, these were generally just able-bodied men aged eighteen to fifty, and the impressment of slaves was only periodic and strictly limited in duration (as was the conscription of free blacks until early 1864). The many black people remaining in the city's wartime labor pool were much sought after by employers, and some found their own niches in private enterprise. Hucksters, most of them free black women, regularly visited the various army camps and the busy railroad stations, peddling sandwiches, hard-boiled eggs, pies, gingerbread, baked apples, and other homemade snacks. The influx of troops also brought a measure of prosperity to black prostitutes and other service providers, such as the slave Walker, who guided soldiers (presumably for a fee) to groggeries willing to serve them. The city's peripatetic newspaper vendors, long a common sight on the sidewalks and in the markets and railroad stations, were by 1864 all or nearly all slaves or free blacks. More and more cookshops and tippling houses were opened, or taken over, by blacks. One black woman, discovering that many white women were glad to part with their old dresses and other apparel for cash and that other women were willing to buy them, opened a used-clothing store.[39]

White Richmonders took note of blacks' increased spending in the war years. It was a bad sign, they thought: too much money in black hands could only lead to trouble. Whites were suspicious about the source of all that cash, too, wondering how much of it was ill gotten. Reporting on the proceedings of the mayor's court one day in October 1863, the *Examiner* remarked that the large number of blacks charged with larceny was evidence of "how the negroes [have] obtained the means to gratify the spirit of extravagance, which [has] manifested itself among them since the war [began]. Negroes—

[including] slaves—buy delicacies in the markets that white people cannot afford; they ride in hacks, which white people cannot afford, and dress in raiment that nobody ought to afford [in] these war-times." A year later the same paper fulminated against "another symptom of the breaking down of the barriers that, until this war, kept the negro in his proper sphere. Now ladies and gentlemen at auctions are forced to bid in competition with swa[r]-thy negroes, who monopolize the most eligible positions [on the floor] and claim the nod of the auctioneer"; auction houses, the writer advised, should "adopt a stringent rule excluding negroes."[40]

The city authorities, employing whatever laws were available, tried to suppress the black population's conspicuous consumption. A slave named Moses was hauled before the mayor in March 1863, charged with publicly smoking a cigar; for this infraction he suffered five lashes at the whipping post. Later that year another slave, John, was sentenced to a lashing for the same offense, prompting the *Dispatch* to remind its readers that "smoking in the streets is a privilege not allowed to negroes." Especially rankling to whites was the increasingly common sight of black people being chauffeured about in hacks. The editor of the *Dispatch* denounced the practice in November 1863: "Negroes," he said, "should be kept in their places." Three months later the city council amended the ordinance forbidding slaves to ride in hacks without the express permission of their master; now free blacks, too, were barred from hiring a hack or licensed carriage—unless "in a funeral procession."[41]

Whites saw other signs, too, that convinced them that black assertiveness was on the rise and deference on the wane. In late 1862 the *Enquirer* reported that Wash Gordon, a well-known bartender at an upscale saloon catering to whites, was under arrest "for growing t[o]o large for one of his color, and using insolent and provoking language to Mr. William Mitchell, a white person. Wash has been considered one of the few respectable free darkies in the city, but, unluckily, he has begun to lead a bad example for the emulation of his kind." Such instances of impertinent language were multiplying, whites believed, along with instances of impertinent behavior, especially failure to yield the sidewalks and flagstone crossings to whites. In November 1863 Mayor Mayo reminded the police of the sidewalk ordinance and, according to the *Dispatch*, "directed the chief to enforce it rigidly from this time [on, even] if he had to call to his aid all the force of the night and day departments." The editor applauded this dictum, commenting that if the law was observed, "ladies will not be rudely run against by mulatto wenches, who have become exceedingly insolent." Later that month a slave woman named Indiana was brought before the mayor by Officer Perrin of the day police, who testified, as the *Examiner* reported, that he had seen her crossing on the flagstones at an intersection "and though she saw some ladies coming across the street, did not pretend to give way, but going straight up against one of the ladies, compelled her to go out into the street, which was very muddy." Five lashes, decreed the mayor, who then took that opportunity to deliver another harangue about black uppityness and to vow that he would "teach all negroes to know their places."[42]

Mayo also declared war on illicit black gatherings, which he was certain were becoming more frequent. Even those for ostensibly innocent purposes such as holiday celebrations, he believed, were corrupting influences, allowing slaves and free blacks to avoid the eyes and ears of whites and to do and say whatever they liked. Other whites agreed and added curfew violations to the list of proliferating black delinquencies. "Negroes go a-gadding at night, from one end of the corporation to the other," one newspaper editor complained. "Slave[s] mingle with free [blacks] and in the counsel of the multitude there is mischief." At the mayor's bidding, the police redoubled their vigilance. A raid on a home by the night watch in December 1861 netted twenty-two blacks celebrating Christmas; the women were released after their fine was paid, but the men were whipped. A card-playing party attended by seventeen black men in September 1863 ended abruptly at one o'clock in the morning with the appearance of the night watch; all seventeen received lashes. There were many such raids as the war continued. The police also cracked down on self-hiring. Between January 1862 and December 1864, eighty-five slaves were arrested for that crime; during a comparable period in the late antebellum era, the number had been three.[43]

Free people of color, in particular, came under increased scrutiny. Those caught without proper registration papers generally went to the whipping post; a few were let off with fines, but if unable to pay went to jail; and a good many of the able-bodied men were turned over to the army's Engineer Bureau for fortification labor. Nonresident free blacks who came to the city temporarily, to sell produce in the markets, for example, attracted extra suspicion because they were strangers. Wary even of those whose registration papers were in order, the city council decreed in the summer of 1863 that no free black could enter the city for any reason "unless he shall first obtain from a Justice of the Peace of the county in which he resides a certificate of good character and loyalty." The police were instructed to arrest all lacking such a certificate, and the mayor was empowered to have them whipped.[44]

The mingling of free blacks with slaves worried whites. The improper

White Supremacy and Black Resistance

mingling of whites with slaves or free blacks was even more disturbing. This was a matter of both morality and racial control, and the Richmond authorities had always been quick to suppress it. They remained alert during the war, determined to chastise white people who degraded themselves with intimate relations across the color line or who encouraged black people to defy the rules of caste and determined, of course, to chastise the blacks involved. Sexual transgressions came to light quite often. In September 1863 alone, as reported in the newspapers, a white woman "was committed to the cage on the charge of associating with a negro, who was also locked up"; a pair of white men "were required to give security to be of good behaviour for being caught in a house on Cary street, with two filthy negro women"; and a Louisiana soldier detailed as a carpenter was arrested at a house on Jefferson Street where, by his own admission, "he had been cohabiting for twelve months" with an enslaved woman who "is [the] . . . mother of a child three days old, of which he [is] the father." In March 1865 a white man named John Farrar spent a night in the cage and then went before the mayor, charged with "lewdly and lasciviously associating and cohabiting with Ann, a slave woman"; Ann likewise faced the mayor's wrath. Less intimate interracial fraternizing could also provoke the authorities. A free black cookshop proprietor named William Ferguson was arrested in 1864 for "keeping a disorderly house," that being his shop, where, it was alleged, "white men and negroes sit at the same table and devour delicacies." The mayor generally came down hard on culprits of these sorts. One exception was a white man named George Norton, charged in January 1865 with "walking the streets on Monday night arm-in-arm with a negro woman"; his case was dismissed after he convinced the mayor "that he was very drunk at the time."[45]

Further evidence of what white Richmonders saw as the erosion of white dominance and black subservience in the war years was the proliferation of petty and felonious theft by slaves and free blacks. The editor of the *Examiner* railed about it repeatedly. In November 1863 he cited four cases that had come before the hustings court in a single day; this appalling record would, he thought, afford his readers "a faint idea of the amount of thieving now being practiced by the negro population of this city." In June 1864 he noted the recent rash of nighttime thefts from vegetable gardens; several of the perpetrators, all of them black, had been caught in the act and shot, which the editor hoped would "have a salutary effect upon the negro population, and restrain them in the exercise of their theiving [*sic*] propensities." Two weeks later, under the headline CRIME AMONG THE NEGROES, he condemned the "headlong and headstrong tendency of our servile population to burglary, theft and pilfering generally" and claimed that the problem had "multiplied ten fold within the past three years."[46]

What to do about black thievery was a question much on the minds of whites. The mayor's answer was, for the lesser offenses, to lay on the whip more generously. Other offenses he referred to the hustings court, which had several punishments to choose from, including flogging, the penitentiary, and (for slaves) sale and removal from the state. For guilty free blacks there was another option. In 1860 the general assembly had authorized courts to enslave, and sell to the highest bidder, any free black person convicted of a felony. Whether the legislators intended this law to be invoked broadly or only for particularly heinous crimes is a moot question; in any event, as worries about racial control mounted during the war, the Richmond Hustings Court availed itself of the law with increasing frequency. In 1863 alone, of the twelve free blacks found guilty of grand larceny, eight were subsequently enslaved and sold; in 1864, of sixteen found guilty, thirteen were enslaved and sold. The condemned included men, women, and at least one child, and in many cases their crimes were relatively minor. Nathaniel Drayton lost his freedom and went to the auction block for stealing fifteen dollars in cash and a watch worth thirty dollars. Sylvester Brown, who had made off with two calves, was enslaved and sold for $4,010. Sarah Edmondson, sentenced to slavery for stealing a dressing gown worth twenty-five dollars, cost her purchaser just $980—but then, she was only fifteen years old.[47]

As far as whites could tell, however, none of these punishments was doing much to stem the deluge of black theft. Some, including the *Examiner*'s editor, eventually concluded that the courts were simply too lenient. "Negroes are whipped," he wrote in July 1864, "[or] sent to work out a term in the chain gang, jail or penitentiary, but no sooner have they expiated their offence than they seem to make all haste to repeat their experience by repeating their crime, and come up before the Mayor again with a nod of recognition." There was but one effective deterrent, the editor insisted—the death penalty—and it ought to be inflicted mercilessly on the worst offenders.[48]

He got his wish a few months later when two slaves were hanged for burglary. Ben, owned by John H. Gentry, had been found guilty in the hustings court of taking shoes and boots valued at $2,500 from a store on Cary Street. William, the property of a Goochland County man and apparently hired out in Richmond, had broken into the home of a white woman and made off with a large quantity of clothing. On the morning of 21 October 1864, the two were taken from the jail, placed in a wagon that held their coffins, and escorted to the execution site by various officials and the Public Guard. A crowd of several thousand awaited them there, mostly blacks. Both men made statements from the gallows, neither denying his guilt. The execution was a particularly gruesome one: the fall did not snap their necks, and the men slowly strangled to death, "their bodies . . . twitching and heaving," as one witness recorded, for nearly half an hour. The *Examiner* informed its readers that this was "the first instance of hanging for burglary within the jurisdiction of the courts of Richmond."[49]

The most troublesome thieves, in the minds of whites, were the slaves who stole themselves. The huge wartime expansion of the city's population created opportunities for slaves to slip away from their owners or employers, settle in quietly among friends or strangers in some teeming neighborhood in another part of town, and elude detection for weeks or even months. A young man named Henry deserted his master, who lived on Seventeenth Street, in late September 1861; two weeks later he was still on the loose despite his master's efforts to track him down, which included posting an ad in the *Dispatch*: "He is probably passing for free, or may have a forged pass. He may be among some of the [army] camps, as he was seen about the reservoir last week." That same issue of the paper printed a reward offer for eighteen-year-old Virginius, who had run off a month earlier from the hotel that hired him: "He has been seen at the Old Market house, selling from a country cart." Three years later, a middle-aged woman named Celia Jackson left her master; he subsequently learned that "she has been hiring herself out in Rocketts as a washer-woman," but he still could not get his hands on her.[50]

Another enslaved man named Henry disappeared inside the city for two months, despite being sought not only by his owner and his employer but by the police. In July 1864 he had gone to the woman who hired him (and who in turn hired him out to others for various jobs), insisting that there was not enough work in Richmond to keep him busy. He asked for a pass to nearby Chesterfield County, where, he said, he could find a job; she obliged, and off he went. Instead of leaving the city, however, he went underground, apparently with the aim of supporting himself by theft. One night about a week later, he and five other black men broke into a dwelling through a basement window and made off with $2,000 worth of stored bacon, flour, sugar, butter, rice, and other provisions, some of which they sold to a grocer. The police soon tracked down Henry's five accomplices, but he evaded capture; he was, however, identified and a warrant was issued for his arrest. Weeks passed with no sighting of him, but then the police got a break: an anonymous note revealing his hideout. It was in the attic of a house on Main Street, where his mother lived; the police arrested him there.[51]

There were certainly many others like Celia Jackson and Henry in the Rebel capital, lying low, dodging pursuers, and living by honest or dishonest work. The *Examiner*'s editor thought so: In March 1863 he complained of "the herd of runaway negroes now accumulated in Richmond." They numbered, he claimed, "at least a thousand." That was a mere guess, of course, but perhaps not an unreasonable one. Whatever the actual number, it was swelled by fugitives from the surrounding rural areas who made their way to the city and lost themselves in its crowded streets, alleys, and neighborhoods.[52]

Some of the runaways in Richmond avoided apprehension with the help of vaguely worded passes provided by careless masters. (Slaves who sneaked away just for a night to gather with friends also found these useful.) The *Dispatch* reminded its readers in June 1863 that passes should be specific, bearing a date, naming the slave, and designating the exact place he or she was permitted to visit and the exact time he or she was to return home; if the pass was meant to cover regular visits, it should be endorsed on the back by the owner of the place visited. As slaves had always known, however, passes like that, which could withstand the scrutiny of even the most suspicious policeman or Public Guardsman, could be had for a price from a forger. A few very literate slaves and free blacks — and even some whites — offered that service. In November 1863 a tip led a county constable to a "negro shanty on Broad street," where he nabbed a young white man in the act of writing passes for slaves. The man confessed that he did this regularly, for a fee, and even employed black agents to spread the word among the city's enslaved populace.[53]

Whites suspected — and it was no doubt true, at least in the first year or so of the war, when many newly formed military units camped in and around the city before being sent to the front — that some of the missing slaves had attached themselves to troops and departed with them. They were welcomed by enlisted men and officers who wanted cooks, launderers, or body servants and who were not inclined to inquire too closely about a willing black person's legal availability. This was likely how a sixteen-year-old named Bob eluded his owner, Robert Haxall, in October 1861, after running off from the factory where he had been put to work. "There is reason to believe," Haxall announced in a newspaper ad, that "he may have gone, [pretending to be] a free boy, with a company of soldiers, who left town on the Central Railroad on Wednesday last."[54]

Bob and others who got away from Richmond by taking up with Confederate troops were lost to their owners but not, of course, lost to Southern slavery. Some slaves, however, escaped both the city and slavery by fleeing to the Yankees. The majority of these self-emancipators made their break for freedom when large Union army forces were near the city, that is, in the spring and summer of 1862 and from June 1864 to the war's end, their number increasing sharply during the Confederacy's last few months of existence. In December 1864 the *Examiner* reported a virtual "exodus of negroes" from Richmond: "A dozen cases are reported to the police every twenty-four hours." Over the course of the war, the escapees numbered many hundreds. Some were aided by pass forgers or by the same sorts of smugglers who, for a fee, spirited army deserters, conscripts, and desperate white civilians out of the city and into Yankee-held territory.[55]

Escape attempts were never undertaken lightly, even when the Union army was close. Many slaves who dreamed of freedom in the Yankee lines hesitated at the thought of leaving behind kith and kin, perhaps never to see them again. The risk of being caught trying to get away was another powerful deterrent. In and beyond the city, civil and military officials were ever alert for runaways. The potential capturers who had to be evaded along the route to freedom included the city police and Public Guard, provost guardsmen and detectives, Rebel army pickets and cavalry scouts, and county slave patrols. Escape attempts were not for the fainthearted.[56]

Many failed, usually with harsh consequences for the unlucky fugitives. On a Saturday night in January 1865, a group of slaves trying to abscond in two wagons escorted by three white men (no doubt hired smugglers) was intercepted by provost marshal detectives on the Nine Mile Road three miles from Richmond. The little caravan abruptly halted; the whites and two or three of the blacks scattered into the darkness, but the remaining seven men and two women were taken into custody, returned to the city, and lodged in Castle Thunder to await their masters' retribution. On a Thursday night about seven weeks later, another group of runaways met a similar fate on the Darbytown Road. This time none got away: the detectives who pounced on them arrested all seven women and four men, along with the three free black men hired to guide them to the Yankees. All fourteen were locked up in the Castle.[57]

Escape attempts, even the failed ones, deeply troubled white Richmonders. But they inflicted no mortal wound on the institution of slavery. Despite the hemorrhaging, and despite the challenges to racial control from black people who took advantage of wartime crowding, anonymity, and economic opportunity, the mechanisms of white supremacy remained intact. Until the moment Union troops marched into the city, slavery endured.

WHITE SOCIETY AND
ITS DISCONTENTS

No rigid lines of caste divided Richmond's white folk, but class distinctions had always been apparent in the city. Friction between the classes, perceptible but not disruptive in the antebellum years, was aggravated by the travails and transformations of war. Anxiety, resentment, and anger grew to the simmering point. Midway through the war these passions boiled over in the form of lower-class mob violence, frightening the upper classes and the authorities and forcing on them the realization that the sufferance of the white masses had its limits. Protests of other sorts over the next two years reiterated that lesson. Compelled to act, the authorities applied both the velvet-gloved hand of appeasement and the iron fist of force. But class tensions persisted, further unsettling a city already riven by discord and haunted by fear.

The upper classes of white Richmond made up a small elite and a larger middle class, readily distinguishable from the rest of white society by their genteel manners and language, good education, and stylish dress. Elite and middle-class men did not engage in manual labor; most were merchants, industrialists, bankers, lawyers, doctors, ministers, teachers, or clerks. Moreover, their wives did not work outside the home, except in benevolent activities. Their children almost all attended school until at least age seventeen or eighteen, a good many of the sons (but few of the daughters) going on from there to college. Together the two upper classes owned the majority of real estate in the city and almost all the slaves, and they generally relied on servants (mostly blacks, whether owned or hired, but in some cases lower-class whites) to make their domestic lives comfortable and allow them leisure time. The elite and upper-middle-class families of late antebellum Richmond owned or rented houses as a rule, many of them clustered in the fashionable central part of the city on Cary, Franklin, Marshall, and Grace Streets. Lesser middle-class folk lived in single-family housing in outlying neighborhoods or in boardinghouses, the latter being the domicile of choice for men starting their careers.[1]

A distinguished lineage was not required for membership in the antebellum elite, although it helped. George Wythe Randolph, a prominent lawyer and city councilman who later served for eight months as Confederate secretary of war, was a grandson of Thomas Jefferson. Joseph Anderson's family background, by contrast, was modest; he won his way into the elite circle through professional accomplishments, obtaining a West Point education, making a mark in civil engineering and business, and eventually acquiring the Tredegar Iron Works and building it into one of the Old South's premier industrial establishments. The elite men of Richmond, though few in number, were a powerful, arguably predominant, presence in the city's economic, political, and social life. Anderson, for example, was not only a captain of industry but a bank director, an officer of the Richmond Board of Trade, a state legislator, a city councilman, a school trustee, and a leading lay churchman. Almost all the city's elites were wealthy. Anderson was one of the richest men in the South, worth some $755,000 in 1860. The great majority of Richmond's antebellum elites owned slaves, although not usually in large numbers. Unlike the planter elites who dominated most of the South outside the cities and towns, these business and professional men generally relied on slaves only for domestic service, not for producing wealth.[2]

Middle-class Richmonders could boast of no exalted family trees or great fortunes, and their professional standing, political and economic influence, and social status were overshadowed by those of the elite. But as a group they enjoyed a measure of prominence and power in the city, although individually they ran the gamut from notable to obscure. Typical of the antebellum upper-middle class was William Brent, who made a living as a merchant but also served on the board of directors of a bank and an insurance company. Virginia born and forty years old in 1860, he lived in a rented house on Fifth Street in the Second Ward with his wife, Caroline, their four children, two elderly white boarders, and several slaves (among them the pious, self-taught, freedom-seeking Thomas Johnson). The oldest child, eighteen-year-old Thomas Brent, was employed as a clerk. The family was well-off, although not rich: William Brent's mercantile stock, home furnishings, slaves, and other personal property (he owned no real estate) were worth about $25,000. A couple of blocks from the Brents was a small boarding establishment known as the Arlington House, home to an assortment of people typical of the city's lower-middle class. Operated by a Southern-born couple in their sixties named McCreary, who rented the building, it sheltered four other men and one woman: S. H. Gordon, a thirty-eight-year-old, English-born bookkeeper, and his twenty-four-year-old wife, Sarah, a Virginian; Charles Kent, a tobacconist and Virginia native in his twenties; an Italian-born physician named Ascoli, in his thirties; and a Belgian-born teacher, age twenty-nine, named Peple. None of them, including the McCrearys, owned any real estate or slaves, or any other property to speak of, although the McCrearys no doubt hired servants to help with the cooking and housekeeping.[3]

The distinction between elite and middle-class white Richmonders was never as sharply drawn as that between those two upper classes, on the one hand, and the white lower classes, on the other, the latter constituting the majority of the city's whites. The lower classes were made up of skilled artisans, semiskilled and unskilled laborers, and their families. Foreign-born men and women without much formal education comprised a considerable portion of the lower classes, Germans being especially well represented among the artisans and Irish among the unskilled.[4]

Most members of the artisan class lived comfortably, although few were really prosperous. Home ownership was common among them, but slave ownership was uncommon and most got along without domestic servants. The artisan folk were, moreover, almost all literate, albeit uncultured by upper-class standards. Richard Taylor, a carpenter, epitomized in some ways Richmond's antebellum white artisans. A native of the Old Dominion, forty-three years old in 1860, he owned a house in the Third Ward worth $1,500, along with, presumably, some home furnishings and the tools of his trade, but no other substantial property. Living with him was his wife, Virginia, and their eight children, ranging in age from two to sixteen. Both Richard and Virginia were literate and they saw to it that their children were, too, but they were satisfied with a basic grounding in reading, writing, and ciphering, leaving higher education to the upper classes. The two sons and two daughters between ages six and twelve all attended school in 1860; the two eldest children, fourteen-year-old Thomas and sixteen-year-old Edith, had by then ended their schooling and taken work, Thomas as an apprentice carpenter (likely under his father's tutelage) and Edith as a seamstress. As was the rule among the wives of artisans, Virginia did not take gainful employment but devoted herself to child-raising and other domestic duties.[5]

The unskilled and semiskilled white workers of antebellum Richmond, with few exceptions, owned no real estate and very little property of any other sort, although they were not for the most part indigent. They generally lived in boardinghouses or tenements, and a good many were illiterate or nearly so. Irish-born Patrick Whalen, who identified himself to the 1860 census taker as a laborer, was typical of such men. He and his wife, Margaret, also a native of the Auld Sod, resided in rented accommodations three doors from Richard and Virginia Taylor. Both were thirty-two years old, and they were raising three children, the oldest age three, all born in Virginia. Also in the household was a fifty-year-old Irish-born widow named Ellen Burgess, perhaps Margaret's mother. She could read and write, but neither Patrick nor Margaret could do so, and none of the three owned any property worth the census taker's notice. The family apparently subsisted on Patrick's wages alone, for neither of the women claimed an occupation. Many other women of the unskilled or semiskilled class, however, took remunerative work to supplement their husbands' meager earnings, and some supported themselves and their families alone. One was twenty-eight-year-old Susan Henderson, a propertyless Virginia native who rented a place (likely a single room) in the Third Ward and took in sewing for a living. She was a single mother, perhaps a widow: the only other member of her household was her four-year-old daughter, Ida. Chances were slim that Ida and the three little Whalens would get a sound elementary education as they grew, much less any higher schooling. Such children, whose parents eked out a living not far from the edge of poverty, were often put to work at a very early age.[6]

Upper-class antebellum Richmonders were quite status-conscious. They referred to themselves as "ladies" and "gentlemen," in contrast to the "women" and "men" of the lower ranks; and they embraced certain customs that set them apart from the masses, including Sunday promenades on Capitol Square and, among the ladies, daytime social visits to one another's homes. Many gentlemen had a prickly sense of honor that manifested itself now and then in dueling (illegal but usually winked at, or only lightly punished, by the authorities). The upper classes also assumed certain entitlements, among them the right to run the city. The municipal council was made up overwhelmingly of upper-class men, and Mayor Joseph Mayo was a scion of one of the city's oldest and most distinguished families. In public matters the mayor and councilmen typically spoke for the upper classes, as did most of the city's newspaper editors.[7]

In their face-to-face dealings with the plain folk, ladies and gentlemen were often condescending but not rudely so. They were generally polite to all lower-class whites and genuinely paternalistic and benevolent toward the very poor — at least the "deserving" poor, whom misfortune had rendered helpless. Privately, however, many elite and middle-class Richmonders were haughtily disdainful of the rough manners, coarse and ungrammatical language, and cultural ignorance of the commoners. They were also a little fearful, not of the lower classes as a whole but of the unpropertied, less "respectable" sorts, whom they regarded as a rabble given to drink, rowdiness, and crime. While they did not worry about a plebeian uprising comparable to the imagined slave insurrection that gave them nightmares, their concerns provoked the city authorities to crack down in the late antebellum era on lower-class drunkenness, unruliness, and violence.[8]

Richmonders of the common sort may have found the condescension of the upper classes annoying, but the spirit and the reforms of the Jacksonian era had given them enough self-respect and political clout that they could ignore it. They were no less sensitive to class distinctions than were the elites and middle class, but they were generally content with their status and, while respectful for the most part toward gentlefolk, did not humble themselves in their presence. All white males who had reached age twenty-one and had established residency in the state and the city could vote and hold office, and the great majority of such men of every social rank exercised their franchise in every election. Local politics in Richmond in the late antebellum years was lively and contentious but never class based. A few artisans were elected to city offices, including the council, but plain-folk voters were basically satisfied to let upper-class men occupy the seats of power, knowing that officeholders were well aware of their dependency on those voters and had to take their concerns seriously.[9]

Economic and social factors also eased class friction in the prewar years. While the disparities of wealth in the city might stir envy among the less favored, they rarely stirred anger. The necessities of life were relatively plentiful and cheap and available to all. Even the unskilled, except for a few of the least fortunate, could earn enough to get by; if they were forced to live austerely (as indeed most were), still they had a roof over their heads to keep them dry, wood or coal in the fireplace or stove to warm them, clothing sufficient for work, relaxation, and church, and enough food to avoid hunger. They did not suffer. For another thing, self-segregation kept the classes apart in certain ways and thus less likely to irritate each other. Drinkers and gamblers generally patronized establishments that catered to their own class, either posh and genteel or unpretentious and earthy. Theatergoing also followed class lines: certain theaters were avoided by the elite and middle class, and even in those attended by all sorts (notably the Richmond), ladies and gentlemen sat apart from the common folk. Certain churches, volunteer militia companies, and fraternal, benevolent, and trade associations likewise attracted people of a particular class (although others extended their embrace across class lines).[10]

The great influx of outsiders beginning in the spring of 1861, along with the departure of many longtime residents, ruffled the city's white class structure but did not fundamentally upset it. Newcomers at first found some of the established Richmonders resentful and aloof, but before long the intruders were absorbed into the city's existing social classes. Among the upper crust, for example, Jefferson and Varina Davis and James and Mary Chesnut, having demonstrated their elite credentials and the requisite patrician attitudes, were acknowledged as peers and made welcome, and so on down the ranks. The shape, tone, tenets, and internal dynamics of Richmond's white society remained basically intact despite the turnover in its constituency.[11]

That said, it is also true that the war brought white Richmonders into contact with one another in new ways and under altered conditions that underscored class distinctions, heightened class consciousness, and intensified class friction. Women's voluntary work for the war effort was one example. Carried out mostly through organizations such as the Ladies' Aid Society (directed by Mary Randolph, wife of George Wythe Randolph) and the Ladies' Defense Association (founded by Maria G. Clopton, well-to-do widow of a Richmond judge), such work was almost wholly the province of upper-class women, who had free time for it. Lower-class women who participated generally did so for wages. Ellen Mordecai described the bustle of activity, and suggested its class dimension, in a letter of June 1861: "All the ladies in town who can, and the number is great, are working for the soldiers, who flock from all parts of the South requiring . . . tents, uniform[s], havelocks, &c. We meet in the basements of the various churches and make what is needed like the working women some of whom we employ to help us. . . . I have been working at St. Paul's with other ladies." At least one lady restricted her benevolence to soldiers of her own class. Early in the war, when the overwhelmed Medical Bureau was calling on Richmonders to care for wounded men in their homes, a young girl named Jennie witnessed this scene: "An ambulance drove up to our next door neighbors' and the lady of the house was asked if she would take in some wounded. She inquired, 'Who have you there? I only take in the officers.'" (The other men were not neglected: Jennie's mother "stepped forward and said, 'Give me the privates.'")[12]

Work inside the army hospitals, where gentry and plain folk came together in an intense atmosphere, likewise highlighted class distinctions and sometimes stirred antagonisms. Rubbing elbows with one another daily and in the most intimate circumstances, the classes often rubbed each other the wrong way. The memoir of Phoebe Pember, well-bred daughter of a rich merchant, revealed her condescension toward, and frequent exasperation with, the women and men of the lower sort with whom she dealt as a chief matron at Chimborazo—beginning on page 1, where she remarked that, once hospital employment was open to white women, "a few, very few ladies, and a great many inefficient and uneducated women, hardly above the [un-skilled] laboring classes, applied for and filled the offices." When hiring female subordinates herself, she was drawn to "ladies of education and position" but generally chose from among "the common class of respectable servants," assuming that "they would be more amenable to authority." She described the first nurse she hired as "a cross-looking woman from North Carolina, painfully ugly, or rather what is termed hard-featured." The woman turned out to be unamenable to Pember's authority (and perhaps put off by her aristocratic demeanor): she acted "indignant," complained "loudly" about her duties, and (to Pember's relief) quit after one day on the job.[13]

Pember was devoted to the care of her patients, but they, too, could get on her nerves. The appearance, manners, and language of the yeomen and poor whites who predominated among the Rebel army's rank and file often offended her elite sensibilities. In the hospital she endured their uncouth-ness quietly (as she did that of the nurses), but in her memoir she vented her disgust. "The mass of patients were uneducated men," she wrote, "who had lived by the sweat of their brow." One of them she described as "an up-country Georgian, . . . lean, yellow, attenuated [sic], with wispy strands of hair hanging over his high, thin cheek-bones"; his fingernails "were like claws." When she urged him to let the staff cut his hair, he replied that "I can't git my hair cut, kase as how I promised my mammy that I would let it grow till the war be over. Oh, it's onlucky to cut it!" That was merely amusing; his explanation for refusing to let his nails be trimmed was revolting: "I aren't got any spoon, and I use them instead."[14]

Such men were not just crude and ignorant, Pember thought, but in some ways morally deficient. They struck her, for one thing, as ungrateful. Rarely did they offer a word or sign of appreciation for the good care they were receiving, leading her to conclude that "gratitude is an exotic plant, reared in a refined atmosphere, kept free from coarse contact and nourished by unselfishness. Common natures look only with surprise at great sacrifices and cunningly avail themselves of the benefits they bestow, but give nothing in return." Lower-class men also seemed callously insensitive to the suffering and death of others, even comrades. She recounted an instance when a very young soldier in one of her wards succumbed to a slow death. As she stood there, having just witnessed the boy's poignant last moments, she noticed a patient in a nearby bed insistently trying to get her attention. Assuming he was as moved as she by what had just occurred, she turned to him solicitously, only to find that all he wanted was something to eat. When she offered to have him moved away from the corpse, "he treated the suggestion with contempt," telling her, "Don't make no sort of difference to *me*; they dies all around *me* in the field — [it] don't trouble *me*."[15]

Skepticism about the virtue of the plain folk, or at least the lowlier portion of them, was in fact common among the upper classes. The issue of poor relief, ever more pressing as the war went on, especially provoked the doubters. In June 1864 the *Examiner* applauded the municipal relief committee's decision to rely on policemen to determine exactly who was worthy of assistance: "The police have a thorough acquaintance with the several localit[i]es where want is to be found; [they] know who are the deserving and who are the undeserving poor, and can make their awards accordingly. It has happened heretofore that swindling old hags, living in down town dens, by a sad tale of poverty and want, have drawn supplies, both from the city and the Young Men's Christian Association, and sold the same at speculator's rates." These parasites, the *Examiner* asserted in a later editorial, were "nearly all Irish and German."[16]

Also common among the upper classes was an assumption of entitlement to privilege. Claims to preferential treatment multiplied as Richmonders faced new challenges during the war. A South Carolina plantation mistress — who spent two months in 1864 at the bedside of her wounded son (an infantry officer) in a Richmond hospital — complained in a letter to a relative that "there is less chance for a gentleman in these Hospitals than you would think reasonable. The mass [of patients] are so animal & vulgar, & the rules & regulations are made for the mass." The *Examiner*, inveterate spokesman for the better sort, often expressed a similar attitude. In January 1864, noting "the present crowded condition of the jail," the editor decried the promiscuous mingling of the classes there and urged the municipal authorities to devise "some arrangement . . . that would obviate the necessity of thrusting in among thieves, murderers and vagabonds, gentlemen by instinct and education." Men of quality held in jail on yet unproved charges should be confined separately. "A human being would stand as much chance in a den of hyenas and hungry wolves, as does a respectable, well-dressed person among the utterly abandoned, God forsaken mob of crime and criminality concentrated in the jail. . . . Like the devils in hell, they rejoice when a victim, superior to themselves, falls into their pit."[17]

Some did not hesitate to request favors of a sort that few among the common folk would have dreamed of asking for. In late May 1862, with the Union army approaching Richmond and the Confederate government frantically impressing every civilian-owned draft animal and vehicle for military use, Alice Haxall, wife of one of the city's richest businessmen, sent a note to the secretary of war asking that her carriage be exempted. Her son was serving at the front, she explained, and if he should be wounded she must be able to go quickly to his aid. And besides that, she said, one of the city's leading clerics, the Reverend Charles Minnegerode of St. Paul's Episcopal Church, often borrowed the carriage to minister to hospitalized soldiers. In early 1863, a lady named Mary Forbes petitioned the secretary of war for help in recovering the body of her brother, a colonel killed the previous summer at Second Manassas and buried on the field. With that area now in enemy hands, she said, it would be necessary for a detail of Confederate troops to go there under flag of truce, "identify the body, take charge of it, & bring it to Richmond for interment," and she asked that the appropriate orders be given—even naming the eight soldiers who should be assigned to the task. Like Alice Haxall, Mary Forbes bolstered her case by name-dropping, noting that the deceased officer was a son-in-law of a prominent Southern politician.[18]

Even as they asserted claims to privilege, many upper-class Richmonders grappled with wartime economic difficulties that threatened their social status. While the very wealthy were largely immune from such worries, certain others, particularly merchants and clerks whose business was disrupted and refugees who had had to leave careers and property behind, experienced downward occupational mobility—as did, in a sense, the ladies forced to take office or hospital jobs and thus forgo the customs of social visiting and benevolent work. Even those who held on to their upper-class occupations sometimes struggled to maintain the lifestyle they were accustomed to at home. Cramped and seedy accommodations, skimpy meals, and little or no hired or enslaved help were the fate of some Richmonders of the better sort as the war went on.[19]

Especially troubling to some was the problem of clothing. A large wardrobe of fine, clean, fashionable apparel for every occasion was a hallmark of the upper classes, a signifier of status no less important than refined manners and a good education. But wartime scarcity and inflation, fueled especially by the ravenous military demand for cloth and leather, put appropriate clothing increasingly out of reach of many ladies and gentlemen. War Department clerk John Jones's diary chronicled the escalating cost of clothes as meticulously as it did that of other necessities. A new pair of gentleman's boots, Jones recorded, went for $30 in May 1862, $50 by November of that year, $100 in September 1863, and $200 in May 1864. A new dress shirt, $12 in late 1862, cost $30 a year later. By that time a "genteel suit of clothes" could not be had from a tailor for less than $700—almost half a year's salary for many government clerks, more than that for some. "None but the opulent," Jones lamented in January 1863, "can obtain a sufficiency of . . . raiment."[20]

Like many others of his station, Jones tried to keep up appearances but had to settle for less than he thought proper. Reluctantly he gave up buying new clothes and turned instead to the secondhand market, acquiring a pair of used shoes in January 1864, a good-quality but out-of-style coat three months later, and two undershirts late that year ($15 apiece, $35 less than new ones were then retailing for); his wife also made him an undershirt from one of her old petticoats. Jones and others also resorted to repeatedly patching and mending what they had—Congressman Warren Akin, for one, darned his own socks—although the rising cost of thread made even that expensive. Some people simply went without: War Department clerk Henri Garidel, who was himself struggling to remain suitably attired, observed in September 1863 that, with children's shoes now selling for $45 a pair, "you often see children in Richmond from the best families with beautiful clothes that have lasted for some time [but with] bare feet." Those who had to pay for laundering often made do with less: Congressman Akin confessed in a letter to his wife in 1864 that he was now wearing his shirts three or four days before sending them to the laundress, socks a week, and underwear two weeks.[21]

Such expedients could not, of course, wholly disguise the truth. "Many are becoming very shabby in appearance," Jones observed in the fall of 1863. He was one of them: "How shabby my clothes have become," he wrote eight months later. "The wonder is that we are not naked, after wearing the same garments three or four years." He endured the humiliation stoically (a patriotic sacrifice, he told himself), but others took it hard. Henri Garidel, depressed by homesickness and the state of the nation in 1865, remarked that the "pitiful" condition of his clothes "made my heart even heavier."[22]

Status anxiety undoubtedly made some upper-class Richmonders more sensitive to class distinctions and fussier about maintaining them. As the war continued, elite and middle-class people complained increasingly about common folk who enjoyed undeserved privileges, rudely challenged their betters, or otherwise violated expectations. Catherine Cochran expressed resentment that so many skilled laboring people were making good money and living relatively well while many government clerks were unable to feed and clothe their families decently and keep their homes heated in winter. The *Examiner* published a lengthy account of a mayor's court case involving a poverty-stricken working-class woman named Harriet Hovan, who had presumed to bring "a charge of annoyance and abuse" against "two respectable ladies (whose names we omit)." According to the newspaper, Hovan—"an ant[e]diluvian hag" (she was in fact only thirty-eight)—had illegally taken up residence in a building owned by the ladies and was obstinately resisting eviction. The article's derisive paraphrase of her testimony left readers in no doubt about her coarseness, unworthiness, and effrontery: "She was the same as a widow; she didn't live with her husband; he had been holding a position in the chain gang, and was now resting from his labours in Castle Thunder. These women . . . kept annoying and abusing her in every possible way, just to drive her out . . . but she wouldn't be driven. . . . [They] called her names which seriously damaged her character. She could prove her good character, she could. . . . It was not her fault that she was dependent on charity." Fortunately for the good order of society, the authorities were not fooled. A policeman "gave the ladies accused an excellent character for respectability and quietness, while his testimony as to their accuser was directly the opposite." The mayor then dismissed the case contemptuously, telling Hovan "to hush and go along to the Poor House, if she could do no better."[23]

Especially rankling to upper-class monitors of wartime social relations was the increasing visibility and assertiveness of prostitutes. In Richmond, as in other American cities, prostitution was more a class issue than a moral or criminal one. It had always been tolerated—in fact, prostitution per se was not even illegal in the city—but it was closely circumscribed. Sex workers, whether vulgar streetwalkers or elegant denizens of posh bordellos, were regarded by "respectable" Richmonders as degraded and were expected to stay out of public view, or at least to confine their activities to certain tacitly approved venues. When they transgressed boundaries, the authorities could and did use the law to rein them in, charging them with disorderly conduct, keeping a disorderly house, vagrancy, and such.[24]

Transgressions multiplied during the war, as did the number of prostitutes. In May 1862, the *Dispatch* complained that Cyprians were "disporting themselves extensively on the sidewalks and in hacks, open carriages, &c., in the streets" and inflicting their "impudence" on good citizens with "smirks and smiles, winks, and . . . remarks not of a choice kind, in a loud voice." Mayor Mayo, having by then made up his mind to suppress this growing evil, had already ordered the arrest for vagrancy of "one lewd character . . . for obtruding herself in an obnoxious attitude before decent people."[25]

That was but one early salvo in a continuing battle that the mayor and police never won. Four months later, a young woman "calling herself Emma Marsh" went before the mayor's court, charged with "being a person of evil name, fame, &c., and indulging in horseback exercise on one of the public streets of the city in company with a person said to be a Lieutenant in the army, to the disgust of decent people, and against the peace and dignity of the Commonwealth." The mayor, who had himself witnessed this outrage, gave Marsh a tongue-lashing, levied a $150 peace bond on her, and jailed her pending posting of the bond. Other prostitutes of the refined sort felt the mayor's wrath when they were caught promenading with Confederate officers in Capitol Square ("unblushing strumpets," he called them, enacting "shameless exhibitions"), occupying boxes in the dress circle of the theater ("They know full well that they have no right to introduce themselves into public places resorted to by virtuous women"), or taking rooms in reputable hotels and boardinghouses (a scandalous, intolerable "mingling of outcast society with respectable society").[26]

Meanwhile, sex workers of the vulgar sort were also flaunting themselves. Griffin's Island in the James River, crossed by a bridge connecting Richmond and Manchester, had by the summer of 1863 become notorious for "the depravity of its inhabitants," as the *Dispatch* put it. A collection of squalid doggeries and shacks there accommodated "lewd women and wicked men," the sight of whom could not be avoided by anyone using the bridge. "If such creatures must be tolerated," the editor urged, "let them find their abodes and places of amusement in such localities as not to offend the decent and virtuous; and if they will thrust themselves before the public, they ought to be punished."[27]

Upper-class concern about lower-class "misbehavior" spiked in the late spring and early summer of 1862, its main focus now being the potential for serious disorder among the most dangerous substratum of white society, the propertyless, miscreant "riffraff," especially the men. These sorts, in the view of Richmond's gentlefolk, had not only swelled in number since the war began, thanks to the influx of undesirables from Baltimore, New Orleans, and elsewhere, but had gotten increasingly out of hand, their ruffianism and criminality fueled by the proliferating saloons. The imposition of martial law and prohibition on 1 March 1862, and the subsequent crackdown on drinking, quieted the city and soothed upper-class anxiety. But by mid-May, the provost guard and municipal police were easing up, and proletarian drunkenness, unruliness, and lawlessness seemed to be again on the upswing. "The old order of rowdyism is returning," the *Enquirer*'s editor declared, "and every night has some free fight or noisy out-door bacchanal to record." The authorities must restrain the "lower orders of society": "Rowdyism should be put down and kept down."[28]

As a huge Union army advanced up the Peninsula and closed in on Richmond that spring, the gentry's fears mounted. The very real possibility that the Confederate government and army would have to abandon the city raised the specter of anarchy. On 12 May a prominent attorney named John H. Gilmer wrote to a city councilman to offer some advice. If the worst came to pass, he said, it "will be absolutely necessary to preserve order and keep down the lawless spirit of inovation [*sic*], which may reasonably be apprehended from the evil disposed elements of civil and social disorganization. . . . In the sad event of a lawless outbrake [*sic*], our people, and property, will be at the mercy of the mob, ever disposed on such occasions to destroy and pillage." It being doubtful that the small city police force and state Public Guard could subdue any substantial body of rioters, and uncertain whether the militia could or would be deployed, "how is this element to be checked?" Gilmer recommended that the council immediately raise and arm a municipal military force of reliable, able-bodied men that would stand ready "to preserve order, protect property and restrain the evil disposed." The council duly considered this proposal and at a specially called meeting on 28 May authorized the creation of a battalion of 500 men "for the purpose of keeping order in the City and guarding the public property, prisons, and bridges in the present emergency."[29]

One month later, Robert E. Lee's army launched the counteroffensive that drove the enemy back down the Peninsula and saved the capital. As the threat of evacuation and anarchy and mobs receded, the municipal battalion was disbanded. Less than a year after that, however, in early April 1863, Richmond did experience mob violence.

It came as a stunning surprise to the upper classes and the authorities, for it was not occasioned by any Confederate abandonment of the city; nor was it carried out by the "rabble," nor even primarily by men. The rioters were mostly "respectable" lower-class women, some of them from the prop-

White Society and Its Discontents

ertyless, unskilled ranks of society but a good many from the propertied artisan ranks. And the disturbance began as an organized demonstration against
high food prices and hunger—afflictions that the common people of Richmond had until then endured quietly, or at least not loudly enough to attract
the notice of the higher ranks.[30]

By that time, many of the plain folk not only were unable to feed themselves adequately but were convinced that the burden of privation was
grossly malapportioned. Most upper-class Richmonders seemed to be eating well enough, a few even sumptuously. It was true that some, especially
government clerks with families, were struggling to avert starvation. It was
also true that some of the humbler citizens, particularly draft-exempt skilled
workers, were subsisting quite comfortably. But on the whole it seemed to
the common people—and it was hard for anyone to deny, as a general proposition—that the lower one's social rank the louder one's stomach growled.
Further fueling their resentment was their certainty that the extreme scarcity
and astronomical price of food were artificial, engendered not by unavoidable shortages but solely by the unconscionable hoarding of greedy speculators and extortionists (unrestrained by government) and by the War Department's excessive stockpiling of rations.

In the latter days of March, a thirty-seven-year-old Second Market
huckster named Mary Jackson went around the market, other parts of the
city, and the suburbs drumming up interest in a mass meeting of women to
protest the food crisis. On the evening of 1 April, 300 or more gathered at a
Baptist church in the working-class neighborhood of Oregon Hill. Jackson
spoke from the pulpit, calling on those assembled to act the next day. They
should arm themselves, she said, and then march through the city's business
district ordering every provision merchant to sell to them at "government
prices," that is, at the same low rate that the War Department paid farmers for
impressed goods; if the demand was refused, the women should take what
they needed by force.

Early the following morning, a Thursday, a crowd of about the same
size assembled on Capitol Square. All were lower-class women or girls, save
for a few boys. Many wielded axes, hatchets, knives, or clubs; some, including Mary Jackson, carried pistols. Clerk Jones, who happened on the scene
and wondered what was going on, was told by a "young woman, seemingly
emaciated, . . . that they were going to find something to eat." Another witness heard Mary Jackson declare that "the women intended to have bread
or blood" and would "shoot down every man who attempted to frustrate
their plans."

Someone else in the crowd spoke up, urging that before confronting the merchants they seek an audience with Governor John Letcher. A number of women subsequently saw the governor at the Capitol and made known their grievances. He told them to go home. The protestors then exited the square and marched silently down Ninth Street. They were followed by a larger assemblage of onlookers, perhaps 1,000, including many men.

Reaching Cary Street, the women turned east. By now they had become a larcenous mob, seizing carts and wagons found along the way. Near the corner of Twelfth, some of them entered a large wholesale establishment and a government warehouse and carried off foodstuffs, including bacon and hams; others looted a shoe store. Continuing along Cary, the women robbed more shops and storage buildings, sometimes threatening the proprietors with their weapons. Some carried off their plunder in the vehicles they had commandeered.

Mayor Mayo was alerted and soon arrived on the scene. He formally read the Riot Act and ordered the women to cease and desist. They ignored him. The pillaging subsequently spread northward to Main and Franklin, some of it done by men (including men in uniform) who had originally tagged along just to watch. Governor Letcher and President Davis appeared and repeatedly tried to dissuade the rioters, with no more success than the mayor.

The police being helpless to stem this surge, the governor called out the Public Guard, which scattered the mob at bayonet point. The violence was suppressed by eleven o'clock, two hours after the women marched out of Capitol Square. Probably no more than two or three dozen establishments had been looted and only a few people had been injured, none fatally.

It was, as urban riots go, a minor incident. But coming as it did without warning, from a direction so unexpected, and in the very capital of the Confederacy, it unsettled the authorities profoundly. No sooner had the mob been swept from the streets than the secretary of war, fearful that news of the event would "embarrass our cause, and . . . encourage our enemies," dispatched a note to the telegraph company asking that "nothing relative to the unfortunate disturbance which occurred in the city to-day . . . be sent over the telegraph lines in any direction for any purpose" and a note to every Richmond newspaper asking that the press "avoid all reference directly or indirectly to the affair."[31]

That same day, the city council held an emergency meeting on the matter. The mayor and the governor attended by invitation. The councilmen quickly passed a series of resolutions. These instructed the mayor to arrest

White Society and Its Discontents

and bring to trial all the rioters and their abettors (only a few people had been arrested on the scene), authorized a reward of fifty dollars to any citizen who helped identify and convict the guilty, empowered the committee on police to enlarge the police force, and assured the citizenry "that every power possessed by the authorities will be exercised to the utmost limit to prevent any repetition of the riot."[32]

Fear of an imminent renewal of violence gripped municipal, state, and Confederate officials in the days that followed. On 3 April small groups of women gathered on street corners along Main decrying the food shortage, prompting army authorities to send in troops of the City Battalion to disperse them. The next day, as diarist Judith McGuire recorded, "a repetition was expected, and the cannon was in place to rake the streets, but [the women] thought discretion the better part of valour, and staid at home." Two days later the commander of the Richmond garrison force declined to send one of his units on a proposed expedition a short distance down the Peninsula, "owing to the continually threatened riots in Richmond." On 10 April, as a rumor circulated that another riot would erupt that night, the mayor called on the governor to ready a military force to suppress it; the governor in turn called on the army, which obligingly ordered two infantry battalions manning the fortifications to move immediately into the capital.[33]

During those tense days the authorities acted forcefully, not only to avert further rioting but to stifle any public expression of sympathy for the rioters. Isabella Ould, a blacksmith's wife, was arrested on the steps of city hall on 3 April for "using incendiary language"; she had been overheard moments earlier saying that the protestors had done nothing wrong, for seizing food was better than begging for it. She was immediately brought before the mayor, who declared that such remarks "incite . . . people to riot and lawlessness" and levied a $500 peace bond on her. The next day a physician was arrested simply for uttering the cryptic comment that there was "a power behind the throne greater than the throne."[34]

Meanwhile the police were rounding up people implicated in the outbreak. Despite the fifty-dollar enticement, few of the rioters or their abettors were brought to justice. All who could be identified and apprehended— forty-four women and twenty-nine men—went before the mayor's court, the first of them on 3 April and the last on 11 April. Some were charged not with rioting or looting but with ancillary crimes such as receiving property stolen by rioters. The mayor closely examined all seventy-three and the witnesses against them, freed a good many of the accused for insufficient evidence of guilt, and turned the rest over to the hustings court or circuit court on misdemeanor or felony charges. Some of these awaited trial in jail, and others made bail; a few who made bail disappeared from the city before trial.[35]

The two higher courts heard the cases that spring, exonerating many of the defendants but ultimately convicting at least sixteen: eleven women and two men for misdemeanors and one woman and two men for felonies. Some of those found guilty received stiff sentences. Forty-year-old Mary Duke, who had been seen among the mob on Franklin and Main Streets brandishing a pistol, was fined $100 and ordered to jail for six months. Cpl. William Lusk, a wounded Mississippi infantryman, age twenty-five, convalescing at Winder Hospital—but fit enough to have left the hospital, joined the rioters, broken into and pillaged two stores, and violently resisted arrest—was fined $100 and sentenced to a year in jail. Twenty-four-year-old Virgil Jones, a recently cashiered Public Guardsman who had forced his way into a wholesale establishment, threatened the proprietors, and carried off a large quantity of bacon, was condemned to three years in the penitentiary. Frail, sixty-five-year-old Mary Johnson (not to be confused with ringleader Mary Jackson) had mustered the strength on 2 April to threaten two store owners with a hatchet and make off with a sizable amount of their bacon; her age and infirmity notwithstanding, she was sentenced to the penitentiary for five years.[36]

The riot shook not just government and military leaders but all upper-class Richmonders: "A frightful spectacle," War Department clerk Jones called it, "and perhaps an ominous one." But privately Jones intimated that the rioters were not wholly to blame, for they had good reason to protest "the evil of scarcity," an evil that he agreed was conjured up by predatory speculators and incompetent or corrupt quartermasters. Another who harbored a modicum of sympathy was habeas corpus commissioner Sydney S. Baxter, who on his own initiative investigated the causes of the riot and reported confidentially to Jefferson Davis on 4 April: some of the rioters, Baxter concluded, were truly "suffering great privations."[37]

Jones and Baxter represented a small minority. Most upper-class Richmonders damned the rioters without qualification. The city councilmen declared in their 2 April meeting that between their own exertions and the benevolent societies' ministrations, the poor had always been sufficiently provided for, even amid wartime stringencies; thus the "riot was uncalled for and did not come from those who are really needy, but from base and unworthy women instigated by worthless men who are a disgrace to the City." These notions—that no one was really going hungry in Richmond and that the rioters were not respectable citizens but the vicious dregs of society—were voiced repeatedly by the better sort in the days that followed. The *Examiner* broke its silence on the riot on 4 April with an editorial touting the city's "large appropriations for the poor" and depicting the rioters as "a handful of prostitutes, professional thieves, Irish and Yankee hags, [and] gallows-birds from all lands but our own . . . with a woman huckster at their head," all undoubtedly stirred up by "emissaries of the Federal Government." A congressman characterized them as a "a mingled crowd of bad men and women" engaged not in a protest against hunger but in a mere "plundering expedition"—as evidenced by the fact that they stole not just food "but shoes, boots, hats, brooms, dry goods, [and] milliners' trimmings." He, too, thought "the whole affair was gotten up by some few bad men who from unpatriotic motives wanted to . . . encourage our enemies." Commissioner Baxter asserted, even as he acknowledged the suffering of some, that most of the rioters were motivated only by "the desire to plunder."[38]

No sooner had the city council proclaimed the riot unjustified, however, than it set about reforming poor relief. Whether this was prompted by some muted, guilty suspicion that the city's efforts thus far had in fact been inadequate or was intended simply to refine what was considered a substantially satisfactory system is uncertain. Whatever the case, at their very next meeting, on 4 April, the councilmen created an ad hoc committee to devise "some plan for the relief of the meritorious poor of the City"—with the proviso that the plan "exclud[e] from such relief all who render themselves unworthy of it by riotous and disorderly conduct." Five days later, at a special meeting requested by the mayor and attended by him, the council appropriated $20,000 to assist indigent wives and children of soldiers in the field. On 13 April it passed an ordinance (the work of the ad hoc committee) establishing a city-operated market stall where the worthy poor could pick up a weekly dole of food. More legislation later in the war improved the system of relief and expanded the number of Richmonders entitled to it.[39]

While with one hand the authorities appeased the needy, with the other they continued to guard against further eruptions of mass violence. In mid-May the council instructed its committee on police to come up with "some more effectual plan for the defence of the City, so as to suppress riots, mobs, and insurrections." By early July, a force of volunteers had been created to act as a police auxiliary. It comprised two companies of 100 men each, all draft-exempt or detailed. For at least the next six months, squads of these volunteers patrolled the city nightly, keeping an eye out for burglars, garroters, and black curfew violators but mainly making a show of force to deter potential rioters.[40]

Richmond's next lower-class protest was, however, peaceful — although vehement enough to command the attention and rattle the nerves of the upper classes. On the evening of 19 September 1863, in response to a well-publicized call to action, a large assemblage of workingmen convened in a room of city hall to air their grievances. First among these, as the *Examiner* reported, was "the spirit of extortion and speculation now so rife in the community." The attendees appointed a committee of five to compose a resolution expressing the sense of the meeting. Promptly written and adopted, it condemned the "exorbitant and unprecedented prices of the necessaries of life . . . brought about partly by the mismanagement of legislation — Confederate and State — and the great and unprecedented range which speculation has taken by a combination of capital against labor." It furthermore called on the state legislature to "relieve us from the iron grasp of the e[x]tortioner and the *money changer*" by outlawing "speculation in the prime necessaries of life." At two subsequent meetings, on 3 October and 10 October, the workers reiterated their complaints and demands. A railroad mechanic named Theophilous Reaves ardently addressed the crowd, declaring that "the doctor and lawyer and professional man were all [doing] well enough"; now "the time had come for the labouring man to assert his rights." More resolutions were passed. One deplored the "abject posture to which . . . we who labor have been reduced" by being robbed of the means of self-sustenance and manly independence. Another reminded the authorities that "it is the duty of the Government to take care of the unfortunate, not the rich."[41]

Respectfully worded but seething with class resentment, the workers' remonstrances frightened the already jittery upper classes. Diarizing about the 19 September meeting, John Jones worried that its true purpose might have been "subverting the government." On the eve of the 10 October meeting, he recorded a rumor that the workingmen "have ulterior objects in view; and as some ten or twelve hundred of them belong to the militia, and have muskets in their possession, mischief may grow out of it." Mayor Mayo was concerned enough to accede to the workers' request, at their 3 October meeting, to come before them and speak; he went on for half an hour, assuring them (as the *Dispatch* reported) of his "heartfelt sympathy with the objects of the meeting, and promis[ing] all the aid in his power to further their plans." The workers' militancy stoked the better sorts' fears of broader lower-class unrest and a repetition of the events of 2 April. Jones, convinced that the hunger crisis had not been resolved by the city council's poor-relief reforms immediately following the riot, warned President Davis on 30 Sep-

White Society and Its Discontents

tember that unless some "speedy remedy" was contrived there would surely be "an explosion of some sort among the non-producing classes" of the city. Five weeks later he was still anticipating a resurgence of rioting at any moment: "People will not perish for food in the midst of plenty."[42]

The tangible results of the workingmen's protests were minimal. The city council was spurred to enact, in mid-October, further poor-relief measures; these failed to satisfy the workers, however, for they wanted not charity (except for the helpless) but their accustomed economic independence, which they insisted could be restored only by stifling inflation. Their key specific demand—a state law capping the prices of all commodities sold in Richmond—was rejected by the legislature after heavy lobbying against it by the city's businessmen, supported by almost all the newspapers.[43]

A flurry of rumors in January 1864 further unsettled the upper classes and the authorities. No overt demonstration of lower-class discontent triggered this alarm. The rumors were perhaps baseless, but they were nonetheless disturbing. Clerk Jones heard from a Subsistence Bureau officer on the fourteenth that army food depots and those in charge of them were in danger: "It is believed there will be a riot . . . [and] Col. Northrop, the Commissary-General, may be immolated by the mob." The next day Jones sensed "a feverish anxiety in the city on the question of subsistence, and . . . fear of an outbreak." On the twenty-sixth he wrote that "an outbreak of the prisoners [of war on Belle Isle] is apprehended," for they had now gone eleven days without meat, "and if they were to rise, it is feared some of the inhabitants of the city would join them, for they, too, have no meat—many of them—or bread either. They believe the famine is owing to the imbecility, or worse, of the government. A riot would be a dangerous occurrence, now: the city battalion would not fire on the people—and if they did, the army might break up, and avenge their slaughtered kindred. It is a perilous time."[44]

Aggravating the anxiety was a bill then moving through Congress, and almost certain to pass, that would extend the draft age limits and restrict exemptions. This threatened to take away many of the auxiliary policemen who had been patrolling the city since July. Councilman N. B. Hill, chairman of the committee on police, pleaded with the secretary of war in late January to delay conscripting these men as long as possible after the bill passed and, once they were enrolled, to detail them or other new draftees to the Richmond police force; otherwise, said Hill, "our City will be unprotected." Anticipating the worst, however, the municipal authorities had already set about forming another auxiliary, or at least trying to. On 11 January the council empowered the mayor "to raise one or more volunteer companies of mounted police for the protection of the City." Three days later Mayo wrote Jefferson Davis to explain. This force, he said, which would number about 200 men, was desperately needed, for the day police and night watch were egregiously undermanned. It would patrol not only the city but also the suburbs and could assist the army in the event of a Yankee raid "or any other emergency." Moreover, it would not drain army resources: the volunteers would all be draft-exempt and would furnish their own horses, equipage, and forage, the majority of them being "men of property."[45]

Class tensions disturbed Richmond for the remainder of the war, waxing and waning to some extent as food shortages intensified or eased but never disappearing. "Writings upon the walls of the houses at the corners of the streets were observed this morning," J. B. Jones wrote in late February 1864, "indicating a riot, if there be no amelioration of the famine." On 2 April — the anniversary of the bread riot — the president of the Virginia Central Railroad warned the secretary of war of the danger posed by "the existing and increasing destitution among thousands [in the city]. I do not speak extravagantly when I say we are 'treading on a volcano' which may burst out ere long in a fearful uprising of the people." In late May, Jones noted that "an armed guard is now a fixture before the President's house." The guard's purpose was confirmed that summer by a Richmonder who fled to the Union army lines and told an interrogator that there was "much dissatisfaction in the city. Women congregate before Jeff. Davis' house and the mayor's office, demanding meal, and . . . great suffering exists."[46]

The early days of spring 1865 saw yet another surge of anxiety about mob violence, as a rumor circulated that the Confederate government and army would soon abandon the capital. On 9 March the state legislature gave the city permission to form "an armed volunteer police force." (By now, apparently, the two companies of auxiliary foot police organized in 1863 had been disbanded and the mounted auxiliary authorized in January 1864 had either been disbanded or had never been organized, thus leaving the day police and night watch as the only municipal police units.) The city council asked the mayor to recruit at least 200 volunteers — all to be over the conscription age limit of fifty but under sixty — and to petition the Confederate or state government for arms. Enrollment began on 17 March. The *Examiner* reported that "some of our most respectable citizens came forward and gave *impetus* to the movement by putting down their names." This force, the newspaper explained, would "act in conjunction with [the regular police] in preserving the peace and property of the city."[47]

While hunger was the primary irritant rankling the lower classes in wartime Richmond, it was not the only one. Conscription also stirred resentment, as it did everywhere else in the Confederacy. As with the food shortage, it was not just the hardships imposed by conscription that provoked the plain folk but their belief that those hardships were shared unequally across class lines. The law sanctioning substitutes benefited only the well-off. Exemptions were granted mostly to the well educated. Many elite and middle-class men in military service were detailed as bureaucrats or assigned to quartermaster or commissary duty or such, keeping them safely behind the lines. Meanwhile, virtually all draft-eligible unskilled and semiskilled workers, and all but the lucky few artisans detailed to war production jobs, went into the ranks and faced enemy bullets. Over time the government eliminated some of the most glaring inequities in the draft laws (substitution, for example, was abolished at the end of 1863), and there was no denying that a great many upper-class men served at the front and faced those same bullets. Still, the common people sensed that they were doing more than their fair share of fighting and dying.[48]

"The curses of the poor man will ever rest upon you." Thus began an impassioned letter to the secretary of war dated 19 March 1864, sent from Richmond, written in pencil in an inelegant hand, and signed simply "A true soldier." The writer may have been a longtime Richmond resident, for he revealed considerable familiarity with the city. In any event, he was posted there now, perhaps as a member of the garrison force or a hospital convalescent, but he had enlisted in 1861 and for much of the time since had been at the front. A man of the working classes (although more articulate than most), he could no longer contain his rage over the wrongs he perceived:

> The rich man — the gentleman — you give exemptions, but the poor
> man you have dragged from his starving wife and children like cattle
> to a slaughter pen. . . . I am poor — my family are suffering, and yet
> see the numbers of men *lounging on the streets of Richmond* protected
> by exemption papers given by *you*. How is it, Sir, that so many men
> keep out of the army when you can travel the whole country and
> not find one poor man at home. None but the rich can stay at home.
> Show me a banker or broker that is in the war — or a merchant. Their
> gold has bought their exemption. Even the Ambulance Committee
> are exempted. And for what. Because they are rich. Why shouldn't
> they be in the army. Why should poor men be made to do the fighting
> when rich men are the men who have property at stake. Mr. Secretary
> Seddon, I am a soldier — I intend to be one until we are free but I

say I am tired of the injustice of your government. I ask you now if you can expect me to fight the Yankees in the next battle with the true enthusiasm of the soldier when I see my family and little ones suffering[,] when the rich man is in his luxury at home, and has never shouldered his musket or shared an hour's [danger?] ever in this war[,] . . . [and] when we see that the *poor* man is [illegible] made food for gunpowder. . . . Let those who have been at home — many of them doing nothing but making money — come out and help to do the fighting. The poor man has borne the burden long enough.[49]

The letter was consigned to the War Department's files without comment by Seddon or anyone else. But the rage and disaffection it voiced were by no means confined to that anonymous soldier. They were felt by many Richmonders of humble status, and they could not be ignored by those in authority.

Whether the Rebel capital was moving toward a violent rupture between the classes or was forestalling such a rupture indefinitely through the combination of increasingly generous poor relief and increasingly repressive policing is a moot question. The Confederate government and army began withdrawing from the city on the evening of 2 April 1865 — the second anniversary of the bread riot. The precautions taken by the municipal government in anticipation of this calamity proved useless. The police, regular and auxiliary, were nowhere to be seen that night as mobs ransacked the business district.

LONGING, SUFFERING, AND DEATH

The Confederate capital was not only a bustling center of government, war, and industry but a mournful sphere of longing, suffering, and death. These were omnipresent in the city, inescapable and profoundly important aspects of the wartime experience. With the enormous influx of strangers, the proliferation of army hospitals, and the ceaseless killing and maiming on the battlefields, Richmond was transformed into a gigantic theater of tragedy, the embodiment of the Rebel nation's sorrow and pain.

Many newcomers, military and civilian, white and black, had left loved ones behind, and their sojourn in the capital was often saddened by their estrangement. Henri Garidel, a refugee from New Orleans, filled his diary with poignant expressions of yearning for his wife, Elodie ("Lolo," he called her), and their young children. Every morning on arising, and every night on retiring, he kissed the photograph of the children that he kept by his bed. He regretted having no picture of Elodie: "How I would kiss it with all my heart. . . . Dear Lolo. I love her so much. Now I know it more than ever. My heart is too heavy." Seeing other families together only burdened his heart more. "I can't bear to go out in the street," he wrote as the first anniversary of his departure from home approached. "When I see a man with his wife or his children, it makes me unbearably sad."[1]

Many of the homesick reunited with loved ones in the land of Nod. Rebel Richmond was a city of nostalgic dreams. "Dearest, last night I dreamed of meeting you at home," wrote Pvt. Harvey Luttrell, a disabled Alabama infantryman detailed to Howard's Grove Hospital, in a letter to his wife. "And after a sweet embrace I hurried to the [children's] bed with you, to see our four cherubs, who were all sleeping not knowing that I was present. The emotions of gladness were so great as to awaken me almost immediately." Congressman Warren Akin confided to his wife in Georgia that "I had a delicious dream about you last night. I dreamed I was at home and you had your arms around me. When I waked up how sorry I was it was a dream." Eight days later he wistfully described another intimate rendezvous: "I was lying down and you were lying at my back hugging me. O how good and pleasant it was; but it was only a dream." Henri Garidel's repose was often interrupted: "I wake up all the time, dreaming about my dear family." These nighttime encounters might bring pleasure or pain in the light of day. Luttrell was certain that his dream presaged a joyful reunion in the flesh: "Oh Surely, our meeting will be a happy one." Akin's dreams only fueled his longing: "O, my darling, what would I not give to be with you this evening!" he wrote after recounting his second one. "And how I do want to see the children. . . . One hour with you all would be worth a great deal to me." Garidel's were agonizing: "I dreamed all night that I was talking to my dear Lolo," he recorded one morning. "It is going to kill me today to think about that."[2]

Some of those yearning for home and family fell into deep depression — melancholia, it was called. One of these, it appears, was Pvt. James D. Ragan of the Fifty-First Georgia Infantry. In 1862 he wrote to Jefferson Davis in a penciled scrawl from his bed at Chimborazo, imploring the president to let him go home. He had been hospitalized for the last three months, originally for intermittent fever but now for severe hemorrhoids — "the Bludey Piles," he termed them. His wife, whom he had not seen since he enlisted seven months earlier, had recently given birth and "is very low[.] She has the fever, and my Sister Rote me to come home if I wanted to see her." But his surgeon "says he cant Recomend a Furlow for the Piles." Ragan insisted that he was no shirker but a good soldier: "I have allways tride to do my Deuty — I have never bin onder arest for nothing." All he asked now was "a Furlow for a few Days." Surely the president could sympathize with his plight: "Just supose you wer plast [i.e., placed] as I am[.] how wood you feal if you were denied perhaps the last chanse on Erth to ever see your Wife." Ragan got no closer to home than Danville, Virginia, however. Very soon after writing this letter he was transferred to a hospital in that city. The surgeons there apparently sensed that this soldier's maladies were not just physical. Within days he was sent back to Richmond, not to Chimborazo but to General Hospital

No. 13, a former tobacco factory on Twentieth Street. This facility had a dual role: caring for Castle Thunder prisoners who fell ill and serving as what was perhaps the only Confederate psychiatric institution. Also called the Lunatic Hospital, it treated government wards suffering from mental disorders, a great many of whom undoubtedly were melancholic. Assuming that that was Private Ragan's affliction, his stay at No. 13 may have proved beneficial, for he was discharged about a month after admission (his piles having apparently subsided too) and rejoined his regiment at the front. His plaintive letter to the commander in chief had, in the meantime, been filed away unanswered.[3]

Henri Garidel also struggled with nostalgia-induced depression, but he found little relief. By October 1863, five months after saying goodbye to Lolo and the children, he was not just sad but despondent: "I am close to going crazy.... My thoughts are too black." He tried numbing his mind with brandy and comforting his heart with prayer, but neither seemed to help. The following April he was "still very depressed. It is my normal state [now]. I am sure that it will pass when I see my loved ones again." But that longed-for reunion was far off; the immediate future appeared to him "in a very black light." His emotional anguish took a physical toll. Donning a pair of trousers he had not worn for some time, he "was frightened to see how much weight I have lost. My pants were much too big for me.... You can actually see me withering away, and I get paler every day. My dear wife and my dear children are never out of my mind's eye." He even fantasized about suicide. Eventually, however, his deep Catholic faith asserted itself, bringing a measure of solace. Immersing himself in his job at the War Department helped a bit too. But he remained "in the grips of a deep melancholia," and in February 1865 professed that he lacked "the courage to bear all this."[4]

Melancholia could in fact not just torment but destroy its victims. Chief matron Phoebe Pember witnessed a number of such cases at Chimborazo and wrote of them feelingly, indeed angrily, in her memoir. "That *maladie du pays* called commonly nostalgia, the home-sickness which wrings the heart and impoverishes the blood, killed many a brave soldier." She recalled "stand[ing] helpless and powerless by the bed of the sufferer, knowing that a week's furlough would make his heart sing for joy, and save his wife from widowhood." But the Medical Bureau was stingy with furloughs — unconscionably so, she thought, in these instances of severe depression provoked by pining for home. Nor did General Hospital No. 13 take in every soldier thus afflicted. (And even had it done so, whatever it provided was a poor substitute for the ministrations of a loving wife, mother, or sister.) Thus, all Pember could do was care for the stricken men as attentively and tenderly as possible. It was never enough: "However carefully the appetite might be pampered, or stimulants prepared and given, the food never nourished, the drink never strengthened.... I have watched a victim, helpless, hopeless and motionless, simply receive into his mouth daily a few spoonfuls of nourishment, making no other movement." The outcome was always the same: "The decay would be gradual, but death was inevitable."[5]

Confederate Richmond writhed with physical as well as emotional pain. The hundreds of thousands of sick and wounded soldiers received there over the course of the war made the city a locus of bodily suffering on a scale never before known in America. Tens of thousands of other Richmond folk witnessed these epic scenes of misery. This suffering, and the beholding and contemplation of it, pervaded the capital and marked it distinctively.

It did not take long for the sufferers to start arriving. Mary Chesnut, returning to the city on 12 July 1861 from a visit to northern Virginia, had a disturbing "glimpse of war" as she stepped off the train: some 200 uniformed men with "pale, ghastly faces" lying on the platform awaiting transportation to a hospital. She and other Richmonders had prepared themselves for battle casualties, but no serious engagement had yet been fought near the capital; these were "sick soldiers—not wounded.... So here is one of the horrors of war we had not reckoned on." It was, she thought, "the saddest sight. The memory of it is hard to shake off."[6]

These sufferers had been sent from Manassas Junction or the Shenandoah Valley, where Confederate field forces were gathering. But by this time, Richmond was already struggling to care for the many sick soldiers belonging to units bivouacked in and around the city. Measles was especially prevalent, along with fevers and diarrhea. The Medical Bureau was in its infancy; surgeons were scarce, and some of those on hand were themselves ailing. Citizens came forward to help nurse the sick, in some cases taking them into their own homes.[7]

The battle at Manassas on 21 July generated the first of many waves of wounded men that would inundate the capital through the war. The already strained resources of the Medical Bureau were overwhelmed. The day after the battle, at a meeting of citizens at city hall chaired by the mayor, an aid committee was established and steps taken to send agents to the battlefield to help evacuate the wounded to Richmond and to locate facilities in the city—private homes, especially—where they could be cared for. The casualties began arriving by rail on 23 July. Committee members met them at the Virginia Central depot and oversaw their dispersal to the various places made available. These efforts were impeded, however, by the swarms of other citizens who showed up wanting to help or just to gawk at the spectacle. "If all who have no business there would stay away," the *Dispatch* remarked, "it would be a great deal better."[8]

As summer gave way to fall, the wounded who recovered were sent back to their units or, if permanently disabled, sent home, but Richmond remained crowded with the sick. Measles continued its ravages. Typhoid appeared, too, along with a host of other camp diseases. On 23 August, Mary Chesnut visited several hospitals with her friend Mary Randolph, head of the Ladies' Aid Society. The experience left Chesnut badly shaken. "Oh, such a day! . . . I can never again shut out of view the sights I saw of human misery." General Hospital No. 3, a onetime tobacco factory on Ninth Street, "was the worst. Long rows of ill men on cots. Ill of typhoid fever, of every human ailment . . . wounds being dressed—all horrors, to be taken in at one glance." General Hospital No. 8, formerly the Saint Charles Hotel on Main Street, was hardly better: "Horrors upon horrors. . . . Awful smells, awful sights." There Chesnut fainted and had to be carried back to her carriage.[9]

Over time the Confederate field forces in Virginia improved their ability to evacuate the sick and wounded to Richmond. They were greatly aided by an efficient, well-equipped association of Richmond citizens evolved from the hastily organized committee of July 1861 and eventually known as the Ambulance Corps. Meanwhile, the Confederate, state, and private hospitals established in the capital were expanding and improving their ability to care for patients, with the help of benevolent organizations. But neither the army nor the civilian volunteers nor the hospitals were prepared for the bloodbath of the late spring and early summer of 1862.[10]

The Battle of Seven Pines (31 May–1 June) was fought just five miles east of Richmond. Soon after the opening volleys of cannon fire were heard in the city, there began what one witness described as "the ghastly procession of wounded brought in from the field." They numbered in the thousands. Army ambulances being too few, many arrived in civilian vehicles impressed by the government or driven by owners responding to the government's appeal for help. Richmonders witnessed scenes they could theretofore hardly have imagined. "Here a van with four or five desperately wounded stretched on its floor," Thomas De Leon wrote, "now a buggy with a faint and bandaged form resting on the driver." No less shocking than the gruesome caravans was the sight of bleeding men coming in on their own for want of transportation. Constance Cary saw many "so black with gunpowder as to be unrecognizable . . . limping in on foot."[11]

Frantically the Medical Bureau and civilian volunteers scrambled to secure shelter and treatment for the sufferers. Warehouses, stores, and homes opened to receive them as the hospitals quickly filled. The government called on citizens to serve as nurses and to donate bandages, food, ice, and all manner of other supplies. The "ghastly procession" on the streets was succeeded by ghastly sights inside the hospitals and makeshift infirmaries. Constance Cary, searching for a kinsman reportedly wounded, "tramped down Main Street [on 1 June] . . . from one scene of horror to another." At the former Saint Charles Hotel, she saw "men in every stage of mutilation, lying waiting for the surgeons upon bare [floor]boards," some with "bandaged faces stiff with blood and thick with flies." Thomas De Leon was likewise appalled by the scenes inside the hospitals: patients "distorted with agony," doctors "bare-armed and bloody." He and many other Richmonders would have earnestly seconded Constance Cary's avowal: "The impression of that day was ineffaceable."[12]

Many of the wounded were still being cared for when the Seven Days' Battles (25 June–1 July) erupted, these, too, fought very near the city. Richmonders who thought they had seen the worst of war's horrors now witnessed a bloodletting roughly three times the magnitude of Seven Pines. All the awful scenes spawned by that battle were reenacted on a more monstrous scale. "The carnage is frightful," diarist Judith McGuire recorded on the night of 27 June. "The citizens — gentlemen as well as ladies — have been fully occupied in the hospitals. Kent, Paine & Co. have thrown open their spacious [mercantile] building for the use of the wounded." Memoirist Sallie Brock Putnam recalled how the summer heat aggravated the misery of the wounded and fostered not only erysipelas and gangrene among them but also other diseases among men still in the ranks, prostrating many whom Yankee bullets and shells had missed: "Our hospitals were loathsome with the bloated, disfigured countenances of the victims. . . . Sickening odors filled the atmosphere. . . . The month of July of 1862 can never be forgotten in Richmond. We lived in one immense hospital."[13]

Every subsequent major battle in the eastern theater likewise inundated the capital with maimed, festering, groaning human wreckage and engraved horrific memories on Richmonders' consciousness. There was no getting used to such sights and sounds and smells, no matter how common they became.

These periodic deluges swamped the Medical Bureau and the Ambulance Corps. After mid-1862, however, both generally coped well during the intervals between battles, when the steady stream of sick soldiers and the occasional influx of modest numbers of those wounded in lesser engagements were all that had to be dealt with. From August 1862 on, with one brief exception (June 1864), the Army of Northern Virginia operated at a considerable distance from the capital, and the sick and wounded were brought to the city by rail, escorted from the field hospitals and tended in transit by Ambulance Corps members and by doctors and ministers who volunteered to help. Some were transported in specially fitted-out ambulance cars. They were met at the Richmond depots by other corps members and Medical Bureau personnel, advance notice of their arrival having been telegraphed. The bureau maintained a fleet of horse-drawn ambulances in the city, supplemented by others owned by the corps; these conveyed the suffering soldiers as speedily and comfortably as possible from the trains to the Receiving Hospital (formerly Seabrook's Warehouse) at the corner of Grace and Seventeenth. There the patients were registered, treated, bathed, and then dispatched to other hospitals or hospital divisions according to their state of residence.[14]

This efficient system invariably broke down under the strain of big battles. In the wake of Fredericksburg (13 December 1862), the southward shipment of the wounded on the Richmond, Fredericksburg, and Potomac Railroad was delayed in some cases up to six hours by the northward shipment of army supplies. Longer delays occurred at the line's Richmond depot (on Broad at Eighth) due to the limited number of ambulances, despite the government's hurried impressment of hotel omnibuses and citizens' wagons as substitutes. Some of the sufferers were forced to lie overnight in the cars near the depot awaiting transportation to the Receiving Hospital; this in turn delayed the return of the cars to the battlefield to fetch more. The railroad's president, convinced that the War Department had fallen down on the job, informed the secretary of war indignantly on 18 December of "the protracted suffering" of "our brave soldiers . . . kept [in the cars] without light, fire, food or medical or surgical care 12 hours or more . . . in the streets of the Capital of the Confederacy!" They endured further delays at the Receiving Hospital, where overworked surgeons, nurses, and clerks fell behind in registering and treating them, and more still when they finally got to their assigned hospitals and found the staffs there likewise overwhelmed.[15]

Most horrific of all was the Overland Campaign (early May–late June 1864), eight weeks of slaughter that began near Fredericksburg and ended at Petersburg, embracing four battles and innumerable smaller actions and compiling a butcher's bill far exceeding that of any other campaign of the war. By 20 May, nearly 5,000 wounded Confederates had passed through the Receiving Hospital; many thousands more would follow. In June, for the first time since the Seven Days' Battles, the combat came so close to Richmond that the casualties were brought in by horse-drawn ambulances. Day after day, Constance Cary saw them "disgorging their ghastly contents, some of the wounded uttering pitiful prayers to be left to die in peace, some mercifully in [a] stupor." The hospital attendants enrolled in the Local Defense Forces were summoned to duty in the trenches, obliging the Medical Bureau to call for female volunteers to assist the surgeons and nurses. Many citizens did show up at the hospitals, but some came just to gawk; the *Examiner* warned that while those willing to help were welcome, "idle visitors" at this critical time were a nuisance and would not be tolerated.[16]

Even Phoebe Pember was stunned by the carnage of the Overland Campaign. She recounted walking home at night from Chimborazo past a railroad depot and seeing men lying all around, "some on stretchers, others on the bare bricks, or laid on a thin blanket, suffering from wounds hastily wrapped around with strips of coarse, unbleached, galling bandages of homespun cotton, on which the blood had congealed and stiffened until every crease cut like a knife." By 22 June more than 600 patients were crammed into her division of the hospital; she had had to relegate most of the convalescents to sleeping on the floor in order to free up beds for the incoming wounded.[17]

These frantic periods in the wake of battle aside, patients were generally very well tended. They were comfortably lodged, too, for the most part, especially those assigned to the airy, spacious, single-story wards of the encampment hospitals. But no matter how clean, uncrowded, efficient, and well designed the hospital, certain discomforts were unavoidable. Even the best-ventilated ward could not dispel Richmond's fierce summer heat. Lice were hard to keep at bay, flies impossible. Bedsores plagued many nonambulatory patients. A visitor described those of a soldier bedridden for weeks: "They realize the worst accounts I ever heard of such things — back bone [visible] quite through. It is frightful to see."[18]

Pain was of course omnipresent in the hospitals, in quiet times and hectic times alike, despite the liberal administration of opiates. And there was little or nothing the doctors and nurses could do to palliate most miseries of other sorts, such as those accompanying dysentery, measles, and pneumonia. Nor could they do much to really heal their patients besides clean and bandage wounds, set broken bones, amputate shattered limbs, provide nutritious meals, and ensure plenty of bedrest. Mostly they relied on the ailing body to heal itself.

That could be an excruciatingly slow process. Many soldiers endured lengthy, agonizing stays in the hospital. W. B. Martin, a patient at Chimbo-

Longing, Suffering, and Death

razo, recounted his travails in a letter of December 1862: "I have met with this Misfortune to get the rim of my Belly Brok[e] or as I [know] no other name By which to call it I am rupturd and am in agrate pane nearly all of the time and hav Bin in the horsepittle over 2 Months." Nineteen-year-old private William Moore, a North Carolinian, felt a bullet smash into his right ankle on 26 June 1862, during the Seven Days' Battles. Admitted the next day to General Hospital No. 24 on Main Street, he was still there five months later, for the wound would not heal properly.[19]

Few endured torments exceeding those of W. Mason Smith, a young infantry lieutenant wounded on 3 June 1864 near Richmond. He was taken to Stuart Hospital, where his case baffled the medical staff. A bullet had penetrated his abdominal wall, not severing any organ but burying itself so deep that the surgeons, despite repeated probing, could not find it. They surmised that it had lodged against a nerve, for it generated horrific pain and paralyzed Smith's legs, but they could not extract it. To these afflictions were added pneumonia and fever. As the weeks passed, hopes for Smith's recovery alternately rose and fell; he would seem to be on the mend one day only to relapse the next. Never was he free of pain, despite frequent doses of opiates and brandy. His widowed mother, Eliza, rushed to Richmond from her home in South Carolina immediately on learning of his injury and thereafter sat beside him every day, doing what she could to ease his misery and chronicling his tribulations in letters to relatives. On 10 July she described him as "motionless & very weak." On 19–20 July he had "a bad night, a restless day, & such cold sweats as threaten to melt him altogether." On 23 July she wrote of his "intense pain in the groin & leg on the slightest movement of the body or limbs." The next day, "his fever continues, also his motionlessness; one leg from Rheumatism stiff & swollen, the other shriveled." On 29 July: "He is completely paralyzed still & his bed sores are frightful." On 30 July: "I was talking yesterday & he begged me to stop, saying 'Mamma it hurts me to think.'" On 1 August: "[He] is suffering dreadfully with pain in the groin. . . . It will be 2 months on Wednesday since his wound, & he has never moved below his waist voluntarily." On 7 or 8 August: "He wakes up constantly giving signs of uncontrollable pain. . . . [He said] it was better to be shot through the heart & be spared the suffering." On 12 August: "Motion is torture. He is drugged with Morphine all the time yet feels the pain; wakes up screaming."[20]

Smith was succored throughout his ordeal not only by his mother and the hospital staff but by his faith. "Mason's mind is tranquil," Eliza wrote. "He is very grateful to God for his mercies & finds comfort in two or three hymns being repeated to him every now and then." Many other sufferers also found a measure of relief in communion with God. One was twenty-seven-year-old David Core. A teacher by profession and a musician in the Second Florida Infantry band, he fell ill with "Typhoid Pneumonia" on 12 September 1862, when the regiment was in the Shenandoah Valley. Shuttled from one hospital to another for weeks, he ended up in Richmond, where on 22 October he was admitted to General Hospital No. 11 on Nineteenth Street. For the next month he was too sick even to write his wife, finally mustering the strength to do so on 20 November. (She would read this letter joyously, despite its unpleasant news, for she had earlier received a report that he had died in Winchester.) He had experienced terrible trials and was still very ill, he told her, yet he felt that through it all he had been safeguarded "by the protecting arm of the almighty." The promise of an eternity in heaven, "where sorrow and affliction and parting is not known," made his present woes seem but "light afflictions . . . [lasting only] for a moment." Core's faith would continue to sustain him in the following weeks; not until 30 December was he well enough to return to duty.[21]

Especially fortunate were the patients who, like Mason Smith, had kinfolk or friends on hand to help nurse them. Every day passenger trains brought in anxious loved ones of soldiers hospitalized in Richmond, their numbers swelling in the wake of battles. They came from far and near, many at great expense and sacrifice. Lucy Randolph, a fifty-two-year-old mother of six children, traveled over 120 miles from Clarke County, in the Shenandoah Valley, to tend her sick son. She wrote movingly of how she "felt the privilege of being with him, & consequently sympathized more sincerely with those deprived of such faithful attentions" as only a family member could offer. She and others like her could "minister to their [loved ones'] ease & comfort, read to them from the holy pages of God's word, [and] speak words of entreaty, comfort & encouragement."[22]

The emotional and spiritual nurture that relatives and friends provided undoubtedly benefited patients, as did the bodily ministrations such as fanning them in the summer heat and shooing away the ever-present flies. Recognizing this, hospitals generally welcomed such caregivers. But not always. Sometimes, especially when visiting in groups, they got in the way of doctors and nurses and disturbed other patients. Many brought food or drink for their ailing loved one that violated his prescribed diet. Some among the poorer sort, having arrived in Richmond penniless or nearly so, expected to be lodged and fed at the hospital. Phoebe Pember felt compassion for the "wives, sisters, cousins, aunts, and whole families" that showed up daily in her wards, but they frequently exasperated her. "Generally their only idea of kindness was giving sick men what food they would take in any quantity and of every quality. . . . Whenever rules circumscribed their plans they abused the government, then the hospital and then myself." When one impoverished family asked for a night's lodging, "I imprudently housed them in my laundry. They entrenched themselves there for six days, making predatory incursions into my kitchen."[23]

However irksome on occasion, the presence of family and friends at the bedside of a sick or wounded soldier was generally deemed a blessing—and not only because it could help restore his bodily health. It could also help assure his eternal welfare if he should die. Most hospital patients in Richmond recovered, but tens of thousands did not. Death was a daily visitor in the wards. A dying soldier fortunate enough to be attended by kinfolk and friends could achieve what Americans of that era extolled as a "good death."[24]

A good death was one whose approach was recognized, contemplated, and ultimately accepted by both the dying person and his assembled loved ones. It was not an abrupt extinction but a gradual sunset, affording him the opportunity to say last words and express final wishes and affording them the opportunity to evaluate the state of his soul and, if necessary, to help perfect it in anticipation of imminent judgment. Those assembled witnessed these final days, hours, and minutes attentively, scrutinizing the departing man's every word and gesture, encouraging professions of his awareness, resignation, and faith, and offering advice and prayers. They hovered uneasily until fully satisfied that he had submitted humbly to his fate and had earned a place in heaven. There they would reunite with him when their own time came.[25]

Mason Smith died a good death. He believed at the time of his injury on 3 June that he would not survive—"I am killed," he exclaimed as he collapsed to the ground—for abdominal wounds were almost invariably fatal. Surgeons at the field hospital he was carried to confirmed his judgment, telling him he had at most three or four days to live. But the seemingly miraculous passage of the bullet around, not through, his vital organs, once it was verified by the doctors at Stuart Hospital, gave hope for his recovery. Thereafter he returned to the contemplation of death only periodically, when his condition deteriorated; but these episodes came more frequently as the weeks passed.[26]

His mother, who joined him on 9 or 10 June, subsequently chronicled his spiritual journey as meticulously as she did his physical setbacks and rallies, and she chronicled her own journey as well. At one point in early July, "I thought Mason's hours numbered & his Drs. were very anxious too. His pulse sunk so, that I made up my mind to be prepared to see God do his own work & only prayed that it might be a gentle departure. . . . [Mason said] that he did not wish to die, but was not afraid if so God willed it." On 20 July, following their regular morning prayers, Mason "told me he knew he was in God's hands always, & that he is prepared to abide His decision even if he has to die." August brought more and more signs that recovery was unlikely, spurring more and more earnest conversations between mother and son and somber introspection by both. "I feel in a tight place," Eliza wrote on the seventh or eighth, "but God is good, & both I & my child belong to Him. . . . For the first time last night [Mason] lost self-control & wished to die; asked for anything that would end his sufferings. He said yesterday that Death is not to be feared, but that the sufferings leading to it tried him severely. [May] God help my boy, & He will."

By the ninth she was almost certain that the end was near, having received a pessimistic report from a doctor. Three days later any remaining doubt vanished: "My boy is dying, slowly, but surely. . . . Perhaps a few hours may bring rest for his tortured body, & I *believe* safety for his soul." When the end came at last, on the evening of Tuesday, 16 August, Mason too was fully prepared. On the previous Saturday morning, the thirteenth, he had acknowledged death's imminent arrival. "He was quite resigned to going," Eliza informed a kinswoman on the twentieth, "[and] expected to die on Sunday. . . . It was quite time that his Soul should be released from a poor suffering body. . . . [I] have not had one cry since it happened & feel as if there were nothing to cry about." To her other children she wrote, "My Son, & your Brother, [is] gone for all time but safe for Eternity."

A good death was denied the great majority of soldiers whose lives ended in a Richmond hospital. Volunteer nurse Judith McGuire described in her diary a more typical passing, that of a very young Alabamian who succumbed to illness in April 1862 after six weeks of suffering, intermittently aware of his fate but with no loved one in attendance to aid in his journey to the next world: "I closed his eyes last night at ten o'clock. . . . Poor little boy! He was but fifteen, and should never have left his home. It was sad to pack his knapsack, with his little gray suit, and coloured shirts, so neatly stitched by his poor mother, of whom he so often spoke, calling to [the nurses] in delirium, 'Mother, mother,' or, 'Mother, come here.'" Many nurses and matrons, including McGuire, endeavored to stand in for a family member or friend, although rarely could they devote much attention to any one soldier with so many others in need. Phoebe Pember, impressed by the stoicism of a desperately wounded soldier brought to one of her wards, singled him out: "[For] five days and nights I . . . fed [him] with my own hands, . . . cheering him by words and smiles." But the doctors told her he was doomed, and by the sixth day he had sensed it himself and "the hope had died out of his [eyes]. . . . What comfort could I give [then]? Only silently open the Bible, and read to him without comment the ever-living promises of his Maker." With his final breaths he spoke of his mother, thanked Pember for her kindness, and assured her that they would meet in heaven. Had he remained unaware of his fate, Pember would have informed him of it, so he could ready himself and make his peace with God. She had to perform that awful task on many occasions; of all her duties at Chimborazo, she wrote in her memoir, that was the worst.[27]

Once the soul fled, there were further obligations. Nearly as important as a good death at the end of an earthly life were proper observances at the beginning of an eternal life. The body must be prepared for interment, funeral services held, and the deceased commemorated. But the exigencies of war and the vast number of soldier deaths complicated these tasks.[28]

Difficulties notwithstanding, the postmortem obligations were faithfully performed by many devoted survivors of soldiers who died in Richmond or whose bodies were brought there from battlefields. When Pvt. Henry Pechaud of the Washington Artillery Battalion of Louisiana was killed, his kinsmen and friends in the capital's close-knit community of New Orleans refugees rallied to their duty. Pechaud died on 16 May 1864, in an engagement at Drewry's Bluff, a few miles south of the capital, his heart pierced by a shell fragment. Word of his death reached the city that day. The next afternoon Henri Garidel and eight other men secured a coffin, boarded a steamboat, traveled down the James to the vicinity of the battlefield, and then set out on foot, lugging the coffin, to retrieve the young man's remains. Hours later they located his hastily dug grave. After disinterring the body, they hired a wagon and driver to haul it to the steamboat landing. That evening, back in Richmond, they laid it out in the home of one of their group, washed it, and dressed it in good, clean clothes. They did not rest until it was respectably prepared for burial—although by then, as Garidel wrote in his diary, "it had already started to smell."[29]

Those who readied corpses for interment usually sought, like Garidel and his friends, to recreate the deceased's earthly appearance at its best, for the body would be displayed at the funeral to afford those assembled a last look at the departed. But in some cases survivors chose to underscore the deceased's patriotic sacrifice by presenting his corpse unaltered. Constance Cary told of the funeral of Randolph Fairfax, a young artilleryman slain at the Battle of Fredericksburg. His parents in Richmond had had his body disinterred, after two days in a battlefield grave, and brought to them. Urged to embellish the corpse according to custom, Fairfax's father replied, "No. Let my son sleep his long sleep as he fell at the post of duty." And so he did: At the service in St. James's Church, Cary wrote, "he was placed, uncoffined, on a bier before the altar. . . . He wore still the coarse flannel shirt, stained with battle smoke, in which he fell, and across him was thrown the blanket that had been his winding-sheet." His "golden curls [were] matted with the clay of his rude sepulcher." Plainly visible was "the cruel mark on the temple made by the piece of shell" that killed him.[30]

At the funeral of a departed soldier, his virtues were enumerated and his loved ones were assured that his new abode was in heaven. This was especially important in cases such as those of Henry Pechaud and Randolph Fairfax, who were denied a good death. Affirming the noble character, Christian devotion, and patriotic service of the deceased helped assuage the disappointment and anxiety of kinfolk and friends deprived of a proper deathbed farewell. Obituaries served the same purpose. One of the thousands published in the capital's newspapers during the war was that of Sgt. Robert M. Tabb. A native Richmonder, he had enlisted just nine days after the news of Fort Sumter reached the city. His regiment, the Twenty-First Virginia Infantry, subsequently saw much hard fighting with the Army of Northern Virginia, through which Tabb passed unscathed until 19 October 1864. On that day, the unit went into action at the Battle of Cedar Creek and, as recounted in the obituary, "the color bearer having been shot down, [Tabb] immediately grasped the flag, and whilst urging his comrades on, with the shout of 'Victory' on his lips, fell, pierced by the ball of a sharpshooter, and thus instantly yielded up his spirit to his God." The anonymous writer, a friend of Tabb's since childhood, testified that the deceased had "been early taught the ways of piety and truth" and "numbered himself with the people of God, worshipping in the First Presbyterian church." His faith abided during the war: "To his fidel[i]ty as a [C]hristian soldier, his captain and comrades testify." Never had the writer known "a better, purer spirit. . . . It must be an unspeakable comfort to his stricken widow and family . . . that though in that sad hour [of his death] there was none even to 'Kiss him for his Mother[,]' he is only 'absent from the body and present with the Lord.'"[31]

With the funeral held and the obituary published, the commemoration of the fallen soldier ideally continued, for months or even years, with the

Longing, Suffering, and Death

wearing of mourning garb by his close female kin. No one could walk the streets of wartime Richmond without seeing numbers of such women. A new recruit at one of the local army camps in the fall of 1862 found it "truly astonishing how many ladies are seen in mourning in Richmond and I am told that almost all would be but for the want of black mater[ial]." In 1864, newly hired Commissary Bureau clerk Judith McGuire commented in her diary on her fellow female employees: "It is melancholy to see how many wear mourning for brothers or other relatives, the victims of war."[32]

Many survivors of soldiers who died in or around Richmond but who had lived elsewhere chose to have their remains brought home, to carry out the postmortem rituals there. Early in the war, before the number of deaths surged, the War Department provided at government expense a shipping container, rail transportation, and sometimes even an escort for the body of any deceased soldier whose family requested that it be sent to them. This practice soon became unfeasible and was ended, but bodies continued to be retrieved from the capital by families elsewhere in the South who could afford the cost.[33]

The bereaved could avail themselves of helpful goods and services offered by Richmond entrepreneurs. The number of undertakers in the city multiplied during the war in response to the huge demand for local burials and for retrieval and shipment of remains. A week after the Battle of Fredericksburg, the proprietor of a mortuary establishment on Broad Street advertised in the *Dispatch* his readiness not only to conduct funeral services and interments in the city but also to "disinter and furnish Coffins, with Boxes, for deceased soldiers, so that they can be transported to any part of the Confederacy." In the fall of 1861, Bowers's Foundry at Ninth and Cary began manufacturing metallic coffins, previously available only from the North; these could be hermetically sealed to prevent the escape of odors during shipment. An alternative was provided by William Maclure, who billed himself as an "Embalming Surgeon" and addressed his advertisements to those "desiring to have the bodies of their deceased friends, on the field of battle or elsewhere, disinterred, embalmed, disinfected, . . . and sent home"; the products of his scientific process could, he promised, "be sent any distance, even in the warmest weather," and would arrive at their destination "looking as natural as cases will admit." (Richmond was one of the very few places in the Confederate South where this service could be procured; practiced in America in the 1850s but uncommon until the war, embalming was confined mostly to the Union states and occupied territory.)[34]

The deaths of certain prominent men in military service occasioned impressive public observances in Richmond. Capt. O. Jennings Wise was one of the first so honored. The son of a Virginia governor and, during the two years just before the war, the outspoken editor of the *Enquirer* (he fought eight duels in that brief span, defending his often acerbic pronouncements), Wise had assumed command of the Richmond Light Infantry Blues in April 1861. Wounded and taken prisoner when the enemy attacked Roanoke Island, North Carolina, in early 1862, he lived just long enough to confirm his pugnacious reputation, telling his captors (according to a report soon reaching Richmond) "that the South could never be subjugated. [The North] might exterminate us, but every man, woman, and child would prefer death to abject subjugation." His body, handed over by the enemy under flag of truce, was carried north, arriving in Richmond by train on the evening of 14 February. Met at the depot by a great assemblage of citizens and a military escort of Public Guardsmen and cavalry, it was taken to the Senate chamber of the Capitol to lie in state. The next day thousands of Richmonders passed solemnly through the chamber to gaze on the face of the hero. On the morning of the sixteenth, a Sunday, a large cortege of soldiers, citizens, and civic officials, including the mayor and city councilmen, accompanied the flag-draped casket in its hearse to St. James's Church. There the Reverend Joshua Peterkin preached from the text of the Lord's Prayer ("Thy will be done") to an audience that crammed the pews and spilled out into the street. When this service concluded, the cortege reassembled and then proceeded at a stately pace to Hollywood Cemetery, just beyond the city's western limit, where an Episcopal burial service was held, accompanied by Masonic and military honors.[35]

The patriots thus commemorated in wartime Richmond were not all native sons. As the nation's capital, the city was also the scene of public obsequies for some of the preeminent Confederate military martyrs who hailed from elsewhere, most notably Stonewall Jackson (in May 1863) and J. E. B. Stuart (May 1864), along with more modest rites for many lesser notables. "Day after day," Constance Cary recalled of the spring and summer of 1862, "one heard the wailing dirge of military bands preceding a soldier's funeral. One could not number those sad pageants in our leafy streets: the coffin with its cap and sword and gloves, the riderless horse with empty boots in the stirrups of an army saddle! Such soldiers as could be spared from the front marching with arms reversed and crape-shrouded banners, passers-by standing with bare bent heads." Near the end of that year, the editor of the *Whig* remarked that a "military funeral, in our city, has become a familiar sight — so common, indeed, as scarcely to excite attention."[36]

Exciting even less attention were the burials of the many thousands of ordinary soldiers who died in Richmond hospitals with no family or friends on hand to see to the customary postmortem rites. Deprived of a good death, these men were then deprived of a befitting funeral. The nation they gave their lives for did what it could to lay them respectfully to rest, but, struggling to defeat the enemy, it could devote little attention to the physical remains of its fallen defenders.[37]

For these martyrs, the journey to the grave began with the summoning of a surgeon to the bed where the still-warm corpse lay. After a perfunctory examination, he signed a death certificate. A steward then removed the deceased's hospital gown and affixed to his underwear a slip of paper recording his name, rank, and unit. (His outer clothing — pants, shirt, jacket, shoes — would be retrieved from hospital storage but he would not wear these articles to the grave, for they were needed elsewhere: washed and mended, they would be reissued to the ragged troops in the field.) A clerk registered the death in the hospital's record books and dispatched letters of notification to the deceased's unit commander and his next of kin, if known; the latter were advised to file the paperwork necessary to receive any pay due the soldier and any personal possessions he left behind. Attendants took the body from the ward, conveying it on a stretcher to the "dead house," a shed where corpses awaited removal to the interment ground. "I see dead bodies carried by the windows two or three times a day," wrote Eliza Smith as she tended her dying son at Stuart Hospital. She thought it disgraceful that they were stripped of clothing "*almost* if not entirely," thus to be buried "like animals."[38]

Coffins were stored nearby — plain wooden boxes provided by the Quartermaster Bureau, which contracted for them by the thousands (paying, in 1862, $2.90 apiece). Each corpse was placed into one of these at the dead house. At least once a day a large, sturdy wagon of the sort used to haul lumber or furniture would pull up at the dead house and the accumulated bodies would be loaded onto it. The wagon would then trundle off to the burial ground, the coffins (as one witness observed) "piled up [on it] like ordinary boxes of goods." Oakwood Cemetery, at the northern end of Thirty-First Street, was the usual destination for the dead of hospitals on the eastern side of the city, including Chimborazo and Howard's Grove; for the others it was Hollywood. A clerk at the cemetery entered into a record book the name, rank, and unit of each man delivered for interment and the precise site where he would be placed, having in mind especially the family members who might at some later date visit the cemetery or have the remains disinterred and brought home.[39]

Army chaplains were assigned to both Oakwood and Hollywood, their duty being to say a few appropriate words over each coffin as it was lowered into the ground by the cemetery's gravediggers. Generally, no one besides the chaplain and the laborers attended this last rite. After the grave was filled, the bare mound of earth atop it remained for some time the only marker. But eventually a simple wooden headboard with the deceased's name and unit painted on it was emplaced — engraved stone markers being out of the question, given the War Department's limited means.[40]

Sometimes the number of deaths surged beyond the cemeteries' capacity to keep up. The problem was aggravated by the labor shortage. Both Hollywood (privately owned) and Oakwood (municipal) set aside acreage for soldier burials not paid for by the deceased's survivors. The War Department oversaw these interments and paid the cemeteries a modest fee for each, but it provided no personnel to carry them out besides the wagon drivers who delivered the coffins and the chaplains who performed services; the cemeteries' laborers and clerks were expected to do the rest. As conscription took away able-bodied men, the cemeteries scrambled to find replacements. Draft-exempt Irishmen were hired to dig graves; penitentiary convicts and runaway slaves recaptured from the Yankees were put to work too. But these proved insufficient at certain critical times. Coffins sometimes sat unburied for a day or more, their contents festering and bloating. To speed interments at Oakwood, its directors ended the practice of digging individual graves for soldiers in favor of trenches. The overburdened chaplains sometimes had to forgo individual attention to each burial and instead, as one explained, "have one service for several bodies [placed] in adjacent graves . . . or have a general service over the coffins, while still above ground."[41]

Civilians also died in wartime Richmond, of course, but after 1861 those deaths were vastly outnumbered by soldiers' deaths. The superintendent of Hollywood Cemetery stated in September 1864 that his twelve-man burial squad was devoting almost all its time to interring Confederate soldiers. The plot of two acres set aside at Hollywood for the War Department in 1861 was quickly filled; it was enlarged in 1862 and by 1863 held the remains of well over 2,000 soldiers. Oakwood, its reserved section likewise enlarged after 1861, absorbed even greater numbers: more than 7,000 by 1863 and at least 16,000 by the war's end.[42]

Richmond's cemeteries, especially the breathtakingly situated and elegantly landscaped Hollywood, had long been popular places of visitation, not solely for the purpose of paying respects at a loved one's grave but also for recreational strolls and for the tranquil contemplation of nature, beauty, history, and mortality. They remained so during the war. In early July 1861, the *Dispatch* noted a recent increase of visitors to Hollywood and extolled the cemetery's virtues: "It is a treasury filled with grand and holy memories—a little Eden, perfumed with flowers—the offerings of affection on the altar of memory, roofed by trees planted by nature and art, and glorious in its quiet loveliness." A year later that newspaper advised its readers that "nothing is better adapted for exciting purifying reflections than a visit to the [Richmond] cemeteries," for they "are capable of conveying instruction which should make the visitor wiser and better ere he leaves." Henri Garidel, who spent a Sunday afternoon at Hollywood in September 1863, was awe-struck: "I couldn't possibly describe the beauty of this spot. It must be seen to be believed. From up there you have the most beautiful panorama of the whole city. . . . There are some lovely monuments."[43]

By then, however, the war was marring the beauty of the cemeteries and altering the nature of the contemplation they inspired. Before the war, as the *Enquirer* pointed out in an October 1862 essay on Hollywood, "this pleasant burial ground was one elysium of charming plots and beautiful monuments. Scarcely a grave was without its marble and its light of laughing flowers. Now through its north-western expanse [the soldiers' section] the yellow earth rises in thickly folding billows over dead roses of chivalry, from every State . . . in the South. The same feelings of sadness arise [now as before], but not in the same train of retrospective musing, when we contemplate these bare and melancholy graves. . . . Men in the first full glow of health and youth, the soul of honor and of patriotism, blessed with friends and fortune . . . sleep there; and when they lay down, no friend was near, no fortune brought them the care and kindness of the home's affection. . . . All that war can suggest . . . floats like a vision over each turfless grave." Artilleryman B. W. Jones, serving with the city garrison, frequently visited Oakwood, where several of his comrades were buried. There he meditated on their sacrifice and that of all the other soldiers who lay there—some of whose headboards were marked "Unknown": "They are not, and can never be, forgotten. Their deeds and self-devotion to the cause they loved, will endear them to the hearts of their countrymen, and of posterity, so long as men love liberty, or have manhood enough to honor the brave." Such musings were also common among the non-Richmonders who went out of their way to visit the cemeteries when passing through the city. There were many: as the *Dispatch* said of Oakwood in 1863, "Nearly every stranger has a father, brother, son, or friend, now inhabiting that vast 'city of the dead.'"[44]

As Oakwood and Hollywood metamorphosed from local burial grounds to national shrines — revered symbols of the war's meaning and cost — the occasional desecrations that both cemeteries had always suffered provoked even greater public indignation. The theft of flowers from graves, sometimes just minutes after they had been placed, became increasingly common; some of the perpetrators were said to be women wanting to adorn themselves or their homes for free or to get a little cash by reselling the flowers. Burial services were now and then interrupted by the noise of shotguns fired by boys hunting in the nearby woods. Poor people were seen bathing in the stream that ran through Hollywood. Cows and goats found their way into Hollywood, too, grazing among the burial plots. The city's newspapers angrily reported these and other outrages. When soldiers' coffins piled up unburied at Oakwood, the *Dispatch* scolded its managers: "This is a great evil, and should at once be remedied — Surely enough hands can be obtained to perform the rite of sepulture — the last testimonial of respect which can be rendered to the unfortunate men who have fallen in the defence of our country."[45]

The spring of 1865 brought an end to the martyrdom of Confederate soldiers in Richmond. The last coffins were hauled to the reserved sections of Oakwood and Hollywood, the last trenches filled in, the last headboards emplaced. But the cemeteries did not relinquish their exalted status in the minds of a great many Southerners. They would become the holiest shrines of the Lost Cause.

1-10 APRIL 1865

War Department clerk John Jones chronicled the death of Confederate Richmond in 1865 as vividly as he had chronicled its short life. It was not a lingering death, nor a quiet one, but abrupt and violent. Jones crammed his diary with details of all he saw and heard.[1]

The first hint that the Rebel capital was in extremis came on 1 April, a Saturday. "We have vague and incoherent accounts from excited couriers," Jones wrote after arriving at work that morning. These told "of fighting, without result," at the Petersburg front, where Lee's army had held out against siege for more than nine months. "It is rumored that a battle will probably occur in that vicinity to-day." Such reports commanded the closest attention, for if Petersburg fell, Richmond could no longer be held.

The next day revealed that the worst had come to pass. "The tocsin was sounded this morning at daybreak, and the militia ordered to the fortifications" to replace regular troops being hurriedly shifted to Petersburg at Lee's command. This, Jones knew, "can only indicate an emergency of alarming importance." There was no report from Lee yet, but "a street rumor says there was bloody fighting yesterday a little beyond Petersburg. . . . An intense excitement prevails." President Davis was called away from the Sunday morning service at St. Paul's by an urgent message from the War Department. The Local Defense Forces were summoned to duty alongside the militia. By early afternoon it was confirmed that the Union army had cut Petersburg's last rail line to the south and Lee was abandoning that city. A telegram from him advised the secretary of war to evacuate Richmond without delay. Locomotives and cars were marshaled at the Richmond and Danville Railroad depot to carry government archives and essential personnel to safety. Jones was told by his superiors that he and other War Department employees could leave or stay as they chose; those with families in the city, like Jones, were advised to stay.

As afternoon turned to evening, Jones left his office and walked the streets, trying to gauge the public mood now that word had spread that the Confederate government and army were pulling out. He kept an eye especially on black Richmonders: "The negroes stand about mostly silent, as if wondering what will be their fate. They make no demonstrations of joy." By now the excitement of the morning hours had given way to tense expectation. As night fell, "all is yet quiet. . . . How long will this continue? When will the enemy come?"

Over the next few hours the president and many other Confederate officials boarded the trains and departed, intending to reestablish the government elsewhere. Jones decided to stay, "awaiting my fate, whatever it may be." The fortifications were abandoned during the night. A lot of the troops in and around the city deserted, but others marched away to join Lee's army as it fled westward from Petersburg.

In the predawn darkness of Monday, 3 April, Jones was awakened by "two tremendous explosions, seeming to startle the very earth." He got dressed and left his house, anxious to learn what had happened overnight. He heard that the detonations were the work of retreating troops destroying munitions. He heard, too, that government records that could not be carried off had been put to the torch and that rations left behind in the army depots had been given away to the populace. The city government, anticipating drunken mobs, had appointed citizen committees to raid the saloons and pour all the liquor they found into the street. "Women and boys, black and white, were seen filling pitchers and buckets from the gutters."

Soon Jones noticed "a dark volume of smoke ris[ing] from the southeastern section of the city, and spread[ing] like a pall over the zenith. It proceeds from the tobacco warehouse, ignited [by retreating troops], I suppose, hours ago, and now just bursting forth." At eight thirty, and continuing for over an hour, "the armory, arsenal, and laboratory[,] . . . which had been previously fired, gave forth terrific sounds from thousands of bursting shells. . . . The pavements are filled with pulverized glass. . . . Flour mills have taken fire from the burning government warehouses, and the flames are spreading through the lower part of the city. A great conflagration is apprehended." He heard reports of pillaging and saw "two negro women laden with plunder."

By now Richmond was in Yankee hands. Jones learned that municipal officials had formally surrendered the city to approaching Federal troops; by nine o'clock there were several hundred occupying Capitol Square and thousands more on the way. At eleven Jones walked to the square, finding the streets "filled with *negro troops*, cavalry and infantry," who were being "cheered by hundreds of [Richmond] negroes [gathered] at the corners."

The Union forces quickly restored order and helped extinguish the fires. On the morning of 4 April, Jones ventured out to survey the damage: "Some seven hundred [buildings], from Main Street to the canal, comprising the most valuable stores, and the best business establishments, were consumed. All the bridges across the James were destroyed." Continuing on, he saw thousands of black people "idl[ing] in the streets, or lying in the Capitol Square, or crowding about [the Federal] headquarters, at the Capitol." He found that no one was accepting Confederate money now—not that that mattered much, for no stores or markets were open for business.

With no job to go to, Jones continued to roam the streets in the following days, recording his observations. "The people are kinder to each other," he noted on 8 April, "sharing provisions, etc." He also transcribed second-hand reports, including a rumor late on the ninth that Lee had surrendered his army. It was confirmed the next day, whereupon Jones acknowledged that the Confederacy was essentially dead. With its demise, keeping up his daily writing seemed pointless: "My Diary is surely drawing to a close, and I feel as one about to take leave of some old familiar associate. . . . I never supposed it would end in this way."

What Jones meant was that he never expected to end his diary with the Confederacy's downfall. He had always intended to end it with the conclusion of the Rebel war for independence (a victorious conclusion, he presumed) and to publish a version of it that would take its place among the premier accounts of the founding of the new nation. He did eventually publish it, and it is certainly a premier account—not of the founding of a new nation, of course, but of the collapse of that dream.

The wrenching changes that Jones and other Richmonders grappled with from April 1861 through March 1865 proved as transitory as the Confederate States of America. Postwar Richmond was a far cry from the city they knew during the eventful war years. No longer a bustling national capital, prolific munitions producer, or fiercely defended military citadel, it withered in size and prominence. Its population, in early 1865 at least 80,000 and likely 100,000 or more, dwindled by 1870 to 51,000 (despite an annexation in 1867 that nearly doubled the area of the city). At the turn of the twentieth century, the city's inhabitants still numbered only 85,000.[2]

The exodus of residents right after the war, although disappointing to the city boosters who envisioned a grand metropolis on the James, was a blessing in at least one respect: it eased the demand on housing, lowering its cost and reducing the claustrophobic crowding. And, too, the intense competition over resources between government and citizenry, which halted construction of civilian housing during the war, ceased with the flight of the Confederate government and army, allowing the city's residential space to expand.

Richmonders could be thankful for other blessings as well, once war gave way to peace in 1865. For one thing, their hunger pangs abated. No longer constricted by sea and land blockades and the demands of the Rebel War Department, the food supply available to the populace increased. Meanwhile, the swift rehabilitation of the railroads, canal, roads, and bridges restored the channels by which provisions came to the city.

As stomachs filled, the anger of the white lower classes subsided. Their discontent was alleviated, too, by the extinction of the Confederate government, whose commandments many had reviled as inequitable. Nor did the upper classes mourn the passing of the Rebel authorities' most onerous dictates — passports, impressment, conscription, and the rest. The Union occupiers did impose martial law on the city, but it was short-lived and comparatively undemanding.

Richmonders welcomed also the ebbing of crime and disorder, which subsided after the war to a tolerable, if not comfortable, level. But most welcome of all was the cessation of battlefield slaughter, which saved the lives of men still in the ranks and brought an end to the ghastly scenes of suffering and death at Richmond's railroad stations and army hospitals.

Not all was well in postwar Richmond, however. Industry and commerce — deprived now of military demand, crippled by the fiery destruction of nine-tenths of the business district, and squeezed by structural changes in the American economy — languished. The total value of Richmond's manufactured products in 1870 was 15 percent less than in 1860 (not even taking into account national inflation over that decade) and vastly less than in any year from 1862 through 1864. The number of workers employed in manufacturing in 1870 (6,966) was hardly greater than in 1860 (6,833) and but a small fraction of the number employed in the war years. Of those at work in 1870, only 687 were women; during the war there had had been many thousands. Moreover, the positions that had opened up for educated white women as Confederate government clerks and hospital matrons vanished with the war's end, and few comparable professional positions were offered to women in the city for many years to come.

The most striking contrast between the city at peace and the city at war was the absence of slavery — a revolutionary consequence of the war, decried or celebrated depending on the color of one's skin. While appreciably enlarging their sphere of autonomy during the conflict, the black men and women of Richmond remained subjugated by law and custom until Yankee troops seized the city. But from that day forward, through the years of Reconstruction, black Richmonders made the most of their freedom, radically altering the city's social, economic, and political landscape. Their assertiveness was bitterly contested, however, and the post-Reconstruction decades brought a white backlash that nullified many of their gains. But never again did they wear chains as heavy and strong as those that bound them before April 1865.

The Civil War years were a unique moment in Richmond's history, a time of tribulations and transformations the likes of which were never seen before or since in that city — or any other city in America. So remarkable was this moment that many men and women who lived through it (John Jones among them) were moved in the postwar years to publish their wartime diaries or write memoirs of their experiences. Almost all were white, upper-class, and pro-Confederate, and their books naturally viewed things from that perspective. The memoirists generally wrote with their audience much in mind, that audience being people of their own kind who relished tales of eminent politicians, dashing army officers, and glamorous belles and who looked back nostalgically on the Lost Cause, preferring to forget its rough underside.

The common folk of wartime Richmond, white and black, were but dimly visible in these accounts, and where visible were often caricatured. The same is true of the Richmond newspapers and city council minutes of the war years, which along with the published diaries and memoirs were the sources most relied on by the twentieth-century historians who wrote general studies of Richmond during the Civil War. Those historians did not by any means ignore the common people, but their portrayal of them was sketchy at best.

Since the 1980s a number of scholars have adopted new perspectives and exploited previously untapped sources to produce articles, book chapters, and dissertations that wonderfully illuminate the experience of Civil War Richmond's plain folk. But the public memory of what happened in the Confederate capital is still dominated by the traditional heroes and their deeds.

Anyone who strolls along the city's famous Monument Avenue will see impressive bronze statues of Jefferson Davis, Robert E. Lee, and other exalted leaders of the Confederacy. But no other Civil War figures are memorialized there, not the working-class women who took to the streets to protest food prices or were burned to death in the laboratory explosion; not the laborers and clerks who manned factories and offices and endured long weeks in the fortifications with the Local Defense Forces; not the dispossessed refugees who crammed into cold, dingy, expensive rented rooms and felt lucky to have them; not the black men and women who dodged night watchmen, detectives, and Rebel pickets to meet in secret fellowship or flee to the Union lines; and not the humble privates who lay in agony in the hospitals with wounds, pneumonia, and hernias and with no loved ones sitting near to brush away the flies.

This book has summoned those obscure and mostly forgotten Richmonders from the wings and placed them at center stage. With this new cast, the drama of Civil War Richmond takes on a fresh aspect and richer meaning.

Acknowledgments

This book embodies the work of many hands and minds besides my own. I'm glad to have the opportunity here to thank those who have helped me along the path from inception to research and writing and finally to publication.

Three good friends of mine, who are also fine historians, read the whole book manuscript and offered valuable suggestions for improvement: I gratefully tip my Tennessee Vols cap to John Cimprich, Ernie Freeberg, and Nelson Lankford. Another very appreciative tip of the Big Orange cap goes to the two anonymous readers for the University of North Carolina Press.

I'm once again in debt to Lisa Adams of the Garamond Agency, who not only has guided me through the intricacies of book proposals and contract negotiations on this and other projects but also has provided expert editorial help all along the way to publication. Many thanks, Lisa.

Two friends have assisted me greatly with research. Dean S. Thomas has been teaching me things about the Civil War since he and I were college students and licensed battlefield guides at Gettysburg in the 1960s; his expertise on Confederate munitions manufacture, in particular, has helped me better understand wartime Richmond. Robert L. Glaze, armed with his own expertise on the Civil War, hit the road to do archival research for me; I could not have asked for a more astute and tireless reader of manuscript collections.

University of Tennessee Library staff members have assisted me in ways too numerous to list, particularly those in Special Collections and the Hoskins Reading Room. I'm grateful as well to the librarians and archivists at all the other research institutions that I've called on for help.

This is my second book published by UNC Press, and in both cases the press staff members have been a joy to work with. Mark Simpson-Vos, my editor on this project, has been especially helpful, offering not only keen critical evaluation but also the enthusiasm and flexibility that authors want and need.

My family continues to be a fount of encouragement, strength, guidance, and good fellowship. No words I can think of can fully express my gratitude for this. I'll just say, simply and inadequately: thanks, Jeanie, mom, and all of you.

Notes

ABBREVIATIONS

CPRCBF   Confederate Papers Relating to Citizens or Business Firms. M 346, RG 109. National Archives, Washington, D.C.

CSR   Compiled Service Records of Confederate Soldiers. M 251 (Florida), M 266 (Georgia), M 267 (South Carolina), M 269 (Mississippi), M 270 (North Carolina), M 320 (Louisiana), M 324 (Virginia), RG 109. National Archives, Washington, D.C.

Dispatch   *Daily Dispatch* (Richmond)

1860 Census   Eighth Census, 1860. Manuscript Returns of Free Inhabitants. M 653, RG 29. National Archives, Washington, D.C.

Enquirer   *Daily Richmond Enquirer*

Examiner   *Daily Richmond Examiner*

LRCSW   Letters Received by the Confederate Secretary of War, 1861–65. M 437, RG 109. National Archives, Washington, D.C.

Whig   *Daily Richmond Whig*

WOTR   *War of the Rebellion: A Compilation of the Official Records of the Union and Confederate Armies.* 128 vols. Washington, D.C.: Government Printing Office, 1880–1901.

PROLOGUE

1. *Richmond Enquirer* (semiweekly edition), 11 April 1861; *Dispatch*, 11, 12 April 1861.
2. *Dispatch*, 11 April 1861; *Richmond Enquirer* (semiweekly edition), 11 April 1861.
3. *Dispatch*, 12 April 1861.
4. *Richmond Enquirer* (semiweekly edition), 11 April 1861.
5. *Dispatch*, 11, 12 April 1861.

CHAPTER 1

1. File 113-1861, LRCSW; Third Ward, Richmond, Henrico County, Virginia, p. 190/633 (James Wright), 1860 Census. For other examples of Richmond men offering their

services to the Confederate army before the outbreak of war, see files 658-1861 and 665-1861, LRCSW.

2. General histories of the city include Dabney, *Richmond*; Manarin and Dowdey, *History of Henrico County*; and Tyler-McGraw, *At the Falls*. On the antebellum era specifically, see Goldfield, *Urban Growth*; Kimball, *American City, Southern Place*; and Chesson, *Richmond after the War*, chap. 1.

3. Manufacturing statistics are in United States Bureau of the Census, *Statistics*, xviii.

4. Chesson and Roberts, *Exile in Richmond*, 44. A good, if rather florid, description of the city in 1861 is in De Leon, *Four Years*, 85–91.

5. Benjamin Washington Jones, *Under the Stars*, 56–57.

6. Jones, 56–57; Lankford, *Irishman in Dixie*, 39; Chesson and Roberts, *Exile in Richmond*, 251, 275, 289, 310, 311; Elsa Barkley Brown and Kimball, "Mapping the Terrain," 297, 302; Scott, *Old Richmond Neighborhoods*, 23–283 passim.

7. Scott, *Old Richmond Neighborhoods*, 23–283 passim; Tyler-McGraw, *At the Falls*, 114; Elsa Barkley Brown and Kimball, "Mapping the Terrain," 302; Wade, *Slavery in the Cities*, 327; McLeod, "Not Forgetting the Land," 38.

8. *Dispatch*, 8 November 1860. Of the many studies of Lower and Upper South responses to Lincoln's election, four that are particularly informative are Channing, *Crisis of Fear*; Crofts, *Reluctant Confederates*; Dew, *Apostles of Disunion*; and Lankford, *Cry Havoc!* On Virginia specifically, see Shanks, *Secession Movement in Virginia*; and Link, *Roots of Secession*. A contemporary Richmonder's explication of the arguments for secession before the outbreak of war is in Norwood, *God and Our Country*, 7–9.

9. J. B. Jones, *Rebel War Clerk's Diary*, 1:16–17.

10. Emma Mordecai to sister, 21 April 1861, Alfred Mordecai Papers; Jacob Bechtel to George Bechtel, 24 April 1861, Bechtel Papers.

11. J. B. Jones, *Rebel War Clerk's Diary*, 1:18–20; Granniss Diary, 15, 18 April 1861; Putnam, *Richmond during the War*, 19–22; Emory M. Thomas, *Confederate State of Richmond*, 4–12; Furgurson, *Ashes of Glory*, 31–37.

12. Emma Mordecai to sister, 21 April 1861, Alfred Mordecai Papers.

13. Crofts, *Reluctant Confederates*, esp. 308–23; Lankford, *Cry Havoc!*, esp. chaps. 4, 9; Emory M. Thomas, *Confederate State of Richmond*, 1–14; Davis, "Richmond Becomes the Capital," 116–22.

14. Davis, "Richmond Becomes the Capital," 113–29; Emory M. Thomas, *Confederate State of Richmond*, 32–34.

15. Jacob Bechtel to George Bechtel, 1, 24 April, 7, 17 May 1861, Bechtel Papers; Third Ward, Richmond, Henrico County, Virginia, p. 195/639 (Jacob H. Becktel [*sic*]), 1860 Census.

16. Hoge, *Moses Drury Hoge*, 146; Tucker, *Southern Church Justified*, 8.

17. Kimball, *American City, Southern Place*, 235–36; Manarin, *Richmond at War*, 48–49n, 83; H. H. Fauntleroy to John Letcher, 11 June 1861, MR 4745, Letcher Executive Papers; Richmond County, Virginia, p. 5/261 (Henry H. Fauntleroy), 1860 Census. Manarin and Wallace, *Richmond Volunteers*, has a complete list and history of all the artillery, infantry, and cavalry companies and batteries recruited in Richmond, with rosters of members. Some of these were preexisting volunteer militia units; others were formed after the war began.

18. Files 797-1861, 5782-1861, 8157-1861, D-626-1862, and O-31-1862, LRCSW; West Ward, Petersburg, Virginia, p. 247/415 (William Oliver family), and Western Subdivision,

Henrico County, Virginia, p. 172 (John N. Powell family), 1860 Census; Bailey, *Henrico Home Front*, 102, 176.

19. Manarin, *Richmond at War*, 59–60, 67–68n; Ellis, "Richmond 'Home Guard,'" 57–60. Another failed attempt, in March 1862, to get the army to accept a Richmond unit restricted to local defense (a company called the Metropolitan Guard) is documented in file B-109-1862, LRCSW.

20. Powhatan Weisiger to James Seddon, 9 April 1864, Civil War Letters Collection; Third Ward, Richmond, Henrico County, Virginia, p. 18/462 (Powhatan Weisiger), 1860 Census; files 11144-1862, D-97-1862, P-7-1862, and P-42-1862, LRCSW. Powhatan Weisiger did finally enlist, in March 1862; he served with a light artillery battery for at least a year, after which he was detailed to a job in Richmond. See Powhatan Weisiger file, Capt. Ellet's Company, Virginia Light Artillery, CSR/Virginia.

21. On the City Battalion—which was a regular, full-time army unit, not a part of the Local Defense Forces (although sometimes mistakenly identified as such)—see Radley, *Rebel Watchdog*, 305–7; Manarin, *Richmond at War*, 186–87n, 203; *Dispatch*, 4 February, 4 March 1863; and Twenty-Fifth Battalion, Infantry, CSR/Virginia.

22. Barber, "'Sisters of the Capital,'" 176–205, 182–87; Ellen Mordecai to Alfred Mordecai, 6 June 1861, Alfred Mordecai Papers; file W-164-1862, LRCSW; *Examiner*, 2 September 1861; Hubard Diary, 15, 18 December 1861; Green, *Chimborazo*, 104–5; McGuire, *Diary*, 97–98, 119, 251; Wiggins, *Journals of Josiah Gorgas*, 66, 67; Mumper, *I Wrote You Word*, 6; J. B. Jones, *Rebel War Clerk's Diary*, 1:131; Harrison, *Recollections*, 82–83; Furgurson, *Ashes of Glory*, 81–83; Bridges, "Juliet Opie Hopkins," 84–99.

23. *Dispatch*, 1, 15 August 1861, 20 February 1862; *Examiner*, 19 March 1864; "Richmond Ambulance Corps"; petition of the Committee of the Association for the Relief of Maimed Soldiers, 30 January 1865, Legislative Petitions of the General Assembly; Record Book of the Confederate Soldiers Home Hospital; files M-101-1864 and H-78-1865, LRCSW; Hoge, *Moses Drury Hoge*, 147–56; Furgurson, *Ashes of Glory*, 159–60, 179–80, 217. For more on the Ambulance Corps, see chapter 10.

24. McGuire, *Diary*, 108; Bagby Diary, 12 March 1862; Norwood, *God and Our Country*, 10.

25. Fisher, *History and Reminiscences*, 268–71; Tucker, *Southern Church Justified*, 8; Doggett, *Nation's Ebenezer*, 8; Estill, "Diary," 38:284, 39:43, 49; McGuire, *Diary*, 96, 98, 262, 266. The most comprehensive study of religion in the Confederacy is Rable, *God's Almost Chosen People*.

26. McGuire, *Diary*, 97–98.

27. Phoebe Pember to [?], 22 June 1864, Pember Letters; Chesson and Roberts, *Exile in Richmond*, 63, 76, 99, 101, 123, 131, 133, 136, 154–55, 156, 219, 220, 225, 228, 231, 324; J. B. Jones, *Rebel War Clerk's Diary*, 1:127, 276, 307, 2:162, 188, 195, 201, 202, 203, 295; McGuire, *Diary*, 282; *Dispatch*, 7 June, 10 July 1861, 2 April, 7, 12, 16 October 1863; *Examiner*, 7 September, 7 October 1863; Lankford, *Irishman in Dixie*, 44; Wiggins, *Journals of Josiah Gorgas*, 105; Blackiston, *Refugees in Richmond*, 32.

28. *Whig*, 16 July, 12 August, 1861, 5 November 1862; Manarin, *Richmond at War*, 194, 202, 208, 265, 356, 502; *Dispatch*, 21 August, 12 September, 5 October 1861, 25 July, 19 August 1863, 18 June 1864; *Examiner*, 3 August 1864; Chesson and Roberts, *Exile in Richmond*, 55, 57, 155, 156, 167, 172, 273, 274n.

29. Putnam, *Richmond during the War*, 315; Chesson and Roberts, *Exile in Richmond*, 234, 236, 310–11; Lankford, *Irishman in Dixie*, 38–39; Trask, *Two Months*, 74–75, 81.

30. J. B. Jones, *Rebel War Clerk's Diary*, 1:141, 200, 278, 2:101, 136, 235; Wiley, *Letters of Warren Akin*, 50, 55, 56, 79, 90; *Whig*, 27 December 1862, 7 March 1865; *Sentinel*, 12 August 1863; Lankford, *Irishman in Dixie*, 38, 44; McGuire, *Diary*, 250–51; Paca, "'Tim's Black Book,'" 457; Harrison, *Recollections*, 84; Woodward, *Mary Chesnut's Civil War*, 107, 109.

31. Fisher, *History and Reminiscences*, 297–98; Norwood, *God and Our Country*, 10–11.

32. Blackiston, *Refugees in Richmond*, 35; Katharine M. Jones, *Ladies of Richmond*, 167.

33. Maury Diary, 20 February, 12 March 1865; Wiley, *Letters of Warren Akin*, 88–89.

CHAPTER 2

1. *Dispatch*, 16 August 1861.

2. Putnam, *Richmond during the War*, 27; McGuire, *Diary*, 88; Trask, *Two Months*, 78.

3. McLeod, "Not Forgetting the Land," 38; J. B. Jones, *Rebel War Clerk's Diary*, 1:277; *Dispatch*, 4 August 1863; Trask, *Two Months*, 75; Emory M. Thomas, *Confederate State of Richmond*, 128; Dabney, *Richmond*, 182; Wiggins, *Journals of Josiah Gorgas*, 98–99.

4. Emory M. Thomas, *Confederate State of Richmond*, 12, 35–36; Manarin and Dowdey, *History of Henrico County*, 250; J. B. Jones, *Rebel War Clerk's Diary*, 1:27, 30, 48; *Dispatch*, 7, 11 June, 20 September 1861; Mumper, *I Wrote You Word*, 2; Day, *Down South*, 1:98; Jacob Bechtel to George Bechtel, 24 April 1861, Bechtel Papers; Putnam, *Richmond during the War*, 33–34; *Examiner*, 16 September 1861.

5. Martis, *Historical Atlas of the Congresses*, 2, 9, 32, 34; Van Riper and Scheiber, "Confederate Civil Service."

6. Van Riper and Scheiber, "Confederate Civil Service," 454; *Stranger's Guide*, 1–31; files 1913-1861 and T-128-1864, LRCSW; *City Intelligencer*, 1–23; Green, *Chimborazo*, 19; *Examiner*, 23 November 1863, 3 June 1864.

7. J. B. Jones, *Rebel War Clerk's Diary*, 1:48, 368, 2:429, 445; Moore, *Conscription and Conflict*, 114–16; Manarin and Dowdey, *History of Henrico County*, 243, 250; *Examiner*, 20 February 1865; *Stranger's Guide*, 12; file A-224-1864, LRCSW.

8. *WOTR*, ser. 1, 18:751, 27(3):1029, 1067, 29(2):783, 811, 33:1157–59, 42(3):1197, 46(2):1112.

9. Coles, "Richmond, the Confederate Hospital City," 71–91; Waitt, *Confederate Military Hospitals*, 5–40.

10. *Dispatch*, 25, 31 July 1861, 2 June 1862, 17 July 1863, 16 May 1864; *Richmond Semi-Weekly Examiner*, 4 July 1862; J. B. Jones, *Rebel War Clerk's Diary*, 1:158–59, 378; *Examiner*, 9 May 1863, 16 May 1864; Younger, *Inside the Confederate Government*, 57; files C-750-1862, C-224-1863, M-548-1863, M-181-1864, and M-422-1864, LRCSW; Coles, "Richmond, the Confederate Hospital City," 72; Robert McPhaill to William Smith, 9 March 1865, MR 5024, William Smith Executive Papers.

11. Dew, *Ironmaker to the Confederacy*, 90–92, 262; J. R. Anderson and Company, Crenshaw and Company, Haxall, Crenshaw, and Company, Belvidere Manufacturing Company, Philip Rahm, Adolphus J. Rahm, and Old Dominion Iron and Nail Works files, CPRCBF; *Enquirer*, 16 October 1861; Takagi, "Rearing Wolves," 128, 130–31.

12. Julius Baumgarten file, CPRCBF; *Examiner*, 22 July 1864.

13. Massey, *Refugee Life*; Putnam, *Richmond during the War*, 201, 320.

14. Ash, *When the Yankees Came*, esp. chap. 1 and pp. 237–41. Refugees in Richmond from Maryland and Northern states are noted in files 7247-1861, E-33-1863, and

H-507-1863, LRCSW; *Dispatch*, 23 April 1863; and J. B. Jones, *Rebel War Clerk's Diary*, 1:67. Refugees from the Eastern Shore are noted in files S-884-1862 and J-9-1863, LRCSW. Those from the Shenandoah Valley and northeastern Virginia are noted in Francis Snapp to James Seddon, 7 November 1863, Civil War Letters Collection; file D-107-1864, LRCSW; *Enquirer*, 26 April, 24 November 1862; J. B. Jones, *Rebel War Clerk's Diary*, 1:195; and McGuire, *Diary*, vii. Those from the Peninsula and other areas of southeastern Virginia are noted in files B-1257-1862, T-82-1863, and P-258-1864, LRCSW; and *Dispatch*, 3, 29 June 1863. New Orleans refugees are noted in files D-144-1864, M-450-1864, and F-37-1865, LRCSW; and Chesson and Roberts, *Exile in Richmond*, 1–11, 105.

15. *Enquirer*, 24 November 1862; J. B. Jones, *Rebel War Clerk's Diary*, 1:195; Emma Mordecai Diaries, 4 July 1864; *Dispatch*, 29 June 1863; file H-507-1863, LRCSW; Eleventh Ward, Baltimore, Maryland, p. 36 (Robert Hough), 1860 Census.

16. Files D-107-1864 and E-33-1863, LRCSW; Martinsburg, Berkeley County, Virginia, p. 168 (John A. Dugan), and Fourteenth Ward, Baltimore, Maryland, pp. 80–81 (Susan Yerby), 1860 Census; *City Intelligencer*, 8–9.

17. Francis Snapp to James Seddon, 7 November 1863, Civil War Letters Collection; Harpers Ferry, Jefferson County, Virginia, pp. 204–5 (Francis Snapp), 1860 Census.

18. File D-144-1864, LRCSW; Jefferson City, Jefferson Parish, Louisiana, p. 77 (Joseph Deady), 1860 Census. Other examples are in files T-82-1863, B-733-1864, M-474-1864, and F-37-1865, LRCSW.

19. File W-529-1862, LRCSW; *Dispatch*, 28 December 1863.

20. *WOTR*, ser. 2, 2:1431; files M-151-1863 and E-55-1864, LRCSW; Carrollton, Kansas District, Carroll County, Georgia, p. 3/563 (L. C. McCalman), 1860 Census.

21. Casstevens, *George W. Alexander*, 39–48; *Dispatch*, 14, 18 August 1862.

22. Casstevens, *George W. Alexander*, 43, 47–48, 50–51, 74, 79; Zombek, "Paternalism and Imprisonment"; Neely, *Southern Rights*, 87–89; *WOTR*, ser. 2, 2:1431, 7:206–7; *Dispatch*, 10 April 1862. For examples of various types of prisoners and lengths of incarceration, see Peyton Wise to George Alexander, 22 May 1863, in C.S.A. Army, Department of Henrico Papers; and files B-315-1862, R-712-1862, A-366-1863, C-728-1863, C-770-1863, H-495-1863, L-230-1864, and W-338-1864, LRCSW.

23. Neely, *Southern Rights*, 136–40; Jordan, *Black Confederates*, 80, 281; Casstevens, *George W. Alexander*, 82–83; report of I. H. Carrington, 22 August 1863, in C.S.A. Army, Department of Henrico Papers; files C-604-1863, S-24-1863, and L-89-1864, LRCSW; *Dispatch*, 20 April 1863, 23 July (which notes the arrival in Richmond of fugitive slaves caught in Tennessee), 27 August 1864; *Examiner*, 21 June 1864. Some recaptured fugitive slaves were held in other Confederate facilities in Richmond, including Camp Lee and Libby Prison. See *WOTR*, ser. 2, 5:844–45; file C-615-1864, LRCSW; *Dispatch*, 2 October 1862; *Examiner*, 28 December 1863; Jordan, *Black Confederates*, 79–80; and Ash, "Wall around Slavery," 64.

24. *Dispatch*, 25 April 1863; *Examiner*, 4 November 1863; file V-62-1864, LRCSW.

25. Casstevens, *George W. Alexander*, 50–51, 74; *Dispatch*, 5 November 1862; *WOTR*, ser. 2, 7:206–7.

26. Radley, *Rebel Watchdog*, 171; *WOTR*, ser. 2, 6:544, 852, 8:1004; Blakey, *General John H. Winder*, 155, 156; Casstevens, *George W. Alexander*, 33, 42; *Dispatch* 27 March 1862.

27. *Dispatch*, 24 July 1861, 2 June, 19 December 1862, 16, 19 May 1864; *Examiner*, 30 June 1862; *Richmond Semi-Weekly Examiner*, 4 July 1862; J. B. Jones, *Rebel War Clerk's*

Diary, 1:67, 139, 315, 318, 321. Prisoners from the Battles of Murfreesboro (Tennessee) and Chickamauga (Georgia) are noted in Jones, 1:240, 2:59. Black prisoners are noted in *Dispatch*, 27 August 1864; and Jordan, *Black Confederates*, 281.

28. Blakey, *General John H. Winder*, 153–74; Radley, *Rebel Watchdog*, 172–73, 175; *Dispatch*, 4 November 1861, 27 March, 19, 31 December 1862; *WOTR*, ser. 2, 4:821, 6:439, 852, 8:71; J. B. Jones, *Rebel War Clerk's Diary*, 2:91, 94.

29. Martinez, *Confederate Slave Impressment*, esp. 1–17, 20–21, 26–27, 33–34.

30. Martinez, esp. 143, 150–51; J. B. Jones, *Rebel War Clerk's Diary*, 1:183, 237, 2:183.

31. *Dispatch*, 24 September 1862; *Enquirer*, 18 October 1862; J. B. Jones, *Rebel War Clerk's Diary*, 1:192, 195.

32. Dabney, *Richmond*, 111–12; Takagi, "Rearing Wolves," 38, 78; Furgurson, *Ashes of Glory*, 20–21; *Enquirer*, 18 October 1862.

33. *Enquirer*, 25 April 1862; Trask, *Two Months*, 86.

34. *Dispatch*, 13 February, 30 September 1862.

35. McMurry, *Two Great Rebel Armies*, 74–86, 112–13; G. W. Bassett Jr. to Robert Lee, [26 April 1861], George Carrington to John Letcher, 27 April 1861, and John Harvie to John Letcher, 27 April 1861, MR 4730, Letcher Executive Papers; Ashland, St. Paul's Parish, Hanover County, Virginia, p. 75/397 (G. W. Bassett), 1860 Census.

36. File 1614-1861, LRCSW; Huntersville, Pocahontas County, Virginia, p. 90 (William Skeen), 1860 Census; *Examiner*, 10 October 1863. For other examples, see files 3019-1861, M-41-1862, M-42-1862, and M-68-1862, LRCSW.

37. Lange, "Changed Name," 146/153; file 1613-1861, LRCSW.

38. Files 3657-1861, M-299-1862, M-1632-1862, and S-446-1863, LRCSW.

39. Files A-515-1862 and 9462-1862, LRCSW.

40. File H-521-1864, LRCSW; Western Subdivision, Henrico County, Virginia, p. 74 (J. [*sic*] H. Hutton), 1860 Census.

41. Files R-509-1862, W-437-1862, W-493-1862, G-13-1865, and J-191/2-1865, LRCSW; *Dispatch*, 12 July 1862; *Enquirer*, 30 July 1861; J. B. Jones, *Rebel War Clerk's Diary*, 1:142; Pember, *Southern Woman's Story*, 51; Green, *Chimborazo*, 76; White Post, Clarke County, Virginia, p. 66/662 (R. C. Randolph), 1860 Census; McDonald, *Diary with Reminiscences*, 237–41.

42. Trask, *Two Months*, 74; *City Intelligencer*; *Stranger's Guide*; Vanfelson, *Little Red Book*.

43. *Dispatch*, 31 July 1861, 28 June 1862; *Enquirer*, 31 July 1861; Crocker, "Army Intelligence Office," 118–19; files C-750-1862 and C-810-1862, LRCSW; *City Intelligencer*, 18; *Stranger's Guide*, 13. See also Green (*Chimborazo*, 76) on the assistance provided by that hospital to visiting kinfolk.

44. *WOTR*, ser. 1, 33:1277, 1279–80, ser. 2, 6:438–39, 455–56.

45. Manarin, *Richmond at War*, 191n, 581, 581–82n; J. B. Jones, *Rebel War Clerk's Diary*, 1:226; *WOTR*, ser. 1, 33:1277, 1279–80, ser. 2, 6:438–39, 455–56; Younger, *Inside the Confederate Government*, 145–46; file L-328-1864, LRCSW.

46. J. B. Jones, *Rebel War Clerk's Diary*, 2:189, 192; Younger, *Inside the Confederate Government*, 145–46; McGuire, *Diary*, 259–60; *WOTR*, ser. 1, 33:1279–80, ser. 2, 6:455–56, 925–26; Radley, *Rebel Watchdog*, 173, 175.

47. Younger, *Inside the Confederate Government*, 145–46; *WOTR*, ser. 1, 33:1279–80.

48. Manarin, *Richmond at War*, 581, 581–82n; file L-328-1864, LRCSW; *WOTR*, ser. 1, 33:1279–80.

49. *WOTR*, ser. 1, 33:1279–80; Younger, *Inside the Confederate Government*, 145–46; Radley, *Rebel Watchdog*, 175.

50. Younger, *Inside the Confederate Government*, 145–46; J. B. Jones, *Rebel War Clerk's Diary*, 2:188, 189; McGuire, *Diary*, 259; Putnam, *Richmond during the War*, 288–89; Woodward, *Mary Chesnut's Civil War*, 596; Chesson and Roberts, *Exile in Richmond*, 118, 119–20.

51. *Dispatch*, 16 August 1861; Trask, *Two Months*, 80. Halttunen (*Confidence Men*, 34–36) offers interesting context on mid-nineteenth-century Americans' concerns about the increasing anonymity of society in the growing cities.

CHAPTER 3

1. J. B. Jones, *Rebel War Clerk's Diary*, 1:226; McGuire, *Diary*, 238, 258.

2. Goldfield, *Urban Growth*, 46, 48, 199; Hopley, *Life in the South*, 1:135; Putnam, *Richmond during the War*, 78; Elsa Barkley Brown and Kimball, "Mapping the Terrain," 302; Sutherland, *Expansion of Everyday Life*, 48–50; Gamber, *Boardinghouse in Nineteenth-Century America*; Takagi, "Rearing Wolves," 40–41.

3. Scott, *Old Richmond Neighborhoods*, 23–283 passim, esp. 91–92, 203, 251; Dabney, *Richmond*, 82; Manarin, *Richmond at War*, 146, 510–11; Chesson and Roberts, *Exile in Richmond*, 44; Hopley, *Life in the South*, 1:144–45; Kimball, "African-Virginians," 125–29; Takagi, "Rearing Wolves," 39–40; Elsa Barkley Brown and Kimball, "Mapping the Terrain," 302; *Examiner*, 21 November 1863.

4. John and George Gibson, Haxall, Crenshaw, and Company, and Samuel C. Robinson files, CPRCBF; file E-93-1862, LRCSW; J. S. Shriver to William Smith, 12 February 1864, MR 5015, William Smith Executive Papers; Pember, *Southern Woman's Story*, 18.

5. Old Dominion Iron and Nail Works Company, Samuel C. Robinson, Talbott and Brother, Adolphus J. Rahm, and William A. Mountcastle files, CPRCBF; files A-374-1862 and B-94-1864, LRCSW; J. B. Jones, *Rebel War Clerk's Diary*, 2:197; Pember, *Southern Woman's Story*, 18.

6. Old Dominion Iron and Nail Works Company and Virginia Iron Manufacturing Company files, CPRCBF; Putnam, *Richmond during the War*, 315. The skilled-labor shortage is further discussed in chapter 5.

7. Manarin, *Richmond at War*, 5–6; *Examiner*, 3 June 1864; Crenshaw and Company, Dunlop, Moncure, and Company, Ritchie and Dunnavant, and Selden and Miller files, CPRCBF; files G-112-1862, W-829-1862, C-487-1863, and G-36-1863, LRCSW; *WOTR*, ser. 2, 3:756, 6:322–23; Waitt, *Confederate Military Hospitals*, 5–18; *City Intelligencer*, 16, 17.

8. De Leon, *Four Years*, 87; Putnam, *Richmond during the War*, 78, 320; *Dispatch*, 29 October 1863; Chesson and Roberts, *Exile in Richmond*, 91, 284, 295, 303–4.

9. *Dispatch*, 21 March 1863, 24 March 1862; *Examiner*, 30 October 1863; McGuire, *Diary*, 240–41, 299, 309–10; Chesson and Roberts, *Exile in Richmond*, 331, 334.

10. *Dispatch*, 15 November 1862, 19 September 1863; J. B. Jones, *Rebel War Clerk's Diary*, 1:257; McGuire, *Diary*, 240–41; Harrison, *Recollections*, 116; Woodward, *Mary Chesnut's Civil War*, 429–30.

11. Wiley, *Letters of Warren Akin*, 13, 36, 36–37, 37n, 60, 62, 90, 93; Second Ward, Richmond, Henrico County, Virginia, p. 218/426 (George W. Gretter), 1860 Census.

12. McGuire, *Diary*, 88.

13. Chesson and Roberts, *Exile in Richmond*, 46, 284, 296, 302–8 passim, 316, 317.

14. *Examiner*, 10 December 1863; Elsa Barkley Brown and Kimball, "Mapping the Terrain," 302; Takagi, *"Rearing Wolves,"* 39–41.

15. John and George Gibson file, CPRCBF; file G-262-1864, LRCSW; J. B. Jones, *Rebel War Clerk's Diary*, 2:35; *Enquirer*, 2 December 1862.

16. James Holloway to Annie Holloway, 19, 26 August 1862, Holloway Papers; Burton Harrison to A. J. Quinche, 21 March 1862, Harrison Family Papers; McGuire, *Diary*, vii–viii, 87–88.

17. McGuire, *Diary*, 88–89, 90–91, 92, 93.

18. *Dispatch*, 24 March, 5 May, 8, 15 November 1862, 6 June, 19 September 1863; Woodward, *Mary Chesnut's Civil War*, 429.

19. Chesson and Roberts, *Exile in Richmond*, 108, 148, 202, 246, 255–84 passim, 295–334 passim. Boarding arrangements are further discussed in chapter 4.

20. Withers Diary, 6, 28 March 1863; file L-185-1862, LRCSW; *Dispatch*, 3 February 1862; Chesson and Roberts, *Exile in Richmond*, 47.

21. *Dispatch*, 29 October 1863.

22. Wiley, *Letters of Warren Akin*, 36–37; J. B. Jones, *Rebel War Clerk's Diary*, 1:266–67; Phoebe Pember to Mrs. J. F. Gilmer, 20 October, 30 December 1863, Pember Letters; First Ward, Richmond, Henrico County, Virginia, p. 106 (Samuel Skinner), 1860 Census.

23. *Whig*, 6 January 1863; files S-759-1862, S-555-1863, C-553-1864, and T-38-1865, LRCSW; *Dispatch*, 24 March 1862; J. B. Jones, *Rebel War Clerk's Diary*, 1:47, 128, 235, 237, 2:170; *Examiner*, 9 May 1864; Chesson and Roberts, *Exile in Richmond*, 104, 127; McGuire, *Diary*, 307; Wiley, *Letters of Warren Akin*, 5.

24. J. B. Jones, *Rebel War Clerk's Diary*, 1:265–66; Woodward, *Mary Chesnut's Civil War*, 429; McGuire, *Diary*, 258, 298–99, 309–10; Chesson and Roberts, *Exile in Richmond*, 46, 104, 265, 283, 284, 294–95; James H. Mondy file, First Battalion, Infantry, Local Defense Troops, CSR/Virginia; Eastern Division, Henrico County, Virginia, p. 187/849 (James Munday [*sic*]), 1860 Census.

25. J. B. Jones, *Rebel War Clerk's Diary*, 1:235, 257, 2:46, 123, 372; Wiley, *Letters of Warren Akin*, 5; Chesson and Roberts, *Exile in Richmond*, 284.

26. Woodward, *Mary Chesnut's Civil War*, 106, 122, 123; *City Intelligencer*, 5, 8–11, 22; Wiley, *Letters of Warren Akin*, 5; Chesson and Roberts, *Exile in Richmond*, 69, 71n; Clark, "Confederate Officer Visits Richmond," 88–89; Goldfield, *Urban Growth*, 107; Manarin, *Richmond at War*, 453; Macon, *Life Gleanings*, 26.

27. John P. Ballard and Spotswood Hotel files, CPRCBF; *Examiner*, 6 March 1863, 24 March 1865; Wiley, *Letters of Warren Akin*, 5, 35; Williams, *William Alexander Graham*, 90.

28. J. B. Jones, *Rebel War Clerk's Diary*, 1:225; Bailey, *Henrico Home Front*, 232–33; T. R. Loockerman (also spelled "Lockerman") file, Third Infantry Regiment, Local Defense Troops, CSR/Virginia; Federalsburg, Caroline County, Maryland, p. 316 (Thomas Lockerman), 1860 Census; files J-53-1862 and H-194-1862, LRCSW; Ordnance Depot superintendent to Josiah Gorgas, 23 February 1863, 90:192–93, Letters Sent by the Richmond Arsenal.

29. J. B. Jones, *Rebel War Clerk's Diary*, 1:114; file C-1771/2-1864, LRCSW; McGuire, *Diary*, 251; Chesson and Roberts, *Exile in Richmond*, 11, 44; Pember, *Southern Woman's Story*, xiii; Katharine M. Jones, *Ladies of Richmond*, 99–100; Waitt, *Confederate Military Hospitals*, 5; Harrison, *Recollections*, 182–84.

30. *Examiner*, 21 November 1863; *Dispatch*, 11 April, 26 October 1863.

31. *Dispatch*, 15, 16 October 1861, 31 January 1862, 1 July 1863; *Examiner*, 25 June 1864.

32. Macon, *Life Gleanings*, 26; Trask, *Two Months*, 74; *Dispatch*, 24 March 1862; Wiley, *Letters of Warren Akin*, 5. For examples of visitors to the city who stayed in a hotel, see files 1614-1861, 3019-1861, 9462-1862, B-1121-1862, C-725-1862, K-214-1862, M-299-1862, and M-1254-1862, LRCSW.

33. Pember *Southern Woman's Story*, 51–53; file H-476-1863, LRCSW; *Dispatch*, 18 July 1862; John M. Watkins file, Third Infantry Regiment, CSR/North Carolina.

34. *Dispatch*, 13, 20, 22 February, 10 June, 30 September 1862; *Stranger's Guide*, 26; Benjamin Washington Jones, *Under the Stars*, 157–59.

35. May 1861 contracts, John and George Gibson file, CPRCBF; Day, *Down South*, 1:86; Williams and Hamilton, *Papers*, 501; Benjamin Washington Jones, *Under the Stars*, 60, 228; Martinez, *Confederate Slave Impressment*, 51, 56–57, 60, 70.

36. Coles, "Richmond, the Confederate Hospital City," 71–75; Waitt, *Confederate Military Hospitals*, 1–40; Green, *Chimborazo*, 43–46; Louisiana Soldiers' Relief Association, *Louisiana Soldiers' Relief Association*; Trask, *Two Months*, 80; Bridges, "Juliet Opie Hopkins," 89–90.

37. Green, *Chimborazo*, 9–12, 17–18, 66–70, 72, 90, 92, 114–15; Coles, "Richmond, the Confederate Hospital City," 75–87.

38. Blakey, *General John H. Winder*, 153–74.

39. WOTR, ser. 2, 6:545, 546, 588, 1087–88, 7:80, 870; Blakey, *General John H. Winder*, 156–72 passim; file B-94-1864, LRCSW.

40. Wheelan, *Libby Prison Breakout*, 31–35; Manarin, *Richmond at War*, 583; Blakey, *General John H. Winder*, 155–74 passim; WOTR, ser. 2, 6:241, 262–63, 301–2, 354, 510, 544–45.

41. WOTR, ser. 2, 5:876–909, 7:204, 8:93–94; Casstevens, *George W. Alexander*, 48–51, 62, 66, 68, 97–99, 107–24; file C-604-1863, LRCSW; Blakey, *General John H. Winder*, 144, 145.

42. *Dispatch*, 6 November 1861, 15 October 1863; *Examiner*, 25 September 1863, 22 November 1864; J. B. Jones, *Rebel War Clerk's Diary*, 1:104, 155, 161, 196, 219, 283, 294, 329, 2:5, 8, 56, 77, 118, 398, 400, 408; Johnston, *Virginia Railroads*, 124–26; files W-893-1862, J-241-1863, S-555-1863, M-245-1864, and T-38-1865, LRCSW; Benjamin Washington Jones, *Under the Stars*, 54–55; WOTR, ser. 2, 8:93–94; claim 2903 (Francis Adams), Barred and Disallowed Case Files; Green, *Chimborazo*, 9–10, 92–93; Manarin, *Richmond at War*, 230–31, 240.

43. Manarin and Dowdey, *History of Henrico County*, 232–34; Dew, *Ironmaker to the Confederacy*, 34, 149–50; Chesson and Roberts, *Exile in Richmond*, 108, 109n, 273; Midlothian Coal Mining Company file, CPRCBF; files D-440-1862, L-750-1862, W-893-1862, M-267-1863, and S-555-1863, LRCSW; *Second Annual Directory*, 226; J. B. Jones, *Rebel War Clerk's Diary*, 1:155, 161, 196, 219, 283, 329, 2:5, 8, 77, 118, 328, 381; Manarin, *Richmond at War*, 230–31, 240.

44. *Charters and Ordinances*, 107–23; Goldfield, *Urban Growth*, 150–51; *Stranger's Guide*, 31; files H-541-1863, G-128-1864, and R-261-1864, LRCSW; Manarin, *Richmond at War*, 111n, 240n, 241, 275, 297, 377, 445, 477–78, 501, 542, 542–43n, 577; Richmond City Gas Works file, CPRCBF; *Examiner*, 21 November, 28 December 1864; Trask, *Two Months*, 74–75; Woodward, *Mary Chesnut's Civil War*, 569; Chesson and Roberts, *Exile in Richmond*, 234, 236, 285.

CHAPTER 4

1. Younger, *Inside the Confederate Government*, xxiii, 116; Goff, *Confederate Supply*, 10–11, 156, 171, 228, 247–48.

2. Craven, *Soil Exhaustion*, 139–61; files D-460-1862, L-2001/2-1863, and D-86-1864, LRCSW; claim 12429 (Isaac Sykes), Southern Claims Commission Approved Claims; claims 3798 (Sedden P. Akin) and 2903 (Francis Adams), Barred and Disallowed Case Files; Goldfield, *Urban Growth*, 187, 189; Robert, *Tobacco Kingdom*, 29–31.

3. Wooster, *Politicians, Planters*, 99–100, 102; Richmond and Charlottesville Turnpike Company and Richmond, Williamsburg, and Central Turnpike Company files, CPRCBF.

4. Goldfield, *Urban Growth*, 187, 189–91; *City Intelligencer*, 22; Black, *Railroads of the Confederacy*, 12–25, 72–73; Johnston, *Virginia Railroads*, 9–19; Brewer, *Confederate Negro*, 74, 79–94.

5. Brewer, *Confederate Negro*, 71, 74–77; Robert, *Tobacco Kingdom*, 59–61; James River and Kanawha Company file, CPRCBF; files E-11-1862, E-40-1862, and S-709-1863, LRCSW; Chesson and Roberts, *Exile in Richmond*, 78, 79n.

6. Goldfield, *Urban Growth*, 192–93; Craven, *Soil Exhaustion*, 132; *Examiner*, 4 November 1863; *Charters and Ordinances*, 17–18; file J-280-1863, LRCSW; Day, *Down South*, 1:133.

7. *Charters and Ordinances*, 123–32; Manarin, *Richmond at War*, esp. 198, 364, 365; *Stranger's Guide*, 31; Chesson and Roberts, *Exile in Richmond*, 62; *Examiner*, 24 April 1863; Chesson, "Harlots or Heroines?," 139, 143, 153–54.

8. Manarin, *Richmond at War*, 17–18, 17–18n, 138, 198; *Charters and Ordinances*, 132–44; Goldfield, *Urban Growth*, 151; *Stranger's Guide*, 31; Chesson and Roberts, *Exile in Richmond*, 56, 78, 282, 336.

9. J. B. Jones, *Rebel War Clerk's Diary*, 1:261. The Subsistence Bureau's policy was that at all times there should be stockpiled in Richmond no less than a ten-day supply of rations for 100,000 troops; see Goff, *Confederate Supply*, 77, 234.

10. Goff, *Confederate Supply*, 104–11; Johnston, *Virginia Railroads*, esp. 193, 227; Brewer, *Confederate Negro*, 75, 79–80; Hurt, *Agriculture and the Confederacy*, 67, 121; *Dispatch*, 4 August 1863; D. Von Groning to Alfred Paul, 28 June 1862, Von Groning Letterbook; Manarin, *Richmond at War*, 189n; J. B. Jones, *Rebel War Clerk's Diary*, 1:207, 240–41; Richmond and Petersburg Railroad Company, Virginia Central Railroad Company, and James River and Kanawha Company files, CPRCBF; *WOTR*, ser. 1, 46(2):1224–25.

11. Haxall, Crenshaw, and Company file, CPRCBF; Goldfield, *Urban Growth*, 193; J. B. Jones, *Rebel War Clerk's Diary*, 1:207, 267–68; files D-677-1862 and W-164-1863, LRCSW; Blakey, *General John H. Winder*, 161; Younger, *Inside the Confederate Government*, 41; *Examiner*, 4 November 1863, 23 May 1864.

12. Files B-783-1863, L-134-1863, and S-307-1864, LRCSW; Blakey, *General John H. Winder*, 156, 161; J. B. Jones, *Rebel War Clerk's Diary*, 1:240, 2:124; Younger, *Inside the Confederate Government*, 41.

13. Files D-671-1862, D-677-1862, and L-134-1863, LRCSW; Manarin, *Richmond at War*, 414; Younger, *Inside the Confederate Government*, 41; J. B. Jones, *Rebel War Clerk's Diary*, 1:279; Goff, *Confederate Supply*, 100.

14. *WOTR*, ser. 2, 6:438, 455; Blair, *Virginia's Private War*, 97; file D-677-1862, LRCSW.

15. Gates, *Agriculture*, 22–23, 74–76; Hurt, *Agriculture and the Confederacy*, 60, 64, 75–76, 135, 146–47, 150–51; D. Von Groning to Messrs. Homer and Sprague, 1 June 1861, and to Alfred Paul, 28 June 1862, Von Groning Letterbook; files W-1057-1862, W-1064-1862,

H-494-1863, H-497-1863, S-92-1864, S-263-1864, and W-126-1864, LRCSW; Martinez, *Confederate Slave Impressment*, 72–97; Jordan, *Black Confederates*, 69–82; Bailey, *Henrico Home Front*, 95–103, 171–78, 222–26.

16. Ash, *When the Yankees Came*; Hurt, *Agriculture and the Confederacy*, 56, 61, 64, 69–70; [?] to J. S. Preston, 14 May 1864, Coke Papers; file J-91-1863, LRCSW; J. B. Jones, *Rebel War Clerk's Diary*, 2:217; Bailey, *Henrico Home Front*, 222.

17. Ash, *When the Yankees Came*, 92–94; Hurt, *Agriculture and the Confederacy*, 145–46, 205–7; claims 12427 (William James), 12428 (Henry Sykes), 12429 (Isaac Sykes), 14990 (James Duke), and 17877 (Isabella Atkins), Southern Claims Commission Approved Claims.

18. *Dispatch*, 4, 6 August 1863; *Examiner*, 12 July 1864; Benjamin Washington Jones, *Under the Stars*, 160–61; files 2882-1861, A-331-1862, C-730-1862, D-460-1862, H-811-1862, J-210-1862, P-517-1862, L-169-1863, L-2001/2-1863, S-183-1863, and P-151-1864, LRCSW; *WOTR*, ser. 1, 11(3):526; Hurt, *Agriculture and the Confederacy*, 138.

19. Goff, *Confederate Supply*, 85–87, 96–104, 154–55, 168–75, 220–21; Gates, *Agriculture*, 46–59, 63–69; Blair, *Virginia's Private War*, 71–73, 112–20; Younger, *Inside the Confederate Government*, 107–8; files G-90-1862, K-118-1863, L-88-1863, S-292-1863, and P-213-1864, LRCSW; D. Von Groning to Alfred Paul, 28 June 1862, Von Groning Letterbook; *Dispatch*, 15 October 1863, 27 April 1864; *Examiner*, 9 May 1863; J. B. Jones, *Rebel War Clerk's Diary*, 1:315; Ryan, *Yankee Spy*, 49.

20. D. Von Groning to Alfred Paul, 28 June 1862, Von Groning Letterbook; Richmond and Charlottesville Turnpike Company, Richmond, Williamsburg, and Central Turnpike Company, and William B. Winston files, CPRCBF; files T-448-1862 and E-121-1863, LRCSW; *Richmond Semi-Weekly Examiner*, 4 July 1862; Manarin, *Richmond at War*, 451.

21. Files F-206-1862, P-324-1862, T-448-1862, and E-121-1863, LRCSW; Trask, *Two Months*, 88; J. B. Jones, *Rebel War Clerk's Diary*, 1:278; *Dispatch*, 25 June, 17 July 1863. Manchester, directly across the river from Richmond and connected to it by three bridges, served as the southern transportation gateway to the capital.

22. Black, *Railroads of the Confederacy*, 124–30, 215–17; Johnston, *Virginia Railroads*, 10, 12, 13, 19, 64, 65–66, 69–70, 122–26, 129–30, 134, 193–94, 224–26, 235–37; *WOTR*, ser. 1, 18: 951–52; files W-832-1862, D-5-1863, D-164-1863, E-34-1863, F-158-1863, and H-321-1863, LRCSW; H. D. Whitcomb to F. W. Sims, 15 February, 7 April 1864, in Virginia Central Railroad Company file, CPRCBF.

23. Black, *Railroads of the Confederacy*, 125, 133; Johnston, *Virginia Railroads*, 13, 118, 126–30, 230–31; E. H. Gill to F. W. Sims, 7 March 1864, in Richmond and Petersburg Railroad Company file, CPRCBF; files F-477-1862 and F-158-1863, LRCSW; *WOTR*, ser. 1, 18: 951–52.

24. Brewer, *Confederate Negro*, 75–79; file P-181-1864, LRCSW.

25. *WOTR*, ser. 1, 46(2):525, 1040, 1041; J. B. Jones, *Rebel War Clerk's Diary*, 2:408; chief engineer to president and board of directors, 18 March 1865, in James River and Kanawha Company file, CPRCBF; Johnston, *Virginia Railroads*, 236–37; Jordan, *Black Confederates*, 54; Brewer, *Confederate Negro*, 78.

26. J. B. Jones, *Rebel War Clerk's Diary*, 1:104, 240, 250, 261, 267, 275, 2:168–69, 218, 391, 432, 457; D. Von Groning to Alfred Paul, 28 June 1862, Von Groning Letterbook; Hurt, *Agriculture and the Confederacy*, 292; Katharine M. Jones, *Ladies of Richmond*, 264; Putnam, *Richmond during the War*, 303; file R-31-1864, LRCSW.

27. J. B. Jones, *Rebel War Clerk's Diary*, 1:294; Chesson and Roberts, *Exile in Richmond*,

55, 91, 124n; files E-33-1863 and S-555-1863, LRCSW; *Dispatch*, 19 September 1863; *Examiner*, 6 March 1863; Katharine M. Jones, *Ladies of Richmond*, 265.

28. Cochran Recollections, vol. 2, February 1864; J. B. Jones, *Rebel War Clerk's Diary*, 1:294; Ordnance Depot superintendent to Josiah Gorgas, 7 April 1863, 90:274, Letters Sent by Richmond Arsenal; Chesson and Roberts, *Exile in Richmond*, 55, 91, 108–9, 255, 259.

29. Putnam, *Richmond during the War*, 252; *Dispatch*, 15 October 1864; Takagi, "Rearing Wolves," 42; *Examiner*, 10 March, 1, 23 November 1864, 24 March 1865; Chesson and Roberts, *Exile in Richmond*, 53; Philip F. Brown, *Reminiscences of the War*, 47, 52; Day, *Down South*, 1:109–10; *Enquirer*, 26 April 1862.

30. Richmond City Water Works file, CPRCBF; Chesson and Roberts, *Exile in Richmond*, 56, 115, 282, 336; file C-402-1864, LRCSW; Green, *Chimborazo*, 12; Manarin, *Richmond at War*, 17–18, 17–18n, 138, 195, 198, 295–96, 329, 347, 371, 423–25, 557–58.

31. Emory M. Thomas, *Confederate State of Richmond*, 87, 105–6; Blakey, *General John H. Winder*, 120, 129–30; *Enquirer*, 25 April 1862; *Dispatch*, 1 May 1862; Steger, "'United to Support,'" 320–35; Manarin, *Richmond at War*, 387–88, 387–88n.

32. Manarin, *Richmond at War*, 189–90n; file S-502-1862, LRCSW; Emory M. Thomas, "To Feed the Citizens," 27.

33. Bill, *Beleaguered City*, 229; J. B. Jones, *Rebel War Clerk's Diary*, 1:202, 240, 2:156; McGuire, *Diary*, 328; Woodward, *Mary Chestnut's Civil War*, 434, 487, 500, 515, 548, 551, 554.

34. J. B. Jones, *Rebel War Clerk's Diary*, 1:291; Younger, *Inside the Confederate Government*, 108; *Examiner*, 10 December 1863; *Dispatch*, 16 July 1861; Chesson and Roberts, *Exile in Richmond*, 168, 172; Cochran Recollections, vol. 2, Christmas 1863.

35. Putnam, *Richmond during the War*, 343–44; Younger, *Inside the Confederate Government*, 43, 108, 117; Cochran Recollections, vol. 2, Christmas 1863; W. S. Downer to Josiah Gorgas, 28 November 1862, 90:41, Letters Sent by the Richmond Arsenal; Chesson and Roberts, *Exile in Richmond*, 161, 300, 324; files B-727-1862, C-265-1862, C-810-1862, D-434-1862, G-710-1862, H-194-1862, S-555-1863, W-415-1863, B-700-1864, D-107-1864, and L-329-1864, LRCSW; Manarin, *Richmond at War*, 292–93; J. B. Jones, *Rebel War Clerk's Diary*, 1:55, 266, 381, 2:41, 170, 335.

36. Time Book of the Richmond Arsenal, January 1863; *Examiner*, 5, 7 December 1863; *Sentinel*, 24 October 1863; files D-434-1862, A-306-1863, C-214-1863, M-805-1863, H-169-1864, and K-27-1864, LRCSW; *Dispatch*, 5 October 1863; *Enquirer*, 18 October 1862.

37. Files T-38-1865 and W-29-1865, LRCSW; Chesson and Roberts, *Exile in Richmond*, 324.

38. Blakey, *General John H. Winder*, 155–72 passim; Martinez, *Confederate Slave Impressment*, 51–55, 70; *WOTR*, ser. 2, 6:241–42, 262–63, 278–79, 439–40, 456, 497–98, 544–46, 1087, 7:117, 205–7; Casstevens, *George W. Alexander*, 67; files B-78-1863, H-226-1863, W-338-1864, and P-30-1865, LRCSW; J. B. Jones, *Rebel War Clerk's Diary*, 2:73, 94, 135; Benjamin Washington Jones, *Under the Stars*, 160–61.

39. Dew, *Ironmaker to the Confederacy*, 241–42; files C-553-1864, G-154-1864, H-172-1864, L-67-1864, and S-477-1864, LRCSW; *WOTR*, ser. 1, 40(3):747–48; *Examiner*, 9 May 1864; Richard Habersham to father, 1 February 1864, Habersham Family Papers; Green, *Chimborazo*, 98; Wiley, *Life of Johnny Reb*, 110–11, 136.

40. Green, *Chimborazo*, 98–104; Louisiana Soldiers' Relief Association, *Louisiana*

Soldiers' Relief Association, 5–7; *Examiner*, 4 November 1863; Pember, *Southern Woman's Story*, 45–46.

41. Putnam, *Richmond during the War*, 253; McGuire, *Diary*, 238–39, 244, 298.

42. File A-306-1863, LRCSW.

43. Chesson and Roberts, *Exile in Richmond*, 362; J. B. Jones, *Rebel War Clerk's Diary*, 1:266, 274, 283, 306, 332, 358–59, 2:9, 17, 28, 50, 135, 170, 239, 246–47.

44. *Examiner*, 20 March 1863, 23 April 1864; Green, *Chimborazo*, 98–99; Patrick H. Starke and George Watt and Company files, CPRCBF; file L-217-1864, LRCSW.

45. Dew, *Ironmaker to the Confederacy*, 154–61, 167–68, 170, 172, 241–42, 243; files D-340-1863, W-117-1863, F-8-1864, and S-477-1864, LRCSW; *Examiner*, 12 November 1863.

46. Files B-810-1863, E-33-1863, K-118-1863, W-654-1863, B-175-1864, G-262-1864, L-105-1864, O-45-1864, O-46-1864, and O-50-1864, LRCSW.

47. Files A-342-1863, S-555-1863, A-84-1864, D-107-1864, D-115-1864, J-120-1864, K-27-1864, L-329-1864, S-477-1864, T-170-1864, and T-38-1865, LRCSW; J. B. Jones, *Rebel War Clerk's Diary*, 2:247, 255, 267, 320, 377; Monroe et al., *Papers of Jefferson Davis*, 11:216; Emory M. Thomas, "To Feed the Citizens," 29; Chesson and Roberts, *Exile in Richmond*, 327; *Examiner*, 23 November 1863; *Sentinel*, 24 November 1863.

48. Ludwell H. Johnson, "Trading with the Union"; J. B. Jones, *Rebel War Clerk's Diary*, 1:271; Putnam, *Richmond during the War*, 203–4; files D-362-1863 and C-570-1864, LRCSW; claim 3229 (Christian Burging), Barred and Disallowed Case Files.

49. Files H-687-1862, B-379-1864, D-144-1864, M-474-1864, F-37-1865, K-29-1865, LRCSW.

50. Emory M. Thomas, "To Feed the Citizens," 27; Naragon, "Ballots, Bullets, and Blood," 326–28; Manarin, *Richmond at War*, 72–73, 95, 108, 165, 247–48, 247–248n, 408, 526n, 589; *Examiner*, 22 October 1863, 26 November, 2 December 1864; files M-432-1863, T-288-1863, and M-137-1864, LRCSW; *Dispatch*, 18 September 1861, 26 November, 1, 2 December 1864. Early in the war the city turned the almshouse over to the Confederate government, which used it as an army hospital; it was returned to city control in 1864. In the meantime, the inmates were housed elsewhere. See Chesson, *Richmond after the War*, 32–33; *Dispatch*, 5 October 1863; *Stranger's Guide*, 31; and file R-70-1864, LRCSW.

51. Manarin, *Richmond at War*, 317, 320–21, 335–37; Emory M. Thomas, "To Feed the Citizens," 27–28; Naragon, "Ballots, Bullets, and Blood," 326–27. The bread riot of April 1863 is discussed in chapter 9.

52. Manarin, *Richmond at War*, 382, 383–84, 451, 471, 484, 526n; file B-747-1863, LRCSW; *Examiner*, 22 October 1863; *Dispatch*, 16 June 1864; Emory M. Thomas, "To Feed the Citizens," 28–29; Naragon, "Ballots, Bullets, and Blood," 327–28; Younger, *Inside the Confederate Government*, 116.

53. *Dispatch*, 26 June 1863; *Examiner*, 5 December 1863; Cochran Recollections, vol. 2, February 1864; McGuire, *Diary*, 253–54, 324; Putnam, *Richmond during the War*, 343–44; J. B. Jones, *Rebel War Clerk's Diary*, 1:196, 200, 2:135, 244, 270, 399; Younger, *Inside the Confederate Government*, 108. In the last months of 1863, two Richmond newspapers mentioned the presence of beggars but insisted that they were not evidence of real want in the city. In one case, a number of people, mostly women, were going from door to door asking for handouts. But, as the *Dispatch* explained, they were really thieves who were casing houses with the intention of slipping inside to steal. The *Examiner* noted a number of crippled men in uniform who "hobble around doffing their caps to every one they meet

with . . . [a] tale of distress and want." Pointing out that there were several places in the city where disabled soldiers could get free meals, the editor none-too-subtly implied that these men were trying to get money to buy liquor and advised citizens approached by them to summon the provost guard. A few weeks later that editor argued that because of the abundance of jobs in the city there was far less begging than before the war; indeed, "with the exception of one or two mendicants, with whom begging has become a second nature, street-begging has ceased to be an institution in Richmond." See *Dispatch*, 23 November 1863; and *Examiner*, 15 September, 5 December 1863. John Jones's last diary entry on the subject (26 January 1865) was this: "Still, there are no beggars in the streets, except a few women of foreign or Northern birth." On the success of Confederate, state, and local efforts to feed the hungry in the state as a whole, see Blair, *Virginia's Private War*.

CHAPTER 5

1. *Examiner*, 5 December 1863. See also *Dispatch*, 26 June 1863; and McGuire, *Diary*, 254. The prewar labor surplus is noted also in Dew, *Ironmaker to the Confederacy*, 90.

2. Manarin, *Richmond at War*, 105; Day, *Down South*, 1:107; Lange, "Changed Name," 141/149; D. Von Groning to Messrs. Homer and Sprague, 1 June 1861, Von Groning Letterbook; files 3428-1861 and G-36-1863, LRCSW; Robert, *Tobacco Kingdom*, 190, 197; Takagi, "Rearing Wolves," 133–34.

3. Bruce, *Virginia Iron Manufacture*, 344; Dew, *Ironmaker to the Confederacy*, 90–91; J. B. Jones, *Rebel War Clerk's Diary*, 1:55, 67.

4. Steger, "'United to Support,'" 247–48; Dean S. Thomas, *Confederate Arsenals*, 3:886; Joseph Anderson to John Letcher, 27 April, 6 May 1861, MR 4735, Letcher Executive Papers; Dew, *Ironmaker to the Confederacy*, 92–93; files 3747-1861, 4169-1861, and 5374-1861, LRCSW.

5. Dew, *Ironmaker to the Confederacy*, 92–94; Bruce, *Virginia Iron Manufacture*, 358–59; files 5786-1861, 6068-1861, and 6362-1861, LRCSW. On exemptions from state militia duty, see Boney, *John Letcher*, 136, 141; Bruce, *Virginia Iron Manufacture*, 358; Manarin, *Richmond at War*, 131–32; and M. J. Michelbacher to John Letcher, 18 July 1861, MR 4750, Letcher Executive Papers.

6. Files 6067-1861, 6127-1861, 6131-1861, 6340-1861, and 6362-1861, LRCSW; Dew, *Ironmaker to the Confederacy*, 93–94.

7. Steger, "'United to Support,'" 274–75; Takagi, "Rearing Wolves," 127, 128, 130–31; Dew, *Ironmaker to the Confederacy*, 91–92; Brewer, *Confederate Negro*, 52–53, 59, 80–81, 96–97; Green, *Chimborazo*, 19, 41–42, 47.

8. United States Bureau of the Census, *Statistics*, xviii; Steger, "'United to Support,'" 261–64; Barber, "'Sisters of the Capital,'" 139–41; Goldfield, *Urban Growth*, 125; Bruce, *Virginia Iron Manufacture*, 360; Dew, *Ironmaker to the Confederacy*, 91; Dean S. Thomas, *Confederate Arsenals*, 3:882–84; files 2323-1861, 10481-1862, and G-124-1862; LRCSW; *Whig*, 9, 22 July, 1 October 1861; *Enquirer*, 16 October 1861; *Dispatch*, 28 January 1862.

9. Moore, *Conscription and Conflict*, esp. 12–14, 27–30, 52–53, 66–69; Goff, *Confederate Supply*, 42, 93–96; Dew, *Ironmaker to the Confederacy*, 144–45, 229–30.

10. Moore, *Conscription and Conflict*, esp. 44–45, 45n, 69n, 76–78, 83–84, 140, 308; Goff, *Confederate Supply*, 94–96, 159–64, 222–23; Dew, *Ironmaker to the Confederacy*, 145, 237–38, 243–45; J. B. Jones, *Rebel War Clerk's Diary*, 2:300; Younger, *Inside the Confederate Government*, 176–77, 181; Ordnance Depot superintendent to W. J. Willey, 14 February

1863, 90:166, Letters Sent by the Richmond Arsenal; Special Orders, Camp of Instruction; Whitlock Recollections, 110–11, 121–22.

11. Mathias Altmeyer file, CPRCBF; file J-15-1863, LRCSW.

12. Files T-261-1863 and V-81-1864, LRCSW; Miller, "Alabama Merchant."

13. John Coke to enrolling officer, 21 July 1864, Coke Papers; file S-25-1865, LRCSW; Ordnance Depot superintendent to E. Griswold, 25 September 1863, 90:567, Letters Sent by the Richmond Arsenal.

14. P. K. White to secretary of war, 21 January 1864, Civil War Letters Collection; P. K. White and John and George Gibson files, CPRCBF; files A-255-1862, G-775-1862, and H-495-1863, LRCSW; James Dinwiddie to John Kane, 11 November 1864, and to Josiah Gorgas, 5 January 1865, 911/2:143, 272, Letters Sent by the Richmond Arsenal; Dean S. Thomas, *Confederate Arsenals*, 3:948; Dew, *Ironmaker to the Confederacy*, 144–45, 228–38, 248–49.

15. Files E-149-1862, E-197-1862, E-34-1863, H-287-1863, H-321-1863, and E-70-1864, LRCSW; Black, *Railroads of the Confederacy*, 128–30, 215–17.

16. Files D-366-1862, D-637-1862, E-113-1862, L-505-1862, and E-19-1863, LRCSW; T. H. Langdon to John Coke, 30 July 1863, Civil War Letters Collection; Moore, *Conscription and Conflict*, 140.

17. Mitchell and Tyler to secretary of war, 14 January 1864, Civil War Letters Collection; file G-60-1864, LRCSW.

18. File T-1-1863, LRCSW.

19. Files W-1057-1862, W-1064-1862, W-1109-1862, and W-48-1863, LRCSW.

20. Files B-1538-1862, C-1278-1862, J-234-1862, M-860-1862, and N-232-1862, LRCSW.

21. Moore, *Conscription and Conflict*, 53, 67–69, 83–84; John Overall to John Preston, 1 October 1863, Circulars and Correspondence Received; file W-300-1864, LRCSW.

22. John Overall to John Preston, 1 October 1863, Circulars and Correspondence Received; *Examiner*, 23 November 1863; *Sentinel*, 24 November 1863; files A-439-1862, K-89-1863, B-154-1864, C-90-1864, L-22-1864, and T-128-1864, LRCSW; Dew, *Ironmaker to the Confederacy*, 234; Monroe et al., *Papers of Jefferson Davis*, 11:260–61.

23. *WOTR*, ser. 2, 5:841, 969; files W-1064-1862 and C-848-1863, LRCSW.

24. File C-770-1863, LRCSW.

25. Dew, *Ironmaker to the Confederacy*, 234–35; J. B. Jones, *Rebel War Clerk's Diary*, 2:354; *Examiner*, 11 December 1863; file C-728-1863, LRCSW.

26. Brewer, *Confederate Negro*, 52–63, 78, 82, 86, 90–91, 93–94; Takagi, "Rearing Wolves," 127, 128; Latimore, "Always a Minority," 96–104; Dew, *Ironmaker to the Confederacy*, 238–39, 250–64; file W-1057-1862, LRCSW; Manarin, *Richmond at War*, 231, 296–97.

27. Brewer, *Confederate Negro*, 18–22, 29, 32–34, 36–41, 96–120; Jordan, *Black Confederates*, 55; Green, *Chimborazo*, 46–49; file P-192-1863, LRCSW.

28. Brewer, *Confederate Negro*, 6–14; Martinez, *Confederate Slave Impressment*, esp. 7–11; Latimore, "Always a Minority," 94–96.

29. "Conscription Report of free negroes," May 1864, and extracts from special orders, April–May 1864, Coke Papers; endorsement, 15 April 1864, on application of J. B. Reed, Endorsements on Letters Received.

30. Johnston, *Virginia Railroads*, 225; files M-752-1863, S-464-1863, C-609-1864, and M-245-1864, LRCSW; Dew, *Ironmaker to the Confederacy*, 256–58; Brewer, *Confederate Negro*, 99–100.

31. Barber, "'Sisters of the Capital,'" 103–4, 107–8, 140, 145, 151, 155–56; *Dispatch*,

1 January 1863; *Enquirer*, 6 January 1863; *Sentinel*, 24 November 1863; Time Book of the Richmond Arsenal, January 1863; Third Ward, Richmond, Henrico County, Virginia, p. 59/503 (Elizth [*sic*] Ashmore), 1860 Census; files A-306-1863, C-810-1863, and M-805-1863, LRCSW; J. B. Jones, *Rebel War Clerk's Diary*, 2:357; *Examiner*, 25 June 1864.

32. Barber, "'Sisters of the Capital,'" 83–84, 103–5, 107, 119–22; Hilde, *Worth a Dozen Men*; Pember, *Southern Woman's Story*, ix, 1–3; files L-123-1864 and W-292-1864, LRCSW; J. B. Jones, *Rebel War Clerk's Diary*, 2:140, 179, 338; Welton, "My Heart," 233; *Examiner*, 5 November 1863.

33. *Dispatch*, 25 June 1864; *Examiner*, 11 November 1864.

34. E. S. Gay and H. Ker to John Letcher, 5 November 1862, MR 4770, Letcher Executive Papers; files G-710-1862, S-555-1863, A-59-1864, D-107-1864, and D-115-1864, LRCSW; *Examiner*, 10 December 1863; Monroe et al., *Papers of Jefferson Davis*, 9:404.

35. *Examiner*, 10 December 1863; files A-342-1863, B-599-1863, LRCSW.

36. File O-35-1864, LRCSW; Barber, "'Sisters of the Capital,'" 129–31; Putnam, *Richmond during the War*, 175; Chesson and Roberts, *Exile in Richmond*, 123, 352.

37. Pember, *Southern Woman's Story*, 3, 10–11, 37–44.

38. J. B. Jones, *Rebel War Clerk's Diary*, 2:106; McGuire, *Diary*, 238; Monroe et al., *Papers of Jefferson Davis*, 10:596.

39. Files T-82-1863 and B-379-1864, LRCSW; Ninth District, Baltimore, Maryland, p. 142/645 (Catherine V. Baxley), 1860 Census.

40. Files A-306-1863 and M-805-1863, LRCSW; *Dispatch*, 22 July, 2, 5 November 1863, 6 May 1864.

41. W. S. Downer to Josiah Gorgas, 28 November 1862, 90:41, and 7 April 1863, 90: 274, Letters Sent by the Richmond Arsenal; files G-775-1862, T-225-1863, and G-82-1864, LRCSW.

42. File D-468-1862, LRCSW; *WOTR*, ser. 2, 4:872; H. A. Hamilton to John Coke, 7 October 1863, W. L Brown to John Coke, 9, 12 June 1863, and Samson and Pae to Josiah Gorgas, 20 August 1863, Civil War Letters Collection; R. B. Wright to John Coke, 22 June 1863, Coke Papers; W. S. Downer to J. H. Winder, 31 July 1863, 90:471–72, and James Dinwiddie to W. L. Brown, 7 March 1865, 92:22, Letters Sent by the Richmond Arsenal.

43. Steger, "'United to Support,'" 250–56; Naragon, "Ballots, Bullets, and Blood," 319; Johnston, *Virginia Railroads*, 69–70; Younger, *Inside the Confederate Government*, 98; J. B. Jones, *Rebel War Clerk's Diary*, 2:21, 22; Martis, *Historical Atlas*, 2.

44. *Examiner*, 7 December 1863; Barber, "'Sisters of the Capital,'" 145–46.

45. *Dispatch*, 5 August 1864; Mitchell, *Hollywood Cemetery*, 59; Jordan, *Black Confederates*, 50–51.

46. Latimore, "Always a Minority," 93–94; *Dispatch*, 15, 16 July, 3, 7, 9 August 1861; claim 20403 (Isaac Pleasants), Southern Claims Commission Approved Claims; claim 20414 (Joseph Atkins), Barred and Disallowed Case Files; file R-85-1864, LRCSW; Brewer, *Confederate Negro*, 135–36, 152–55; Martinez, *Confederate Slave Impressment*, 64–65.

47. File T-539-1862, LRCSW.

48. *WOTR*, ser. 1, 27(3):862, 33:1301, 42(3):1370; *Dispatch*, 10 June 1863. The Local Defense Forces were sometimes referred to as the Local Defense Troops. The battalions were designated the First through the Sixth. In September 1864, the Second and Sixth were consolidated to form the Second Regiment and the Third was redesignated the Third Regiment. For details on the organization of the LDF, see CSR/Virginia for these units: First Battalion, Infantry, Local Defense Troops; Second Battalion, Infantry, Local Defense

Troops; Second Infantry Regiment, Local Defense Troops; Third Infantry Regiment, Local Defense Troops; Fourth Battalion, Infantry, Local Defense Troops; Fifth Battalion, Infantry, Local Defense Troops; and Sixth (Tredegar) Battalion, Infantry, Local Defense Troops.

49. *WOTR*, ser. 1, 27(3):862, 33:1301; Monroe et al., *Papers of Jefferson Davis*, 9:254; J. B. Jones, *Rebel War Clerk's Diary*, 2:70–71, 330, 331. For examples of younger and older enlistees, see Jacob Orme Jr. file, First Battalion, Infantry, Local Defense Troops (age fourteen when enrolled in June 1863), and A. W. Johnson file, Fourth Battalion, Infantry, Local Defense Troops (age fifty-seven when enrolled in June 1863), CSR/Virginia.

50. *WOTR*, ser. 1, 27(3):1067, 33:1301, 42(3):1197; *Examiner*, 7 September, 7 October 1863; *Dispatch*, 12 October 1863.

51. Younger, *Inside the Confederate Government*, 78, 102; Chesson and Roberts, *Exile in Richmond*, 107, 107n; *WOTR*, ser. 1, 27(3):977; Wiggins, *Journals of Josiah Gorgas*, 79; Welton, "My Heart," 211–13; J. B. Jones, *Rebel War Clerk's Diary*, 2:40–41, 162–63; W. S. Downer to Josiah Gorgas, 6 January 1864, 90:756–57, Letters Sent by the Richmond Arsenal; files C-810-1863, A-59-1864, and G-124-1864, LRCSW; St. Clair F. Sutherland file, Third Infantry Regiment, Local Defense Troops, CSR/Virginia.

52. Welton, "My Heart," 226, 228; J. B. Jones, *Rebel War Clerk's Diary*, 2:200–232 passim, 237, 296; Thomas Long, Charles A. Rose, and W. H. Crews files, Third Infantry Regiment, Local Defense Troops, CSR/Virginia; Monroe et al., *Papers of Jefferson Davis*, 11:260–61; Wiggins, *Journals of Josiah Gorgas*, 105; Chesson and Roberts, *Exile in Richmond*, 164, 351; files A-215-1864, A-132-1864, B-498-1864, C-603-1864, N-56-1864, B-45-1865, and S-47-1865, LRCSW; *WOTR*, ser. 1, 40(2):686; *Examiner*, 30 June 1864; J. R. Anderson and Company file, CPRCBF.

53. Welton, "My Heart," 226, 228; L. W. Caldwell file, Third Infantry Regiment, Local Defense Troops, CSR/Virginia; Monroe et al., *Papers of Jefferson Davis*, 11:448; files A-133-1864, A-233-1864, S-47-1865, LRCSW; J. B. Jones, *Rebel War Clerk's Diary*, 2:314, 330, 331–32. There was much dissatisfaction, too, among those Richmonders (numbering in the latter part of the war probably fewer than 1,000, mostly men and boys too old or young for Confederate military service) who were required to serve in the three state militia regiments based in the city. Mustered for duty by the governor's order now and then to assist the Confederate army, these troops were mostly assigned to guarding Richmond's bridges, government office buildings, and prisons but on occasion were sent to the fortifications. See governor's message, 4 February 1864, MR 5015, William Smith Executive Papers; Boney, *John Letcher*, 159–60, 194–95; Fahrner, "William 'Extra Billy' Smith," 69–72; *Dispatch*, 18, 19 March, 12 July 1862, 6 July, 2 December 1863; *Examiner*, 7 October 1863, 30 May, 19 August 1864; and *WOTR*, ser. 1, 46(2):1140–41.

54. J. C. White to officer in charge of Castle Thunder, 9 February 1864, in C.S.A. Army, Department of Henrico Papers; Wiggins, *Journals of Josiah Gorgas*, 128; J. B. Jones, *Rebel War Clerk's Diary*, 2:332, 370; file S-68-1865, LRCSW.

55. File G-124-1864, LRCSW; Welton, "My Heart," 211–13; J. W. Blunt file, First Battalion, Infantry, Local Defense Troops, and J. H. Bechtel file, Third Infantry Regiment, Local Defense Troops, CSR/Virginia; J. B. Jones, *Rebel War Clerk's Diary*, 2:163, 300; Chesson and Roberts, *Exile in Richmond*, 107, 229, 230n; *Examiner*, 6 October 1864. Why Bechtel had not been conscripted by June 1863 is unclear. He was of draft age and, as a bookstore clerk, would have been ineligible for an occupational exemption. Perhaps he had a medical condition serious enough to persuade the examining board to excuse him from duty but

not serious enough to keep him from joining the LDF (which would have been voluntary in his case at that time).

56. *Dispatch*, 4 July 1861, 28 January, 6 February, 6 August 1862; Hubard Diary, 3 July 1861, 13, 15 February 1862; *Examiner*, 24 November 1864.

57. Dean S. Thomas, *Confederate Arsenals*, 3:915–30; Time Book of the Richmond Arsenal, January, February 1863; *Dispatch*, 5 January 1863; *Enquirer*, 6 January 1863.

58. Dean S. Thomas, *Confederate Arsenals*, 3:921–30.

59. *Dispatch*, 14, 16, 31 March, 13 April 1863; *Sentinel*, 14, 16, 18 March, 13 April 1863; Dean S. Thomas, *Confederate Arsenals*, 3:921–30; Time Book of the Richmond Arsenal, March 1863.

60. *Dispatch*, 14, 24, 26 March 1863; Dean S. Thomas, *Confederate Arsenals*, 3:928.

CHAPTER 6

1. Lange, "Changed Name," 142/150; Mehrlander, *Germans of Charleston*, 242–44; Kimball, *American City, Southern Place*, 55, 213, 231–33; Second Ward, Richmond, Henrico County, Virginia, p. 100/309 (Robt. A. Granniss), 1860 Census.

2. Botts, *Great Rebellion*, 279, 281–82; Furguson, *Ashes of Glory*, 29, 43, 112–13, 118, 120; Ryan, *Yankee Spy*; Varon, *Southern Lady*; Kimball, *American City, Southern Place*, 242–46; Stuart, "Samuel Ruth"; Stuart, "Colonel Ulric Dahlgren"; Stuart, "Of Spies and Borrowed Names"; claim 14990 (James Duke), Southern Claims Commission Approved Claims; First Ward, Richmond, Henrico County, Virginia, p. 86 (D. W. Hughes), 1860 Census; *WOTR*, ser. 1, 42(2):1050.

3. Takagi, *"Rearing Wolves,"* 142–43; Latimore, "Always a Minority," 91–93, 105–7; Berlin et al., *Destruction of Slavery*, 727–28; Thomas L. Johnson, *Africa for Christ*, 25–26.

4. *Dispatch*, 19, 20 April 1861.

5. Manarin, *Richmond at War*, 30–31, 32, 36; *Dispatch*, 18 June 1861.

6. *Dispatch*, 23 April, 4, 8, 24 May 1861; Lange, "Changed Name," 144/151.

7. Jacob Bechtel to George Bechtel, 24 April, 17 May, 10 June 1861, Bechtel Papers.

8. D. Von Groning to Messrs. Gildemeister and Reis, 3 June 1861, Von Groning Letterbook; Harriet Baker to John Letcher, 18 May 1861, MR 4740, Letcher Executive Papers.

9. *Dispatch*, 20 May 1861; Dew, *Ironmaker to the Confederacy*, 94–95.

10. File G-231-1862, LRCSW; *Enquirer*, 7 June 1861; Naragon, "Ballots, Bullets, and Blood," 307; Neely, *Southern Rights*, 80–98.

11. *Dispatch*, 3, 11 May 1861; claim 14990 (James Duke), Southern Claims Commission Approved Claims; Steger, "'United to Support,'" 390–91.

12. *Examiner*, 16 July 1861.

13. *WOTR*, ser. 2, 2:1368–70; Neely, *Southern Rights*, 146–48; *Enquirer*, 22 February 1862.

14. J. B. Jones, *Rebel War Clerk's Diary*, 1:71, 73, 90, 96; claim 14990 (James Duke), Southern Claims Commission Approved Claims; *Enquirer*, 22 February 1862; files 7243-1861, 10450-1862, 10552-1862, and A-18-1862, LRCSW.

15. Emory M. Thomas, *Confederate State of Richmond*, 81; Richardson, *Compilation*, 1:220; Radley, *Rebel Watchdog*, 178–82. Davis's proclamation of 1 March embraced not just the city but also the area in a radius of ten miles around it.

16. Emory M. Thomas, *Confederate State of Richmond*, 82; Casstevens, *George W.*

Alexander, 41; *Enquirer*, 3–7 March 1862; Botts, *Great Rebellion*, 279–94; Furgurson, *Ashes of Glory*, 112–13, 115; Mehrlander, *Germans of Charleston*, 244, 246.

17. J. B. Jones, *Rebel War Clerk's Diary*, 1:120, 347; *WOTR*, ser. 1, 51(2):493, ser. 2, 4:888; file G-717-1862, LRCSW; Emory M. Thomas, *Confederate State of Richmond*, 82–83; Blakey, *General John H. Winder*, 122, 127–29, 139–40; Radley, *Rebel Watchdog*, 183; Neely, *Southern Rights*, 80–88, 91; claim 14990 (James Duke), Southern Claims Commission Approved Claims.

18. Richardson, *Compilation*, 1:220–21; Blakey, *General John H. Winder*, 120, 121–22, 124, 126, 151; Neely, *Southern Rights*, 2–6; Emory M. Thomas, *Confederate State of Richmond*, 82; Radley, *Rebel Watchdog*, 37, 56, 74–76, 77–79, 181–82, 183–84, 234–37; *Enquirer*, 5 March 1862; *Examiner*, 5 April 1864; *Dispatch*, 1 May 1863; report of I. H. Carrington, 23 July 1863, in C.S.A. Army, Department of Henrico Papers; Philip F. Brown, *Reminiscences of the War*, 44–46; file G-717-1862, LRCSW.

19. J. B. Jones, *Rebel War Clerk's Diary*, 1:272, 287, 2:174; files A-122-1862, B-470-1862, C-309-1862, V-35-1862, A-74-1863, A-1341/2-1863, and W-294-1863, LRCSW.

20. File A-74-1863, LRCSW; J. B. Jones, *Rebel War Clerk's Diary*, 1:222.

21. J. B. Jones, *Rebel War Clerk's Diary*, 1:144; file A-357-1863, LRCSW; Radley, *Rebel Watchdog*, 52, 150, 153.

22. Files C-628-1862, C-766-1862, S-440-1863, and S-25-1865, LRCSW; *Dispatch*, 16 January, 1 May 1863; Chesson and Roberts, *Exile in Richmond*, 227; Philip F. Brown, *Reminiscences of the War*, 42–43; J. B. Jones, *Rebel War Clerk's Diary*, 2:296.

23. *Dispatch*, 30 October 1863, 29 April, 28 June 1864.

24. Philip Weber Sr. to T. G. Peyton, 23 June 1864, and attached statements, Civil War Letters Collection; First Ward, Richmond, Henrico County, Virginia, p. 44 (Philip Weber), 1860 Census.

25. "A Lover of Public Justice" to John Coke, 14 March 1864, Coke Papers; Southern District, Chesterfield County, Virginia, p. 117 (H. C. G. Timmerman), 1860 Census.

26. *Sentinel*, 5 April 1864; *Examiner*, 5 April 1864.

27. Files A-133-1864, A-233-1864, and S-68-1865, LRCSW; J. B. Jones, *Rebel War Clerk's Diary*, 2:331–32; Steger, "'United to Support,'" 345–47; Monroe et al., *Papers of Jefferson Davis*, 11:110, 448.

28. *Dispatch*, 9 July 1864, 2 January 1865; Welton, *"My Heart,"* 245; Samuel Brequet, M. C. Green, and Patrick Quaide files, First Battalion, Infantry, Local Defense Troops, CSR/ Virginia; *WOTR*, ser. 1, 42(3):1179; J. B. Jones, *Rebel War Clerk's Diary*, 2:247, 323.

29. John Yakel file, Sixth (Tredegar) Battalion, Infantry, Local Defense Troops, and Patrick Gaul file, Fifth Battalion, Infantry, Local Defense Troops, CSR/Virginia; claim 14990 (James Duke), Southern Claims Commission Approved Claims; file S-486-1864, LRCSW; report of I. H. Carrington, 29 January 1864, in C.S.A. Army, Department of Henrico Papers; *WOTR*, ser. 1, 42(2):735, 881, 912.

30. *Dispatch*, 8, 13 February, 1864; *Whig*, 29 June 1864.

31. For examples of people wanting to leave in order to better their economic circumstances, see files M-862-1863, S-466-1863, A-49-1864, A-59-1864, D-144-1864, H-169-1864, M-77-1864, and M-450-1864, LRCSW. Men motivated by rumors of changes in the conscription law are noted in files F-158-1863 and H-488-1863, LRCSW; and J. B. Jones, *Rebel War Clerk's Diary*, 1:268–69, 270, 379, 2:107. Examples of women desiring to follow their husbands to Union territory are recorded in file K-29-1865, LRCSW; and *Examiner*, 8 July 1864.

32. Files M-862-1863, A-59-1864, C-429-1864, C-436-1864, C-517-1864, C-570-1864, C-571-1864, C-590-1864, H-169-1864, L-22-1864, and C-57-1865, LRCSW; Ordnance Depot superintendent to John Winder, 24 December 1863, 90:738, Letters Sent by the Richmond Arsenal. The foreign-born Richmonders who were recognized as having the right to leave the Confederacy included natives of Maryland and other nonseceding slave states.

33. *Examiner*, 22, 27 July 1864; file C-429-1864, LRCSW.

34. Files G-370-1863, C-436-1864, C-570-1864, L-22-1864, and C-57-1865, LRCSW; claim 3229 (Christian Burging), Barred and Disallowed Case Files; *Examiner*, 27 July 1864. Some of the hired wagoners were apparently "blockade runners," men who were granted passports to travel into Union-occupied territory and procure food and other supplies to bring back to Richmond (as discussed in chapter 4). The blockade-running ships that operated out of Wilmington and other ports did not sail to Europe but to some closer neutral site such as Nassau; there the traveler could take passage on a Europe-bound vessel.

35. Files D-345-1863, S-466-1863, B-506-1864, M-77-1864, M-510-1864, and K-29-1865, LRCSW. The inconsistency of the policy regarding wives of soldiers is illustrated in files D-144-1864 and M-450-1864, LRCSW, concerning two Richmond women who were in essentially the same circumstances as Macauley but who, in the summer of 1864, were granted passports to Union-occupied New Orleans, where they had family.

36. Files D-345-1863, G-370-1863, S-466-1863, A-202-1864, B-506-1864, C-91-1864, C-100-1864, G-57-1864, M-77-1864, and S-486-1864, LRCSW; *Examiner*, 20 November 1863; W. L. Pettit file, Fourth Battalion, Infantry, Local Defense Troops, CSR/Virginia; City of Norfolk, Norfolk County, Virginia, p. 148 (W. L. Pettit), 1860 Census.

37. Files S-466-1863, B-506-1864, M-77-1864, S-47-1865, LRCSW; Manarin, *Richmond at War*, 581, 581–82n.

38. File A-49-1864, LRCSW.

39. Welton, *"My Heart,"* 238; J. B. Jones, *Rebel War Clerk's Diary*, 2:359.

40. Younger, *Inside the Confederate Government*, 183; Maury Diary, 6, 20 February, 12 March 1865; McGuire, *Diary*, 332; Thomas Tredway to daughter, 16 February 1865, Tredway Papers; J. B. Jones, *Rebel War Clerk's Diary*, 2:411, 415, 429, 444; Wiggins, *Journals of Josiah Gorgas*, 147, 151, 153, 156; Chesson and Roberts, *Exile in Richmond*, 331, 332, 344; Tunnell, *"'Patriotic Press,'"* 35–50; *WOTR*, ser. 1, 46(2):115, 475.

41. Chesson and Roberts, *Exile in Richmond*, 322; Wiggins, *Journals of Josiah Gorgas*, 153, 155.

CHAPTER 7

1. File G-717-1862, LRCSW; *Whig*, 2 August 1861; *Examiner*, 16 September 1861; *Dispatch*, 25 June, 14 September, 19 November 1861, 16 August 1862, 3, 23 July 1863.

2. *Dispatch*, 28 January, 23 May 1862; Manarin, *Richmond at War*, 61; Neely, *Southern Rights*, 30–31; Philip F. Brown, *Reminiscences of the War*, 45–48.

3. *Dispatch*, 2, 9 June 1863; *Examiner*, 26 September 1863, 10 November 1864.

4. *Examiner*, 9 June 1864; *Dispatch*, 9 June, 23 November 1863, 20 June 1864; J. B. Jones, *Rebel War Clerk's Diary*, 2:101, 120, 185, 400; Cei, "Law Enforcement in Richmond," 51.

5. *Dispatch*, 20 June 1864; *Examiner*, 6 October 1863, 9 June 1864; Jordan, *Black Confederates*, 174, 175–76.

6. Scott, *Old Richmond Neighborhoods*, 77; Goldfield, *Urban Growth*, 145–46; Cei,

"Law Enforcement in Richmond," 47; Marten, *Children's Civil War*, 163, 168. Civil War-era Richmond had no public school system of the modern sort, but the city council did support one free primary school in each of the city's three wards, along with a free high school operated on the "Lancasterian" model. The students enrolled in these institutions were almost all poor; the majority of schoolchildren in the city attended privately run or church-run schools, a few of which took in some students whose parents could not pay tuition. While no statistics are available, it is likely that the typical poor child in the city during the war received very little or no schooling and that even better-off children suffered from their parents' declining ability to pay tuition as inflation ate away at income. Education in the wartime capital was hindered also by a shortage of teachers and facilities. See Dabney, *Richmond*, 140, 145–46; Goldfield, *Urban Growth*, 165–68; Emory M. Thomas, *Confederate State of Richmond*, 29–30, 132; and Weddell, *St. Paul's Church*, 1:148, 150–51.

7. File P-226-1863, LRCSW; *Dispatch*, 8 June, 18 September, 11 October, 19 November 1861, 3 February 1862; *Examiner*, 21 April 1863, 20 January, 24, 27 June 1864.

8. *Dispatch*, 19 November 1861, 2 July 1863; *Whig*, 2 August 1864; *Examiner*, 14 May 1864.

9. *Dispatch*, 23 April, 11 June 1863; Chesson and Roberts, *Exile in Richmond*, 292; *Examiner*, 28 December 1863, 24 June, 19, 28 December 1864.

10. Trask, *Two Months*, 75; Paca, "'Tim's Black Book,'" 461; *Dispatch*, 8, 9 June 1863; Manarin, *Richmond at War*, 420; Chesson and Roberts, *Exile in Richmond*, 241; Williams and Hamilton, *Papers*, 502; Wiley, *Letters of Warren Akin*, 35, 56, 60.

11. *Dispatch*, 28 January 1862; Trask, *Two Months*, 75; Putnam, *Richmond during the War*, 36–37.

12. Putnam, *Richmond during the War*, 37; hustings court grand jury report, 22 February 1864, and governor's report to general assembly, 26 February 1864, MR 5015, William Smith Executive Papers.

13. William to Mattie, 21 May 1861, Howitzer Company Collection; *Dispatch*, 10, 17 July 1861; *Rules and Regulations*; Paca, "'Tim's Black Book,'" 460; Philip F. Brown, *Reminiscences of the War*, 47; *Enquirer*, 7 March 1862; Benjamin Washington Jones, *Under the Stars*, 158; file S-25-1865, LRCSW.

14. *Dispatch*, 20 May, 5, 14 November 1861; Manarin, *Richmond at War*, 31, 127.

15. Richardson, *Compilation*, 1:220–21; Blakey, *General John H. Winder*, 122; *Enquirer*, 4, 5 March 1862; *Dispatch*, 5, 21 March 1862.

16. Blakey, *General John H. Winder*, 124; *Dispatch*, 26 March, 16 August 1862; *Enquirer*, 13 March, 24 May 1862.

17. *Dispatch*, 13 March, 20 April, 20 June, 3 July 1863; *Examiner*, 4 March 1863; Manarin, *Richmond at War*, 407.

18. Governor's report to general assembly, 26 February 1864, MR 5015, William Smith Executive Papers; *Sentinel*, 2 May 1864; Wiley, *Letters of Warren Akin*, 52.

19. *Charters and Ordinances*, 149–55; Manarin, *Richmond at War*, 94, 103, 202, 242, 404–5; file M-356-1864, LRCSW; *Dispatch*, 3 February 1864. The army was willing to keep up the strength of the police force to a certain extent by detailing some conscripted policemen to the force; see Special Order 55, 7 March 1865, vol. 228, Special Orders, Camp of Instruction.

20. Campbell, *Slavery on Trial*, 29; *Dispatch*, 31 October, 7 November 1862, 3 January, 9 June 1863, 3 February 1864; *Enquirer*, 13 March, 1 December 1862; *Whig*, 10 November 1862.

21. *Dispatch*, 28 July 1863, 1 January 1864; Campbell, *Slavery on Trial*, 22–24, 28–29, 55; *Charters and Ordinances*, 153; *Stranger's Guide*, 3, 21.

22. Campbell, *Slavery on Trial*, 55, 67; *Dispatch*, 11 October, 19 November 1861, 21 July 1863; *Stranger's Guide*, 31; Manarin, *Richmond at War*, 270.

23. *Dispatch*, 23 May 1861, 20 November 1862, 3 February, 27 June 1863; Manarin, *Richmond at War*, 233, 234; *Whig*, 5 November 1862.

24. Statement of Richmond Hustings Court magistrates, 12 February 1864, MR 5015, William Smith Executive Papers; file L-20-1863, LRCSW.

25. Files A-92-1862 and H-549-1862, LRCSW.

26. J. B. Jones, *Rebel War Clerk's Diary*, 1:200; files S-113-1864 and S-307-1864, LRCSW.

27. J. B. Jones, *Rebel War Clerk's Diary*, 1:93, 332, 353, 2:102, 225, 373; files A-92-1862, J-120-1862, A-86-1864, and A-166-1864, LRCSW.

28. Blakey, *General John H. Winder*, 122, 141; J. B. Jones, *Rebel War Clerk's Diary*, 1:71, 115, 150, 166, 167, 170, 178, 179; Lange, "Changed Name," 146/153; *Whig*, 5 November 1862.

29. The anxiety about "speculators" and "extortionists" was not particular to Richmond but a Confederacy-wide phenomenon; see Faust, *Creation of Confederate Nationalism*, 41–57.

30. J. B. Jones, *Rebel War Clerk's Diary*, 1:164, 183, 250, 272, 288, 2:9, 28, 183, 264; *Dispatch*, 19, 21 September 1863; *Examiner*, 21 September 1863; Norwood, *God and Our Country*, 13; file A-374-1862, LRCSW; Maury Diary, 25 February 1865.

31. File H-46-1865, LRCSW; J. B. Jones, *Rebel War Clerk's Diary*, 2:183, 373–74; *Dispatch*, 20 March 1862.

32. Berman, *Richmond's Jewry*, 176–80, 184–88; Kimball, *American City, Southern Place*, 52–53, 250–51; *Dispatch*, 14 September 1861; J. B. Jones, *Rebel War Clerk's Diary*, 1:78, 88, 128, 221, 362.

33. Hustings court grand jury report, 22 February 1864, and governor's report to general assembly, 26 February 1864, MR 5015, William Smith Executive Papers; Blackiston, *Refugees in Richmond*, 35; *Dispatch*, 19 September 1863.

34. Kimball, *American City, Southern Place*, 48, 192; *Dispatch*, 4 November 1861; file C-1029-1862, LRCSW; Third Ward, Richmond, Henrico County, Virginia, p. 25/46 (William H. Christian), 1860 Census.

35. Macon, *Life Gleanings*, 37; Kimball, *American City, Southern Place*, 46–47, 250; Day, *Down South*, 1:98–99; De Leon, *Four Years*, 238–39; Furgurson, *Ashes of Glory*, 99–100; Chesson and Roberts, *Exile in Richmond*, 357.

36. *Examiner*, 24 October, 17 December 1863; Furgurson, *Ashes of Glory*, 99–100; Chesson and Roberts, *Exile in Richmond*, 357.

37. Kimball, *American City, Southern Place*, 44; *Stranger's Guide*, 31; *Whig*, 11, 16 December 1861; *Dispatch*, 5, 6 June 1863; *Examiner*, 24 October 1863, 6 October 1864, 21 January 1865; Jordan, *Black Confederates*, 151–52; Furgurson, *Ashes of Glory*, 103.

38. Burrows, *New Richmond Theatre*, 3–16; *Whig*, 3 January 1862; Furgurson, *Ashes of Glory*, 102–3, 180–81.

39. Benjamin Washington Jones, *Under the Stars*, 116.

40. Woodward, *Mary Chesnut's Civil War*, 430, 492, 507–8. The friend who promised to keep James away from home while Mary and other friends drank and played cards was none other than Varina Davis, the first lady of the Confederacy, who with her husband hosted a dinner that evening that James was expected to attend.

41. De Leon, *Four Years*, 151; Chesson and Roberts, *Exile in Richmond*, 211, 212n; Harrison, *Recollections*, 187–88.

42. Chesson and Roberts, *Exile in Richmond*, 43–44; Katharine M. Jones, *Ladies of Richmond*, 209; file B-379-1864, LRCSW; *Dispatch*, 27 June 1863; Barber, "'Sisters of the Capital,'" 100–101; Pember, *Southern Woman's Story*, 18–19.

43. Norwood, *God and Our Country*, 12; Blackiston, *Refugees in Richmond*, 50; Benjamin Washington Jones, *Under the Stars*, 87–88.

44. Benjamin Washington Jones, *Under the Stars*, 87.

45. Blackiston, *Refugees in Richmond*, 35; J. B. Jones, *Rebel War Clerk's Diary*, 2:183; Norwood, *God and Our Country*, 12–15; Faust, *Creation of Confederate Nationalism*, 44–45.

CHAPTER 8

1. Thomas L. Johnson, *Africa for Christ*, 9–11, 16.

2. Johnson, 11–12.

3. General studies of enslaved Southerners during the war that emphasize the diversity of their experiences include Litwack, *Been in the Storm*; Berlin et al., *Destruction of Slavery*; and Ash, *Black Experience*.

4. Takagi, "Rearing Wolves," is a comprehensive study of slaves and slavery in Richmond from the early national period through the Civil War. On the city's free black population in the late antebellum and war years, see Latimore, "Always a Minority."

5. Tucker, *Southern Church Justified*, 10–16.

6. Tucker, 10–16. See also Norwood, *God and Our Country*, 8–9.

7. *Whig*, 11 January 1862; *Dispatch*, 29 June 1861; Berlin, *Slaves without Masters*, 347–49.

8. Takagi, "Rearing Wolves," 112, 115; Wade, *Slavery in the Cities*, 106; Campbell, *Slavery on Trial*, esp. xi; Latimore, "Always a Minority," 122.

9. *Charters and Ordinances*, 194–98; Wade, *Slavery in the Cities*, 107–8; Jordan, *Black Confederates*, 169; Thomas L. Johnson, *Africa for Christ*, 23; Day, *Down South*, 1:143; Takagi, "Rearing Wolves," 115; Latimore, "Always a Minority," 122; Campbell, *Slavery on Trial*, 53; Hadden, *Slave Patrols*, 57.

10. *Charters and Ordinances*, 195–98; Wade, *Slavery in the Cities*, 107–8; Takagi, "Rearing Wolves," 114, 115.

11. Campbell, *Slavery on Trial*, 27–29; Randolph, *From Slave Cabin*, 81–82.

12. Thomas L. Johnson, *Africa for Christ*, 11, 13–14, 16, 18, 25; Second Ward, Richmond, Henrico County, Virginia, p. 111/319 (Wm. Brent and family), 1860 Census.

13. File L-105-1864, LRCSW; Furgurson, *Ashes of Glory*, 283–84; First Ward, Richmond, Henrico County, Virginia, p. 72 (S. Omahundres [*sic*], Coriner [*sic*] Hinton), 1860 Census.

14. Petition for pardon of William, 4 April 1864, and trial record of *Commonwealth v. William, a Slave*, MR 5017, William Smith Executive Papers. The governor rejected Doggett's petition. Another example of paternalism and profit at work was the much boasted-of hospital for slaves that opened in Richmond in 1860; a privately owned facility with forty beds, clean and airy wards, and a staff of six physicians, it offered slave owners a place where (for five dollars a week per patient) they could be sure their sick and injured bondsmen would be well cared for—and healed as quickly as possible so they could get back to work. See Jordan, *Black Confederates*, 96; and Starobin, *Industrial Slavery*, 71.

15. Latimore, "Always a Minority," 69; Takagi, "Rearing Wolves," 104–5; Ryland, "Origin

and History," 252–53; O'Brien, "Factory, Church, and Community," 525–26, 531; Berlin, *Slaves without Masters*, 300; Thomas L. Johnson, *Africa for Christ*, 22; Gen. 16:9.

16. Hopley, *Life in the South*, 1:145, 180–81. For an eyewitness description of a slave auction in Richmond in 1862, see Malet, *Errand to the South*, 291–92.

17. *Examiner*, 17, 18, 20 August, 14 October, 16 November 1864, 19 January 1865; Second Ward, Richmond, Henrico County, Virginia, p. 34/240 (J. N. and Abigail Hoeflich [sic]), 1860 Census; Jordan, *Black Confederates*, 176. Hoeflick and his wife, Abigail, were both subsequently charged in the hustings court with involuntary homicide. But by the time the case came to trial, Abigail had left the city and gone to the North; unable to determine which of the two had actually inflicted the whippings, the jury acquitted Jacob. For other examples of the extreme abuse of slaves, see *Dispatch*, 21 May 1861; and *Enquirer*, 5 September 1861.

18. *Examiner*, 6 July 1864.

19. J. B. Jones, *Rebel War Clerk's Diary*, 1:202; *Dispatch*, 11 June 1861. See also *Examiner*, 24 October 1863; and Woodward, *Mary Chesnut's Civil War*, 165.

20. Files C-327-1864 and S-295-1864, LRCSW.

21. Hopley, *Life in the South*, 1:144; Woodward, *Mary Chesnut's Civil War*, 535. See also *Dispatch*, 22 July 1863; and *Examiner*, 19 December 1864.

22. Hopley, *Life in the South*, 1:165.

23. McCurry, *Confederate Reckoning*, 31–32, 137, 144, 225, 239; D. Von Groning to Messrs. Gildemeister and Reis, 3 July 1861, Von Groning Letterbook; J. B. Jones, *Rebel War Clerk's Diary*, 2:212.

24. Thomas L. Johnson, *Africa for Christ*, 19, 24, 25–26; Hopley, *Life in the South*, 1:181.

25. Hopley, *Life in the South*, 1:180; Malet, *Errand to the South*, 169, 291–92. See also Woodward, *Mary Chesnut's Civil War*, 132.

26. Hopley, *Life in the South*, 1:144–45, 158–62, 190; *Dispatch*, 10 January 1863.

27. Randolph, *From Slave Cabin*, 87–88; O'Brien, "Factory, Church, and Community," 531; Thomas L. Johnson, *Africa for Christ*, 19–24.

28. Takagi, "Rearing Wolves," 103, 106–7; White, *Richmond Baptists Working Together*, 15–16; O'Brien, "Factory, Church, and Community," 521–22, 523–27; Latimore, "Always a Minority," 68–69, 74, 80–81; Campbell, *Slavery on Trial*, 179–80; Ryland, "Origin and History," 247–54, 261–62; Berlin, *Slaves without Masters*, 295, 297; *Examiner*, 24 November 1863; *Dispatch*, 9 July, 17 August 1863; Minute Book, 15 September 1861, 14 August 1864, Ebenezer Baptist Church Records.

29. Ryland, "Origin and History," 249, 251, 254, 258–59; O'Brien, "Factory, Church, and Community," 522–23, 525, 527–28; Latimore, "Always a Minority," 69–73, 80; Tyler-McGraw and Kimball, *In Bondage and Freedom*, 37–38; Hopley, *Life in the South*, 1:187–91.

30. Latimore, "Always a Minority," 77–78; Ryland, "Origin and History," 256, 257, 258, 262; Hopley, *Life in the South*, 1:189; O'Brien, "Factory, Church, and Community," 530–31; Takagi, "Rearing Wolves," 106; Minute Book, 13 November 1864, Ebenezer Baptist Church Records; *Dispatch*, 17 August 1863; *Religious Herald*, 30 July 1863; Tyler-McGraw and Kimball, *In Bondage and Freedom*, 40–42.

31. Campbell, *Slavery on Trial*, 180–84; Latimore, "Always a Minority," 74–77; O'Brien, "Factory, Church, and Community," 528–30; Minute Book, 8 September, 8 December 1861, 9 February, 6 June, 9 November, 14 December 1862, [?] January 1864, 12 February 1865, Ebenezer Baptist Church Records.

32. Berlin, *Slaves without Masters*, 310–12, 313; Tyler-McGraw and Kimball, *In Bondage*

and *Freedom*, 40, 41, 49–51; Woodward, *Mary Chesnut's Civil War*, 458; Takagi, "Rearing Wolves," 96–101.

33. Berlin, *Slaves without Masters*, 146–48, 311–12, 327–28; Woodward, *Mary Chesnut's Civil War*, 526, 564; Maris-Wolf, *Family Bonds*, 8, 10; Takagi, "Rearing Wolves," 116–20, 122–23; Latimore, "Always a Minority," 83; Campbell, *Slavery on Trial*, 22.

34. O'Brien, "Factory, Church, and Community," 521, 525–26; Jordan, *Black Confederates*, 101; Hopley, *Life in the South*, 1:159–60; Ryland, "Origin and History," 252–53; Thomas L. Johnson, *Africa for Christ*, 16–18, 23–24, 25.

35. Gutman, *Black Family*, 230–56; Minute Book, 1861–65, Ebenezer Baptist Church Records; Harrison, *Recollections*, 70. Mrs. Davis missed the joke, assuming (as the pranksters no doubt intended) that it was a solecism occasioned by black ignorance.

36. Hopley, *Life in the South*, 1:153, 187–88, 191; Day, *Down South*, 1:141; Malet, *Errand to the South*, 169; *Examiner*, 9 May, 6, 24 October 1863; *Dispatch*, 11 November 1863; Ryland, "Origin and History," 251, 260–61, 270–72; Latimore, "Always a Minority," 72–73; O'Brien, "Factory, Church, and Community," 530–31.

37. Berlin, *Slaves without Masters*, 235–39, 242–43; Kimball, "African-Virginians," 122; Ryland, "Origin and History," 270–72; Hopley, *Life in the South*, 1:187; Takagi, "Rearing Wolves," 117, 120–23; Day, *Down South*, 1:110; Putnam, *Richmond during the War*, 264–66; Woodward, *Mary Chesnut's Civil War*, 544.

38. Berlin, *Slaves without Masters*, 248–49; Tyler-McGraw and Kimball, *In Bondage and Freedom*, 35, 49; Second Ward, Richmond, Henrico County, Virginia, p. 205/413 (Fields Cook), 1860 Census.

39. Steger, "'United to Support,'" 351–54; Katharine M. Jones, *Ladies of Richmond*, 209; Benjamin Washington Jones, *Under the Stars*, 226; Manarin, *Richmond at War*, 518–19n; Jordan, *Black Confederates*, 130–31; *Dispatch*, 25 June 1861; Woodward, *Mary Chesnut's Civil War*, 588.

40. *Examiner*, 6 October 1863, 2 December 1864.

41. Steger, "'United to Support,'" 354; *Dispatch*, 11, 24 November 1863; *Examiner*, 9 May 1863; Manarin, *Richmond at War*, 426.

42. *Enquirer*, 15 December 1862; *Dispatch*, 18 June, 10 September 1861, 6, 24 November 1863; *Examiner*, 24 November 1863.

43. *Enquirer*, 26 November 1861; Jordan, *Black Confederates*, 156, 169–70; *Examiner*, 28, 29 September 1863; Steger, "'United to Support,'" 355; Takagi, "Rearing Wolves," 136.

44. Latimore, "Always a Minority," 138–42; Manarin, *Richmond at War*, 346.

45. Emory M. Thomas, *Confederate State of Richmond*, 28–29; *Examiner*, 8, 28, 29 September 1863, 21 March 1865; Jordan, *Black Confederates*, 204; *Dispatch*, 18 January 1865.

46. *Examiner*, 11 November 1863, 21 June, 6 July 1864. See also Putnam, *Richmond during the War*, 264–66; and Manarin, *Richmond at War*, 545–46.

47. Latimore, "Always a Minority," 122, 145–46; *Enquirer*, 10 December 1863; *Examiner*, 13 November 1863. Other examples are in *Dispatch*, 13 May 1862, 13 January 1863; *Examiner*, 11 November 1863; and trial record of *Commonwealth v. James Butler*, and governor's endorsement, 11 April 1864, MR 5017, William Smith Executive Papers.

48. *Examiner*, 6 July 1864.

49. *Enquirer*, 21 October 1864; *Examiner*, 21, 22 October 1864; *Dispatch*, 21, 22 October 1864; Jordan, *Black Confederates*, 164.

50. *Dispatch*, 7 October 1861, 30 March 1863, 24 September 1864.

51. Trial record of *Commonwealth v. Henry, a Slave*, filed with 28 October 1864 papers, MR 5022, William Smith Executive Papers. The hustings court, taking into account Henry's previous conviction for theft (for which he had received thirty-nine lashes), decided that Richmond was better off without him and sentenced him to sale and transportation out of the state.

52. *Examiner*, 4 March 1863; *Dispatch*, 30 March 1863.

53. Steger, "'United to Support,'" 356–57; *Dispatch*, 27 June, 21 November 1863; *Examiner*, 21 November 1863.

54. *Dispatch*, 7, 14 October 1861.

55. Takagi, *"Rearing Wolves,"* 141; Jordan, *Black Confederates*, 69–70, 76; Martinez, *Confederate Slave Impressment*, 64; Putnam, *Richmond during the War*, 264–66; *Examiner*, 19, 21 December 1864. Reports and evidence of the forgery of passes to aid escape to Union lines and of the smuggling of slaves out of the city are in the trial record of *Commonwealth v. William, a Slave*, filed with 23 April 1864 papers, MR 5017, William Smith Executive Papers; file K-58-1864, LRCSW; *Dispatch*, 22 July 1863, 21 January 1865; and Steger, "'United to Support,'" 356–57.

56. *Dispatch*, 9 January 1865; *Enquirer*, 25 February 1865; file H-80-1864, LRCSW; Takagi, *"Rearing Wolves,"* 141; Martinez, *Confederate Slave Impressment*, 65; Ash, "Wall around Slavery," 55–73. The Henrico County authorities kept slave patrols active, despite severe manpower shortages, throughout the war; see Bailey, *Henrico Home Front*, 6–7, 16, 20, 48–49, 78, 79, 110, 123, 182–83, 190, 193, 217, 227.

57. *Dispatch*, 9 January 1865; *Enquirer*, 25 February 1865.

CHAPTER 9

1. Emory M. Thomas, *Confederate State of Richmond*, 24–25; Goldfield, *Urban Growth*, chap. 2; Tyler-McGraw, *At the Falls*, 113–14; Shackelford, *George Wythe Randolph*, 96–97.

2. Tyler-McGraw, *At the Falls*, 114; Emory M. Thomas, *Confederate State of Richmond*, 24–25; Luskey, "'Debt of Honor,'" 21–22; Shackelford, *George Wythe Randolph*, 80–81, 82, 87, 98; Dew, *Ironmaker to the Confederacy*, 4–18, 144; Goldfield, *Urban Growth*, 30, 32, 38–40. Goldfield describes the small coterie of elite men of antebellum Richmond as an "interlocking directorate" controlling the city's leading economic, political, and social institutions. It should be noted that Joseph Anderson's slaveholding was an exception to the rule; he owned sixty slaves in 1860, employing them not only at home but in his manufacturing enterprises. See Third Ward, Richmond, Henrico County, Virginia, pp. 33–34 (Jos. R. Anderson), in Eighth Census, 1860, Manuscript Returns of Slaves; and Dew, *Ironmaker to the Confederacy*, 262–63.

3. Emory M. Thomas, *Confederate State of Richmond*, 25; Second Ward, Richmond, Henrico County, Virginia, pp. 111/319 (Wm. Brent and family), 110/317 (Wm. McCrery [*sic*] and household), 1860 Census; *Dispatch*, 16 April 1861, 23 May 1862; *Second Annual Directory*, 55, 152; Second Ward, Richmond, Henrico County, Virginia, p. 24/40 (Wm. Brent), in Eighth Census, 1860, Manuscript Returns of Slaves.

4. Emory M. Thomas, *Confederate State of Richmond*, 25–26; Tyler-McGraw, *At the Falls*, 114; Goldfield, *Urban Growth*, 124–25.

5. Third Ward, Richmond, Henrico County, Virginia, p. 173/617 (Richard Taylor and family), 1860 Census.

6. Third Ward, Richmond, Henrico County, Virginia, pp. 172/617 (Patk. Whalen and

family), 56/501 (Susan M. Henderson and family), 1860 Census. On schools available to those of modest means in Richmond, see chapter 7, note 6.

7. Pember, *Southern Woman's Story*, 1; Ellen Mordecai to Alfred Mordecai, 6 June 1861, Alfred Mordecai Papers; Luskey, "'Debt of Honor,'" chaps. 1–3; Bill, *Beleaguered City*, 16–17; Furgurson, *Ashes of Glory*, 9, 27–28; Emory M. Thomas, *Confederate State of Richmond*, 19–20; Manarin, *Richmond at War*, 627–36; Dabney, *Richmond*, 17.

8. Goldfield, *Urban Growth*, 160–65; Campbell, *Slavery on Trial*, 64, 67.

9. Emory M. Thomas, *Confederate State of Richmond*, 20, 26; Steger, "'United to Support,'" chap. 2; McGuire, *Diary*, 98–100; Wooster, *Politicians, Planters*, 2–6; Naragon, "Ballots, Bullets, and Blood," chap. 4; Manarin, *Richmond at War*, 628.

10. Emory M. Thomas, *Confederate State of Richmond*, 24; Day, *Down South*, 1:99; Luskey, "'Debt of Honor,'" 50–67; Putnam, *Richmond during the War*, 190–91; Kimball, *American City, Southern Place*, 48, 188–90.

11. De Leon, *Four Years*, 156–57; Luskey, "'Debt of Honor,'" 19, 28, 32–34. The Chesnuts, newcomers from South Carolina, were adopted into the social circle of George and Mary Randolph, as were refugees Constance Cary and Hetty Cary. See Woodward, *Mary Chesnut's Civil War*, 119, 119n, 120, 145, 158, 431, 475n, 477, 524, 533, 538, 540; and Harrison, *Recollections*.

12. Shackelford, *George Wythe Randolph*, 84–85; Luskey, "'Debt of Honor,'" 197–98; Fox Hill District, Elizabeth City County, Virginia, p. 32/630 (Maria G. Clopton), 1860 Census; files C-327-1864 and S-295-1864, LRCSW; Ellen Mordecai to Alfred Mordecai, 6 June 1861, Alfred Mordecai Papers; Katharine M. Jones, *Ladies of Richmond*, 133–34.

13. Schurr, "Inside the Confederate Hospital," 104–7; Pember, *Southern Woman's Story*, ix, 1, 18–19; Second District, City of Savannah, Chatham County, Georgia, p. 141 (Jacob C. Levy), 1860 Census.

14. Pember, *Southern Woman's Story*, 13–16.

15. Pember, 13–14, 17–18.

16. *Examiner*, 17 June, 8 July 1864.

17. Daniel E. Huger Smith, Smith, and Childs, *Mason Smith Family Letters*, 105; *Examiner*, 23 January 1864.

18. Files H-489-1862 and F-98-1863, LRCSW; Kimball, *American City, Southern Place*, 56; Second Ward, Richmond, Henrico County, Virginia, p. 150/358 (Wm. H. Haxall and family), 1860 Census. The hard-pressed Confederate authorities did not necessarily grant such requests—both Haxall's and Forbes's letters were simply filed away unanswered.

19. For downward occupational mobility, see the example of refugee Francis R. Snapp, noted in chapter 2, and the various examples of ladies taking jobs in chapter 5. For examples of upper-class Richmonders in reduced domestic circumstances, see chapters 3 and 4.

20. Luskey, "'Debt of Honor,'" chap. 3, esp. pp. 120–21, 125–26; *Examiner*, 21 October 1863; J. B. Jones, *Rebel War Clerk's Diary*, 1:128, 192, 198, 240, 2:28, 56, 90, 101, 212. See also file G-90-1863, LRCSW; McGuire, *Diary*, 242–43; Trask, *Two Months*, 84; Woodward, *Mary Chesnut's Civil War*, 579; and Cochran Recollections, vol. 2, February 1864.

21. J. B. Jones, *Rebel War Clerk's Diary*, 2:17, 77, 90, 125, 132, 192, 328–29; Wiley, *Letters of Warren Akin*, 43, 55–56, 79, 90; file S-555-1863, LRCSW; Chesson and Roberts, *Exile in Richmond*, 58, 318, 319, 321, 324, 328, 330, 338; Cochran Recollections, vol. 2, Christmas 1863.

22. J. B. Jones, *Rebel War Clerk's Diary*, 1:278, 2:77, 235; Chesson and Roberts, *Exile in Richmond*, 294, 315.

23. Cochran Recollections, vol. 2, Christmas 1863; *Examiner*, 29 June 1864; First Ward, Richmond, Henrico County, Virginia, p. 199 (Harriet Hovan), 1860 Census.

24. Barber, "Depraved and Abandoned Women," 155–63; Campbell, *Slavery on Trial*, 64–66.

25. Barber, "Depraved and Abandoned Women," 163–67; Luskey, "'Debt of Honor,'" 129–33; *Dispatch*, 6, 13 May 1862.

26. *Dispatch*, 8 September 1862; *Examiner*, 27 April, 1 September, 10 October, 20 November 1863, 22 August 1864.

27. *Dispatch*, 1 July 1863.

28. *Enquirer*, 13, 24 May 1862. On drinking, disorder, and prohibition, see chapter 7.

29. Manarin, *Richmond at War*, 172–73, 179, 185, 187. The council appointed officers for the battalion on 28 May but soon after resolved to put the matter on hold until it could be ascertained whether the governor intended to call out the militia—in which event, the council decided, the battalion would be unnecessary. It is not clear whether any rank-and-file members were actually recruited or any arms procured for the battalion before the project was scrapped.

30. This and the following seven paragraphs are based on these sources: Chesson, "Harlots or Heroines?"; McCurry, *Confederate Reckoning*, 184–90; Barber, "'Sisters of the Capital,'" 263–64, 269–73; Steger, "'United to Support,'" 286–91, 296–301; J. B. Jones, *Rebel War Clerk's Diary*, 1:284–86; and *Examiner*, 24, 27 April 1863. (See also chapter 4 on the food problem.) Chesson and McCurry speculate—quite reasonably, in the absence of direct evidence—that the protestors were inspired by reports (some published in the city's newspapers) of food riots in several other Confederate cities in March 1863. I have found no evidence that the Richmond authorities or upper classes were concerned about potential mob violence in the city that month (or any time before then, except in the late spring and early summer of 1862), in spite of the disturbances elsewhere. The city council explicitly denied that there had been any indication of real suffering from hunger among the white citizenry before the riot; see Manarin, *Richmond at War*, 311–12.

31. WOTR, ser. 1, 18:958. The Richmond press honored this request for self-censorship for exactly one day. No mention of the riot appeared in any of the city papers on 3 April, but on 4 April the *Examiner* published an editorial condemning the riot and a lengthy report on the 3 April mayor's court examinations of accused rioters. A telegraph report of the riot went out while it was still in progress, that is, before the secretary's request reached the telegraph company. See Chesson, "Harlots or Heroines?," 169; J. B. Jones, *Rebel War Clerk's Diary*, 1:286; Pryor, *Reminiscences*, 239; and *Examiner*, 4 April 1863.

32. Manarin, *Richmond at War*, 311–13.

33. J. B. Jones, *Rebel War Clerk's Diary*, 1:286, 290; McGuire, *Diary*, 203–4; WOTR, ser. 1, 18:965, 977–78. The War Department had declined to intervene during the actual riot on 2 April. Although the governor requested that the City Battalion be deployed that day, and two local military commanders likewise urged sending in some of the garrison force to subdue the rioters, the secretary of war opined that it was a city and state matter and refused to provide any troops. See file R-125-1863, LRCSW; and J. B. Jones, *Rebel War Clerk's Diary*, 1:286.

34. *Examiner*, 4, 6 April 1863; Southern District, Pittsylvania County, Virginia, p. 132 (Thomas Ould and family), 1860 Census; Chesson, "Harlots or Heroines?," 169; J. B. Jones, *Rebel War Clerk's Diary*, 1:287. Interrogated by the mayor, the physician said that the power he referred to was "the people," whereupon he was released.

35. Chesson, "Harlots or Heroines?," 155, 158–60; *Examiner*, 4, 13 April 1863.

36. Chesson, "Harlots or Heroines?," 153–54, 164–68; *Examiner*, 15 May 1863; file F-159-1863, LRCSW; William J. Lusk file, Seventeenth Infantry Regiment, CSR/Mississippi; trial record of *Commonwealth v. Virgil Jones*, May–June 1863, and associated documents, February 1864, and trial record of *Commonwealth v. Mary Johnson*, May–October 1863, and associated documents, January 1864, MR 5015, William Smith Executive Papers. Mary Duke's case was reconsidered by Governor Letcher on appeal; she was freed after serving three months in jail. Letcher declined to alter William Lusk's sentence on appeal, but Lusk was released from jail sometime between November 1863 and January 1864 and rejoined his regiment. Letcher's successor, Governor William Smith, pardoned Mary Johnson in January 1864, after she had served at least three months in the penitentiary (her case had not been finally adjudicated until October 1863). In February 1864, Smith pardoned Virgil Jones, who had been in the penitentiary since his conviction the previous spring. Mary Jackson, the central figure in the riot, was apparently tried on a misdemeanor charge, but the court records have been lost and the outcome of her case is unknown.

37. J. B. Jones, *Rebel War Clerk's Diary*, 1:286; file B-296-1863, LRCSW.

38. Manarin, *Richmond at War*, 311–12; *Examiner*, 4 April 1863; Estill, "Diary," 39:46–47; file B-296-1863, LRCSW. See also McGuire, *Diary*, 204; Wiggins, *Journals of Josiah Gorgas*, 59, 60; Barber, "'Sisters of the Capital,'" 266–68; Luskey, "'Debt of Honor,'" 223–29; Sheehan-Dean, "Politics," 23; and Steger, "'United to Support,'" 294–96.

39. Manarin, *Richmond at War*, 314–15, 317, 320–22; Emory M. Thomas, "To Feed the Citizens," 27–29. For details on the post-riot poor-relief measures, see chapter 4.

40. Manarin, *Richmond at War*, 325; *Dispatch*, 8 July 1863; file H-80-1864, LRCSW.

41. *Dispatch*, 19, 21 September, 5, 12 October 1863; *Examiner*, 21 September, 12 October 1863; Steger, "'United to Support,'" 320–27; Naragon, "Ballots, Bullets, and Blood," 315–16; Third Ward, Richmond, Henrico County, Virginia, p. 166 (Thos. J. Laprade), 1860 Census.

42. J. B. Jones, *Rebel War Clerk's Diary*, 2:48, 61–62, 66, 90, 91; *Dispatch*, 5 October 1863; file J-305-1863, LRCSW.

43. Manarin, *Richmond at War*, 382, 383–84; Naragon, "Ballots, Bullets, and Blood," 315–17; Steger, "'United to Support,'" 327–35.

44. J. B. Jones, *Rebel War Clerk's Diary*, 2:128, 129, 135–36.

45. Files H-80-1864 and M-356-1864, LRCSW; Manarin, *Richmond at War*, 416. I have found no mention of this mounted force after January 1864, leading me to suspect that it was never actually organized, perhaps because the War Department declined to sanction or arm it, or because it was not authorized by the state government, or because the exemptions claimed by some of the prospective volunteers were abolished. Nor have I found any mention after January 1864 of the two companies of auxiliary foot police formed in 1863, leading me to suspect that they were disbanded after the conscription law amendments passed in February 1864. (See below on the organization of another auxiliary in March 1865.)

46. J. B. Jones, *Rebel War Clerk's Diary*, 2:159, 218; file F-73-1864, LRCSW; WOTR, ser. 1, 42(2):522.

47. Manarin, *Richmond at War*, 580–81; *Examiner*, 18 March 1865.

48. Moore, *Conscription and Conflict*; Blair, *Virginia's Private War*, 55–60, 81–84, 102–7, 126–28.

49. File A-89-1864, LRCSW. See also file A-166-1864, LRCSW. The members of the

Ambulance Committee (generally called the Ambulance Corps) to whom the letter writer referred were technically not exempted from military service, if draftable, but rather were conscripted and then detailed to the corps. See chapter 10.

CHAPTER 10

1. Chesson and Roberts, *Exile in Richmond*, 58, 62, 63, 65, 66, 76, 77, 130, 131, 145, 325. See also files B-634-1863, B-154-1864, and W-29-1865, LRCSW; and McGuire, *Diary*, 254. For helpful historical background, see Anderson, "Dying of Nostalgia"; and Clarke, "So Lonesome."

2. Miller, "Alabama Merchant," 198; Wiley, *Letters of Warren Akin*, 80, 92; Chesson and Roberts, *Exile in Richmond*, 271, 325, 362.

3. File R-622-1862, LRCSW; James D. Ragan file, Fifty-First Infantry Regiment, CSR/Georgia; Waitt, *Confederate Military Hospitals*, 14. When admitted to General Hospital No. 13, Ragan was listed as suffering only from diarrhea, but there would have been no reason to assign him to that particular hospital unless he was suspected of having a mental disorder.

4. Chesson and Roberts, *Exile in Richmond*, 91, 113, 114, 117, 120, 130, 131, 145, 147, 148, 162, 322, 325.

5. Pember, *Southern Woman's Story*, 54.

6. Woodward, *Mary Chesnut's Civil War*, 99–100.

7. Mumper, *I Wrote You Word*, 1, 3, 6–7; files 2692-1861, 2777-1861, and 3092-1861, LRCSW; Woodward, *Mary Chesnut's Civil War*, 100.

8. File 2443-1861, LRCSW; Lange, "Changed Name," 149/156; *Dispatch*, 23, 25 July 1861.

9. Mumper, *I Wrote You Word*, 11, 14; Woodward, *Mary Chesnut's Civil War*, 158; Waitt, *Confederate Military Hospitals*, 11, 12–13.

10. Green, *Chimborazo*, 1–8; Coles, "Richmond, the Confederate Hospital City"; Bridges, "Juliet Opie Hopkins," 83–95; Putnam, *Richmond during the War*, 135. On the Ambulance Corps, see *Examiner*, 19, 23 March 1864; "Richmond Ambulance Corps"; Manarin, *Richmond at War*, 172; files E-159-1862 and G-329-1862, LRCSW; John Reily to Samuel French, 4 December 1862, French Letterbook; *WOTR*, ser. 1, 27(3):873; and *Whig*, 27 June 1864.

11. Harrison, *Recollections*, 82; *Dispatch*, 3 June 1862; Putnam, *Richmond during the War*, 134–35; De Leon, *Four Years*, 199; J. B. Jones, *Rebel War Clerk's Diary*, 1:130, 131, 132.

12. *Dispatch*, 3 June 1862; J. B. Jones, *Rebel War Clerk's Diary*, 1:131; Putnam, *Richmond during the War*, 135; Harrison, *Recollections*, 82–83; De Leon, *Four Years*, 199–200.

13. *Dispatch*, 30 June 1862; *Richmond Semi-Weekly Examiner*, 4 July 1862; J. B. Jones, *Rebel War Clerk's Diary*, 1:140–41; Lange, "Changed Name," 159/166; James Holloway to Annie Holloway, 2 July 1862, Holloway Papers; McGuire, *Diary*, 125; Putnam, *Richmond during the War*, 150, 151, 154.

14. *Dispatch*, 20 December 1862, 13 July, 23 October 1863; *Examiner*, 19 November 1863, 19, 23 March, 7 May 1864; *Enquirer*, 16 December 1862; *WOTR*, ser. 1, 27(3):873; Pember, *Southern Woman's Story*, 23; H. D. Whitcomb to Major Ashe, 29 October 1861, Virginia Central Railroad Company file, CPRCBF; files D-689-1862, P-507-1862, and W-415-1863, LRCSW; Waitt, *Confederate Military Hospitals*, 13; *Stranger's Guide*, 28; *Sentinel*, 23 November 1863. The army valued the services of the Ambulance Corps so highly that it was willing to detail a considerable number of conscripts to it (some twenty-six in early

1864); see Special Order 1, 1 January 1864, and Special Order 7, 8 January 1864, vol. 223, Special Orders, Camp of Instruction.

15. *Enquirer*, 16 December 1862; *Dispatch*, 17 December 1862; *Stranger's Guide*, 24; receipt, 19 December 1862, John P. Ballard file, CPRCBF; file D-689-1862, LRCSW.

16. Cunningham, *Doctors in Gray*, 125; Harrison, *Recollections*, 186; *Examiner*, 16, 17 May 1864; endorsement, 7 May 1864, on letter of W. A. Carrington, Endorsements on Letters Received.

17. Pember, *Southern Woman's Story*, 59; Phoebe Pember to [?], 22 June 1864, Pember Letters.

18. File A-310-1862, LRCSW; Emma Mordecai Diaries, 9 June 1864; Chesson and Roberts, *Exile in Richmond*, 11, 53; Daniel E. Huger Smith, Smith, and Childs, *Mason Smith Family Letters*, 112, 120, 121, 123.

19. Files M-1563-1862 and M-1607-1862, LRCSW; William Moore file, First Infantry Regiment, CSR/North Carolina; Waitt, *Confederate Military Hospitals*, 17.

20. Daniel E. Huger Smith, Smith, and Childs, *Mason Smith Family Letters*, 96–132; William Mason Smith file, Twenty-Seventh Infantry Regiment, CSR/South Carolina.

21. Daniel E. Huger Smith, Smith, and Childs, *Mason Smith Family Letters*, 106; file C-1314-1862, LRCSW; between Sopchoppy and St. Marks Rivers, Wakulla County, Florida, p. 36 (David W. Core), 1860 Census; David W. Core file, Second Infantry Regiment, CSR/Florida; Waitt, *Confederate Military Hospitals*, 13–14. See also McGuire, *Diary*, 97, 315.

22. *Enquirer*, 30, 31 July 1861; *Dispatch*, 31 July 1861, 12 July 1862; McGuire, *Diary*, 316; J. B. Jones, *Rebel War Clerk's Diary*, 1:142; files C-1134-1862 and R-509-1862, LRCSW; White Post, Clarke County, Virginia, p. 66/662 (Lucy M. Randolph), 1860 Census.

23. Green, *Chimborazo*, 76–77; Emma Mordecai Diaries, 7, 8, 9 June 1864; *Examiner*, 16 May 1864; file 6165-1861, LRCSW; Pember, *Southern Woman's Story*, 51–54.

24. At Chimborazo, for example, of the 23,849 patients whose ultimate disposition is recorded, some 2,717 died—a mortality rate of 11.39 percent. Applying this rate to the whole number of patients admitted to that hospital (77,889) suggests that altogether nearly 9,000 men may have died there. Applying it to the estimated number of patients treated in all Richmond hospitals combined (between 200,000 and 300,000) yields a death toll of roughly 23,000 to 34,000—on average, between sixteen and twenty-three per day over the course of the war. The true number of deaths may well be significantly higher, for not all the hospitals were as effective as Chimborazo. See Green, *Chimborazo*, 114; and Coles, "Richmond, the Confederate Hospital City," 72.

25. Faust, *This Republic of Suffering*, chap. 1; Schantz, *Awaiting the Heavenly Country*, chaps. 1, 2; Rable, *God's Almost Chosen People*, 176–78.

26. This and the next two paragraphs are drawn from Daniel E. Huger Smith, Smith, and Childs, *Mason Smith Family Letters*, 96–137.

27. File R-509-1862, LRCSW; McGuire, *Diary*, 96, 97, 104–5; Pember, *Southern Woman's Story*, 24–25, 61.

28. Sutherland, *Expansion of Everyday Life*, 126–31; Faust, *This Republic of Suffering*, chap. 1.

29. Chesson and Roberts, *Exile in Richmond*, 140, 141–42; *Whig*, 27 June 1864; Henry Peychand [*sic*] file, Washington Artillery Battalion, CSR/Louisiana. See also McDonald, *Diary with Reminiscences*, 239–41.

30. Halttunen, *Confidence Men*, 170–72; Faust, *This Republic of Suffering*, 93–94; J. B. Jones, *Rebel War Clerk's Diary*, 2:214; Harrison, *Recollections*, 95–96.

31. Faust, *This Republic of Suffering*, 30, 161–64; Hubard Diary, 16 July 1861; J. B. Jones, *Rebel War Clerk's Diary*, 2:214; *Examiner*, 4 November 1864; Robert M. Tabb file, Twenty-First Infantry Regiment, CSR/Virginia.

32. Faust, *This Republic of Suffering*, 146–51; Lange, "Changed Name," 162/169; J. B. Jones, *Rebel War Clerk's Diary*, 2:136; Lankford, *Irishman in Dixie*, 38, 44; Paca, "'Tim's Black Book,'" 457; McGuire, *Diary*, 250–51.

33. McGuire, *Diary*, 311–13; file 8483-1861, LRCSW; receipts, November 1861–January 1862, Richmond and Petersburg Railroad Company file, CPRCBF.

34. Manarin, *Richmond at War*, 353; *Dispatch*, 24 October 1861, 20 December 1862, 31 July 1863; file H-251-1863, LRCSW; *Examiner*, 15 May 1863; Halttunen, *Confidence Men*, 170; Faust, *This Republic of Suffering*, 91–95; Schantz, *Awaiting the Heavenly Country*, 61.

35. Bill, *Beleaguered City*, 16, 39, 99–100; Furgurson, *Ashes of Glory*, 5, 9, 32–33; J. B. Jones, *Rebel War Clerk's Diary*, 1:109–10; *Enquirer*, 15, 17 February 1862; McGuire, *Diary*, 91, 92–93; *Dispatch*, 17 February 1862; Putnam, *Richmond during the War*, 98.

36. *Dispatch*, 24, 25 July 1861, 13 May 1863; *Sentinel*, 13 May 1863; Harrison, *Recollections*, 84, 141; J. B. Jones, *Rebel War Clerk's Diary*, 1:319, 321; Katharine M. Jones, *Ladies of Richmond*, 167–68; Manarin, *Richmond at War*, 322–24, 471–72; Putnam, *Richmond during the War*, 222–24; *Examiner*, 14 May 1864; McGuire, *Diary*, 270–71; *Enquirer*, 17 December 1862; McDonald, *Diary with Reminiscences*, 240–41; *Whig*, 27 December 1862.

37. Harrison, *Recollections*, 188–89.

38. Green, *Chimborazo*, 81; Register of Effects of Deceased Soldiers; Daniel E. Huger Smith, Smith, and Childs, *Mason Smith Family Letters*, 108; file L-505-1862, LRCSW; Noble Beverage file, Twenty-Fifth Battalion, Infantry, CSR/Virginia; Katharine M. Jones, *Ladies of Richmond*, 134.

39. T. H. Langdon to John Coke, 30 July 1863, Civil War Letters Collection; receipt, 14 June 1862, John and George Gibson file, CPRCBF; Kent, *Four Years in Secessia*, 19; Green, *Chimborazo*, 81–82; Mitchell, *Hollywood Cemetery*, 48–49, 51; *Dispatch*, 12 July 1862; file R-642-1862, LRCSW.

40. Mitchell, *Hollywood Cemetery*, 48–49, 59; *Enquirer*, 16 July 1862; Benjamin Washington Jones, *Under the Stars*, 159; Manarin, *Richmond at War*, 214; Green, *Chimborazo*, 82.

41. Mitchell, *Hollywood Cemetery*, 48–49, 51–52, 59; Manarin, *Richmond at War*, 66, 193, 194n, 196, 380; files R-642-1862 and O-50-1864, LRCSW; *Stranger's Guide*, 9; *Dispatch*, 20 August 1861, 10, 12 July, 8 August 1862, 5 August 1864; *Enquirer*, 24 June 1862; Putnam, *Richmond during the War*, 151–52n; Kent, *Four Years in Secessia*, 18–19.

42. File O-50-1864, LRCSW; *Dispatch*, 20 August 1861, 12 July 1862, 27 June 1863; Mitchell, *Hollywood Cemetery*, 48, 51–53; Manarin, *Richmond at War*, 111n, 193, 196, 232, 262; Green, *Chimborazo*, 81–82; Benjamin Washington Jones, *Under the Stars*, 213. Richmond's other municipal burying ground, Shockoe Hill Cemetery, had no section set aside for War Department interments of Confederate soldiers, but it was used for interments of Federal prisoners of war who died in Richmond. See *Dispatch*, 12 November 1861, 19 February 1862.

43. Mitchell, *Hollywood Cemetery*, 3–16, 33–34; Schantz, *Awaiting the Heavenly Country*, chap. 3; Blackiston, *Refugees in Richmond*, 50; *Dispatch*, 1 July 1861, 27 June 1862; Chesson and Roberts, *Exile in Richmond*, 66, 77.

44. *Enquirer*, 16 October 1862; Benjamin Washington Jones, *Under the Stars*, 159–60, 213; *Dispatch*, 27 June 1863.

45. Mitchell, *Hollywood Cemetery*, 57; *Dispatch*, 21 May, 12 July 1862, 4 August, 15 October 1864; *Sentinel*, 18 May, 4 June 1863.

EPILOGUE

1. The following nine paragraphs are based on J. B. Jones, *Rebel War Clerk's Diary*, 2:464–75, supplemented by Lankford, *Richmond Burning*, chaps. 4–12.

2. This and the following six paragraphs are based on Chesson, *Richmond after the War*, esp. xv-xvi, 64–65, 67–68, 115, 117–19, 130–39, 145–46; Tyler-McGraw, *At the Falls*, chap. 7; Naragon, "Ballots, Bullets, and Blood," chaps. 7–9, esp. p. 389; Lankford, *Richmond Burning*; Barber, "'Sisters of the Capital,'" chaps. 7, 8; Cei, "Law Enforcement in Richmond," chap. 4; and Latimore, "Always a Minority," chap. 5. The city's population in 1870 was 35 percent greater than in 1860, but that growth was less than the 38 percent growth of 1850–60. The 1867 annexation abruptly increased the population at that point by almost 30 percent.

Bibliography

MANUSCRIPTS

Bagby, George W. Diary. Virginia Historical Society, Richmond, Va.

Barred and Disallowed Case Files of the Southern Claims Commission, 1871–80. M 1407, RG 233. National Archives II, College Park, Md.

Bechtel, Jacob H. Papers, 1858–62. William L. Clements Library, University of Michigan, Ann Arbor, Mich.

Circulars and Correspondence Received by the Confederate Enrolling Officer at Richmond. E 23, RG 109. National Archives, Washington, D.C.

Civil War Letters Collection. New-York Historical Society, New York, N.Y.

Cochran, Catherine Mary Powell (Noland). Recollections, 1861–65. Virginia Historical Society, Richmond, Va.

Coke, John A. Papers. New-York Historical Society, New York, N.Y.

Compiled Service Records of Confederate Soldiers. M 251 (Florida), M 266 (Georgia), M 267 (South Carolina), M 269 (Mississippi), M 270 (North Carolina), M 320 (Louisiana), M 324 (Virginia), RG 109. National Archives, Washington, D.C.

Confederate Papers Relating to Citizens or Business Firms. M 346, RG 109. National Archives, Washington, D.C.

C.S.A. Army. Department of Henrico Papers, 1861–64. Virginia Historical Society, Richmond, Va.

Ebenezer Baptist Church (Richmond, Va.) Records, 1858–1975. Library of Virginia, Richmond, Va.

Eighth Census, 1860. Manuscript Returns of Free Inhabitants. M 653, RG 29. National Archives, Washington, D.C.

Eighth Census, 1860. Manuscript Returns of Slaves. M 653, RG 29. National Archives, Washington, D.C.

Endorsements on Letters Received, 1864. Records of the Confederate Provost Marshal's Office at Richmond, Virginia, 1862–64. Chap. 9, vol. 1841/2, RG 109. National Archives, Washington, D.C.

French, Samuel Bassett. Letterbook. New-York Historical Society, New York, N.Y.

Granniss, Robert A. Diary. Virginia Historical Society, Richmond, Va.

Habersham Family Papers, 1787–1892. MMC-0609. Library of Congress, Washington, D.C.

Harrison, Burton Norvell. Family Papers, 1812–1926. MSS 25080. Library of Congress, Washington, D.C.

Holloway, Dr. James Montgomery. Papers. Virginia Historical Society, Richmond, Va.

Howitzer Company Collection. New-York Historical Society, New York, N.Y.

Hubard, Maria Mason Tabb. Diary. Virginia Historical Society, Richmond, Va.

Lange, John Gottfried. "The Changed Name, or the Shoemaker of the Old and New World: Thirty Years in Europe and Thirty Years in America." Unpublished memoir. Translated by Ida Windmueller. Virginia Historical Society, Richmond, Va.

Legislative Petitions of the General Assembly, 1776–1865. Library of Virginia, Richmond, Va.

Letcher, John. Executive Papers, 1859–63. Library of Virginia, Richmond, Va.

Letters Received by the Confederate Secretary of War, 1861–65. M 437, RG 109. National Archives, Washington, D.C.

Letters Sent by the Richmond Arsenal (Ordnance Depot), 1862–65. Records of Confederate Ordnance Establishments at Richmond, Virginia, 1861–65. Chap. 4, vols. 90, 91, 91.5, 92, RG 109. National Archives, Washington, D.C.

Maury, Richard Lancelot. Diary. Virginia Historical Society, Richmond, Va.

Mordecai, Alfred. Papers, 1790–1948. 0628 FF. Library of Congress, Washington, D.C.

Mordecai, Emma. Diaries, May 1864–May 1865. Southern Historical Collection, University of North Carolina, Chapel Hill, N.C.

Pember, Phoebe Yates. Letters, 1861–1920. Southern Historical Collection, University of North Carolina, Chapel Hill, N.C.

Record Book of the Confederate Soldiers Home Hospital and the Association for the Relief of Maimed Soldiers in Richmond, Virginia, 1862–65. Chap. 6, vol. 463, RG 109. National Archives, Washington, D.C.

Register of Effects of Deceased Soldiers, General Hospital 24, 1862–64. Chap. 6, vol. 652, RG 109. National Archives, Washington, D.C.

Smith, William. Executive Papers, 1864–65. Library of Virginia, Richmond, Va.

Southern Claims Commission Approved Claims, 1871–80: Virginia. M 2094, RG 217. National Archives II, College Park, Md.

Special Orders, Camp of Instruction, Richmond, Virginia, 1864–65. Chap. 1, vols. 223–29. National Archives, Washington, D.C.

Time Book of the Richmond Arsenal, 1863–65. Records of Confederate Ordnance Establishments at Richmond, Virginia, 1861–65. Chap. 4, vol. 99, RG 109. National Archives, Washington, D.C.

Tredway, Thomas Thweatt. Papers, 1857–65. MSS 1977. Library of Congress, Washington, D.C.

Von Groning, D. Letterbook, 1861–63. MSS 24224. Library of Congress, Washington, D.C.

Whitlock, Philip. Recollections. Virginia Historical Society, Richmond, Va.

Withers, Anita Dwyer. Diary, 1860–65. Southern Historical Collection, University of North Carolina, Chapel Hill, N.C.

NEWSPAPERS

Daily Dispatch (Richmond)
Daily Richmond Enquirer
Daily Richmond Examiner
Daily Richmond Whig

Religious Herald (Richmond)
Richmond Enquirer (semiweekly edition)
Richmond Semi-Weekly Examiner
Sentinel (Richmond)

PUBLISHED PRIMARY SOURCES

Berlin, Ira, Barbara J. Fields, Thavolia Glymph, Joseph P. Reidy, and Leslie S. Rowland, eds. *The Destruction of Slavery*. Cambridge: Cambridge University Press, 1985.

Blackiston, Henry C., ed. *Refugees in Richmond: Civil War Letters of a Virginia Family*. Princeton, N.J.: Princeton University Press, 1989.

Botts, John Minor. *The Great Rebellion: Its Secret History, Rise, Progress, and Disastrous Failure*. New York: Harper and Brother, 1866.

Brown, Philip F. *Reminiscences of the War of 1861–1865*. Richmond, Va.: Whittet and Shepperson, 1917.

Burrows, J. L. *The New Richmond Theatre*. Richmond, Va.: Smith, Bailey, 1863.

The Charters and Ordinances of the City of Richmond. Richmond, Va.: Ellyson's Steam Presses, 1859.

Chesson, Michael Bedout, and Leslie Jean Roberts, eds. *Exile in Richmond: The Confederate Journal of Henri Garidel*. Charlottesville: University Press of Virginia, 2001.

The City Intelligencer; or, Stranger's Guide. Richmond, Va.: Macfarlane and Fergusson, 1862.

Clark, Sam L., ed. "A Confederate Officer Visits Richmond." *Tennessee Historical Quarterly* 11 (1952): 86–91.

Crocker, Rev. W. A. "The Army Intelligence Office." *Confederate Veteran* 8 (1900): 118–19.

Day, Samuel Phillips. *Down South: Or, an Englishman's Experience at the Seat of the American War*. 2 vols. London: Hurst and Blackett, 1862.

De Leon, T. C. *Four Years in Rebel Capitals: An Inside View of Life in the Southern Confederacy from Birth to Death*. Mobile, Ala.: Gossip, 1890.

Doggett, Rev. David Seth. *A Nation's Ebenezer*. Richmond, Va.: Enquirer Book and Job Press, 1862.

Ellis, Thomas H. "The Richmond 'Home Guard' of 1861." *Southern Historical Society Papers* 19 (1891): 57–60.

Estill, Mary S., ed. "The Diary of a Confederate Congressman, 1862–1863." Pts. 1 and 2. *Southwestern Historical Quarterly* 38 (1935): 270–301; 39 (1935): 33–65.

Harrison, Mrs. Burton H. *Recollections Grave and Gay*. New York: C. Scribner's Sons, 1911.

[Hopley, Catherine Cooper]. *Life in the South: [...] From the Spring of 1860 to August 1862*. 2 vols. London: Chapman and Hall, 1863.

Johnson, Thomas L. *Africa for Christ: Twenty-Eight Years a Slave*. London: Alexander and Shepheard, 1892.

[Jones, Benjamin Washington]. *Under the Stars and Bars: A History of the Surry Light Artillery; Recollections of a Private Soldier in the War between the States*. Richmond, Va.: Everett Waddey, 1909.

Jones, J. B. *A Rebel War Clerk's Diary at the Confederate States Capital*. 2 vols. Philadelphia: J. B. Lippincott, 1866.

Jones, Katharine M., ed. *Ladies of Richmond, Confederate Capital*. Indianapolis, Ind.: Bobbs-Merrill, 1962.

Kent, Mrs. E. C. *Four Years in Secessia: A Narrative of a Residence at the South*. Buffalo, N.Y.: Franklin, 1865.

Lankford, Nelson D., ed. *An Irishman in Dixie: Thomas Conolly's Diary of the Fall of the Confederacy*. Columbia: University of South Carolina Press, 1988.

Louisiana Soldiers' Relief Association. *Louisiana Soldiers' Relief Association, and Hospital, in the City of Richmond, Virginia*. Richmond, Va.: Enquirer Book and Job Press, 1862.

Macon, T. J. *Life Gleanings*. Richmond, Va.: W. H. Adams, 1913.

Malet, Rev. William Wyndham. *An Errand to the South in the Summer of 1862*. London: Richard Bentley, 1863.

Manarin, Louis H., ed. *Richmond at War: The Minutes of the City Council, 1861–1865*. Chapel Hill: University of North Carolina Press, 1966.

McDonald, Mrs. Cornelia. *A Diary with Reminiscences of the War and Refugee Life in the Shenandoah Valley, 1860–1865*. Nashville: Cullom and Ghertner, 1935.

[McGuire, Judith W.]. *Diary of a Southern Refugee during the War*. Lincoln: University of Nebraska Press, 1995.

Miller, John D., ed. "An Alabama Merchant in Civil War Richmond: The Harvey Wilkerson Luttrell Letters, 1861–1865." *Alabama Review* 58 (2005): 176–206.

Monroe, Haskell M., Lynda Lasswell Crist, Mary Seaton Dix, and Kenneth H. Williams, eds. *The Papers of Jefferson Davis*. 14 vols. Baton Rouge: Louisiana State University Press, 1971–2015.

Mumper, James A., ed. *I Wrote You Word: The Poignant Letters of Private Holt, John Lee Holt, 1829–1863*. Lynchburg, Va.: H. E. Howard, 1993.

Norwood, William. *God and Our Country*. Richmond, Va.: Smith, Bailey, 1863.

Paca, Edmund C., ed. "'Tim's Black Book': The Civil War Diary of Edward Tilghman Paca, Jr., C.S.A." *Maryland Historical Magazine* 89 (1994): 453–66.

Pember, Phoebe Yates. *A Southern Woman's Story*. Columbia: University of South Carolina Press, 2002.

Pryor, Mrs. Roger A. *Reminiscences of Peace and War*. New York: Macmillan, 1904.

Putnam, Sallie Brock. *Richmond during the War: Four Years of Personal Observation*. Lincoln: University of Nebraska Press, 1996.

Randolph, Rev. Peter. *From Slave Cabin to the Pulpit: The Autobiography of Rev. Peter Randolph*. Boston: James H. Earle, 1893.

Richardson, James D., ed. *A Compilation of the Messages and Papers of the Confederacy Including the Diplomatic Correspondence, 1861–1865*. 2 vols. Nashville: United States Printing, 1906.

Rules and Regulations for the Government of the Command, at the Camp of Instruction, Hermitage Fair Grounds, Richmond, Va. Richmond, Va.: n.p., 1861.

Ryan, David D., ed. *A Yankee Spy in Richmond: The Civil War Diary of "Crazy Bet" Van Lew*. Mechanicsburg, Pa.: Stackpole, 2001.

Ryland, Robert. "Origin and History of the First African Church." In *The First Century of the First Baptist Church of Richmond, Virginia, 1770–1880*, edited by H. A. Tupper, 245–72. Richmond, Va.: Carlton McCarthy, 1880.

Second Annual Directory for the City of Richmond. Richmond, Va.: W. Eugene Ferslew, 1860.

Smith, Daniel E. Huger, Alice R. Huger Smith, and Arney R. Childs, eds. *Mason Smith Family Letters, 1860–1868*. Columbia: University of South Carolina Press, 1950.

The Stranger's Guide and Official Directory for the City of Richmond. Richmond, Va.:
    Geo. P. Evans, 1863.

Trask, Benjamin H., ed. *Two Months in the Confederate States: An Englishman's Travels
    through the South.* Baton Rouge: Louisiana State University Press, 1996.

Tucker, John Randolph. *The Southern Church Justified in Its Support of the South in the
    Present War.* Richmond, Va.: Wm. H. Clemmitt, 1863.

United States Bureau of the Census. *Statistics of the United States* [. . .] *in 1860.* Washington,
    D.C.: Government Printing Office, 1866.

Vanfelson, Charles A. *The Little Red Book, or, Department Directory: For the Use of the Public
    in the Confederate States of America.* Richmond, Va.: Tyler, Wise, and Allegre, 1861.

*War of the Rebellion: A Compilation of the Official Records of the Union and Confederate
    Armies.* 70 vols. in 128. Washington, D.C.: Government Printing Office, 1880–1901.

Welton, J. Michael, ed. *"My Heart Is So Rebellious": The Caldwell Letters, 1861–1865.*
    Warrenton, Va.: Bell Gale Chevigny, 1991.

Wiggins, Sarah Woolfolk, ed. *The Journals of Josiah Gorgas, 1857–1878.* Tuscaloosa:
    University of Alabama Press, 1995.

Wiley, Bell Irvin, ed. *Letters of Warren Akin, Confederate Congressman.* Athens: University
    of Georgia Press, 1959.

Williams, Max R., ed. *The Papers of William Alexander Graham.* Vol. 6, 1864–65. Raleigh:
    North Carolina Department of Cultural Resources, Division of Archives and History,
    1976.

Williams, Max R., and J. G. de Roulhac Hamilton, eds. *The Papers of William Alexander
    Graham.* Vol. 5, 1857–63. Raleigh: North Carolina Office of Archives and History, 1973.

Woodward, C. Vann, ed. *Mary Chesnut's Civil War.* New Haven, Conn.: Yale University
    Press, 1981.

Younger, Edward, ed. *Inside the Confederate Government: The Diary of Robert Garlick Hill
    Kean.* Baton Rouge: Louisiana State University Press, 1993.

SECONDARY SOURCES

Anderson, David. "Dying of Nostalgia: Homesickness in the Union Army during the
    Civil War." *Civil War History* 56 (2010): 247–82.

Ash, Stephen V. *The Black Experience in the Civil War South.* Santa Barbara, Ca.: Praeger,
    2010.

———. "A Wall around Slavery: Safeguarding the Peculiar Institution on the
    Confederate Periphery, 1861–1865." In *Nineteenth-Century America: Essays in Honor
    of Paul H. Bergeron,* edited by W. Todd Groce and Stephen V. Ash, 55–73. Knoxville:
    University of Tennessee Press, 2005.

———. *When the Yankees Came: Conflict and Chaos in the Occupied South, 1861–1865.*
    Chapel Hill: University of North Carolina Press, 1995.

Bailey, James H. *Henrico Home Front, 1861–1865: A Picture of Life in Henrico County,
    Virginia, from May, 1861, through April, 1865.* Richmond, Va.: Whittet and Shepperson,
    1963.

Barber, E[dna] Susan. "Depraved and Abandoned Women: Prostitution in Richmond,
    Virginia, across the Civil War." In *Neither Lady nor Slave: Working Women of the
    Old South,* edited by Susanna Delfino and Michelle Gillespie, 155–73. Chapel Hill:
    University of North Carolina Press, 2002.

————. "'Sisters of the Capital': White Women in Richmond, Virginia, 1860–1880." PhD diss., University of Maryland, 1997.

Berlin, Ira. *Slaves without Masters: The Free Negro in the Antebellum South*. New York: Vintage, 1976.

Berman, Myron. *Richmond's Jewry, 1769–1976: Shabbat in Shockoe*. Charlottesville: University Press of Virginia, 1979.

Bill, Alfred Hoyt. *The Beleaguered City: Richmond, 1861–1865*. New York: Alfred A. Knopf, 1946.

Black, Robert C., III. *The Railroads of the Confederacy*. Chapel Hill: University of North Carolina Press, 1952.

Blair, William. *Virginia's Private War: Feeding Body and Soul in the Confederacy, 1861–1865*. New York: Oxford University Press, 1998.

Blakey, Arch Fredric. *General John H. Winder, C.S.A.* Gainesville: University of Florida Press, 1990.

Boney, F. N. *John Letcher of Virginia: The Story of Virginia's Civil War Governor*. University: University of Alabama Press, 1966.

Brewer, James H. *The Confederate Negro: Virginia's Craftsmen and Military Laborers, 1861–1865*. Tuscaloosa: University of Alabama Press, 2007.

Bridges, Edwin C. "Juliet Opie Hopkins and Alabama's Civil War Hospitals in Richmond, Virginia." *Alabama Review* 53 (2000): 83–111.

Brown, Elsa Barkley, and Gregg D. Kimball. "Mapping the Terrain of Black Richmond." *Journal of Urban History* 21 (1995): 296–346.

Bruce, Kathleen. *Virginia Iron Manufacture in the Slave Era*. New York: Century, 1931.

Campbell, James M. *Slavery on Trial: Race, Class, and Criminal Justice in Antebellum Richmond, Virginia*. Gainesville: University Press of Florida, 2007.

Casstevens, Frances Harding. *George W. Alexander and Castle Thunder: A Confederate Prison and Its Commandant*. Jefferson, N.C.: McFarland, 2004.

Cei, Louis Bernard. "Law Enforcement in Richmond: A History of Police-Community Relations, 1737–1974." PhD diss., Florida State University, 1975.

Channing, Steven A. *Crisis of Fear: Secession in South Carolina*. New York: W. W. Norton, 1970.

Chesson, Michael Bedout. "Harlots or Heroines? Another Look at the Richmond Bread Riot." *Virginia Magazine of History and Biography* 92 (1984): 131–75.

————. *Richmond after the War*. Richmond: Virginia State Library, 1981.

Clarke, Frances. "So Lonesome I Could Die: Nostalgia and Debates over Emotional Control in the Civil War North." *Journal of Social History* 41 (2007): 253–82.

Coles, David J. "Richmond, the Confederate Hospital City." In *Virginia at War, 1862*, edited by William C. Davis and James I. Robertson Jr., 71–91. Lexington: University Press of Kentucky, 2007.

Craven, Avery Odelle. *Soil Exhaustion as a Factor in the Agricultural History of Virginia and Maryland*. Urbana: University of Illinois Press, 1926.

Crofts, Daniel W. *Reluctant Confederates: Upper South Unionists in the Secession Crisis*. Chapel Hill: University of North Carolina Press, 1989.

Cunningham, H. H. *Doctors in Gray: The Confederate Medical Service*. Baton Rouge: Louisiana State University Press, 1958.

Dabney, Virginius. *Richmond: The Story of a City*. Charlottesville: University of Virginia Press, 1990.

Davis, William C. "Richmond Becomes the Capital." In *Virginia at War, 1861*, edited by William C. Davis and James I. Robertson Jr., 113–29. Lexington: University Press of Kentucky, 2005.

Dew, Charles B. *Apostles of Disunion: Southern Secession Commissioners and the Causes of the Civil War*. Charlottesville: University Press of Virginia, 2001.

————. *Ironmaker to the Confederacy: Joseph R. Anderson and the Tredegar Iron Works*. Richmond: Library of Virginia, 1999.

Fahrner, Alvin A. "William 'Extra Billy' Smith, Governor of Virginia 1864–1865: A Pillar of the Confederacy." *Virginia Magazine of History and Biography* 74 (1966): 68–87.

Faust, Drew Gilpin. *The Creation of Confederate Nationalism: Ideology and Identity in the Civil War South*. Baton Rouge: Louisiana State University Press, 1988.

————. *This Republic of Suffering: Death and the American Civil War*. New York: Alfred A. Knopf, 2008.

Fisher, George D. *History and Reminiscences of the Monumental Church, Richmond, Va.: From 1814 to 1878*. Richmond, Va.: Whittet and Shepperson, 1880.

Furgurson, Ernest B. *Ashes of Glory: Richmond at War*. New York: A. A. Knopf, 1996.

Gamber, Wendy. *The Boardinghouse in Nineteenth-Century America*. Baltimore: Johns Hopkins University Press, 2007.

Gates, Paul W. *Agriculture and the Civil War*. New York: Alfred A. Knopf, 1965.

Goff, Richard D. *Confederate Supply*. Durham, N.C.: Duke University Press, 1969.

Goldfield, David R. *Urban Growth in the Age of Sectionalism: Virginia, 1847–1861*. Baton Rouge: Louisiana State University Press, 1977.

Green, Carol C. *Chimborazo: The Confederacy's Largest Hospital*. Knoxville: University of Tennessee Press, 2004.

Gutman, Herbert G. *The Black Family in Slavery and Freedom, 1750–1925*. New York: Pantheon, 1976.

Hadden, Sally E. *Slave Patrols: Law and Violence in Virginia and the Carolinas*. Cambridge, Mass.: Harvard University Press, 2001.

Halttunen, Karen. *Confidence Men and Painted Women: A Study of Middle-Class Culture in America, 1830–1870*. New Haven: Yale University Press, 1982.

Hilde, Libra R. *Worth a Dozen Men: Women and Nursing in the Civil War South*. Charlottesville: University Press of Virginia, 2012.

Hoge, Peyton Harrison. *Moses Drury Hoge: Life and Letters*. Richmond, Va.: Presbyterian Committee of Publication, 1899.

Hurt, R. Douglas. *Agriculture and the Confederacy: Policy, Productivity, and Power in the Civil War South*. Chapel Hill: University of North Carolina Press, 2015.

Johnson, Ludwell H. "Trading with the Union: The Evolution of Confederate Policy." *Virginia Magazine of History and Biography* 78 (1970): 308–25.

Johnston, Angus James, II. *Virginia Railroads in the Civil War*. Chapel Hill: University of North Carolina Press, 1961.

Jordan, Ervin L., Jr. *Black Confederates and Afro-Yankees in Civil War Virginia*. Charlottesville: University Press of Virginia, 1995.

Kimball, Gregg D. "African-Virginians and the Vernacular Building Tradition in Richmond City, 1790–1860." *Perspectives in Vernacular Architecture* 4 (1991): 121–29.

————. *American City, Southern Place: A Cultural History of Antebellum Richmond*. Athens: University of Georgia Press, 2003.

Lankford, Nelson D. *Cry Havoc! The Crooked Road to Civil War, 1861*. New York: Viking, 2007.

————. *Richmond Burning: The Last Days of the Confederate Capital*. New York: Viking, 2002.

Latimore, Carey H., IV. "Always a Minority: Richmond Area Free Blacks in the Civil War Era." PhD diss., Emory University, 2005.

Link, William A. *Roots of Secession: Slavery and Politics in Antebellum Virginia*. Chapel Hill: University of North Carolina Press, 2003.

Litwack, Leon F. *Been in the Storm So Long: The Aftermath of Slavery*. New York: Alfred A. Knopf, 1979.

Luskey, Ashley Whitehead. "'A Debt of Honor': Elite Women's Rituals of Cultural Authority in the Confederate Capital." PhD diss., West Virginia University, 2014.

Manarin, Louis H., and Clifford Dowdey. *The History of Henrico County*. Charlottesville: University Press of Virginia, 1984.

Manarin, Louis H., and Lee A. Wallace Jr. *Richmond Volunteers: The Volunteer Companies of the City of Richmond and Henrico County, Virginia, 1861–1865*. Richmond, Va.: Westover, 1969.

Maris-Wolf, Ted. *Family Bonds: Free Blacks and Re-enslavement Law in Antebellum Virginia*. Chapel Hill: University of North Carolina Press, 2015.

Marten, James. *The Children's Civil War*. Chapel Hill: University of North Carolina Press, 1998.

Martinez, Jaime Amanda. *Confederate Slave Impressment in the Upper South*. Chapel Hill: University of North Carolina Press, 2013.

Martis, Kenneth C. *The Historical Atlas of the Congresses of the Confederate States of America, 1861–1865*. New York: Simon and Schuster, 1994.

Massey, Mary Elizabeth. *Refugee Life in the Confederacy*. Baton Rouge: Louisiana State University Press, 1964.

McCurry, Stephanie. *Confederate Reckoning: Power and Politics in the Civil War South*. Cambridge, Mass.: Harvard University Press, 2010.

McLeod, Norman C., Jr. "Not Forgetting the Land We Left: The Irish in Antebellum Richmond." *Virginia Cavalcade* 47 (1998): 36–47.

McMurry, Richard M. *Two Great Rebel Armies: An Essay in Confederate Military History*. Chapel Hill: University of North Carolina Press, 1989.

Mehrlander, Andrea. *The Germans of Charleston, Richmond, and New Orleans during the Civil War Period, 1850–1870*. Berlin: De Gruyter, 2011.

Mitchell, Mary H. *Hollywood Cemetery: The History of a Southern Shrine*. Richmond: Virginia State Library, 1985.

Moore, Albert Burton. *Conscription and Conflict in the Confederacy*. Columbia: University of South Carolina Press, 1996.

Naragon, Michael Douglas. "Ballots, Bullets, and Blood: The Political Transformation of Richmond, Virginia, 1850–1874." PhD diss., University of Pittsburgh, 1996.

Neely, Mark E., Jr. *Southern Rights: Political Prisoners and the Myth of Confederate Constitutionalism*. Charlottesville: University Press of Virginia, 1999.

O'Brien, John T. "Factory, Church, and Community: Blacks in Antebellum Richmond." *Journal of Southern History* 44 (1978): 509–36.

Rable, George C. *God's Almost Chosen People: A Religious History of the American Civil War*. Chapel Hill: University of North Carolina Press, 2010.

Radley, Kenneth. *Rebel Watchdog: The Confederate States Army Provost Guard*. Baton Rouge: Louisiana State University Press, 1989.

"The Richmond Ambulance Corps." *Southern Historical Society Papers* 25 (1897): 113–15.

Robert, Joseph Clarke. *The Tobacco Kingdom: Plantation, Market, and Factory in Virginia and North Carolina, 1800–1860*. Gloucester, Mass.: Peter Smith, 1965.

Schantz, Mark S. *Awaiting the Heavenly Country: The Civil War and America's Culture of Death*. Ithaca, N.Y.: Cornell University Press, 2008.

Schurr, Nancy. "Inside the Confederate Hospital: Community and Conflict during the Civil War." PhD diss., University of Tennessee, 2004.

Scott, Mary Wingfield. *Old Richmond Neighborhoods*. Richmond, Va.: Whittet and Shepperson, 1950.

Shackelford, George Green. *George Wythe Randolph and the Confederate Elite*. Athens: University of Georgia Press, 1988.

Shanks, Henry T. *The Secession Movement in Virginia, 1847–1861*. Richmond, Va.: Garrett and Massie, 1934.

Sheehan-Dean, Aaron. "Politics in Civil War Virginia: Democracy on Trial." In *Virginia at War, 1864*, edited by William C. Davis and James I. Robertson Jr., 15–34. Lexington: University Press of Kentucky, 2009.

Starobin, Robert S. *Industrial Slavery in the Old South*. New York: Oxford University Press, 1970.

Steger, Werner H. " 'United to Support, but Not Combined to Injure': Free Workers and Immigrants in Richmond, Virginia, during the Era of Sectionalism, 1847–1865." PhD diss., George Washington University, 1999.

Stuart, Meriwether. "Colonel Ulric Dahlgren and Richmond's Union Underground, April 1864." *Virginia Magazine of History and Biography* 72 (1964): 152–204.

———. "Of Spies and Borrowed Names: The Identity of Union Operatives in Richmond Known as 'the Phillipses' Discovered." *Virginia Magazine of History and Biography* 89 (1981): 308–27.

———. "Samuel Ruth and General R. E. Lee: Disloyalty and the Line of Supply in Fredericksburg, 1862–1863." *Virginia Magazine of History and Biography* 71 (1963) 35–109.

Sutherland, Daniel E. *The Expansion of Everyday Life, 1860–1876*. New York: Harper and Row, 1989.

Takagi, Midori. *"Rearing Wolves to Our Own Destruction": Slavery in Richmond, Virginia, 1782–1865*. Charlottesville: University Press of Virginia, 1999.

Thomas, Dean S. *Confederate Arsenals, Laboratories, and Ordnance Depots*. 3 vols. Gettysburg, Pa.: Thomas Publications, 2014.

Thomas, Emory M. *The Confederate State of Richmond: A Biography of the Capital*. Baton Rouge: Louisiana State University Press, 1998.

———. "To Feed the Citizens: Welfare in Wartime Richmond." *Virginia Cavalcade* 22 (1972): 22–29.

Tunnell, Ted. "A 'Patriotic Press': Virginia's Confederate Newspapers, 1861–1865." In *Virginia at War, 1864*, edited by William C. Davis and James I. Robertson Jr., 35–50. Lexington: University Press of Kentucky, 2009.

Tyler-McGraw, Marie. *At the Falls: Richmond, Virginia, and Its People*. Chapel Hill: University of North Carolina Press, 1994.

Tyler-McGraw, Marie, and Gregg D. Kimball. *In Bondage and Freedom: Antebellum Black Life in Richmond, Virginia*. Richmond, Va.: Valentine Museum, 1988.

Van Riper, Paul P., and Harry N. Scheiber. "The Confederate Civil Service." *Journal of Southern History* 25 (1959): 448–70.

Varon, Elizabeth R. *Southern Lady, Yankee Spy: The True Story of Elizabeth Van Lew, a Union Agent in the Heart of the Confederacy.* New York: Oxford University Press, 2003.

Wade, Richard C. *Slavery in the Cities: The South, 1820–1860.* New York: Oxford University Press, 1964.

Waitt, Robert W., Jr. *Confederate Military Hospitals in Richmond.* Richmond, Va.: Richmond Civil War Centennial Committee, 2002.

Weddell, Elizabeth Wright. *St. Paul's Church, Richmond, Virginia, Its Historic Years and Memorials.* 2 vols. Richmond, Va.: William Byrd, 1931.

Wheelan, Joseph. *Libby Prison Breakout: The Daring Escape from the Notorious Civil War Prison.* New York: Public Affairs, 2010.

White, Blanche Sydnor. *Richmond Baptists Working Together, 1780–1960.* Richmond, Va.: Richmond Baptist Association, 1961.

Wiley, Bell Irvin. *The Life of Johnny Reb: The Common Soldier of the Confederacy.* Indianapolis, Ind.: Charter, 1962.

Wooster, Ralph A. *Politicians, Planters, and Plain Folk: Courthouse and Statehouse in the Upper South, 1850–1860.* Knoxville: University of Tennessee Press, 1975.

Zombek, Angela M. "Paternalism and Imprisonment at Castle Thunder: Reinforcing Gender Norms in the Confederate Capital." *Civil War History* 63 (2017): 221–52.

Index

Page numbers in italics refer to illustrations.

conscription, conscripts: desertion by, 100–101; enforcement of, 85, 87, 88, 89, 91, 98–99, 131; evasion of, 130–32; exemptions from, 85, 90, 91, 98, 131, 132, 149, 201, 203; food and housing for, 52, 73–74; for fortifications, 29, 39, 52, 73, 84, 93, 100, 176; labor shortages aggravated by, 66, 85, 89, 90, 98, 174; public resentment of, 203; of skilled labor, 39, 66, 86, 98

Conscription Act (1862), 13, 85, 93

Cook, Fields, 173–74

cookshops, 68–69, 173, 174

Core, David, 214

corn, 2, 59, 61, 69, 77

corporal punishment, 55, 100, 146, 162, 163, 164, 175, 176, 178; by slave owners, 165

corruption, 148–50

cotton, 32, 78

Council Chamber Hill, 7

Crenshaw, William, 90

Crenshaw Woolen Mills, 23, 85

Crews, W. H., 102–103

crime, 139–58, 228

Crocker, W. A., 34

Daily Dispatch, 26, 45, 51, 64, 65, 145, 147, 156, 209, 223, 224; blacks viewed by, 161, 175; changing city viewed by, 19, 20, 36; disorderliness deplored by, 140, 142, 143, 152; gambling viewed by, 152–53; poverty viewed by, 49–50; prostitution decried by, 193; slave owners warned by, 180; speculators viewed by, 151; Unionists assailed by, 124

Daily Richmond Enquirer, 43, 98, 126, 145, 175, 194, 220, 223

Daily Richmond Examiner, 31, 50, 102, 104, 136, 165, 176, 212; blacks disdained by, 166, 174–75, 177–78, 180; crime reporting by, 140, 141, 142, 179; fugitive slaves reported by, 181; poor relief viewed skeptically by, 189; prostitution deplored by, 134–35; shortages viewed by, 61, 81, 82, 95; strike at, 99; Unionists assailed by, 127; upper-class interests defended by, 189–90, 192, 199

Dalney, George, 13

dating, unchaperoned, 155–56

Davis, Deupree, and Company, 2

Davis, Jefferson, 12, 13, 20, 34, 41, 57, 73, 133, 152, 156, 167, 187, 202, 225; favors sought from, 27, 32–33, 79, 89, 96–97, 166, 206; habeas corpus suspended by, 128; inauguration of, 172; martial law declared by, 69, 128–129; memorials to, 230; residences of, 48, 51; Richmond arrival of, 10; riot of 1863 and, 196, 198

Davis, Varina, 51, 71, 167, 172–73, 187, 254n40, 257n35

Deady (Louisiana woman), 25–26

death penalty, 169, 178–79

De Kalb, Camille La Valliere, 31

Delano, John, 136

De Leon, Thomas, 155, 209, 210

desertion, 27, 55, 91–92, 100–101, 104, 130–33, 136

Dick (blacksmith), 93

Doggett, D. S., 15

Doggett, Mary, 163–64

domestic servants, 47–48, 84, 182–83

Drayton, Nathaniel, 178

Drewry's Bluff, Va., 217

Dugan, John A., 25

Duke, Mary, 198

Dunlop, Moncure, and Company, 62

Dunn, George, 91

dysentery, 212

Eagle Machine Works, 23, 25

Eastern District Military Prison. *See* Castle Thunder

"eating saloons," 68

Ebenezer Baptist Church, 170–71, 172

Edmondson, Sarah, 178

Edwards, Ann, 27

Ellis, Charles, 87–88

Emancipation Proclamation, 15

embalming, *120*, 133–34, 219

Engineer Bureau, 92

English immigrants, 91

Examiner. See Daily Richmond Examiner

Exchange Hotel, 48, 148

executive branch, 21

Fairfax, Randolph, 218
Farrar, John, 177
Fauntleroy, Henry H., 11
Ferguson, William, 177
Fifteenth Virginia Infantry Regiment, 83
fire of April 1865, 122, 226, 227, 228
firewood, 55–56, 64, 80, 93–94
First African Baptist Church, 164, 170
First Baptist Church, 153
First Market House, 59, *112*
First Virginia Infantry Regiment, 83
Fitzpatrick, John, 104
"floating population," 30, 50
flooding, 1–3, 67, 69
food shortages, 36, 46, 57–80, 150, 202
Forbes, Mary, 190
Ford, W. H., 32
fortifications, 22, 133; black laborers and, 29, 30, 39, 52, 63, 73, 84, 92, 93, 101, 174, 176; lumber used for, 38
Fort Monroe, Va., 135
Fort Sumter, S.C., 9, 12
Forty-Sixth Virginia Infantry Regiment, 89
fraternal organizations, 171, 187
Fredericksburg, Battle of (1862), 23, 211, 218
Fredericksburg, Va., 30, 211
free blacks, 71, 160; affluence among, 173–74; desertion by, 100; enslavement of, 178; as laborers, 23, 29, 39, 59, 66–67, 73, 74, 76, 84, 92–93; registration required of, 162, 171, 176; residential patterns of, 8, 38, 42; slaves and whites mingling with, 176–77; thieving by, 177–78; whites' views of, 161
Frost, George, 2
fugitive slaves, 28, 55, 101, 179–81
funerals, 217–21
furniture making, 43, 92

Gabriel's Rebellion (1800), 161, 162
Gallego Mills, 61
gambling, 152–53
gangs, 54, 141–42
Garidel, Elodie ("Lolo"), 205, 206, 207
Garidel, Henri, 56, 71, 78, 96, 137, 191, 217; Hollywood Cemetery described by, 223;

homesickness of, 205, 206, 207; as tenant, 42, 44–45, 47, 68
garrison force, 22
garroting, 142–43
gas, 56, 125
Gellatly, William, 91
General Hospital No. 3, 209
General Hospital No. 8, 209
General Hospital No. 11, 214
General Hospital No. 13 (Lunatic Hospital), 206–7
General Hospital No. 24, 213
Gentry, John H., 178
George (blacksmith), 93
Germans, 8, 91, 127, 128, 184, 189
Gettysburg, Battle of (1863), 23
Gibson, George, 98
Gibson, John, 98
Gilmer, John H., 194
Goddard, Isaac, 82, 89
Going, Lewis, 27
Gordon, S. H., 184
Gordon, Sarah, 184
Gordon, Wash, 175
Gorgas, Josiah, 137–38
Gormley, John, 141
Gormley, Sarah, 141
government employees, 71–72, 78, 82, 85, 95
Graham, James, 143
grain, 58, 59, 65, 82
Granniss, Robert, 123
gravedigging, 100, 222
Green, George, 142
Green, Philip, 171
Gretter, George, 41, 45
Griffin, George, 50
Griffin's Island, 193
groggeries. *See* saloons

habeas corpus, 128, 143, 145
Hall, E. M., 83
Hallock (storekeeper), 130
Halloran, John, 134
Hargrove, Ann, 79
Harpers Ferry raid (1859), 162
Harris, Ann, 171
Harrison, Burton, 43

Unionists, 123–38
Upshur, Mrs., 47

vandalism, 142
Van Lew, Elizabeth, 123
Vaughan, V. V., 95
vegetables, 58, 59, 64, 71, 76–77, 141
Virginia Central Railroad, 2, 58, 77, 78,
    202; black labor recruited by, 84, 92;
    derailments by, 66; prisoners of war
    transported by, 28; striking workers at, 99
Virginia Iron Manufacturing Company, 77,
    92
Virginius (slave), 179
visitor guides, 33
volunteers, army, 6, 11–12, 82, *110*, 235n19
Von Groning, Daniel, 125, 168

wages, 46, 49, 71–73, 74, 81, 95, 100
Walker (slave), 139–40, 174
War Department, 21, 22, 23, 31, 167;
    conscripts disciplined by, 98–99;
    exemptions granted by, 83–84, 85–87;
    prisons built by, 36; railroads used by,
    60–61; rations stockpiled by, 195
warehouses, 20, 22, 27, 28, 39, 40
Washington, D.C., 3
water supply, 60, 69
Watkins, Eliza, 51
Watkins, John M., 51
Watt, George, 89
Watt, Hugh, 89
Watt and Company, 92
Weber, Philip, 132
Weisiger, Powhatan, 12, 235n20
Werner, Charles, 86

West family, 26
Whalen, Margaret, 184
Whalen, Patrick, 185
Whig (newspaper), 102, 161
Wilderness, Battle of (1864), 23, 135
William (Doggett family slave), 163–64
William (Goochland County slave), 178–79
William (slave and hospital employee), 141
Williams, Betsey, 2
Wilmington, N.C., 135, 151
Winder, John H., 69, *115*, 129, 149–50, 152
Winder Hospital, 23, 49, 75, 77, 92, 141, 198
Wise, O. Jennings, 220
women, black, 76, 84, 163, 174
women, white: abandoned by husbands,
    136; and benevolent work, 14, 187–
    88; class distinctions among, 75, 182,
    184–85, 187, 188, 190; dating by, 155–
    56; discrimination against, 95–96; in
    factories, 72, 76, 84–85, 94, 99–100,
    105; forced to take jobs, 75–76; as
    government employees, 75–76, 96–97,
    156; in mourning, *122*, 218–19; in needle
    trades, 14, 71, 72, 76, 85, 94, 97; as nurses,
    52, 85; postwar, 228–29; as prostitutes, 24,
    49–50, 76, 134–35, 153, 192–93; as rioters,
    194–96; segregation of, 156; in skilled
    positions, 94, 96, 98; theft by, 140, 141
wounded soldiers, 205–17
Wright, James, 5–6, 8

Yerby, Ann, 25
Yerby, Susan, 25
YMCA, 14, 79, 97, 189

Zouaves, 143